D1195574

The Building Program
of Herod the Great

The Building Program
of Herod the Great

Duane W. Roller

UNIVERSITY OF CALIFORNIA PRESS
Berkeley   Los Angeles   London

University of California Press
Berkeley and Los Angeles, California

University of California Press
London, England

Library of Congress Cataloging-in-Publication Data

Roller, Duane W.
    The building program of Herod the Great / Duane W. Roller.
        p.   cm.
    Includes bibliographical references and index.
    ISBN 0–520–20934–6 (cloth : alk. paper)
        1. Architecture, Roman—Palestine.   2. Architecture—Palestine.   3. Herod I, King of
Judea, 73–4 B.C.—Contributions in architecture.   I. Title.
    NA335.P19R65   1998
    722′.7′0933—dc21   96-54003
                                                                                        CIP

Printed in the United States of America
9   8   7   6   5   4   3   2   1

The paper used in this publication meets the minimum requirements of American National
Standard for Information Sciences—Permanence of Paper for Printed Library Materials,
ANSI Z39.48-1984.

CONTENTS

ILLUSTRATIONS AND STEMMATA

Figures follow pages 100 and 192

Maps and city plans follow page 144

LINE DRAWING

Berenike inscription, Berytos / *249*

STEMMATA

PREFACE

*Then Herod . . . was exceedingly angry, and he sent for and killed all the boys
in Bethlehem and all the surroundings who were two years old or less.*

MATT. 2.16.

He who has not seen the Temple of Herod has never seen a beautiful building.

JEWISH PROVERB (BABYLONIAN TALMUD, *BABA-BATHRA* 4A).

I would rather be Herod's pig than his son.

EMPEROR AUGUSTUS, QUOTED BY MACROBIUS, *SATURNALIA* 2.4.11.

Herod the Great, King of Judaea between 40 and 4 B.C., is known in the
Christian nativity story as the attempted murderer of the infant Jesus. Christian tradition thereafter considered Herod the supreme criminal, and by
the end of antiquity, he was remembered almost solely for his role in the
Nativity rather than as a client king of Rome's.[1] Works of art such as the
Massacre of the Innocents by Pieter Bruegel the Elder[2] have perpetuated and
popularized the image of Herod as one of the world's great villains.

It is not the purpose of this work to assess the character of Herod or to
place him within the religious traditions of Judaea, tasks that have been better performed by others.[3] One expects that Herod's virtues and vices were

---

1. Christian writers emphasized his role in the Nativity. Eusebios (*Ecclesiastical History*
1.6.8) suggested that the deterioration of Herod's reign and his terrible death were divine jus-
tice for his persecution of Jesus of Nazareth, which came to be an accepted point of view in
Christian theology.

2. Now in the Kunsthistorisches Museum, Vienna.

3. Biographies of Herod are numerous, from Walter Otto's lengthy *RE* article, whose
"Zeittafel für Herodes I" is invaluable, to Abraham Schalit's *KH* and Michael Grant's more popular *Herod the Great* (London, 1971). In addition, other works particularly valuable for biographical data include Hugo Willrich, *Der Haus des Herodes Zwischen Jerusalem und Rom* (Heidelberg, 1929); Jones, *Herods*; A. Momigliano, "Herod of Judaea," in *CAH*, 1st ed., corrected
(1966), 10: 316–39; Stewart Perowne, *The Life and Times of Herod the Great* (London, 1956);
Menahem Stern, "The Reign of Herod," in *HP*, 71–123; Schürer (NEV), 1: 287–329 is a particularly straightforward and well-documented summary. Most recently, see Martin Goodman,
"Judaea," in *CAH*, 2d ed. (1996), 10: 737–50, and Peter Richardson, *Herod: King of the Jews,
Friend of the Romans* (Columbia, S.C., 1996), which has an unusually complete discussion of
the building program (pp. 174–202). Samuel Sandmel's *Herod: Profile of a Tyrant* (Philadelphia, 1967), more of a theological study than a political or artistic one, dismisses Herod's
building program in a sentence (p. 272). On Herod's miserable death, see Thomas Africa,

little different from those of other dynasts and client kings of the Hellenistic-Roman East. He certainly was more adept than many, as he successfully survived the twists and turns of the Roman civil war from Pompey through Augustus, successively supporting Caesar, Cassius, and Antonius and Cleopatra. He created the model Roman client kingdom of the East, largely based on the Egypt of Antonius and Cleopatra, fostering a Greco-Roman cultural climate, with scholars, a library, artists, and, above all, monumental architecture. It is the architecture of Herod that is the focus of this study, especially the Roman basis of his building program and his overlooked contributions to the architectural history of the Greek and Roman world.

Discussions of Herodian architecture are not rare: in fact most treatments of Herod have the requisite summary of his architectural achievements, often lifted bodily from the pages of Josephus. Yet such summaries, however detailed, tend to exclude two important aspects of Herodian architecture: that it extended throughout the eastern Roman world, from western Greece to interior Syria (map 1), and that it was more Roman than Hellenistic in inspiration.

Herod built extensively in his kingdom (map 2) and in the surrounding areas: Josephus catalogued over twenty locations within his territory that saw Herodian constructions. But Josephus listed almost as many places outside Herod's kingdom that also benefited from his building,[4] including Syria, Asia Minor, the Greek islands, and even Athens, Sparta, and perhaps Rome. In fact, Herod's career as a builder began not in Judaea but on Rhodes, before he was king.[5]

Moreover, Herod's architectural inspiration was not from the expected Hellenistic and Eastern sources, but a reflection of the immense rebuilding of late Republican and Augustan Rome. Although hinted at by Kathleen M. Kenyon in a fundamental, yet brief and obscurely published, study,[6] this aspect of Herod's career has never been fully and systematically explored.[7] He was a remarkable innovator, introducing to the East such

---

"Worms and the Death of Kings: A Cautionary Note on Disease and History," *ClAnt* 1 (1982): 9–11; Richard Fenn's *The Death of Herod* (Cambridge, 1992) is a sociological study of the cultural implications of Herod's death. Many other studies of Herod are cited in the main bibliography to this work; a thorough bibliography of modern works on Herod (through 1980) appears in Louis H. Feldman, *Josephus and Modern Scholarship* (Berlin, 1984), 278–303.

4. As a typical example of the attitude toward this part of Herod's career, Abraham Schalit devoted nearly eighty detailed pages in his monumental *KH* to Herod's constructions within his kingdom but barely three, essentially quotations from Josephus, to his buildings in the rest of the Greek and Roman world. Schürer (NEV), 1: 308, likewise acknowledged Herod's work outside his kingdom, but in a single paragraph.

5. *AJ* 14.378.

6. "Some Aspects of the Impact of Rome on Palestine," *JRAS* 1970: 181–91.

7. Rare exceptions are Willrich (supra, n. 3) and David Braund's *Rome and the Friendly King: The Character of Client Kingship* (London, 1984), which also examines the matter of Herod and Rome, with some attention to architectural issues (pp. 75–78, 108–13). Ilana

diverse architectural forms as the Italian podium temple, the Roman theater, the Italian villa, and probably the enclosed portico and amphitheater. In his youth he was inspired by emergent Roman building activities in Syrian and southern Levantine cities and by the unfulfilled eastern architectural legacy of Julius Caesar, but an early visit to Rome in 40 B.C. provided the impetus for a systematic romanizing of the physical aspect of his future kingdom.

Central to this study is the first analytical catalogue of the Herodian architectural program, discussing every site at which he built. It is placed within its context both of the Roman influence, its central focus, and of its continuation of the Roman traditions that had emerged since Syria had become a Roman province and several Roman builders had come to Herod's world.

Also of importance is the intellectual setting: not only the cultural life of Augustan Rome, but Herod's own scholarly circle in Jerusalem, which recreated the defunct scholarly life of the court of Antonius and Cleopatra. It included a number of people who traveled regularly between Rome and Judaea and thus provided Herod with much of his information about Roman happenings.

When Herod died in 4 B.C., he left a significant legacy in the architectural romanization of the East. His dynastic successors and in-laws in other client kingdoms continued with their own Herodian-inspired programs. But he also laid the groundwork for the successive great Roman constructions in the East and even influenced the later architectural development of Rome.

The author's interest in the career of Herod the Great grew out of fieldwork, particularly at Herod's Caesarea, in the late 1970's and early 1980's, and a realization that Herod had never been adequately studied as a royal builder or from the perspective of Rome rather than Judaea. The

---

d'Ancona Porte's "The Art and Architecture of Palestine under Herod the Great: A Survey of the Major Sites" (Ph.D. diss., Harvard University, 1966; see the summary in *HSCP* 26 [1966]: 341–44) is a limited discussion of Herod's architecture within his kingdom, with some allusions to Roman influence, but does not deal with the issue in any systematic or detailed way. Archaeological fieldwork by Ehud Netzer, especially at Herodeion and Jericho, has also raised questions of Roman involvement, even to the point of suggesting that teams of Roman architects were sent from Rome to Judaea. Other fieldwork at a number of sites within Herod's kingdom has revealed specific cases of Roman influence, such as in the harbor technology and urban plan of Caesarea, but this is largely on an ad hoc basis, without consideration of broad questions of inspiration. A brief but incisive discussion of Herodian architecture in Judaea and Syria, which includes acknowledgement of its Roman origins, appears in Ward-Perkins, *RIA*, 309–14. See also John R. Bartlett, *Jews in the Hellenistic World: Josephus, Aristeas, the Sibylline Orations, Eupolemus* (Cambridge Commentaries on the Writings of the Jewish and Christian World, 1.1 [Cambridge, 1985]), 102–10, who saw Herod's architectural activities as more Hellenistic than Roman. As a contrast to those who ignored Herod's architectural achievements, Jones, *Cities*, 270–77, tended to diminish their importance.

Roman East itself is a vital area, which is only recently coming to be studied in detail, inspired by the groundwork of scholars like Glen Bowersock and Fergus Millar, who are encouraging a new interest. It is hoped that in a modest way this first presentation of the totality of Herod's achievements as a royal builder, completed in the year of the 2,000th anniversary of his death, will contribute to an understanding of this most intriguing of environments.

This study is based on personal examination, during repeated trips to the eastern Mediterranean since the late 1970's, of virtually every site at which Herod and his predecessors and dynastic successors built. The project was supported by a National Endowment for the Humanities fellowship and numerous grants and leaves from the Ohio State University. Much of the library research was done at the Harvard College Library, the Library of Congress, the New York Public Library, and the library of the University of California at Berkeley, and the author is particularly grateful to those institutions and their staffs for support. Among the many people who assisted in the improvement of this work the author would like to cite Jeffrey Blakely, Glen Bowersock, Robert J. Bull, Barbara Burrell, Donna M. Distel, Claire Epstein, Kathryn L. Gleason, Marian Gooding, David F. Graf, Philip C. Hammond, Karen Hawley, Robert L. Hohlfelder, cartographer Keehwan Hong, Jan Jordan and the Athenian Agora Excavations, Nikos Kokkinos, Mary Lamprech, Rachel Berchten, Peter Dreyer, and many others at the University of California Press, Janet Larkin and the British Museum, Jodi Magness, Fergus Millar, Krzystof Nawotka, L. Richardson, Jr., (whose topographical seminars at the American Academy in Rome were of major importance in understanding the remains of the Julio-Claudian period), Letitia K. Roller, C. Brian Rose, graduate assistant Joseph G. Schott, Christopher J. Simpson, Abe Socher, Kathy Stedke, Lawrence E. Toombs (who first directed the author toward the Hellenistic-Roman Levant), Cornelius Vermeule and the Boston Museum of Fine Arts, Wendy Watkins and the Center for Epigraphical Studies of the Ohio State University, Katherine Welch, and, particularly, Charles L. Babcock.[8]

I am especially grateful to my father, Duane H. D. Roller, late professor of the history of science at the University of Oklahoma, who not only encouraged my early interest in intellectual history but read and commented on as much of the manuscript as existed before his death.

---

8. Some of the material contained herein was presented as "Herod the Great and the Augustan Literary Circle," at the Classical Association of the Middle West and South, Hamilton, Ontario, April 1991; "Herod the Great and Augustan Rome," at the First International Conference on Ancient World History, Tianjin, China, September 1993; "The Augustan Literary Circle and Herod the Great," at the American Philological Association, Atlanta, December 1995; "New Insights into the Building Program of Herod the Great," at the American Schools of Oriental Research, Philadelphia, November 1995, and the Archaeological Institute of America, New York, December 1996; and "A New Look at the Building Programs of Herod's Descendants," at the American Schools of Oriental Research, New Orleans, November 1996.

ABBREVIATIONS

AA	*Archäologischer Anzeiger*
AAP	*The Aqueducts of Ancient Palestine: Collected Essays,* ed. D. Amit et al. (Jerusalem, 1989)
AASOR	*Annual of the American Schools of Oriental Research*
AbhGött	*Abhandlungen der Akademie der Wissenschaften zu Göttingen*
ADAJ	*Annual of the Department of Antiquities of Jordan*
AEpigr	*L'Année épigraphique*
AJ	Josephus, *Jewish Antiquities*
AJA	*American Journal of Archaeology*
AJP	*American Journal of Philology*
Akten	*Akten des XIII. Internationalen Kongresses für klassiche Archäologie Berlin 1988* (Mainz, 1990)
AM	*Mitteilungen des Deutschen Archäologischen Instituts, Athenische Abteilung*
AnatSt	*Anatolian Studies*
AncW	*The Ancient World*
ANRW	*Aufstieg und Niedergang der römischen Welt*
ANSMN	*American Numismatic Society Museum Notes*
AntW	*Antike Welt*
Apion	Josephus, *Against Apion*
AR	*Archaeological Reports*
ArchDelt	Ἀρχαιολογικόν Δελτίον
ArtB	*The Art Bulletin*
Avi-Yonah, *Holy Land*	Michael Avi-Yonah, *The Holy Land from the Persian to the Arab Conquests (536 B.C. to A.D. 640): A Historical Geography* (rev. ed., Grand Rapids, Mich., 1977)
BAR	*Biblical Archaeology Review*
BAR-IS	*British Archaeological Reports, International Series*
BASOR	*Bulletin of the American Schools of Oriental Research*

BdA	*Bollettino d'arte*
BEFAR	Bibliothèque des Écoles françaises d'Athènes et de Rome
BEO	*Bulletin d'études orientales*
BiblArch	*The Biblical Archaeologist*
BICS	*Bulletin of the Institute of Classical Studies of the University of London*
BJ	Josephus, *Jewish War*
BJb	*Bonner Jahrbücher des Rheinischen Landesmuseums in Bonn und des Vereins von Altertumsfreunden im Rheinlande*
BJPES	*Bulletin of the Jewish Palestine Exploration Society*
BMC	*Catalogue of the Greek Coins in the British Museum*
BMusBeyr	*Bulletin du Musée de Beyrouth*
Bowersock, *Augustus*	G. W. Bowersock, *Augustus and the Greek World* (Oxford, 1965)
Broughton	T. Robert S. Broughton, *The Magistrates of the Roman Republic* (*Philological Monographs of the American Philological Association* 15; New York, 1951–52, 1986)
BSA	*Annual of the British School in Athens*
BSAE	*British School of Archaeology in Egypt, Publications*
BSR	*Papers of the British School in Rome*
BT	*Babylonian Talmud*
BZ	*Byzantinische Zeitschrift*
CaesMarit	*The Joint Expedition to Caesarea Maritima, Excavation Reports* (Lewistown, N.Y.)
CAH	*Cambridge Ancient History*
CEFR	Collection de l'École française de Rome
CIG	*Corpus inscriptionum graecarum*
CIL	*Corpus inscriptionum latinarum*
ClAnt	*Classical Antiquity*
ClRh	*Clara Rhodos*
CMR	*Caesarea Maritima: A Retrospective after Two Millennia* (*Documenta et Monumenta Orientis Antiqui* 21, ed. Avner Raban and Kenneth Holum; Leiden, 1996)
CMS News	*Center for Maritime Studies News*
Coarelli, *Guida*	Filippo Coarelli, *Guide archeologiche Laterza 6: Roma* (Bari, 1980)
Corinth	*Corinth: Results of Excavations Conducted by the American School of Classical Studies at Athens* (Princeton)
cos.	*consul*
cos. suff.	*consul suffectus*
CP	*Classical Philology*
CQ	*Classical Quarterly*
CRAI	*Comptes rendus des séances de l'Académie des inscriptions et belles-lettres* (Paris)
EAEHL	*Encyclopedia of Archaeological Excavations in the Holy Land* (English edition, ed. Michael Avi-Yonah; London, 1975–78)

EchCl	Echos du monde classique: Classical Views
ErIsr	Eretz-Israel
FGrHist	Die Fragmente der griechischen Historiker
GRBS	Greek, Roman, and Byzantine Studies
HA	Historia Augusta
HP	The Herodian Period (The World History of the Jewish People 1.7, ed. Michael Avi-Yonah; New Brunswick, N.J., 1975)
HSCP	Harvard Studies in Classical Philology
HThR	Harvard Theological Review
HUCA	Hebrew Union College Annual
IEJ	Israel Exploration Journal
IG	Inscriptiones graecae
IGRR	Inscriptiones graecae ad res romanas pertinentes
IJNA	International Journal of Nautical Archaeology and Underwater Exploration
ILS	Inscriptiones latinae selectae
IstMitt	Istanbuler Mitteilungen
JAOS	Journal of the American Oriental Society
JARCE	Journal of the American Research Center in Egypt
JC	Jerusalem Cathedra
JEA	Journal of Egyptian Archaeology
JHS	Journal of Hellenic Studies
JNES	Journal of Near Eastern Studies
Jones, Cities	A. H. M. Jones, The Cities of the Eastern Roman Provinces (2d ed., Oxford, 1971)
Jones, Herods	A. H. M. Jones, The Herods of Judaea (Oxford, 1938)
JPOS	Journal of the Palestine Oriental Society
JRA	Journal of Roman Archaeology
JRAS	Journal of the Royal Asiatic Society
JRS	Journal of Roman Studies
JThS	Journal of Theological Studies
KlPauly	Der kleine Pauly. Lexicon der Antike
Life	Josephus, Life
LSJ	H. G. Liddell, R. Scott, and H. Stuart Jones, Greek-English Lexicon (9th ed., Oxford, 1940)
LTUR	Lexicon Topographicum Urbis Romae, ed. Eva. Margareta Steinby (Rome, 1993–)
MAAR	Memoirs of the American Academy in Rome
Magie, RR	David Magie, Roman Rule in Asia Minor to the End of the Third Century after Christ (Princeton, 1950)
MAMA	Monumenta Asiae minoris antiqua
MeditArch	Mediterranean Archaeology: Australian and New Zealand Journal for the Archaeology of the Mediterranean World
MEFRA	Mélanges de l'École française de Rome: Antiquité
Migne, PG	J. P. Migne, Patrologia graeca (Paris, 1928–36)
Migne, PL	J. P. Migne, Patrologia latina (Paris, 1879)

Millar, *RNE*	Fergus Millar, *The Roman Near East, 31 B.C.—A.D. 337* (Cambridge, Mass., 1993)
Nash	E. Nash, *Pictorial Dictionary of Ancient Rome* (2d ed., New York, 1968)
NC	*Numismatic Chronicle*
NEAEHL	*The New Encyclopedia of Archaeological Excavations in the Holy Land*, ed. Ephraim Stern (Jerusalem, 1993)
OGIS	*Orientis Graeci inscriptiones selectae*
Ol.	Olympiad
OLD	*Oxford Latin Dictionary*
OpArch	*Opuscula archaeologica*
OpRom	*Opuscula romana*
Otto, *RE*	Walter Otto, "Herodes I." (#14), *RE* Supp. 2 (1913) 1–158
PalJb	*Palästinajahrbuch*
PECS	*Princeton Encyclopedia of Classical Sites*, ed. R. Stillwell (Princeton, 1976)
PEFQ	*Palestine Exploration Fund Quarterly Statement*
PEQ	*Palestine Exploration Quarterly*
PIR	*Prosopographia imperii romani*
Platner-Ashby	S. B. Platner, *A Topographical Dictionary of Ancient Rome*, completed and revised by Thomas Ashby (London, 1929)
PP	*La parola del passato*
QDAP	*Quarterly of the Department of Antiquities in Palestine*
Rbibl	*Revue biblique*
RE	Pauly-Wissowa, *Real-Encyclopädie der klassischen Altertumswissenschaft*
Reinhold	Meyer Reinhold, *Marcus Agrippa: A Biography* (Geneva, N.Y., 1933)
REL	*Revue des études latines*
RhM	*Rheinisches Museum für Philologie*
Richardson, *NTD*	L. Richardson, Jr., *A New Topographical Dictionary of Ancient Rome* (Baltimore, 1992)
Roddaz	Jean-Michael Roddaz, *Marcus Agrippa* (Rome, 1984)
Schalit, *KH*	Abraham Schalit, *König Herodes: Der Mann und Sein Werk* (Berlin, 1969)
Schürer, *NEV*	Emil Schürer, *The History of the Jewish People in the Age of Jesus Christ (175 B.C.—A.D. 135*, new English version, rev. and ed. Geza Vermes, Fergus Millar, Pamela Vermes, and Matthew Black (Edinburgh, 1973–87)
SEG	*Supplementum epigraphicum gracum*
SIG	*Sylloge inscriptionum graecarum*
Stadion	*Stadion. Zeitschrift für Geschichte des Sports und der Körperkultur* (Cologne)
Sullivan, *NER*	Richard D. Sullivan, *Near Eastern Royalty and Rome, 100–30 B.C.* (*Phoenix* suppl. vol. 24; Toronto, 1990)
Syme, *RR*	Ronald Syme, *The Roman Revolution* (Oxford, 1939)

TAPA	*Transactions of the American Philological Association*
TIR-IP	Yoram Tsafrir, Leah Di Segni, and Judith Green, *Tabula Imperii Romani: Iudaea-Palaestina* (Jerusalem, 1994)
Travlos	J. Travlos, *Pictorial Dictionary of Ancient Athens* (New York, 1971)
Wacholder, *Nicolaus*	Ben Zion Wacholder, *Nicolaus of Damascus* (Berkeley, 1962)
Ward-Perkins, *RIA*	J. B. Ward-Perkins, *Roman Imperial Architecture* (2d ed., Harmondsworth, 1981)
ZDPV	*Zeitschrift der Deutschen Palästina-Vereins*
ZPE	*Zeitschrift für Papyrologie und Epigraphik*

INTRODUCTION

Herod the Great, the son of Antipatros and Kypros, was born around 73 B.C. His family was Idumaean and had been in the service of the rulers of Judaea for at least two generations: his grandfather, who died about the time Herod was born, had been governor of Idumaea in the early first century B.C.[1] His father, who inherited the governorship, married a Nabataean, possibly the daughter of King Aretas III, and this alliance between Idumaea and Nabataea formed the fragile basis of the power their son was to develop. Antipatros was an early, if reluctant, supporter of Roman expansion, one of the first dynasts in the region to seek out Pompey when the latter was advancing through Syria in 64 B.C. Antipatros's position was strengthened during Aulus Gabinius's eastern command in the 50's B.C., a period that would have seen young Herod's introduction both to politics and to Roman commanders.

Herod's career rose with that of his father, who received Roman citizenship from Julius Caesar after Pharsalos; thus Herod also became a citizen. Caesar was to exercise a profound influence on the direction of Herod's architectural endeavors. By 47 B.C., Herod was *strategos* of Galilee. Yet his ethnic background was offensive to many Jews, and difficulties with the Synhedrion in Jerusalem caused him to flee to the governor of Syria, Sextus

1. On the background of Herod's family, see Schürer (NEV), 1: 234; Tessa Rajak, "Justus of Tiberias," *CQ*, n.s., 23 (1973): 366–67. It has recently been suggested that Herod's "Idumaean" origins are of little significance, given the mixed nature of the population of Hellenistic Idumaea, and that the obscure tradition that Herod's family was Askalonian (see further infra, p. 217) makes more sense. This would mean that his ethnic background was more likely Hellenized Phoenician, perhaps making him more acceptable to the Romans and more Roman in his outlook. See Nikos Kokkinos, "The Herodian Dynasty: Origins, Role in Society, and Eclipse" (Ph.D. diss., Oxford University, 1993).

Julius Caesar, thereby beginning a lifelong tradition of seeking Roman protection from domestic political problems. Sextus offered Herod a position in Koile-Syria, but he soon had difficulties of his own and was killed in the summer of 46 B.C. Herod then sought the support of Sextus's relative Julius Caesar, but he too was soon murdered, whereupon Herod effortlessly attached himself to C. Cassius Longinus. Shortly thereafter, Herod's father Antipatros was also assassinated, a result of increasing instability in Judaea after the death of Julius Caesar. Cassius assisted Herod in avenging Antipatros's death and proposed that Herod be named king of Judaea, an office that had been vacant for twenty years.

Cassius did not live long enough to implement the idea, and when the victor of Philippi, Marcus Antonius, arrived in the East late in 42 B.C., he named Herod tetrarch. But the Parthians, ever active along the eastern limits of the Roman sphere of influence, invaded Syria in 40 B.C. and put forward their own candidate for king of Judaea, the Hasmonean claimant Antigonos II. This brought about civil war in Judaea, resulted in the death of Herod's brother Phasael, and encouraged Herod to seek the protection of Cleopatra in Egypt. By the end of the year, however, he decided that going direct to Rome was in his best interest. On his way, he aided in the reconstruction of Rhodes.

In Rome, Herod successfully exploited his previous association with Antonius and other important Romans, and he was promptly named king of Judaea. However, he spent the next three years in a continuing civil war there, which was not settled until 37 B.C., and then only with extensive Roman assistance. Herod's early years as king also coincided with the final stages of the Roman civil war. He attempted to remain neutral while Antonius became more involved with Cleopatra and even gave parts of Herod's kingdom to her. There were also continued problems with other claimants to his throne: Antigonos II had been eliminated in 37 B.C., but the Hasmoneans instigated a revolt in 35 or 34 B.C., and there was war with the Nabataeans in 32–31 B.C. This war and an earthquake in Judaea in the spring of 31 B.C. fortunately prevented Herod from personally aiding Antonius and Cleopatra at Actium late that summer. When Octavian came to Rhodes early the following year, Herod quickly appeared and successfully persuaded him of his future loyalty. He assisted Octavian logistically on his way to Egypt and saw his own kingdom expanded in return. Despite the chaos of these early years of Herod's kingship, his internal architectural program was already well under way, with fortifications ringing his kingdom and palaces erected at Masada and Jerusalem.

The following decade finally saw Herod's external political position secure and the Roman civil war over. His kingdom was never free of conspiracies and claimants to the throne, but these were not yet the problem they would be later in the reign. He had been involved in architectural construction since before he was king, but Octavian's ascendancy after the demise of Antonius and Cleopatra and the devastation of the earthquake of 31 B.C. provided the impetus for an intensive architectural program, which especially flourished in the twenty years between 29 and 9 B.C., It began with the reconstruction of Samaria, renamed Sebaste to honor (in Greek) Octavian's new name of Augustus. Throughout the 20's B.C., there was extensive building inside his kingdom, especially at Jerusalem, Herodeion, and Caesarea. Herod also built in the Greek world, including at the Roman victory city of Nikopolis near Actium. His friendship with Augustus's heir apparent Marcus Vipsanius Agrippa—and the architectural influence it implied—was solidified during Agrippa's residency in Mytilene beginning in 23 B.C. Augustus continued to enlarge Herod's kingdom, especially in 22 B.C., and after the two met in Syria in 20 B.C., Herod regularly sent his sons to Rome to be educated (some of them were housed with Augustus himself) and also encouraged scholars to reside at his own court, especially those set adrift by the collapse of Antonius and Cleopatra. His children were married to other eastern rulers, creating a dynastic network that spread as far as Armenia and lasted until at least the second century A.C.

The peak of Herod's career came in the decade following 20 B.C. That year he began his greatest architectural achievement, the new Temple in Jerusalem. After the dedication of the still-unfinished building, probably in 18 B.C., he made his first trip to Rome as king, to visit his sons and to be received by Augustus. In 15 B.C., Marcus Agrippa made a state visit to Judaea and saw firsthand the romanization of the kingdom; at this time he asked for Herod's assistance on an expedition to the Kimmerian Bosporos. Herod joined Agrippa, and together they made a triumphal tour across Asia Minor. In 12 B.C., Herod was named *agonothetes* of the Olympic Games, in response to generous financial support, and presided at the games while on the way to Rome for the third and last time. In early 9 B.C., Caesarea, his most expansive architectural creation, was dedicated.

The last years of Herod's life were marked by increasingly stormy relations with his family and repeated attempts to involve Augustus in these dynastic problems. As a typical Hellenistic monarch, Herod had complex and often violent family relationships. He was married at least ten times and had over a dozen children, and different parts of his vast family rotated in and out of favor. Executions began with his wife Mariamme in 29 B.C. and eventually included his three eldest sons; the younger ones fared better and survived their father. Augustus—no stranger to family problems—became increasingly displeased at requests for mediation of Herod's domestic difficulties. Herod's original plan was to have his sons by Mariamme, Aristoboulos and Alexandros, succeed him, and although both survived long enough to produce their own dynasties of eastern kings, they were executed for conspiracy in 7 B.C. Favor then passed to the neglected eldest son, Antipatros, but he lost out and was executed in the last months of Herod's life. Herod's violence toward his own children may have given rise to the biblical tale of the Massacre of the Innocents. He then settled on three of his surviving sons, Archelaos (who was to be king), his brother Antipas, of biblical fame (who was to be tetrarch of Galilee), and their half-brother Philippos (as tetrarch of Peraia), as well as bequeathing some territory to his sister Salome. But he also left a conflicting will that named Antipas king.[2]

In the spring of 4 B.C., when he was nearly seventy, Herod died, one of the few members of his family to do so naturally. Quarrels immediately broke out between his sons over the succession. Soon the Judaean religious party was involved, demanding the abolition of the kingship. All appealed to Augustus, who, however, had no patience with any of the petitioners and dissolved Herod's kingdom, giving autonomous powers to Antipas and Philippos, as well as to Archelaos, to whom he denied the title of king, making him merely an *ethnarchos*. Roman military intervention under the command of the legate of Syria, P. Quinctilius Varus, was necessary. The territories of Antipas and Philippos became the nucleus of the kingdom Claudius established in A.D. 41 under the rule of Herod's grandson, Agrippa I. Archelaos proved so incompetent, both internally and in his relations with Rome, that after a decade of increasing impatience Augustus, now totally disgusted, deposed him in A.D. 6 and sent him into obscure retirement at Vienna in Gaul. His territory was turned into the Roman province of Judaea, governed from Herod's Caesarea by a procurator.

LITERARY SOURCES

The extant literary source material for the buildings of Herod the Great consists almost entirely of Flavius Josephus's two major works, the *Jewish War* and the *Jewish Antiquities*. Josephus, who was born around A.D. 37, came to Rome at the beginning of the reign of Vespasian and spent the rest of his life there. He first wrote the *Jewish War*, which was finished late in Vespasian's reign.[3] The *Jewish Antiquities* was written during the latter years of Domitian, and completed in A.D. 93/94.[4] The tone of the two works differs, the *Jewish Antiquities* being less favorable toward Roman policy and ideas

---

2. On the several conflicting wills of Herod, see Harold W. Hoehner, *Herod Antipas* (Society for New Testament Studies Monograph 17 [Cambridge, 1972]), 269–76; David Braund, *Rome and the Friendly King: The Character of Client Kingship* (London, 1984), 139–43.

3. *BJ* 7.158; *Life* 363.

4. *AJ* 20.267. Josephus was fifty-six at this time.

and more nationalistic. Josephus's attitude toward the master romanizer, Herod, is therefore also more negative in it.[5]

Josephus was thus born forty years after Herod's death and wrote a century or more after his great building program. Yet he relied heavily on material contemporary with Herod's reign, especially the works of Herod's confidant Nikolaos of Damaskos, who was mentioned frequently by Josephus, both as a participant in the events of Herod's career and as a source of information about them. Although the actual citations are few—no more than a dozen fragments of the works of Nikolaos were preserved by Josephus—it is probable that Nikolaos was Josephus's major source of information on the Herodian period.

Nikolaos was Herod's most trusted advisor and essentially his ambassador to the Roman government. A brief discussion of his career appears later in the present work.[6] His literary output was extensive, including, in addition to philosophical and scientific works, a biography of Augustus (written some time in the 20's B.C.),[7] and an autobiography, perhaps the earliest work of that genre.[8] His great work was a *History* in 144 books, perhaps the longest universal history written, which by the late second century A.C. was famed as *polybiblos*.[9] Herod persuaded Nikolaos to write it, and Nikolaos was at work by 12 B.C.,[10] but it was not completed until after Herod's death. It covered all human history, beginning with the Assyrians and Babylonians and the Trojan War. The latest datable fragment is from 14 B.C., when Nikolaos traveled with Herod in Ionia,[11] but the history continued for another twenty books, almost certainly to the end of Herod's reign, and probably to the succession struggles after his death. Nikolaos may thus have devoted as

---

5. See Shaye J. D. Cohen, *Josephus In Galilee and Rome: His Vita and Development as a Historian* (Columbia Studies in the Classical Tradition, 8 [Leiden, 1979]), 56–57; John R. Bartlett, *Jews in the Hellenistic World: Josephus, Aristeas, the Sibylline Orations, Eupolemus* (Cambridge Commentaries on the Writings of the Jewish and Christian World, 1.1 [Cambridge, 1985]), 102–3; Seth Schwartz, *Josephus and Judaean Politics* (Columbia Studies in the Classical Tradition, 18 [Leiden, 1990]), 4–22.

6. See infra, pp. 22–23, 61–62; *FGrHist*, # 90; Richard Laqueur, "Nikolaos" (# 20), *RE*, 33 (1936): 362–424; Wacholder, *Nicolaus;* Bowersock, *Augustus*, 134–38; Nikolaos of Damaskos, *Life of Augustus*, ed. Jane Bellemore (Bristol, 1984); Emilio Gabba, "The Historians and Augustus," in *Caesar Augustus: Seven Aspects*, ed. Fergus Millar and Erich Segal (Oxford, 1984), 61–66; Ben Zion Wacholder, "Josephus and Nicolaus of Damascus," in *Josephus, the Bible, and History*, ed. Louis H. Feldman and Gohei Hata (Detroit, 1989), 147–72.

7. Nikolaos, ed. Bellemore (supra, n. 6), xxi–xxii; Wacholder, *Nicolaus*, 25–26; Mark Toher, "The Date of Nicolaus' Βίος Καίσαρος," *GRBS* 26 (1985): 199–206.

8. Wacholder, "Josephus" (supra, n. 6), 148–49.

9. Athenaios 6.54.

10. Nikolaos, fr. 135; Menahem Stern, *Greek and Latin Authors on Jews and Judaism* (Jerusalem, 1974–80), 1: 250–60.

11. Bk. 124 = fr. 81 (*AJ* 12.125–27).

many as thirty books to Herod's era and career,[12] providing an exceedingly detailed account of the southern Levant in the second half of the first century B.C. Yet virtually none of this portion of the history remains: most of the 102 extant fragments concern events of the fifth century B.C. or earlier, and fewer than 10 can be dated to the first century B.C. Nevertheless, it is clear that Josephus used Nikolaos's *History* extensively and critically, often without citation, and corrected him where he deemed necessary.[13]

Other sources offer insights into particular aspects of the Herodian program. John Malalas made detailed comments on Herod's work at Antioch.[14] Moses Khorenats'i discussed Herod and Armenia.[15] There are occasional comments in book 16 of Strabo's *Geography*, but little detail. Strabo's lost *History* was evidently more informative, and it was used by Josephus, although generally for periods previous to Herod's reign.[16] Traditional historians of the Augustan period rarely mentioned Herod: there are slight references, inevitably political, by Appian, Dio, Plutarch, and Tacitus,[17] but only Tacitus commented on Herodian architecture. Some details concerning the Temple in Jerusalem were provided by Philon of Alexandria.[18] Christian texts are equally deficient architecturally, as the familiar nativity story of Matt. 2 demonstrates.[19] Rabbinic literature provides a number of details about the Temple in Jerusalem, but little about other Herodian constructions.[20]

---

12. Wacholder, *Nicolaus*, 61–62.

13. For example, at *AJ* 14.8–10.

14. Malalas 223–24.

15. Moses Khorenats'i, *History of Armenia*, 2: 25–26. For the value of this source, see infra, Appendix 1.

16. *FGrHist* # 91, frs. 4, 6, 7, 10–18. In the present work, citations of Strabo's lengthy extant *Geography* are numerous and are given without title; citations of the lost *History* are rare and are always with title.

17. Appian, *Civil War* 5.75; Dio 49.22, 54.9; Plutarch, *Antonius* 61, 71–72; Tacitus, *Histories* 5.9–12. There is also a reference to the area of Jericho by Horace (*Epistles* 2.2.184), and to Caesarea by Pliny (*Natural History* 5.69).

18. Philon, *Special Laws* 1.71–75, 273; *Embassy to Gaius* 294–300.

19. Christian sources that briefly mention the building program include Sextus Julius Africanus, *Chronography* 17.4 (Sebaste, Caesarea, Antipatris); the *Chronikon Paschale* (Migne, *PG*, 92) 181, 186, 191, 193 (Sebaste, Askalon, Jerusalem, Caesarea, Paneion, Agrippias); Hegesippos (Migne, *PL*, 66) 67 (Jerusalem, Sebaste); Ioannes Lydus, *De magistratibus populi Romani* 3 (Nikopolis); *Itinera Hierosolymitana* (Migne, *PL*, 39) 110 (Herodeion?); Stephanos of Byzantion (s.vv. "Antipatris," "Phasaelis"); Synkellos, *Ekloga chronographika* 548–49, 581, 594 (Sebaste, Jerusalem, Antipatris, Paneion, Agrippias, Herodeion, Gaba). None of these adds anything of significance.

20. Specific references from the Babylonian Talmud regarding the Temple at Jerusalem include *Yoma* (entire tractate), *Sukkah* 51b, *Baba Bathra* 3a–4a, and, from the *Mishna*, *Middot*. BT *'Arakin* 14a referred to Sebaste. On rabbinic literature generally, see Schürer (NEV), 1: 68–122. Generally, the texts are no earlier than the late second century A.C. and thus sub-

Additional sources may have been valuable in their day but have vanished virtually without trace. A certain Ptolemaios wrote *On Herod*;[21] whether the author was one of two men of that name at Herod's court is probable but cannot be determined.[22] The first book contained a discussion of the differences between Jews and Idumaeans, and thus of Herod's ethnic background.

The role of the works of Justus of Tiberias is uncertain. Secretary to King Agrippa II, he was excoriated by Josephus not only for his role in the civil disturbances of the 60's A.C. but as a poor historian. He wrote a history of the Jews, or of the Jewish kings, no longer extant, but which would have been one of the earliest treatments of Herod: Josephus's *Life* was written in response to portions of Justus's work.[23]

Moreover, Herod's own memoirs were known to Josephus.[24] He cited them by name only once, but other passages, especially in book 15 of the *Jewish Antiquities*, speak of actions by Herod in a personal tone that suggests that they are derived from his memoirs. Whether those memoirs were ever published is not known: Josephus may have drawn on them only from the writings of Nikolaos.[25]

Other memoirs were also available to Josephus. Those of Asinius Pollio provided information about events of the 40's B.C.[26] Quintus Dellius's memoirs were used by Strabo[27] and Plutarch,[28] and thus probably by Josephus, although he did not cite them. Yet it is doubtful whether any of these shed much light on the Herodian building program.

Two memoirs that may have provided interesting information do not

---

stantially later than most of the major historial sources. The Babylonian Talmud, in which some of the references to Herodian building occur, is as late as the sixth century A.C. But rabbinic literature relied on a lengthy oral tradition, which could be from as early as the period of Herod himself. Since practically all the above citations relate to the Temple in Jerusalem, which was destroyed before the end of the first century A.C., one may assume that they refer to the time of Herod or not much later.

21. *FGrHist*, # 199. The only source for this work is the lexicographer Ammonios, of uncertain date; see Schürer (NEV), 1: 27–28.

22. Infra, pp. 63–64.

23. *FGrHist*, # 734; *Life* 345–60; Schürer (NEV), 1: 34–37; Rajak (supra, n. 1), 345–68.

24. *AJ* 15.164–74 (= Herod [*FGrHist*, # 236], fr. 1). The account concerns the death of the Hasmonean Hyrkanos II.

25. Schürer (NEV), 1: 26–27. Other possible places where Josephus may have used the memoirs are Herod's letter regarding his meeting with Antonius and Cleopatra and the rebuke of Cleopatra (*AJ* 15.74–79) and the famous speech to Octavian at Rhodes after Actium (*AJ* 15.187–93). See Otto, *RE*, 43–47, and commentary on *FGrHist*, # 236.

26. *AJ* 14.138. Josephus probably did not consult them directly, but used the citations in Strabo's *History*.

27. Strabo 11.13.3.

28. Plutarch, *Antonius* 59.

seem to have been used by Josephus. Those of Marcus Agrippa seem to have been little known even in Josephus's day, and may already have been completed previous to the greatest period of contact between Agrippa and Herod.[29] And nowhere did Josephus hint that he used the memoirs of Augustus, which probably did not deal with the most intensive period of Herodian building either.

In summary, then, the works of Josephus, based largely on the *History* of Nikolaos of Damaskos and Herod's own memoirs, are the major, and almost the exclusive, extant literary source for information about the Herodian building program.[30]

TOPONYMS AND CHRONOLOGICAL PERIODS

There is no good collective toponym for the territory of Herod's kingdom. Although Herod was king of Judaea, his kingdom always included more than Judaea: Galilee, Samaria, Peraia, Idumaea, and parts of southern Syria were all within his borders at various times. The actual boundaries of his kingdom changed, being reduced by Antonius in the 30's B.C. and enlarged by Augustus several times in the 20's B.C.: this means that one cannot speak of "Herod's kingdom" without a temporal reference. Moreover, ancient sources tend to confuse the territorial and ethnic limits of Herod's kingship and are never quite clear—as perhaps the Romans themselves were not certain—as to whether Herod was king of Judaea or king of the Jews. Herod's son Archelaos became *ethnarchos*, an indication that political power could be exercised ethnically as well as territorially.

The only ancient collective term for the area in question is Palestine, but this was anachronistic in Herod's day, and if used at all, tended to be limited to the southwestern coastal areas, the ancient Philistine territory. The best general term for the modern scholar is "southern Levant," which is used throughout this work to describe the territory between Syria and Egypt, on both sides of the Jordan river, although wherever possible ancient regional toponyms such as Judaea or Galilee are preferred.

Another problem occurs in creating a collective term for the period of Herod the Great. Using Herodian as a dynastic name makes little sense: a better one would be "Antipatrid," the name of Herod's father and probably of his grandfather, the latter being the earliest member of the dynasty who

---

29. They were cited only by Seneca (*Epistles* 94.46), Pliny (*Natural History* 7.148 = Agrippa, fr. 1; 36.121 = Agrippa, fr. 3), and in the scholia to Vergil (*Georgics* 2.162 = Agrippa, fr. 2): for the fragments of Agrippa, see Hermann Peter, *Historicum Romanorum Reliquiae* (Stuttgart, 1967), 1: 64–65. See also Horace, *Odes* 1.6; Reinhold, 142; Roddaz, 568–71.

30. Schürer (NEV), 1:43–63. One nonliterary source deserves mention: the mosaic map, dating to the sixth century A.C., on the floor of a church in the city of Madaba in Moab, providing a visible record from late antiquity of a number of Herod's constructions. See Michael Avi-Yonah, *The Madaba Mosaic Map* (Jerusalem, 1954).

can be identified. Yet "Herodian" has consistently been used as the dynastic name. Unfortunately, it has tended to mean the entire period of the dynasty, from 40 B.C. (or even from 64 B.C., a strange nomenclature, which would begin the "Herodian Period" with Pompey) to A.D. 66 or later, placing Herod and his successors (few of whom were named Herod) in one undifferentiated period, which is as if the time from Pompey to Nero in Roman history were treated as a unit. This is far too generalized, and causes serious problems in the interpretation of the physical remains of the southern Levant: the building program of Pompey had little similarity with that of Agrippa II over a century later.

In this work, "Herodian" refers specifically to the period of Herod the Great, from the 40's B.C. to 4 B.C. "Herodian dynasty" is used for Herod and his successors through Agrippa II. But wherever possible the name of the specific dynast or builder is used, in order to distinguish the programs of Herod the Great, his Roman predecessors, and his descendants who were also royal builders in the southern Levant.

TRANSLITERATION

With a certain amount of reluctance, the author has adopted the familiar English "Herod" for the client king of Judaea and his like-named descendants. This is even though the consistent English form of the name for anyone outside the Antipatrid family is "Herodes," directly transliterated (whether from Greek or Latin): examples include the fifth-century B.C. Athenian whose murderer was defended by Antiphon, and the members of the Athenian philanthropic family of the second century A.C. "Herod" came late to English: Chaucer used "Herodes,"[31] and the Master of Wakefield used "Herode."[32] The form "Herod" seems first to appear in the Tyndale Bible of 1525, but indiscriminately with "Herodes" and "Herode." Only with Shakespeare and the King James Bible did "Herod" become the common English form: Shakespeare may have chosen it for metrical reasons. Yet the contemporary popular image of "Herod" is so pervasive that it seems unreasonable to use any other form, despite the fact that doing so violates the author's own precepts concerning transliteration.[33] Elsewhere, names are transliterated directly from Greek or Latin, except in a few cases (e.g., Jerusalem, Athens, Cleopatra), where common English forms exist.

---

31. *Canterbury Tales* 1.3384.

32. *Slaughter of the Innocents* (from the Corpus Christi Cycle produced at Wakefield in the fifteenth and sixteenth centuries).

33. Herod is called "the Great" only at *AJ* 18.130–36, where the term appears three times. The passage is a complex discussion of the descendants of Herod and includes other people named Herod, so the sobriquet may be more a genealogical distinction between the first Herod and his descendants rather than a qualitative expression. Regardless, it has become almost universal.

CHAPTER ONE

Herod's First Trip to Rome

Near the end of 40 B.C., Herod, the tetrarch of Judaea and a Roman citizen, appeared unexpectedly in Rome. He had been so anxious to come to Rome that he ignored the perils of a winter voyage and reports of civil strife in the city: even the persuasive Cleopatra could not keep him from setting forth from Alexandria. His past few years had been difficult. Civil war in Judaea had seen the death of his father and brother. His Roman patron, C. Cassius Longinus, who had promised to name him king of Judaea,[1] had died at Philippi. Yet the young tetrarch felt that he might be helped by another Roman whom he had known and who was now reputed to be a power in Rome, Marcus Antonius. Antonius had been a friend of Herod's father's and had known Herod himself for at least two years, having made him tetrarch. Hence Herod, who may have had some misunderstood concept of the right of *provocatio*,[2] felt that the desperate midwinter journey was his only chance of survival.

His trip was indeed a great success, for after only a week in Rome, he had been named king of Judaea. Herod had been introduced to the Senate, and Antonius had proposed the kingship. Octavian had agreed to support the proposal. Herod left the Senate walking between the two triumvirs, eventually going to Antonius's home for dinner. This auspicious event, in which Herod demonstrated his ability to bring Antonius and Octavian to rare agreement, initiated over thirty years of rule by the greatest builder-dynast Judaea was ever to see. His early visit to Rome was a major influence on the direction of his rule. While in the city, he made a number of lifelong friends,

---

1. *BJ* 1.225; *AJ* 14.280.

2. On the concept of *provocatio*, see A. H. M. Jones, "I Appeal unto Caesar," in *Studies Presented to David Moore Robinson*, 2 (St. Louis, 1953): 918–30.

who were to be of great service to him and would become some of the most powerful figures in Augustan Rome. Herod also became friends with a number of Greek intellectuals, especially those interested in the East and in Jewish history and culture. These were men whom Antonius had cultivated, and they would remain influential long after his death: some of them would eventually reside at Herod's court. And finally, and perhaps most important, Herod saw the physical aspect of the city of Rome at a crucial point in its history, the early stages of the dynamic building program that had begun with Sulla, Pompey, and Caesar and was to continue under Augustus. Herod only spent a single week in Rome, but it was a major formative experience of his life.

The principal sources for Herod's visit are two similar descriptions by Josephus.[3] That in *BJ* is slightly more detailed in describing Herod's perilous journey. He departed for Rome from Alexandria, where his eagerness to leave made him spurn even the hospitality of Cleopatra. His immediate destination was Pamphylia, but a particularly fierce storm, which he barely survived, caused a detour to Rhodes, where damage from the Roman civil war was still visible. Despite his own limited funds, Herod financed the reconstruction of the city, the first documented instance of his talent for urban renewal and rebuilding. He then had a trireme built, sailed for Brundisium, and went directly to Rome, where he told Antonius all that had happened to him.

The midwinter context of the trip is an essential point in Josephus's narrative, and there is no reason to doubt it. Josephus's date of Ol. 184 would mean no later than the winter of 41–40 B.C.,[4] but the consuls mentioned, Cn. Domitius Calvinus (II) and C. Asinius Pollio, are the *consules ordinarii* of 40 B.C.[5] Yet Josephus was often inconsistent about synchronisms between Olympiads and consulships, an inevitable problem, since one began in July and the other in January.[6] Moreover, the winter of 41–40 B.C. is impossible, inasmuch as Antonius was away from Rome (and did not return until the middle of 40 B.C.), and the spirit of cooperation between Antonius and Octavian implicit in Herod's visit can only reflect the situation after the triumvirs' agreement at Brundisium and the marriage of Antonius and Octavia, events of autumn 40 B.C.[7] Thus Herod was in Rome in "midwinter,"

---

3. *BJ* 1.279–85; *AJ* 14.375–89. There are casual references to the event, without detail, by Strabo (16.2.46), Tacitus (*Histories* 5.9), Appian (*Civil War* 5.75), and Dio (49.22).

4. E. J. Bickerman, *Chronology of the Ancient World*, 2d ed. (Ithaca, N.Y., 1980), 120.

5. Broughton, 2: 378.

6. An example is at *AJ* 14.487. This was a constant problem of historians during the Roman period and affected Polybios, Diodoros, and Dionysios of Halikarnassos as well as Josephus (see Bickerman [supra, n. 4], 76).

7. Syme, *RR*, 215–18.

as Josephus put it, and during the consular year of Calvinus and Pollio (40 B.C.), which had begun in Ol. 184. Midwinter implies late in the calendar year, probably the latter part of December.[8]

Herod's reason for going to Rome in December 40 B.C. was to exploit the contact he had already made with Antonius, who was now at the peak of his power.[9] Antonius had known and helped Herod's father, Antipatros, while serving under the Syrian command of Aulus Gabinius (57–55 B.C.). Gabinius was the first Roman to institute a major building program in the southern Levant.[10] Herod had thus at an early age been exposed to the architectural obligations of powerful men.[11]

8. See (for modern sources) Otto, *RE*, 25–26; Schalit, *KH*, 83–88, 146–48; E. Mary Smallwood, *The Jews under Roman Rule* (Studies in Judaism in Late Antiquity, 20 [Leiden, 1976]), 55–56; David Braund, *Rome and the Friendly King: The Character of Client Kingship* (London, 1984), 24–25. Calvinus and Pollio had been replaced by *consules suffecti* by this time (Broughton, 2: 378), but Josephus was dating the year by the *ordinarii*. It is slightly possible, however, that Herod did not come to Rome until February of the following year, as this was the month fixed for the Senate to receive foreign embassies (see Richard J. A. Talbert, *The Senate of Imperial Rome* [Princeton, 1984], 208–9), but it is likely that the urgent nature of the journey would not have allowed him to wait several months, and any date beyond the end of 40 B.C. does violence to the data supplied by Josephus. Nevertheless, a date of 39 B.C. is indicated by Appian (*Civil War* 5.75), who listed Herod among kings appointed by Antonius in that year. Although it should be emphasized that Appian refered to the beginning of Herod's kingship rather than his visit to Rome, various commentators have argued for a 39 B.C. date for the visit, especially W. E. Filmer ("The Chronology of the Reign of Herod the Great," *JThS*, n.s., 17 [1966], 284–98). But 39 B.C. is difficult to reconcile with Josephus's emphasis on the midwinter context of the trip and the major role Antonius played in the events. Antonius was away from Rome in both the winters of 41–40 B.C. and 39–38 B.C. (Dio 48.39; Syme, *RR*, 214–26; Eleanor Goltz Huzar, *Mark Antony: A Biography* [London, 1978], 141) and was in the city only from summer 40 to summer 39: at the latter time he left for two years in Athens. Unless one is to reject the midwinter timing of the trip, near the end of 40 B.C. seems the only possible date. Herod may have been in Rome around the turn of the year (from 40 to 39 B.C.), probably after 10 December, when the tribunes for the new year took office (Bickerman [supra n. 4], 64–65). This may have added to later confusion as to what year he had been in Rome, even if his trip did not actually overlap the two years. In addition, some of the administrative details regarding his appointment as king may not have been completed until the new year.

9. Josephus (*AJ* 14.386–88) indicated that Herod's initial purpose was to persuade the Romans to give the throne to his brother-in-law Aristoboulos III, who as a Hasmonean had a stronger hereditary claim. Regardless of whether this was the original reason, it was soon forgotten, except perhaps by Herod, who before long had Aristoboulos killed (*AJ* 15.53–56). Furthermore, it would not have been difficult for Herod to realize that a stable Rome was in his own best interest (G. W. Bowersock, *Roman Arabia* [Cambridge, Mass., 1983], 38).

10. Gabinius was the most extensive but not the only Roman builder of the late Republic in the southern Levant: see infra, ch. 6.

11. *BJ* 1.165–66; *AJ* 14.87–88. On Gabinius, see Eva Matthews Sanford, "The Career of Aulus Gabinius," *TAPA* 70 (1939): 64–92; Jones, *Cities*, 257–58; Erich S. Gruen, *The Last Generation of the Roman Republic* (reprint, Berkeley, 1995), passim; Richard S. Williams, "The Role of *Amicitia* in the Career of A. Gabinius (cos. 58)," *Phoenix* 32 (1978): 195–210, with previous bibliography; A. N. Sherwin-White, *Roman Foreign Policy in the East, 168 B.C. to A.D. 1* (London, 1984), 271–79.

While serving with Gabinius, Antonius may have met the adolescent Herod. Regardless, young Herod would have heard about the Roman officer who had aided his father. Herod and Antonius met, perhaps for the second time, in Bithynia in 41 B.C., shortly after the battle of Philippi. Herod was now a Roman citizen, and Antonius was in the midst of his fateful two-year stay in the East, which would result in his liaison with Cleopatra.[12] When Antonius arrived in Bithynia, he was approached by a delegation of Jews, who accused Herod of treason and sedition. Herod came to Bithynia to defend himself and appeared before Antonius, who already esteemed him highly. The defense was successful, although money is said to have changed hands. Nevertheless, some weeks later, at Daphne near Antioch, just after Antonius had met Cleopatra, the charge was made again, this time by one hundred of the most powerful Jewish leaders.[13] Again Antonius decided in Herod's favor, citing the previous friendship between himself and Herod's father, and appointed Herod and his brother Phasael tetrarchs. A third accusation against Herod—this time at Tyre by a thousand Jewish leaders—was also unsuccessful.[14] Although Josephus's account of the three confrontations, involving increasingly larger and suspiciously rounded numbers of accusers, is formulaic and probably exaggerated, the result is clear: Antonius consistently supported Herod against his opponents. Herod came to have confidence in Antonius's willingness to help him.

Accompanying Antonius during this eastern trip was a young refugee from the battle of Philippi, M. Valerius Messalla Corvinus.[15] Messalla had been with Cassius in Asia Minor in 42 B.C.,[16] where he may have first met Herod, since Herod and Cassius were in regular contact in the months before Philippi, both involved in avenging the recent murder of Herod's father.[17] What part Messalla played in these events is unknown. But when the Jewish leaders made their second accusation against Herod at Daphne in early 41 B.C., Messalla, who had switched his allegiance from the Republican cause to that of Antonius, knew Herod well enough to speak up in his

12. *BJ* 1.242; *AJ* 14.302–3. Five years earlier, Julius Caesar had bestowed citizenship on Herod's father (*BJ* 1.194, *AJ* 14.137): Charlotte E. Goodfellow, *Roman Citizenship* (Lancaster, Pa., 1935), 93–94. On citizenship given to provincials, see J. P. V. D. Balsdon, *Romans and Aliens* (London, 1979), 82–96.

13. *BJ* 1.243–45; *AJ* 14.324–26.

14. *BJ* 1.245; *AJ* 14.327.

15. Messalla was yet to become the patron of Tibullus, Ovid, and other literati. For modern bibliography on Messalla, see Jacob Hammer, *Prolegomena to an Edition of the Panegyricus Messalae* (New York, 1925); Rudolf Hanslik, "M. Valerius Messalla Corvinus" (# 261), in *RE*, 2d ser., 15 (1955): 131–57; Alfredo Valvo, "M. Valerio Messalla Corvino negli studi più recenti," *ANRW* 2.30 (1982–83): 1663–80; Ronald Syme, *The Augustan Aristocracy* (Oxford, 1986), 200–226.

16. Velleius 2.71; Dio 47.24; Hammer (supra, n. 15), 17–18.

17. *BJ* 1.225–35; *AJ* 14.288–93.

defense. No reason was given by Josephus as to why Messalla might have wished to speak on behalf of Herod: it seems that in a short time Messalla had become impressed with the man.

Messalla was the first of several future followers of Augustus who would come to respect Herod. It is difficult to imagine that young Messalla, who had studied in Athens along with Horace[18] and Cicero's son,[19] did not already have the tastes in the arts and literature that would distinguish him in the Augustan era. He would have shared his interests with a dynamic, culturally inclined personality like Herod. For Herod, association with Messalla would have led to contact with other intellectuals, especially those interested in the East and Jewish affairs. When the tetrarch appeared in Rome at the end of 40 B.C., Messalla, now *praetor suffectus* and a supporter of Octavian,[20] took up his cause and introduced him to the Senate, whose prerogative it was to receive foreign embassies.[21] A certain Atratinos[22] seconded Messalla's introduction. This seems to have been L. Sempronius Atratinus, a supporter of Antonius's, who was probably also *praetor suffectus*.[23] But Messalla was the principal speaker. He noted the services of Herod's father to Rome and mentioned Herod's own good will toward the Romans. He

18. Horace, *Odes* 3.21.

19. Cicero, *Ad Atticum* 12.32.2. See also Lloyd W. Daly, "Roman Study Abroad," *AJP* 71 (1950): 49–53.

20. Broughton, 2: 380; 3: 213–14. By this time Messalla seems to have switched his support to Octavian: Herod's role as a conciliator between the two triumvirs suggests this. In summer 41 B.C., Messalla was still with Antonius in the East, but by 37 B.C., he was commanding part of Octavian's army (Appian, *Civil War* 5.102). In the autumn of 40 B.C., Antonius and Octavian concluded the agreement of Brundisium and Antonius married Octavia, which led to a period of good relations between the two triumvirs, as demonstrated by their cooperation in the matter of Herod several weeks later, and this would not have been a time for a major transfer of allegiance. It has thus reasonably been suggested that Messalla's transfer must have predated the Brundisium agreement, in other words, fallen between summer 41 B.C. and autumn 40 B.C. (Hammer [supra, n. 15], 25–27; Hanslik [supra, n. 15] 139–40), and Messalla was already a partisan of Octavian's by the time Herod came to Rome. If so, it does not seem to have affected his continuing support of Herod, who was still strongly attached to Antonius. See, however, Syme, *Augustan Aristocracy* (supra, n. 15), who suggested that Messalla remained independent of both Octavian and Antonius until as late as 33 or 32 B.C. (pp. 205–8).

21. Polybios 6.13; Cicero, *Ad Quintum fratrem* 2.12.3; on the Senate's role in diplomacy, see Talbert (supra, n. 8), 411–25.

22. *BJ* 1.284; Agratinos or Satrapinos at *AJ* 14.384.

23. *RE*, # 26; Syme, *RR*, 231, 282, 328, 339; Syme, *Augustan Aristocracy* (supra, n. 15) 29, 41, 45, 109, 329, 354; Broughton, 2: 615; F. Münzer, "L. Sempronius Atratinus" (# 26), in *RE*, 2d ser., 2 (1923): 1366–68. Distinguished by the age of seventeen as an orator (56 B.C.), by 40 B.C. he was one of the augurs; in the 30's B.C., he was a naval commander for Antonius and *consul suffectus* in 34 B.C.; in 21 B.C. he celebrated a triumph. He lived until A.D. 7. Although the details of his life and career are scattered, he does not seem to have shown any particular interest in Herod, Hellenism, Judaea, or the East. He probably acted merely as a prominent Antonian partisan in seconding the motion of a prominent Octavian one.

also emphasized that the Parthians were threatening the East. At this point, Antonius, again mentioning the Parthians, proposed that Herod should be named king of Judaea, fulfilling Cassius's promise of three years earlier. Evidently the vote was unanimous in Herod's favor. A procession was then formed to go to the Capitol, led by the consuls and magistrates, with Herod between Antonius and Octavian. A sacrifice was made, the decree was deposited in the Capitol, and a banquet in Herod's honor was given by Antonius.[24]

It is clear that by this time Herod had received the most important introduction of his life, that to Octavian, the future Augustus.[25] It is possible that Antonius introduced the tetrarch to his triumviral colleague, but it is more probable that it was Messalla, the former Antonian, Herod's patron and Octavian's follower, who had introduced Herod to the Senate, who also introduced him to his new patron.

Messalla was the first friend Herod made among the future Augustan aristocracy. Another prominent Augustan who eventually became a close friend was Messalla's associate M. Vipsanius Agrippa.[26] Herod and Agrippa came to have great esteem for each other, said to be second only to their individual esteem for Augustus.[27] Agrippa was an important source for Herod about developments, especially architectural, in Augustan Rome: at the time of Herod's visit, he may already have begun work on the aqueducts of Rome.[28] Documented contact between the two is not until 23–21 B.C., at Mytilene, but by that time Herod and Agrippa are described as already being the best of friends,[29] a statement that implies extensive previous association. The specifics of that earlier contact are unknown, and during the years 39–23 B.C., Agrippa and Herod do not seem ever to have been in the same area.[30] Hence it is probable that they first met at the time of Herod's

---

24. *BJ* 1.284–85; *AJ* 14.384–89.

25. Although interest in Syria and the southern Levant on the part of Octavian is to be be expected, since it was an important element of contemporary Roman foreign policy, he may have had another reason to be particularly aware of that part of the world. His stepfather, L. Marcius Philippus, whom his mother Atia married in 58 B.C. when Octavian was four or five years old, had been governor of Syria in 61–60 B.C. and had rebuilt Gabae, a town probably in the vicinity of Mt. Carmel, renaming it Philippeis. He may also have refounded Pella, in the Jordan valley. Thus Octavian grew up in a household especially knowledgeable about the East, where there was at least one town named after his stepfather. On Philippus, see infra, pp. 179–80.

26. The closeness between Messalla and Agrippa is demonstrated by their later sharing of Antonius's house on the Palatine (Dio 53.27).

27. *BJ* 1.400; *AJ* 15.361.

28. Dio 48.32; Frederick W. Shipley, *Agrippa's Building Activities in Rome* (St. Louis, 1933), 25–28.

29. *AJ* 15.350.

30. For Agrippa's movements in these years, see Dio 51.3; Reinhold, 58–77; Roddaz, 451. Malalas (220–22) placed Agrippa in Syria after Actium, but this was rejected by Glanville

Roman visit of 40 B.C.[31] Agrippa was *praetor urbanus* that year and already a member of the Senate,[32] and if his official duties did not bring him into contact with Herod, they may have met through Messalla. It is unlikely, however, that any intimacy could have developed until after the death of Antonius.[33] Agrippa was one of the few participants in the civil war who never changed sides. He was never with any faction other than the Caesarean one, and he seems to have been a companion of young C. Octavius well before the death of Caesar, perhaps even a childhood friend.[34] Thus Agrippa in 40 B.C. would have found Herod a matter of curiosity and interest, but perhaps little more than yet another of the strange easterners Antonius seemed to collect, not yet worthy of special attention.

After a week in Rome, Herod returned to Judaea. It took him nearly three years to achieve in actuality the kingship Rome had given him. His position was not assured until late 37 B.C.,[35] and then only with the military assistance of Antonius and a large Roman force under the command of C. Sosius, governor of Syria. Sosius actually captured Jerusalem for Herod, for which he triumphed in 34 B.C., rebuilding the temple of Apollo in the Campus Martius, which came to be called Apollo Sosianus.[36] The early career of Sosius is unknown, but as an Antonian he too may have met Herod in 40 B.C.[37]

Despite Herod's lengthy efforts to acquire what Rome had promised, his week in the city was one of the most influential of his life. He already knew Antonius and Messalla, and he now met many of the future leaders of the emergent new era, including Octavian and Agrippa. Messalla and Agrippa could have provided continuing information about the cultural activities of early Augustan Rome. Other prominent personalities, such as Asinius Pollio and Q. Dellius, may also have met Herod. The personal contacts Herod made during that week in 40 B.C. served him both politically and intellectually for many years. These contacts may have included an intellectual circle, centered around Antonius, that was interested in the East, particularly in the culture of Syria and Palestine. These areas had only come within the

---

Downey, *A History of Antioch in Syria from Seleucus to the Arab Conquest* (Princeton, 1961), 172. For Herod's movements, see the *Zeittafel* in Otto, *RE*.

31. Roddaz, 451, but see 66–68, where it is argued that Agrippa had already departed for his command in Gaul before Herod's arrival.

32. Dio 48.20; Reinhold, 21–24; Broughton, 2: 380.

33. Reinhold, 84–85.

34. Nikolaos of Damaskos (*FrGrHist*, # 90), fr. 127, ch. 7.

35. A date of 36 B.C. is prefered by Filmer (supra, n. 8), 285–89.

36. Frederick W. Shipley, "Chronology of the Building Operations in Rome from the Death of Caesar to the Death of Augustus," *MAAR* 9 (1931): 25–28.

37. He may have been quaestor in 39 B.C. or slightly earlier and thus in Rome in late 40 B.C. (Broughton, 2: 387, 3: 200).

Roman sphere during the previous generation, creating a developing interest in Jews and Judaea, which had hitherto been little known to the Romans.[38]

Greek authors as early as Herodotos had been aware of the Jews and Judaea.[39] Probably the first to write a work on the Jews was Hekataios of Abdera, whose extant fragments range from Abraham to his own era, the fourth century B.C.[40] By the first century B.C., a number of Greek historians had discussed these topics.[41] Conspicuous to the Romans would have been Apollonios Molon of Alabanda, seemingly the first after Hekataios of Abdera to write a work specifically on the Jews.[42] Apollonios spent most of his life on Rhodes, where he was the teacher of Caesar and Cicero, and visited Rome as a Rhodian ambassador in the 80's B.C.[43] His work was used by Alexandros Polyhistor of Miletos, who came to Rome in 82 B.C. as a prisoner of war,[44] and wrote *On the Jews*, whose extant fragments indicate a scope from Abraham through Solomon and the prophets down to the Hellenistic dynasts. Another Greek to write about the Jews was Teukros of Kyzikos:[45] a work on Mithradates implies a date contemporary with Alexandros and Apollonios, or toward the middle of the first century B.C. All three were from Asia Minor, and it is probable that the contact between Rome and Judaea at the time of Pompey was a stimulus for these writings.[46]

Before the middle of the first century B.C., Jewish matters and Judaean details were finding their way into the works of Latin authors. Lucretius may have referred to the Dead Sea.[47] Cicero mentioned the Jews several times,

---

38. Harry J. Leon, *The Jews of Ancient Rome* (Philadelphia, 1960), 2–3. The extent of this interest has been overemphasized, however: see Louis H. Feldman, "Asinius Pollio and His Jewish Interests," *TAPA* 84 (1953): 73–80. For intellectual life in Rome in the first century B.C., see, generally, Elizabeth Rawson, *Intellectual Life in the Late Roman Republic* (London, 1985); on the interest in the Jews, see 61–63.

39. Herodotos 2.104–6. For early contacts between the Greek world and the Jews, see Elias J. Bickerman, *The Jews in the Greek Age* (Cambridge, Mass., 1988), 13–19.

40. *FrGrHist*, # 264; *Apion* 1.183. Abraham: *AJ* 1.159; the fourth century B.C.: *Apion* 2.43. See also F. Jacoby, "Hekataios aus Abdera" (# 4), in *RE*, 14 (1912): 2750–69; Walter Spoerri, "Hekataios von Abdera," in *Reallexikon für Antike und Christenthum*, 14 (Stuttgart, 1988): 275–310. The extant fragments attributed to his *Peri Ioudaion* (*FrGrHist*, # 264, frs. 21–24) are probably spurious: see the commentary in *FrGrHist* and Louis H. Feldman, *Jew and Gentile in the Ancient World* (Princeton, 1993), 8–9.

41. References to Jews and Judaism by classical authors have been collected by Mehanem Stern in *Greek and Latin Authors on Jews and Judaism* (Jerusalem, 1974–80).

42. *FrGrHist*, # 728; see also Stern (supra, n. 41), 1: 148–49.

43. Strabo 14.2.13; Valerius Maximus 2.2.3; Plutarch, *Caesar* 3, *Cicero* 4; Cicero, *Brutus* 307–16; George Kennedy, *The Art of Persuasion in Greece* (Princeton, 1963), 326–27; J. Brzoska, "Apollonios" (# 85), in *RE*, 3 (1895): 141–44.

44. *FrGrHist*, # 273, esp. fr. 19.

45. *FrGrHist*, # 274.

46. Stern (supra, n. 41), 1.165.

47. Lucretius 6.756–59.

especially concerning political events since the early 50's B.C.,[48] as did Varro,[49] who was one of the first to discuss Jewish religion. Thus Romans at the end of the Republic were developing an interest in the Jews and Judaea, an interest perhaps originating in the political involvement of Pompey, but soon spreading to curiosity about the social, religious, and natural history of that part of the world. This was the atmosphere in which the Roman aristocrats of the late Republic who were to be the leaders of Augustan Rome grew up.

In addition, the new generation of Roman poets that began to write in the 40's B.C. was interested in the Jews and Judaea. Vergil and Horace are the first extant Latin poets to include definite information about the southern Levant. Vergil was the first to mention Idumaea,[50] and it seems no mere coincidence that notice of Herod's homeland should have appeared in Latin literature shortly after Herod's visit to Rome. Vergil's fourth *Eclogue* is also a product of this period, of the very year of Herod's visit and Asinius Pollio's consulship.[51] Horace referred several times to the Jews and was the first in extant Latin literature to mention Herod himself.[52] Soon the Jews entered Roman historical writing too, in the works of Asinius Pollio.[53]

Moreover, a Jewish community had existed in Rome for some time.[54] Although Valerius Maximus seems to refer to Jews in Rome in the second century B.C., it is not clear whether he meant a permanent community or merely transients.[55] But after Pompey returned from his eastern campaign in 61 B.C., Jewish prisoners of war were a noticeable element in the city.[56] Two years later, in October 59 B.C., Cicero defended L. Valerius Flaccus, who had been charged, among other things, with confiscation of Jewish funds while on a propraetorian command in Asia.[57] Cicero's defense discussed Jewish financial practices at length and described the Jewish community in Rome as a sizable group that was politically active. Fifteen years later, it was particularly prominent at Caesar's funeral.[58] It is no wonder,

---

48. *Pro Flacco* 66–69; *De provinciis consularibus* 10–12.

49. The numerous references were collected by Stern (supra, n. 41), 1: 207–12.

50. *Georgics* 3.12.

51. It has even been suggested that Herod appears in the poem in the guise of Tiphys: see E. Coleiro, "Quis Tiphys?" *Latinitas* 22 (1974): 109–16.

52. *Satires* 1.4.143; 1.5.100; *Epistle* 2.2.184. It has been conjectured that Horace had Jewish ancestry: see William Hardy Alexander, "The Enigma of Horace's Mother," *CP* 37 (1942): 385–97, but see Stern (supra, n. 41), 1: 321–22.

53. *AJ* 14.138 (via Strabo); see also Stern (supra, n. 41), 1: 213–14.

54. See Schürer (NEV), 3: 73–81, on the early Jewish community in Rome.

55. Valerius Maximus 1.3.3; Leon (supra, n. 38), 2–4.

56. Philon, *Embassy to Gaius* 155; Leonard Victor Rutgers, "Roman Policy toward the Jews: Expulsions from the City of Rome during the First Century C.E.," *ClAnt* 13 (1994): 59–60.

57. *Pro Flacco* 66–69.

58. Suetonius, *Divine Julius* 84.

then, that in the late Republic, and into the Augustan era, Jewish culture was of great topicality in Rome, and Herod was thus assured of an interested and informed reception.

This emerging interest in Judaea and Jewish affairs had, by the 40's B.C., influenced the development of a literary and intellectual circle centered around Antonius, whose own interest in things Greek and Eastern was a stimulus to the group. In many ways this was the birth of the literary circle that was to mature over the next twenty years around Augustus. Such literary and intellectual circles were common by the late Republic. Antonius's own grandfather, M. Antonius (cos. 99 B.C.), had brought Menedemos, a rhetorician, to be his guest in Rome,[59] and Pompey, Caesar, Cicero, and Brutus, among many others, had their own circles of Greek scholars.[60] Antonius the triumvir was no exception. When Herod came to Rome in 40 B.C., he would have been particularly interesting to the Greek members of Antonius's circle.[61] These included men such as Alexandros Polyhistor of Miletos, Timagenes of Alexandria, Strabo of Amaseia, and Nikolaos of Damaskos.

59. Cicero, *De oratore* 1.85.

60. Balsdon (supra, n. 12), 54–58. On the topic of Greek intellectuals and Romans generally, see M. H. Crawford, "Greek Intellectuals and the Roman Aristocracy in the First Century B.C.," in *Imperialism in the Ancient World*, ed. P. D. A. Garnsey and C. R. Whittaker (Cambridge, 1978), 193–207; Bowersock, *Augustus*, 10. But not all Greek intellectuals attached themselves to Romans or to other Greeks: a conspicuous exception to the pattern of Roman patronage was Diodoros of Sicily, who was in Rome ca. 56–30 B.C. but remained an outsider and an independent scholar: see Kenneth S. Sacks, *Diodorus Siculus and the First Century* (Princeton, 1990), 184–91.

61. Although the circle consisted of both Greeks and Romans, Herod probably did not speak Latin at this time. As *philoromaios* one might expect him eventually to have learned Latin, which had been known in Judaea since at least the time of Julius Caesar (*AJ* 14.191, 197); in fact, Latin seems to have been somewhat more common in Judaea than in other eastern provinces and kingdoms, perhaps because of a long-standing Jewish antipathy toward Greek, whose teaching was banned on occasion (Smallwood [supra, n. 8], 424; Jorma Kaimio, *The Romans and the Greek Language* [Commentationes Humanarum Litterarum, 64 (Helsinki, 1979)], 115–16; Joseph A. Fitzmyer, "The Languages of Palestine in the First Century A.D.," *Catholic Biblical Quarterly* 32 [1970]: 501–31, and Balsdon [supra, n. 12], 116–45). Even such a hellenophile as Marcus Antonius published decrees in both Greek and Latin in this region (*AJ* 14.319). But there is no evidence of Herod's personal use of the Latin language at any time in his life, and his memoirs (*FrGrHist*, # 236) were probably written in Greek. Latin is not even listed among the accomplishments of the astonishly multilingual Cleopatra, although she spoke at least eight languages (Plutarch, *Antonius* 27). Any desire of Herod to demonstrate his Romanness by speaking Latin would have collided with the desire of Roman aristocrats to speak Greek, and he would have been able to address the Senate in Greek and without an interpreter. Greek ambassadors had addressed the Senate in their native language as early as the time of Pyrrhos of Epeiros, when his advisor Kineas came to Rome in 280 B.C. (Plutarch, *Pyrrhos* 18–21), although it was not until the 80's B.C. that Apollonios Molon became the first to speak without an interpreter (Valerius Maximus 2.2.3). From that time the use of interpreters seems to have been rare, and by the 50's B.C., senators were generally expected to know Greek and to be capable of being addressed in that language (Cicero, *De finibus* 5.89). On this problem generally, see Balsdon (supra, n. 12), 126; Kaimio (supra), 103–10.

Romans in the group included Q. Dellius and a man who even as Herod visited was being commemorated by Vergil, the consul C. Asinius Pollio.

The senior member of the circle was Alexandros Polyhistor.[62] He had come to Rome at the time of Sulla as the slave of a certain Cornelius Lentulus, and he was eventually given his freedom by either Lentulus or Sulla; hence he was known in Rome as Cornelius Alexander. Whether this Cornelius Lentulus was the same as or related to Antonius's stepfather, P. Cornelius Lentulus Sura,[63] cannot be established, since the vast number of Cornelii Lentuli makes the exact identity of Alexandros's owner uncertain.[64] Antonius's stepfather was quaestor in 81 B.C. and had some association with Sulla, but there are other candidates for the role of Alexandros's owner. The best are L. Cornelius Lentulus,[65] a shadowy follower of Sulla's, and Cn. Cornelius Lentulus Clodianus,[66] who fought under Sulla and was consul in 72 B.C. Nevertheless, it is possible that Alexandros was either in the household of the young Antonius or in that of a relative, and it might have been Alexandros who first excited Antonius's interest in the East, through works such as his *On the Jews* and *Aigyptiaka.* Alexandros was still active in the 30's B.C., when he taught C. Julius Hyginus, Augustus's librarian and Ovid's teacher.[67] His eventual death by a fire in his own house was one of the well-known events of the era.

Timagenes of Alexandria,[68] who had come to Rome in 55 B.C. as the prisoner of Aulus Gabinius, was also prominent.[69] Timagenes became an intimate of Antonius's, and introduced him to other Greeks.[70] He eventually became an adherent of Octavian's and went to live in his household, but the two quarreled, and Timagenes went to the home of C. Asinius Pollio, a former pupil, and became known as a wit and raconteur.[71] Timagenes was a

62. *FrGrHist,* # 273; G. Schwartz, "Alexandros von Milet" (# 88), in *RE,* 1 (1894): 1449–52; Rawson (supra, n. 38), see index.

63. F. Münzer, "P. Cornelius Lentulus Sura" (# 240), in *RE,* 7 (1900): 1399–1402; Broughton, 2: 76.

64. He is only identified as "Kornelios Lentoulos" in the *Souda,* and there are thirty Cornelii Lentuli from the first century B.C. listed in *RE.*

65. F. Münzer, "L. Cornelius Lentulus" (# 194), in *RE,* 7 (1900): 1369–71.

66. F. Münzer, "Cn. Cornelius Lentulus Clodianus" (# 216), in *RE,* 7 (1900): 1380–81; Broughton, 2: 116.

67. Suetonius, *On Grammarians* 20.

68. *FrGrHist,* # 88; Bowersock, *Augustus,* 109–10; 124–27; Balsdon (supra, n. 12), 183–85; F. Gisinger, "Timagenes" (# 2), in *RE,* 2d ser., 11 (1936): 1063–73; Marta Sordi, "Timagene di Alessandria: Uno storico ellenocentrico e filobarbaro," *ANRW* 2.30 (1982–83): 775–97.

69. *Souda,* "Timagenes."

70. Plutarch, *Antonius* 72.

71. *Souda,* "Pollion"; Seneca, *Epistles* 91.13; A. B. Bosworth, "Asinius Pollio and Augustus," *Historia* 21 (1972): 445–46; Bowersock, *Augustus,* 110.

prolific writer, and his historical works were available by 29 B.C., when his protégé Strabo of Amaseia began to use them.[72]

Timagenes believed that rulers should benefit from the lessons of history, but felt that Augustus had unfortunately failed to do so, and after their quarrel, he burned his biography of the Princeps.[73] There is no evidence that Timagenes wrote a work specifically on the topic of Judaea and the Jews, but Josephus cited him as a source for Jewish history in the Hellenistic period.[74]

Timagenes was instrumental in introducing Greeks to Antonius as well as in educating a younger generation of both Greeks and Romans. One of the Greeks he brought to Antonius's attention was Alexas of Laodikeia, who was to become the most influential Greek among Antonius's intimates.[75] After Actium he was sent by Antonius to persuade Herod not to join Octavian. It seems unlikely that Antonius would have chosen someone unknown to Herod for this delicate mission; Herod and Alexas may have met as early as the summer of 43 B.C. in Laodikeia, when Herod seems to have been there with Cassius and Messalla. They could have renewed their acquaintance in Rome in 40 B.C., and their paths probably crossed in the following years. Alexas's embassy after Actium was particularly unsuccessful. Herod had already joined Octavian, and he persuaded Alexas to betray Antonius. Alexas then went to Octavian, who ordered him to be returned to Laodikaia and executed. Alexas felt that Herod would save him, and Herod did plead on his behalf, but there evidently had been some previous problem with Alexas, perhaps his persuasiveness in convincing Antonius to abandon Octavia for Cleopatra, and Octavian thus refused to relent.

Timagenes' protégés also included two of the most important writers of the Augustan period,[76] the historian and geographer Strabo of Amaseia[77] and the historian Nikolaos of Damaskos.[78] Strabo and Nikolaos felt that men of public affairs needed a knowledge of geography and history,[79] something learned from Timagenes. This belief was passed on by Nikolaos, at

72. Bowersock, *Augustus*, 125–26.

73. Seneca, *On Anger* 3.23.

74. *Apion* 2.84; *AJ* 13.319, 344.

75. *BJ* 1.393; *AJ* 15.197–98 (emended from Alexandros); Plutarch, *Antonius* 72; B. Niese, "Alexas von Laodikeia" (# 1a), in *RE*, suppl. 1 (1903): 56; Plutarch, *Life of Antony*, ed. C. B. R. Pelling (Cambridge, 1988), 298.

76. Bowersock, *Augustus*, 124.

77. W. Aly, "Strabon von Amaseia" (# 3), in *RE*, 2d ser., 7 (1931): 76–155; W. Aly, *Strabon von Amaseia* (Bonn, 1957); François Lasserre, "Strabon devant l'Empire romain," *ANRW* 2.30 (1982–83): 867–96.

78. Barbara Scardigli, "Asinius Pollio und Nikolaos von Damaskus," *Historia* 32 (1983): 121–23; Bowersock, *Augustus*, 125–26, 137.

79. Strabo 1.1.16; see also 15.1.73; Nikolaos (*FrGrHist*, # 90), fr. 135.

least, to his own protégé Herod. Strabo was in Rome ca. 44–35 B.C. and returned there in 29 B.C. to write his history.[80] The work was used frequently by Josephus as a source for Hellenistic Judaea and thus indicates Strabo's detailed treatment of that region and his early interest in that part of the world. Most of the extant fragments deal heavily with Judaea and show a dependence on Timagenes.[81] Strabo's interest in Judaea may have led to a visit to Herod's court after he finished his history.[82]

His colleague Nikolaos exerted strong influence on Herod.[83] Nikolaos's early life is poorly documented, and there is no direct evidence that he was in Rome in 40 B.C., but his association with the Antonian intellectual circle makes this probable, and he may have renewed acquaintance at that time with Herod, seemingly an old family friend.[84] They had perhaps first met in Damaskos,[85] and their fathers, both named Antipatros, had probably been acquainted since 63 B.C., when Herod's father came to Damaskos on an embassy to Pompey.[86]

Yet contact between Herod and Nikolaos was minimal in the decade after 40 B.C. Nikolaos became the tutor to the children of Antonius and Cleopatra,[87] which might temporarily have affected friendship with Herod, who was in the process of becoming violently opposed to Cleopatra. In 36 B.C., having escorted Antonius to the Euphrates on his Parthian expedition, Cleopatra visited Judaea, where she allegedly attempted to seduce Herod. The latter wisely resisted, however, and even considered killing her, but was dissuaded by his advisors; instead, he sent her on her way laden with gifts.[88] The entire story may be a piece of anti-Cleopatra propaganda designed to

80. *FrGrHist*, # 91; Bowersock, *Augustus*, 123, 126; Syme, *Augustan Aristocracy* (supra, n. 15), 346.

81. See, e.g., *AJ* 13.319 = Strabo fr. 11 = Timagenes fr. 5.

82. Infra, pp. 64–65.

83. Wacholder, *Nicolaus;* Emilio Gabba, "The Historians and Augustus," in *Caesar Augustus: Seven Aspects*, ed. Fergus Millar and Erich Segal (Oxford, 1984), 61–66; Richard Laqueur, "Nikolaos" (# 20), in *RE*, 33 (1936): 362–424; Bowersock, *Augustus*, 135.

84. Wacholder, *Nicolaus*, 23.

85. Ibid., 23.

86. *BJ* 1.131; *AJ* 14.37.

87. Although this is documented only by the obscure Sophronios of Damaskos (patriarch of Jerusalem in the first half of the seventh century A.C.), in a discussion of notable Damascenes (*Account of the Miracles of Saints Cyrus and John* 54 = *FrGrHist*, # 90, T2), and seems to have been ignored by Nikolaos himself, there is no reason to doubt it. Nikolaos, later the devotee and early biographer of Augustus, would not have wanted to call attention to this unfortunate episode from his past, and Sophronios, a compatriot, would have had access to hometown traditions about Nikolaos that might not have been obscured by Augustan attitudes. See also Wacholder, *Nicolaus*, 21–22; Bowersock, *Augustus*, 135.

88. *AJ* 15.96–103.

ingratiate Herod to Augustan Rome.[89] But if there were a growing hostility—and perhaps, like so many, Herod was disturbed at the effect Cleopatra had on Antonius—it might well have kept Herod from developing any close rapport with the tutor of Cleopatra's children.

After Actium and the deaths of Antonius and Cleopatra, the source of animosity between Herod and Nikolaos was removed. Both were now supporters of Octavian, and Nikolaos was in need of a new royal patron. He had spent much of the previous decade in the service of the greatest and most lavish court of the Hellenistic East: it would be only natural for him to have turned his attentions to the neighboring and increasingly opulent court of Herod, whom he had known intermittently for a decade and whose father had known his father. Herod's rule was entering its greatest period, and he was about to turn his court into a cultural center in the best Hellenistic fashion, including development of an intellectual circle around the monarch. The beginning of this program was Nikolaos, a man already comfortable in the exalted circles of both East and West, who was soon to become Herod's daily companion,[90] his liaison with Augustus,[91] and his advisor on how he should behave toward the Roman government and its leaders, principles succinctly summarized in the preface to Nikolaos's *Life of Caesar* (i.e., Augustus), which was probably written in these years.[92]

Alexandros Polyhistor, Timagenes, Strabo, and probably Nikolaos were in Rome in 40 B.C., when Herod arrived. All had established interests in the East, particularly Judaea. All were members of an intellectual circle around Antonius, Herod's patron, and all were knowledgeable about Herod's world, some of them eventually living at his court. And all would have been interested in meeting Herod when he came to Rome.

There were also Romans in Antonius's intellectual circle, most notably C. Asinius Pollio. He seems to have been in the East only briefly in his youth,[93] and there is no evidence for early contact with Herod. In the year of Herod's visit to Rome, he was consul and already a patron of the arts. But whether or not this brought him into personal contact and friendship with Herod has been disputed.

---

89. Wacholder, *Nicolaus* 22. It does not appear in the *Jewish War*, and there is no other evidence of previous hostility to Cleopatra: the two seem to have been on quite good terms as recently as 40 B.C. (*BJ* 1.279; *AJ* 14.375–76). See also Sullivan, *NER*, 226–27.

90. *AJ* 17.99.

91. *AJ* 17.54, 106–27.

92. *Life of Augustus*, ed. Jane Bellemore (Bristol, 1984), xxi–xxii; Gabba (supra, n. 83), 62–63.

93. Cicero, *Ad familiares.* 1.6; J. André, *La vie et l'oeuvre d'Asinius Pollion* (Paris, 1949), 10–11; William C. McDermott, "C. Asinius Pollio, Catullus, and C. Julius Caesar," *AncW* 2 (1979): 55–56.

Pollio reached his maturity in an era when Jews and Judaea were both politically topical in Rome and of great curiosity. He was exposed to the scholarly side of interest in Jewish matters[94] even before his teacher Timagenes[95] came to live in his household after quarreling with Augustus. Born in 76 B.C.,[96] Pollio was a precocious youth[97] at the impressionable age of fourteen when Pompey had his eastern triumph and interest in Jews and Judaea was awakened. A few years later, Timagenes came to Rome, and Pollio gravitated toward the Greek scholar. During these years, Pollio began the political and cultural career that raised him to the consulship in 40 B.C., when he was thirty-six, an event commemorated by Vergil.

Thus by the time of Herod's visit, Pollio had already distinguished himself both as a political leader and as a patron of the arts, and had studied with the Greek intellectual circle interested in Judaea and the East. Herod's arrival in Rome would have been a matter of great interest to Pollio. That a friendship developed between the two, which eventually resulted in Herod's sons being sent to live in Pollio's house, has been presumed without question by some commentators.[98] But there are serious problems with such an assumption, and the matter has, moreover, become entangled with the irrelevant issue of Jewish sympathies in early imperial Rome.[99]

The first problem is whether Herod and Pollio could have met in 40 B.C. Herod's trip to Rome was during Pollio's consular year,[100] but because of the Perusine War, Pollio may never have been in Rome during his consulship.[101] If he did come to Rome, it is most probable that it was late in the year, perhaps after the Brundisium agreement.[102] During this period of optimism, Vergil wrote his fourth *Eclogue*, dedicated to Pollio, which Pollio believed referred to his son Gallus.[103] But sometime in the year, Pollio and his colleague Calvinus were replaced by *consules suffecti*. Pollio resigned in order to become proconsul of Makedonia and to lead a campaign against

94. This is demonstrated in his own writings: see *AJ* 14.138.

95. Timagenes (*FrGrHist*, # 88) fr. 4; Gisinger (supra, n. 68), 1064; Giuseppe Zecchini, "Asinio Pollione: Dall'attività politica alla filessione storiographica," *ANRW* 2.30 (1982–83): 1279–81.

96. André (supra, n. 93), 9–10.

97. Catullus 12; McDermott (supra, n. 93), 55–60.

98. Feldman, *TAPA* (supra, n. 38), 73–80; Schalit, *KH*, 413, 588. Zecchini (supra, n. 95), 1280–81; Louis H. Feldman, "Asinius Pollio and Herod's Sons," *CQ* 35 (1985): 240–43.

99. See the debate over Asinius Pollio's Jewish sympathies: Feldman, *TAPA* (supra, n. 38), 73–80; David Braund, "Four Notes on the Herods," *CQ* 33 (1983): 240–41; Feldman, *CQ* (supra, n. 98), 240–43.

100. *AJ* 14.389.

101. Ronald Syme, "Pollio, Saloninus and Salonae," *CQ* 31 (1937): 41.

102. Appian, *Civil War* 5.65.

103. Syme, *RR*, 218–20.

the Parthini.[104] He returned to celebrate a triumph in either 39 or 38 B.C.[105] As a part of this triumph, he rebuilt the Atrium Libertatis (perhaps a project initiated by Julius Caesar), including an art gallery and Rome's first public library.[106] The sequence of events seems clear: lacking are the precise dates, and that has a bearing on possible contact between Herod and Pollio.

The crucial questions are: was Pollio still in the city when Herod arrived, and did they meet? Josephus's mention of Pollio as consul at the time of Herod's visit cannot be used as evidence,[107] because it is probable that Josephus was merely dating the year by the *consules ordinarii* (as he also dated it by the Olympiad). Immediately before the mention of the two consuls of the year, Josephus wrote that Herod was accompanied to the Capitol by the consuls, here unnamed. One can argue stylistically that these unnamed consuls ought to be the same as the named consuls of a few lines later, but Josephus may not have known the exact dates of transference of power from *consules ordinarii* to *consules suffecti*, and the two mentions of consuls probably came from two different sources: one a Herodian biographical source, probably Nikolaos or Herod's memoirs, and the other a chronographical source.

The matter cannot be determined. Lacking precise evidence as to the exact timing of Pollio's movements in the latter part of 40 B.C., it cannot be said whether the two men came into personal contact at that time. Yet Pollio, the student of Timagenes and Alexandros and the acquaintance of Nikolaos and Antonius, would have wanted to meet Herod and would have done so, if possible. And regardless of whether a meeting occurred, almost immediately thereafter, Herodian references appeared in the literary output of Pollio's friends and artistic clients.[108]

A further problem is whether friendship ever developed. Those who presume a friendship use as their strongest evidence the statement by Josephus that Herod sent his sons Alexandros and Aristoboulos to Rome, where they stayed at the house of Pollio, one of his best friends, and then eventually

104. Syme, *CQ* (supra, n. 101), 41–42; Broughton, 2: 378, 381.

105. It was probably in 30 B.C.: *CIL* I², p. 50; Dio 48.41; Syme, *CQ* (supra, n. 101), 41; Shipley, MAAR (supra, n. 36), 19–21.

106. Ovid, *Tristia* 3.1.71–72; Pliny, *Natural History* 7.115, 35.10, 36.23–25, 33–34; Suetonius, *Augustus* 29; Filippo Coarelli, "Atrium Libertatis," in *LTUR*, 1: 133–35; Filippo Coarelli, "Bibliotheca Asinii Pollionis," in *LTUR*, 1: 196.

107. Nevertheless, it has been so used. See Feldman, *TAPA* (supra, n. 38), 77–78; Zecchini (supra, n. 95), 1281; Mehanem Stern, "The Reign of Herod," *HP*, 85.

108. Vergil, *Georgics* 3.12 is the most conspicuous example. As noted below, the name Pollio was also known in Judaea shortly after this time: a certain Pollio the Pharisee supported Herod when, three years later, he captured Jerusalem (*AJ* 15.3, 370; Schalit, *KH*, 768–71).

lived in the house of Augustus himself.[109] A synchronism with the founding of Caesarea[110] indicates that the sons were sent to Rome in 22 B.C. If Asinius Pollio, the consul of 40 B.C., had been a friend of Herod's for nearly twenty years, it seems reasonable that the sons would have been housed with this family friend and Augustan intimate. They would have been close to the center of power, and they would have benefited from one of the most cultured households in early imperial Rome and from exposure to the venerable Timagenes of Alexandria—the teacher of Herod's court historian Nikolaos—who had been living in Pollio's home since his quarrel with Augustus. There seems no better place for Herod's sons to have been housed.

Unfortunately, Josephus did not identify the host of Herod's sons except as "Pollio." This ambiguity has made possible the argument that the Pollio who housed Alexandros and Aristoboulos was not Asinius Pollio, the consul of 40 B.C., but another Pollio, perhaps a Jew.[111] The arguments against Asinius Pollio include the vagueness of Josephus's identification, spelling variants between this Pollio's name and that of Asinius Pollio elsewhere in *AJ*,[112] and the sending of Herod's other sons to stay in Rome with a "certain Jew," who is never named.[113]

The arguments advanced in opposition to Asinius Pollio as the host of Herod's sons are all weak and inconclusive. The variations in name mean nothing. C. Asinius Pollio was first cited merely as "Asinius."[114] His full name appears only when his consulship is used as a date. Josephus was inconsistent in his use of Roman names, probably reflecting his sources. Julius Caesar was introduced at *AJ* 14.123 merely as "Caesar," and is so

109. *AJ* 15.342–43. On the matter of eastern dynasts sending their sons to Rome to be educated, see Braund, *Rome and the Friendly King* (supra, n. 8), 9–21, and Ann L. Kuttner, *Dynasty and Empire in the Age of Augustus: The Case of the Boscoreale Cups* (Berkeley, 1995), 111–17. The practice began in the early second century B.C.; by Augustus's day, it had become common (Suetonius, *Augustus* 48). Herod sent eight of his nine sons to Rome: only Phasael, probably the youngest, was excepted. See also Harold W. Hoehner, *Herod Antipas* (Cambridge, 1972), 12–17.

110. *AJ* 15.331–42.

111. Questions about the identification were raised by Hugo Willrich, *Das Haus des Herodes Zwischen Jerusalem und Rom* (Heidelberg, 1929), 116–17; see also Braund, *CQ* (supra, n. 99), 240–41.

112. The name appears seven times in *AJ*: 14.389 (the consul of the year of Herod's visit), 15.3, 4 (the Pharisee who helped Herod in the capture of Jerusalem), 15.343 (the host of Herod's sons), twice at 15.370 (the Pharisee again), 19.267 (the emperor Claudius's praetorian prefect). All of these are spelled the same way (Πωλλίων), except the first, which is Πολίων.

113. *AJ* 17.20.

114. *AJ* 14.138.

cited many times in book 14, until, in chapter 188, the name suddenly becomes "Caesar Julius" and then, in chapter 190, "Gaius Julius Caesar." In successive chapters, "Julius Caesar" and "Gaius Caesar" and perhaps even "Julius Gaius" appear indiscriminately, and at his death (chapter 217), he is merely "Gaius." So it is a mistake to make any arguments regarding identification of personalities from the form of a Roman personal name used by Josephus. The spelling variants also settle nothing, especially since the one used for the host of Herod's sons conforms more to the Latin spelling of Asinius Pollio's name than does the specific citation of him as consul. And the housing of Herod's other sons elsewhere many years later is not relevant to the issue at all: given Herod's stormy relations with his older sons by that time, which was to result eventually in their execution, it is unlikely that further sons of Herod's would have been welcome in the same Roman household.

Moreover, every other mention of a Pollio by Josephus is specifically identified so that there will be no confusion with Asinius Pollio: this is the case with the "Pollio the Pharisee" of *AJ* 15.3 and 370 and the Pollio of *AJ* 19.267, identified as Claudius's prefect. Only the Pollio of *AJ* 15.343, the host of Herod's sons, is not further identified. Two Pollios have previously been mentioned: Gaius Asinius Pollio and Pollio the Pharisee. It seems unlikely that the latter, a religious leader in Jerusalem, was the host of Herod's sons in Rome. It seems equally unlikely that the host was a previously unknown Pollio. One is left with Gaius Asinius Pollio. The sons were certainly favored by Augustus, as he eventually housed them himself. This makes it even more probable that the Pollio they initially stayed with (and who had been mentioned immediately previously by Josephus) was the famous Asinius Pollio, rather than a nonentity. Later Herod sent his son Antipatros to Rome in the care of M. Vipsanius Agrippa,[115] and in the following generation, Herod's grandson Agrippa stayed with the imperial family itself.[116] Thus there is ample evidence of the hosting of Herodian offspring by prominent Romans.[117]

Nevertheless, it remains implausibly possible that the sons were sent to live, not with Asinius Pollio, despite the advantages in that distinguished and cultured household, but with an obscure Pollio, perhaps the P. Vedius Pollio who was in Asia after Actium, an Augustan agent described as a Roman equestrian "of libertine parentage."[118] Or they may have stayed with an even less known Pollio, perhaps related to Pollio the Pharisee. If such

---

115. *AJ* 16.86.

116. *AJ* 18.143.

117. Richard D. Sullivan, "The Dynasty of Judaea in the First Century," *ANRW* 2.8 (1977): 305.

118. Ronald Syme, "Who Was Vedius Pollio?" *JRS* 51 (1961): 23–30.

were the case, friendship between Herod and Asinius Pollio may be less likely. But Asinius Pollio is by far the most probable host for the sons: a man of power and influence, close to the Princeps, who had been consul in the year of Herod's first visit to Rome and in whose home lived the teacher of Herod's closest advisor and chronicler. Thus it seems equally probable that Asinius Pollio was himself a friend of Herod's, and had been one since 40 B.C.

The mysterious Q. Dellius, whom Messalla rather inconsistently criticized for his changes of sides in the civil war, and whose relationship with Antonius seems to have been especially close, was an associate of Asinius Pollio's.[119] Although not a particularly sympathetic figure, he too seems to have been on the fringes of the eastern-oriented intellectual circle. Dellius had already gained a certain immortality as the one who introduced Cleopatra to Antonius.[120] It was he whom Antonius sent with Herod, on the latter's return to Judaea after his Roman visit, to help him claim his kingship. Nothing is known about his early life; he is first documented changing allegiance from P. Cornelius Dolabella to Cassius after the assassination of Julius Caesar,[121] at which time he might have come into contact with Herod. But in the 30's B.C. he was at the court of Herod as Antonius's agent. He seems to have become infatuated with the royal women, and he had portraits of them commissioned and sent to Antonius in Egypt as a means of advancing his own interests with both Antonius and the women.[122] Yet he deserted Antonius soon after Actium[123] and seems then to have retired from politics, writing one of the first histories of the later years of the civil war.[124] This must have contained much information about Herod, but all that survives is a quotation by Strabo[125] and a citation in Plutarch's biography of Antonius.[126] Dellius himself survived well into the Augustan era as one of the men most knowledgeable about the East,[127] another example of the eastern-oriented Roman whom Herod attracted during his 40 B.C. visit.

119. G. Wissowa, "Q. Dellius," *RE*, 4 (1901): 2447–48; Bowersock, *Augustus*, 26; T. P. Wiseman, *New Men in the Roman Senate, 139 B.C.—A.D. 14* (Oxford, 1971), # 154; Hermann Bengtson, *Marcus Antonius: Triumvir und Herrscher des Orients* (Munich, 1977), 186–88; Plutarch, *Life of Antony*, ed. Pelling (supra, n. 75), 185. Messalla called him a *desultor* (Seneca, *Suasoriae* 1.7), "a rider in the circus who jumped from one horse to another" (*OLD*).

120. Plutarch, *Antonius* 25.

121. Velleius 2.84.

122. *AJ* 15.25–28; see also *BJ* 1.439.

123. Plutarch, *Antonius* 59.

124. *FrGrHist*, # 124 (and commentary thereon); Syme, *Augustan Aristocracy* (supra, n. 15), 356–57.

125. Strabo 11.13.3 = Dellius fr. 1, discussing Antonius's Parthian campaign.

126. Plutarch, *Antonius* 59 = Dellius fr. 2, discussing his desertion of Antonius after Actium.

127. Bowersock, *Augustus*, 26.

Another important early personal contact of Herod's was with Augustus's wife, Livia. In 40 B.C. she was still married to Tiberius Claudius Nero, so it is improbable that Herod met her then. But within a decade, Livia and the Herodian family were on intimate terms. The closest relationship seems to have been with Herod's sister Salome, who was perhaps about the same age as Livia.

Salome was heavily involved in the palace intrigues of Herod's court.[128] By shortly after the battle of Actium, if not earlier, she had developed a strong friendship with Livia. The fruits of this relationship were first apparent when Salome wanted to marry Syllaios, a Nabataean who was de facto ruler of Nabataea because of the indolence of the king, Obodas. The date is uncertain, but it was after Salome divorced her second husband, Kostobaros, at the time of his revolt, probably around 28 B.C.[129] Syllaios fell in love with Salome at a dinner party at Herod's court, and they quickly became involved. Within a few months, Syllaios formally asked for marriage. But the plans were canceled by Herod when Syllaios refused to convert to Judaism;[130] moreover, Herod was none too eager to strengthen the Nabataeans at his own expense.[131] In the midst of this, Livia intervened. It appears that Livia first tried to persuade Herod to agree to the marriage, but when this angered Herod greatly,[132] Livia then convinced Salome to accept Herod's decision and his insistence that she marry one of his courtiers, Alexas. Salome followed Livia's advice both because she was the wife of Augustus and because she had given her good advice in the past.[133]

Salome also provided Livia with a slave for her household. This was a Jewish lady named Akme, clearly a Herodian mole in the Augustan court, who was able to write Herod directly about happenings in Rome, especially the intrigues of Herod's own family; one of Akme's letters to Herod was quoted by Josephus.[134] She also sent Herod letters Salome had allegedly written Livia. These demonstrate the type of communication that passed between Jerusalem and Rome, even though they turned out to be forgeries by Herod's son Antipatros,[135] who had bribed Akme to send them to Herod. Augustus was not pleased at Akme's intrigues and had her executed.[136]

This incident does not seem to have affected the friendship between Livia and the Herodian family, and when Caesarea was dedicated, Livia

---

128. Schalit, *KH*, 571, called her a "satanische Figur."
129. Otto, *RE, Zeittafel.*
130. *AJ* 16.220–28.
131. Bowersock, *Roman Arabia* (supra, n. 9), 50–51.
132. *BJ* 1.566.
133. *AJ* 17.10.
134. *AJ* 17.134–41.
135. *BJ* 1.641–43.
136. *BJ* 1.661; *AJ* 17.182.

assisted in the financing of the festivities.[137] A city in Peraia was also named Livias, although the date of its foundation is not certain. The respect that Herod showed Livia was for more than the obvious political reasons: in the East, honors had been paid to the wives of Romans since the days of Antonius's wife Fulvia, and cults of Livia were established in eastern cities—many of which were also beneficiaries of Herodian building— as early as 28 B.C.[138] At his death Herod left a large sum to Livia;[139] Salome, who died around A.D. 10, left her the cities of Iamneia, Phasaelis, and Archelais.[140]

Although the relationship between Livia and Herod's family was of interest to Josephus because of the political intrigues involved, it demonstrates Herod's ability to be remarkably well informed about happenings in Rome. As he was constantly indulging in architectural creations, information flowing to Jerusalem from Rome would have been architectural as well as political, as demonstrated by his early knowledge about the Mausolem of Augustus and Livia's interest in the dedication of Caesarea.

Herod remained in contact with many of these Greeks and Romans for years. His later association with Augustus and Nikolaos is well known. The friendship established between Herod and Messalla was of benefit to both, although Herod's difficulties in winning his kingdom and Messalla's activity in the renewed Roman civil war[141] meant no personal contact for a decade after 40 B.C. During these years, however, Messalla's ever-more-prominent role as a partisan of Octavian's and a patron of the arts[142] confirmed Herod's talent for choosing his friends, especially among the rising young men of the emerging Augustan era. The developing artistic consciousness of Augustan Rome, exemplified in men like Messalla, encouraged Herod to establish artistic patronage in his own kingdom. Personal contact was renewed after Actium. Messalla was in Syria in order to strengthen local support for Octavian:[143] his friendship with Herod may even have been a reason he was sent there. Herod was under pressure from Antonius, who had sent Alexas of Laodikeia to keep him loyal;[144] despite this, Herod, probably assisted and persuaded by Messalla, became active in eliminating Antonian support in Syria. Herod was then quick to join Octavian, whom he met at

137. *AJ* 16.139.

138. Gertrude Grether, "Livia and the Roman Imperial Cult," *AJP* 67 (1946), 223–33.

139. *AJ* 17.146, 190.

140. *BJ* 2.167; *AJ* 18.31.

141. Hammer (supra, n. 15), 28–40.

142. Ibid., 43–45.

143. Dio 51.7; Hammer (supra, n. 15), 46–60; see also Syme, *Augustan Aristocracy* (supra, n. 15), 209–10.

144. Plutarch, *Antonius* 72.

Rhodes in early (probably March) 30 B.C. Octavian thanked him for his assistance, and Herod made his famous speech stressing his trait of loyalty, which would now be as strong to Octavian as it had been to Antonius. Octavian then went to Egypt, soon to be joined by Messalla.[145] Herod entertained Octavian en route at Ptolemais and supplied him for the rest of his journey.[146]

Friendship with Agrippa, however minimal in 40 B.C., developed strongly, especially after Actium and the death of Antonius. In these years, when sharing a house with Messalla, Agrippa would have learned much about the king of Judaea, and, given the interest of both in architecture and urban renewal, a rapport might have developed despite the lack of personal contact. Thus by 23 B.C., when the two did meet at Mytilene, Herod could indeed be called Agrippa's close friend. Their own individual building programs were well under way, and the two would have had much to talk about.

Dellius's acquaintance with Herod was of use to Antonius in the 30's B.C., and Dellius was often at Herod's court during those years, but after Antonius's death, he seems to have retired from politics. In the 20's B.C., he was cautioned by Horace,[147] wrote his memoirs,[148] and became proverbial for his changes of side in the civil war; but he had essentially vanished from view. It seems that Herod maintained stronger contact with Asinius Pollio, who also retired from politics, after his triumph in 39 or 38 B.C., and wrote his own histories, which were used, at least indirectly, by Josephus.[149] His role as a patron of the arts continued, for he organized public lectures and encouraged men of letters,[150] housing his own teacher Timagenes, and then, presumably, Herod's sons.

The personal contacts Herod made in 40 B.C. were thus to serve him for the rest of his years.[151] The only exceptions were Antonius, dead within a

---

145. Tibullus 1.7.20–22.

146. *AJ* 15.187–201; *BJ* 1.386–96; see also Hammer (supra, n. 15), 51.

147. Horace, *Odes* 2.3.

148. They went as far as 32 B.C.: see Bengtson (supra, n. 119), 186–87.

149. *AJ* 14.138.

150. Zecchini (supra, n. 95), 1279–81.

151. Herod's Italian interests were not limited to personal contacts and architecture: he also had wine imported from Italy. The excavators at Masada found thirteen amphorae with their labels still readable, recording that in 19 B.C. Herod received a shipment of Philonianum wine (otherwise unknown, but perhaps from the region of Brundisium). He also seems to have had a taste for Aminean, Massic (probably both from Campania), and Tarantine wines, as well as other Italian commodities, including *garum* and apples from Cumae. See Hannah M. Cotton and Joseph Geiger, *Masada*, vol. 2: *The Latin and Greek Documents* (Jerusalem, 1989), 140–67, and Hannah M. Cotton, Omri Lernau, and Yuval Goren. "Fish Sauces from Herodian Masada," *JRA* 9 (1996): 223–38.

decade, and Alexandros Polyhistor, who vanishes from the record by the end of the civil war: he had been in Rome since the time of Sulla and would have been in his seventies, at least, after Actium. But his and Timagenes' pupils Nikolaos and Strabo formed the nucleus of Herod's own intellectual circle in Judaea: Nikolaos from probably shortly after Actium until Herod's death, and Strabo possibly in the 20's B.C.

CHAPTER TWO

What Herod Saw in Rome

When Herod arrived in December 40 B.C., Rome was in the midst of a vibrant building program that was transforming it from an agrarian city-state into an imperial capital. The process had begun over a century earlier—Hellenism had been a feature of Roman taste since the First Punic War[1]—but in the generation before Herod's visit, a new spirit of imperial thinking entered the Roman conception of architecture. This spirit is best exemplified in the rebuilding of the temple of Juppiter on the Capitol after the fire of 83 B.C.,[2] a reconstruction dedicated in 69 B.C.[3] Its columns may have come from the Olympieion in Athens, sent by Sulla.[4] The entire temple was rebuilt on a scale comparable to that of the largest temples of Hellenistic Greece,[5] inspiring the enthusiasm of Cicero.[6] In the thirty years between the completion of the rebuilt Capitoline Temple and Herod's arrival, building continued at a relentless pace. The Basilica Aemilia, Basilica Julia, Curia Julia, Forum Julium, Forum of Augustus, Temple of Divine Julius, Rostra, Saepta Julia, Temple of Saturn, and Theater of Pompey were all rebuilt, completed, started, or conceived in those thirty years. The extent

1. Livy 25.40.2.

2. For the numerous sources, see Platner-Ashby, 299–301.

3. Nash, 1: 530.

4. Pliny, *Natural History* 36.45: but see Frank E. Brown, review of *Etruscan and Roman Architecture*," by Axel Boëthius and J. B. Ward Perkins, *ArtB* 54 (1972): 343. Richardson, *NTD*, 222–23, has convincingly argued that Sulla brought the columns of the Peisistratid, not the Hellenistic, Olympieion.

5. Axel Boëthius, *Etruscan and Early Roman Architecture*, 2d ed. (Harmondsworth, 1978), 47–48.

6. Cicero, *In Verrem* 2.4.68–69; by 45 B.C., however, Cicero complained about what an ignorant Athenian architect was doing to the city (*Ad Atticum* 13.35–36).

of the city at the end of the Republic is shown by Octavian's need to restore eighty-two temples as early as 28 B.C.[7]

Such was the architectural world into which Herod was thrown. He was no stranger to great and monumental cities: he had been received by Antonius in Antioch and by Cleopatra in Alexandria, although neither of these had the vitality that characterized Rome. Antioch, which had experienced a recent spurt of Roman building (by Q. Marcius Rex, Pompey, and Julius Caesar) was Herod's first exposure to the Roman taste for architectural renovation. Alexandria, however, had suffered in the Roman civil wars.[8] Herod was also familiar with Roman architectural patronage closer to home, having seen Gabinius's rebuilding of a dozen southern Levantine cities. And while en route to Rome, Herod assisted in the restoration of Rhodes, still suffering from its resistance to Cassius several years earlier.[9] He also had a ship built with which to reach Brundisium; in later years he did not forget Rhodes's assistance with his transportation needs, repeatedly contributing to its shipbuilding industry.[10]

Herod made the overland journey to Rome from Brundisium along the ancient Via Appia. The highway approached through a low swale, which prevented any distant Hellenistic-style views of the city, but in the vicinity of Rome it was already lined with the tombs that still mark its course. About a mile from the city, Herod would have encountered the elaborate tomb of the Scipios, Rome's greatest philhellene family;[11] and within twenty years, he would build his own monumental dynastic tomb. Just beyond, where the Via Latina joined the Appia, the swale widened into a broad terrace, which gave Herod his first views of Rome. On his right were the bluffs of the Caelian, and ahead, to his left, was the Aventine, surmounted by the ancient Temple of Diana.

Entry into Rome proper was through the Porta Capena, lying between the Caelian and the Aventine. The city walls, centuries old, had been patched and repaired over the years, most recently during the conflict between Marius and Sulla.[12] Once through the walls, Herod had late Republican Rome before him, although the city center was still not visible. Immediately in front was the eastern end of the Circus Maximus. To the right was the valley leading between the Caelian and Palatine to the swampy

---

7. Augustus, *Res gestae* 20.

8. Plutarch, *Caesar* 49; Dio 42.38; Matthias Gelzer, *Caesar: Der Politiker und Staatsmann* (Wiesbaden, 1960), 227.

9. *AJ* 14.377–78.

10. *BJ* 1.424; *AJ* 16.147. On the Rhodian shipping industry, see Lionel Casson, *The Ancient Mariners*, 2d ed. (Princeton, 1991), 138–42, 163–66.

11. Coarelli, *Guida*, 154–61; Boëthius (supra, n. 5), 135; Richardson, *NTD*, 359–60.

12. Coarelli, *Guida*, 10.

depression where, a century later, Nero, partly inspired by Herod, would create the lake of his Domus Aurea. Ahead was the Palatine itself, sprinkled with the houses of the aristocracy. Few public buildings were visible from this point, and Herod would have seen only those on the summit of the Aventine, to his left, and several small temples beyond the Circus and on the corner of the Palatine.

Herod knew at least two influential people in Rome: Antonius and Messalla. Messalla lived at the north of the city, on the Pincian.[13] Although Antonius's ancestral home—later to be occupied jointly by Messalla and Marcus Agrippa[14]—was on the Palatine, Caesar had given him Pompey's house on the Carinae,[15] which Antonius had enhanced with Caesar's furnishings, illegally obtained.[16] This is probably where he received Herod, and it was here that Herod would have been housed during his week in the city.[17]

Where did Herod go and what did he see while in Rome? Literature names only three places: Antonius's home, the Senate, and the Capitol. As noted, Antonius's homes were on the Palatine and Carinae, and the location of the Capitol is indisputable. But where the Senate met in late 40 B.C. is unknown. The Curia Hostilia, the traditional and ancient senate house, had burned down twelve years earlier at the funeral of Clodius, when his supporters had built his funeral pyre out of the furniture of the building,[18] and its successor, the little-known Curia Cornelia, only lasted a few years.[19] Julius Caesar began a new senate house,[20] but the work was so little advanced by the time of his death that Augustus could claim the Curia Julia as his own.[21] At the time of Caesar's assassination, the Senate was meeting in the Curia of Pompey, part of the complex attached to Pompey's theater in the Campus Martius,[22] but after the Ides of March, this was walled off, and eventually it was turned into a latrine.[23] Then the Senate met in a variety of places, especially the Temple of Concordia at the west end of the

13. Richardson, *NTD*, 131.

14. Dio 53.27; Emanuele Papi, "Domus: M. Antonius," in *LTUR*, 2: 34. Its location is not certain, but it has recently been suggested that it was the structure today known as the Casa di Livia (Richardson, *NTD*, 281).

15. Plutarch, *Antonius* 21, 32; Suetonius, *Grammarians* 15; Appian, *Civil War* 2.126; Vincent Jolivet, "Domus Pompeiorum," in *LTUR*, 2: 159–60.

16. Cicero, *Philippic* 3.12.30.

17. *BJ* 1.281; *AJ* 14.379.

18. Cicero, *Pro Milone* 90; Appian, *Civil War* 2.21; Dio 40.49; Richardson, *NTD*, 102.

19. Lily Ross Taylor and Russell T. Scott, "Seating Space in the Roman Senate and the *Senatores Pedarii*," *TAPA* 100 (1969): 537. Whether the Curia Cornelia even existed as a building is disputed: see Filippo Coarelli, "Curia Hostilia," in *LTUR*, 1: 331.

20. Dio 44.5, 45.17; Richardson, *NTD*, 103–4.

21. Augustus, *Res gestae* 19.

22. Suetonius, *Divine Julius* 80–81.

23. Ibid., 88; Dio 47.19.

Forum and the Temple of Juppiter on the Capitol.[24] In October 39 B.C., it was meeting on the Palatine;[25] it was not until August 29 B.C. that the new Curia Julia was dedicated by Octavian.[26] Thus Rome lacked a permanent senate house for over twenty years. But even when a permanent structure was available, the Senate met in many different places.[27] It was not meeting on the Capitol when Herod was declared king (since Herod went to the Capitol after the Senate adjourned), and the most likely candidate is the Temple of Concordia, which was a usual place for meetings after the death of Caesar.[28]

But it is foolish to assume that Herod visited only the three places documented. As in any great city, there were standard places where foreign dignitaries were taken to be impressed. One such was the Theater and Portico of Pompey (fig. 1),[29] which remained one of the famous monuments of Rome for centuries.[30] In Herod's day, it was also one of the newest, having been built only fifteen years previously. This unique complex, which contained the first permanent theater in Rome,[31] was notorious as the site of Caesar's assassination. Pompey is said to have modeled the theater on that at Mytilene, even making plans or a model of the Greek structure, and using Pergamene details.[32] Over half a century later, it was still considered one of Pompey's greatest achievements.[33] Not many years after Herod's visit, Prop-

---

24. Taylor and Scott (supra, n. 19), 557–63.

25. This is documented on an inscription from Aphrodisias, published in Joyce Reynolds, *Aphrodisias and Rome* (*JRS* Monographs, 1 [London, 1982]), document 8, line 4 (pp. 54–91).

26. Dio 51.22; Augustus, *Res gestae* 19.

27. Richard J. A. Talbert, *The Senate of Imperial Rome* (Princeton, 1984), 113–20.

28. Taylor and Scott (supra, n. 19), 559; Richardson, *NTD*, 99.

29. Tacitus, *Annals* 13.54. For problems with its chronology (which do not affect its situation in Herod's day), see Roger B. Ulrich, "Julius Caesar and the Creation of the Forum Iulium," *AJA* 97 (1993): 51.

30. Dio 39.38; Ammianus Marcellius 16.10.14; Nash, 2: 423; Boëthius (supra, n. 5), 205–6; Coarelli, *Guida*, 288–91; Richardson, *NTD*, 383–85.

31. The Theater of Scaurus, dated to 58 B.C., three years before Pompey's structure, although lavish, was overshadowed by the later building and may have been temporary, since it seems not to have survived long, and even its location was soon forgotten (Pliny, *Natural History* 34.36, 36.113–15; Richardson, *NTD*, 385). Regardless, the Theater of Pompey was universally hailed as Rome's first and most impressive theater. Another theater had already been started by the time of Herod's visit. The foundations had been laid by Julius Caesar (Dio 53.30), but construction probably lapsed until twenty years later, when Augustus completed the building (Suetonius, *Augustus* 29; Plutarch, *Marcellus* 30).

32. Plutarch, *Pompey* 42, but see Richardson, *NTD*, 384. For problems in relating the two buildings, whose known remains have few similarities, see Hector Williams, "Notes on Roman Mytilene," in *The Greek Renaissance in the Roman Empire*, ed. Susan Walker and Averil Cameron (*BICS*, suppl. 55 [1989]), 164; an explanation for the seeming inconsistencies has been advanced by L. Richardson, Jr., "A Note on the Architecture of the *Theatrum Pompei*," *AJA* 91 (1987): 123–26.

33. Velleius 2.48

ertius wrote of its shaded gardens and luxuriant fountains, one of the true delights of contemporary Rome.[34] Herod would have been shown this innovative and revolutionary complex with such famous historical associations. Soon he would introduce the theater and portico to Judaea.

In Herod's day, as the architectural efforts of Pompey indicate, the Campus Martius was a developing area, already serving the ambitions of the rival dynasts of the late Republic. Most of the structures for which it was to become famous were as yet unbuilt or unplanned: when Herod returned to Rome a quarter century later, the changes would be profound. The entire Campus was outside the walls, which ran northeast from the river across the Capitol to the Quirinal. Except in its southeastern corner, there were few constructions in the Campus in 40 B.C. Even late in the Augustan period, it retained an open spacious character, covered with grass, in a magnificent setting.[35]

Urbanization of the Campus had begun as early as the third century B.C., when the angle between the city walls and river had begun to be covered with a number of small shrines and structures. These included the Temple of Bellona,[36] which lay near the Circus Flaminius, the largest Republican construction of the early Campus,[37] and temples of Juno and Diana,[38] all buildings of probably the third or early second century B.C.[39] A third-century B.C. Temple of Neptune was in the process of being restored at the time of Herod's visit.[40] Other Republican temples were scattered over the area,[41] as well as two porticoes, that of Octavia and that of Metellus, both from the second century B.C.[42] Little is known about their exact disposition, as the area was heavily rebuilt by Augustus, but they seem to represent the growing late Republican fashion for such structures.[43] The Porticus Octavia may have introduced the Corinthian order into Rome.[44] Herod might not have been particularly impressed with these imitations of what he had seen

34. Propertius 2.32.11–16; on the famous gardens of the complex, see Kathryn L. Gleason, "The Garden Portico of Pompey the Great," *Expedition* 32.2 (1990): 4–13.

35. Strabo 5.3.8. On the area generally, with a good discussion of its urbanization, see T. Peter Wiseman, "Campus Martius," in *LTUR*, 1: 220–24; see also John R. Patterson, "The City of Rome: From Republic to Empire," *JRS* 82 (1992): 197–98.

36. Livy 10.19.17; Ovid, *Fasti* 6.201–4; Pliny, *Natural History* 35.12.

37. Livy 3.54.15.

38. Livy 40.51–52.

39. Nash, 1: 136, 202; Coarelli, *Guida*, 271–72, 280–85.

40. Nash, 2: 120; but see Platner-Ashby, 361.

41. See the list, Coarelli, *Guida*, 272. Only those in the area now known as the Area Sacra di Largo Argentina are visible today.

42. Velleius 1.11, 2.1; Vitruvius 3.2.5; Coarelli, *Guida*, 275–77.

43. Ward-Perkins, *RIA*, 74–75.

44. Pliny, *Natural History* 34.13; Platner-Ashby, 426.

on a grander scale at Antioch and Alexandria, the cities that inspired such structures at Rome. But he may have been shown as a curiosity the Temple of Juppiter Stator within the Porticus Metelli, the earliest marble temple in Rome and the earliest built by a Greek, one Hermodoros of Salamis.[45]

Thus the southeastern portion of the Campus Martius contained a number of small temples, some as much as three hundred years old, scattered around the Circus Flaminius, and of little interest to a visitor such as Herod. But in the years previous to Herod's visit, the character of the Campus had begun to change significantly. Just to the north of the Circus Flaminius complex, Pompey had initiated monumental construction with one of the most impressive and innovative structures in the city. Shortly thereafter, Julius Caesar had conceived of a systematic urbanization of the area,[46] having begun another unusual structure, the Saepta Julia, which stretched to the north at right angles to the theater. Its sheer size—nearly 1,050 Roman feet long—made this the most monumental area of the city until the Augustan development of the Imperial Fora.[47] Construction of the Saepta was planned as early as 54 B.C.,[48] but at the time of Herod's visit it had barely started,[49] and it was not to be completed until 26 B.C. Yet the work in progress on the Saepta well defined the late Republican monumentalizing of the city. Although representative of open political institutions hardly appropriate to Herod's world, as architecture it was particularly relevant, creating, with the Theater of Pompey complex, two sides of a massive quadrangle open to the west and north and allowing an unobstructed view across the grassy lawn to the river. It was a view that the exiled Ovid would fondly remember.[50]

Also in the Campus Martius was the tomb of the Julian family, the Tumulus Iuliae, a forerunner of the Mausoleum of Augustus. Its exact location is unknown, but it was here that the ashes of Julius Caesar were probably placed after the unexpected burning of the body in the Forum (where the Temple of the Divine Julius was to be built) while the funeral cortege was on its way to the Tumulus.[51] As the tomb of the one responsible for his Roman

45. Velleius 1.11; Vitruvius 3.2.5; Coarelli, *Guida*, 276.

46. Cicero, *Ad Atticum* 13.33a.1.

47. Frederick W. Shipley, "Chronology of the Building Operations in Rome from the Death of Caesar to the Death of Augustus," *MAAR* 9 (1931): 18; Nash, 2: 291; Coarelli, *Guida*, 268; Richardson, *NTD*, 340–41. It was one of the first examples of the cross-fertilization between Hellenistic and Italian architecture (Erik Sjöqvist, "Kaisareion: A Study in Architectural Iconography," *OpRom* 1 [1954]: 105).

48. Cicero, *Ad Atticum* 4.17.

49. Dio 53.23.

50. Ovid, *Epistulae ex Ponto* 1.8.33–38.

51. Dio 44.51; Suetonius, *Divine Julius* 84; Richardson, *NTD*, 402. The name refers not to the Julian family but to its first occupant, Julia, the daughter of Julius Caesar and the wife of Pompey the Great.

citizenship, it would have been of interest to Herod, and it is inconceivable that he did not visit it.

Building activity was even more intense in the vicinity of the Forum Romanum,[52] which must have seemed one vast construction zone, with both the Basilica Aemilia and Basilica Julia under construction and repair, the Curia Julia being built, and the site of the temple of Divine Julius already being cleared. The western end, the slope leading up to the Capitol, was the area least under construction in 40 B.C. The Tabularium had been completed nearly forty years before;[53] then as now it provided the Forum with a monumental backdrop in Hellenistic fashion. On the slope below were two Republican temples, that of Saturn to the south and of Concordia to the north, the latter perhaps where the Senate met to declare Herod king. Both temples were allegedly ancient, with the former dated to the early fifth century B.C.[54] and the latter from the following century.[55] But even here the urban renewal of the late Republic had been active: the Temple of Saturn had been plundered by Caesar[56] and then restored by the consul L. Munatius Plancus two years before Herod's visit.[57] Plancus, who fifteen years later was to propose the name "Augustus" for Octavian, would come to know Herod while governor of Syria in the 30's B.C.[58]

The eastern end of the Forum was defined by the ancient Temples of Castor and Vesta. The latter was said to date from the regal period,[59] although its original wooden walls and thatched roof were long gone, probably lost to a fire in the third century B.C.[60] The Temple of Castor originally dated from the early fifth century B.C. In Herod's day the most recent reconstruction had been in 117 B.C., with some repairs as late as the 70's B.C.[61] To the northwest, the heart of the ancient Forum was almost totally under renovation in 40 B.C. The largest structure in this area had long been a basilica, generally known today as the Basilica Aemilia. This uniquely Roman form of architecture,[62] which would first appear in Judaea in Herodian

52. For the status of the Forum Romanum in the last years of the Republic, see Nicolas Purcell, "Forum Romanum (The Imperial Period)," in *LTUR*, 2: 336–39.

53. It was during the consulship of Q. Lutatius Catulus (78 B.C.): for the evidence, see Richardson, *NTD*, 376. For the suggestion that the structure generally known today as the Tabularium was in fact the Atrium Libertatius, see Nicolas Purcell, "*Atrium Libertatis*," *BSR* 61 (1993): 125–55.

54. Platner-Ashby, 463; Nash, 2: 294.

55. Ovid, *Fasti* 1.641–44; Plutarch, *Camillus* 42.

56. Lucan, *Pharsalia* 3.154–68; Pliny, *Natural History* 33.56.

57. Richardson, *NTD*, 343.

58. Suetonius, *Augustus* 7; Appian, *Civil War* 5.144; Schürer (NEV), 1: 252–53.

59. Plutarch, *Numa* 11.

60. Livy 26.27.4; Ovid, *Fasti* 6.261–64, 437–54.

61. Livy 2.20.12, 2.42.5; Cicero, *In Verrem* 2.1.129–54; Richardson, *NTD*, 74–75.

62. Boëthius (supra, n. 5), 149–52. Despite antecedents such as the late third century B.C. Hypostyle Hall on Delos, the basilica in its developed form is purely Roman.

residential constructions, came to dominate the Forum. A basilica had been built on the site in the early second century B.C.,[63] variously called the Fulvia, Aemilia, and Paulli, with the last being the most common name at the end of the Republic and into the early Empire.[64] In 55 B.C., Caesar paid for the restoration of the structure,[65] but the project seems to have dragged on for over twenty years, through the time of Herod's visit, and it was not completed until 34 B.C.[66]

Opposite, on the southern side of the Forum, another great basilica, the Julia, was under construction when Herod visited. It may have been part of the same project that started the restoration of the Basilica Paulli.[67] Construction was well in progress before Caesar's death, but a fire destroyed the uncompleted building, and it was not finished for many years, perhaps not even by the time of the death of Augustus.[68] In the northwest corner of the Forum, west of the Basilica Paulli, was the Curia Julia, started just before Caesar's death.[69] Work on it was probably not far advanced when Herod visited, since Augustus took all the credit for its eventual completion.[70]

Perhaps the most controversial part of the Forum was the eastern end, where Caesar's body had been suddenly cremated.[71] The original memorial, a 20-foot-high column of Numidian marble,[72] had been demolished by revolutionary partisans within the year.[73] There was also a dispute about the memorial altar.[74] Eventually, the site was cleared,[75] and by 42 B.C. the Temple of Divine Julius was authorized.[76] Yet there is no indication of prompt

63. Plautus, *Curculio* 472; Livy 39.44.7; 40.51.5; Richardson, *NTD*, 54–56.

64. Platner-Ashby, 72; the complex building and nomenclature history of the site is summarized by Coarelli, *Guida*, 44–46. See also Eva Margareta Steinby, "Basilica Aemilia," in *LTUR*, 1: 167–68; Heinrich Bauer, "Basilica Fulvia," in *LTUR*, 1: 173–75; Heinrich Bauer, "Basilica Paul(l)i," in *LTUR*, 1: 183–87. Interpretation of the basilica and its predecessors is one of the most disputed elements of the topography of Rome: for a summary of the problems, see Patterson (supra, n. 35), 192–93.

65. Cicero, *Ad Atticum* 4.17; Plutarch, *Caesar* 29; Appian, *Civil War* 2.26.

66. Dio 49.42.

67. Cicero, *Ad Atticum* 14.17.8; Cairoli F. Giuliani and Patrizia Verducci, "Basilica Iulia," in *LTUR*, 1: 177–79.

68. Suetonius, *Augustus* 29; Dio 56.27.

69. Dio 44.5, 45.17, 47.19.

70. Augustus, *Res gestae* 19.

71. This was not the place of intended cremation: the body was being carried through the Forum on its way from Caesar's house in the Subura to a pyre erected in the Campus Martius when it was set afire under mysterious and probably staged circumstances (Suetonius, *Divine Julius* 84).

72. Ibid., 85.

73. Cicero, *Ad Atticum* 14.15, *Philippic* 1.5.

74. Cicero, *Ad familiares* 11.2 (letter of Brutus and Cassius to Antonius); Appian, *Civil War* 1.4, 3.2.

75. Cicero, *Ad Atticum* 14.15.

76. Dio 47.18.

construction[77]—perhaps emotions were still too extreme—and probably all Herod saw was a site in ruins.

Intensive construction was not limited to the Forum proper. Immediately to the northwest, behind the site of the Curia and on the northern slopes of the Capitol, Caesar, attempting to rival Pompey architecturally, had begun the first of the Hellenistic-style enclosed porticoes that were to become the Imperial Fora (fig. 2).[78] Its origin may be reflected in general land purchases and expropriations of 54 B.C.,[79] and construction may have begun three years later.[80] At Pharsalos, Caesar vowed to include a temple of Venus Genetrix in the structure.[81] Although not totally completed, the complex was dedicated in late 46 B.C.[82] A significant part of Roman architectural history, it added to the public space of the Forum Romanum, included shops, and integrated the portico and temple forms. Herod would have visited this greatest of Caesarian architectural monuments, perhaps to enjoy the coolness of its fountains[83] or to admire its impressive collection of art, including works by Arkesilaos[84] and Timomachos.[85] But Herod might have been most intrigued by the golden statue of Cleopatra,[86] who had entertained him lavishly only a few weeks previously.[87]

There were many other elements of contemporary Roman architecture that would have interested Herod. The sewer system of the Cloaca Maxima, which traditionally dated back to the regal period[88] but was probably mostly of the third century B.C. or later,[89] remained one of the wonders of Rome until at least the sixth century A.C.[90] Marcus Agrippa would tour and rebuild

---

77. Augustus, *Res gestae* 19, 21.

78. Ulrich (supra, n. 29), 53–54. It, too, was seen as eastern in inspiration: Appian, *Civil War* 2.102. For a complete summary of recent information on the complex, see Chiara Morselli, "Forum Iulium," in *LTUR*, 2: 299–306.

79. Cicero, *Ad Atticum* 4.17; for the chronology of its construction, see Ulrich (supra, n. 29), 51. But see the objections of Nicolas Purcell (supra, n. 53), who would take Cicero's letter to refer to the west end of the Forum, not the Forum Julium.

80. Suetonius, *Divine Julius* 26.

81. Appian, *Civil War* 2.68–69, 102, 3.28; Dio 43.22.

82. This is despite Dio's assertion, 43.22; see also Augustus, *Res gestae* 20. Caesar had been in Antioch the previous year and had commissioned his Kaisareion in that city, whose Hellenistic forms influenced the Forum Julium (Sjöqvist [supra, n. 47], 105–7). See also infra, pp. 82–83.

83. Ovid, *Ars Amatoria* 1.81–82.

84. Pliny, *Natural History* 35.156.

85. Ibid.,7.126, 35.136.

86. Appian, *Civil War* 2.102; Dio 51.22.

87. *BJ* 1.279.

88. Livy 1.38.6, 1.56.2; Dionysios of Halikarnassos, *Roman Antiquities* 3.67.5, 4.44.1; Pliny, *Natural History* 36.104.

89. Platner-Ashby, 127; Richardson, *NTD*, 91–92.

90. Cassiodorus (Migne, *PL*, 69–70), *Variarum* 3.30.

the sewers in 33 B.C.,[91] and a decade later Herod would begin construction of the most sophisticated sewer system in the East at Caesarea. The great warehouses on the Tiber, known today as the Porticus Aemilia and Emporium,[92] had been constructed early in the second century B.C.,[93] and may have inaugurated concrete construction in Rome:[94] Herod built similar warehouses at Masada and Caesarea.

In addition, there were many potential building projects under discussion in 40 B.C. Two years previously, at Philippi, Octavian had vowed to construct the Temple of Mars Ultor,[95] which in the end took forty years to complete (its delays became proverbial).[96] At the time of Herod's visit, the concept was little formed, and it probably did not yet include the idea of the Forum of Augustus, but it was nevertheless to become one of the most Hellenistic monuments of Augustan Rome, inspired in part by the great temple complexes of Asia Minor.[97] Another topic of discussion might have been Asinius Pollio's plans for restoring the Atrium Libertatis and establishing the first public library in the city.[98] Other projects of the emerging Augustan era must have been suggested or discussed by 40 B.C. Architecture and urban renewal were among the most vital subjects in Rome at this time, and Herod's previous and future interest in these matters makes it a certainty that he avidly sought out information, both visual and oral, on the architectural enhancement of the city. Everywhere Herod went, he was steadily gathering knowledge that would serve him well in his own architectural endeavors. Like Aeneas watching the building of Carthage, he may often have seen without understanding,[99] but the seeds were planted for the Herodian architectural program of the next thirty years.

---

91. Dio 49.43.

92. Nash, 1: 380; 2: 238; Coarelli, *Guida*, 261–62.

93. Livy 35.10.12, 41.27.8.

94. Boethius (supra, n. 5), 126–30.

95. Ovid, *Fasti* 5.569–78; Suetonius, *Augustus* 29.

96. Macrobius, *Saturnalia* 2.4.9.

97. Einar Gjerstad, "Die Ursprungsgeschichte der römischen Kaiserfora," *OpArch* 3 (1944): 40–72.

98. The project, a rebuilding of a long-standing structure, was part of his triumph of 39 or 38 B.C., but one suspects it was under discussion before that date. Ovid, *Tristia* 3.1.72; Pliny, *Natural History* 7.115, 35.10; Suetonius, *Augustus* 29. Its location is uncertain: although conventionally believed to have been where the Basilica Ulpia was later built (Richardson, *NTD*, 41), it has recently been suggested to be the building commonly known as the Tabularium (Purcell [supra, n. 53], 125–55).

99. Vergil, *Aeneid* 8.730.

CHAPTER THREE

Herod and Marcus Agrippa

"Herod was regarded by Caesar as second only to Agrippa, and by Agrippa as second only to Caesar."[1] Many examples of the mutual esteem of Herod and Marcus Vipsanius Agrippa are recorded in the pages of Josephus. Much of the information comes from sources favorable to Herod, which might tend to emphasize the respect in which he was held by the ruling elite of Rome, but the existence of such respect is supported by the extensive time Agrippa and Herod spent together.

Close friendship between them is first documented in the *Autobiography* of Nikolaos of Damaskos, written shortly after the death of Herod in 4 B.C. and describing an incident involving Agrippa's wife Julia in which Nikolaos himself had played a crucial role.[2] In A.D. 40, Herod's grandson King Agrippa I reminded Agrippa's grandson, the emperor Gaius, of their grandfathers' friendship and mutual respect. The letter Agrippa I sent Gaius was quoted or paraphrased, or perhaps even originally written, by Philon of Alexandria, who recorded it in his *Embassy to Gaius*,[3] written early in the reign of Claudius.[4] Josephus is the source for the remaining references, most of which originated with Nikolaos.[5] In *BJ*, citations are few, usually on the topic of honors paid to Agrippa,[6] although the statement about mutual esteem is also included. But in *AJ*, the later work, which is less favorable toward Herod, association of Herod and Agrippa is repeated and frequent.

---

1. *BJ* 1.400; repeated slightly differently at *AJ* 15.361.
2. *FGrHist*, #90, fr. 134. For the incident, see infra, pp. 49–50, 226.
3. Philon, *Embassy to Gaius* 294–97.
4. Philon, *Embassy* 107, 206; Philon, *Philonis Alexandrini Legatio ad Gaium*, ed. and trans. E. Mary Smallwood (Leiden, 1970), 151, 291–92.
5. This is most apparent at *AJ* 16.27–65 (= Nikolaos, fr. 142).
6. *BJ* 1.118, 416.

Contact between the two is of particular importance in an analysis of the Roman basis of Herod's building program. Agrippa was second only to Augustus himself in the erection of public structures, both for the completion of many of the late Republican buildings Herod had seen under construction in 40 B.C., and for further implementation of many aspects of the Augustan enhancement of the physical splendor of Rome.[7] Agrippa's building program may have begun as early as the time of Herod's first visit to Rome, when, according to Dio,[8] he constructed the Aqua Julia.[9] During his aedileship of 33 B.C., he was involved in a wide range of projects, both new and repairs, including public buildings, streets, sewers,[10] aqueducts,[11] and a number of fountains.[12]

Agrippa's building program reached a peak in 26–25 B.C. In 26 B.C., the Saepta Julia, in progress for nearly twenty years, was finally dedicated,[13] and other structures in the Campus Martius, including the Pantheon and Porticus Argonautarum, were completed the following year.[14] In 19 B.C., after Agrippa's return from several years on Mytilene, the Aqua Virgo was finished,[15] and this is probably also the date of completion of the Baths of Agrippa and associated hydraulic structures.[16] Little known today is the Campus Agrippae, containing the Porticus Vipsania,[17] which lay near the Quirinal and was still not completed at the time of Agrippa's death.[18] In the Porticus was the map of the world Agrippa had prepared, which would have shown Herod's kingdom.[19] Also little known are Agrippa's bridge over the Tiber and the Horrea Agrippiana. Yet it would seem that much of Agrippa's work was completed by the time of his Mytilene sojourn and visit with Herod in 23–21 B.C.,[20] and it can be no accident that the most brilliant

---

7. On the topic of Agrippa's building program generally, see Frederick W. Shipley, *Agrippa's Building Activities in Rome* (St. Louis, 1933).

8. Dio 48.32.

9. It is more probable that this did not occur until his aedileship seven years later. Frontinus, *De aquis* 9; Richardson, *NTD*, 17; Dorianna Cattalini, "Aqua Iulia," in *LTUR*, 1: 66–67.

10. Pliny, *Natural History* 36.105; Dio 49.43; Broughton, 2: 415.

11. Frontinus, *De aquis* 9, although Pliny (*Natural History* 36.121) and Dio (48.32, 49.43) dated various of these aqueduct works to between 40 and 19 B.C.

12. Pliny, *Natural History* 36.121.

13. Dio 53.23.

14. Dio 53.27; Richardson, *NTD*, 283, 312.

15. Frontinus, *De aquis* 9; Dio 54.11; Susanna Le Pera, "Aqua Virgo," in *LTUR*, 1: 72–73.

16. Coarelli, *Guida*, 291–92.

17. Platner-Ashby, 90, 430; Shipley, *Agrippa* (supra, n. 7), 73–77; Coarelli, *Guida*, 241, 263; Richardson, *NTD*, 64.

18. Dio 55.8.

19. Pliny, *Natural History* 3.17; O. A. W. Dilke, *Greek and Roman Maps* (Ithaca, N.Y., 1985), 41–53.

20. Shipley, *Agrippa* (supra, n. 7), 14–15; Coarelli, *Guida*, 269.

phase of Herod's own building, including the Temple in Jerusalem and the founding of Caesarea, directly follows the initiation of a period of extensive personal contact between him and Agrippa.

In 40 B.C., when Herod first came to Rome, Agrippa was *praetor urbanus.* There is no documentation that the two met at this time, but the intimacy that existed by 23 B.C. can best be explained by previous meeting and friendship. After 40 B.C., however, there seems to have been no opportunity for their paths to cross again until 23 B.C.,[21] by which time both were established in their careers. Herod had been king for nearly two decades and had seen his dominions enlarged, especially after the death of Cleopatra. His building program was well under way, and he had already attracted Greek scholars to his court. Agrippa had been consul three times and had been crucial in the final disposition of the civil war and in the implementation of Augustus's peaceful revolution. And whatever their early contacts and knowledge of one another, by the winter of 23/22 B.C., they had developed a friendship that would last for the rest of Agrippa's life.

Sometime in 23 B.C., Agrippa was sent by Augustus to the East. The fragmentary historical sources for this mission mix political and personal motives connected with the imperial succession, Augustus's illness that year, and his consolidation of powers.[22] Regardless of the exact reason for Agrippa's departure from Rome, by mid-23 B.C., he had established himself at Mytilene, where he was to remain for nearly two years, perhaps writing his memoirs. Before long, Herod came to visit. According to Josephus, the encounter was in winter, probably the first one Agrippa spent at Mytilene. One can hardly imagine Herod waiting over a year to make a call,[23] as he was already considered one of Agrippa's best friends. Agrippa's existing respect for Herod was soon demonstrated when a contingent from Gadara—the city had been added to Herod's realm after the death of Cleopatra[24]—made charges against Herod: Agrippa would not even listen but sent the delegation in chains to Herod.[25]

21. Unless Malalas (220) was correct in placing Agrippa in Syria after Actium.

22. *AJ* 15.350; Velleius 2.93; Suetonius, *Augustus* 66; Dio 53.32; Davie Magie, "The Mission of Agrippa to the Orient in 23 B.C.," *CP* 3 (1908): 145–52; Reinhold, 78–85, 167–75; Roddaz, 319–31.

23. Some, however, following Otto, *RE*, 70, have argued for the second winter: Hugo Willrich, *Das Haus des Herodes zwischen Jerusalem und Rom* (Heidelberg, 1929), 89; Schalit, *KH*, 424. But see Helmut Halfmann, *Itinera principum* (Heidelberger Althistorische Beiträge und Epigraphische Studien, 2 [Stuttgart, 1986]), 163.

24. *AJ* 15.217.

25. Herod freed them; unfortunately, this generosity only encouraged the Gadarenes, who renewed their appeal when Augustus visited Antioch two years later. This too was in vain (*AJ* 15.356–59). Magie (supra, n. 22), 147–48, assumed that this incident was to cement "the friendship thus formed" (in Mytilene), rather than proof of any prior relationship.

No specific details are available regarding Herod's visit to Agrippa: in fact, sources about Agrippa's entire stay at Mytilene are exceedingly sparse.[26] But the two men, meeting at the locale that allegedly had inspired the remarkable Theater of Pompey in Rome (fig. 1), would have found an immediate rapport in the topic of architecture and urban renewal. Herod would have asked Agrippa for architectural news from Rome, and Agrippa could have told Herod about the recent completion of the Saepta,[27] the progress of construction in the Campus Martius,[28] and what was happening to the plans for the Temple of Mars Ultor. He would have had more than polite interest in Herod's recent completion of Sebaste and his plans for Jerusalem and Caesarea. Since both were involved in the urban renewal of Antioch,[29] they could have shared their ideas. Perhaps arrangements were also begun for Agrippa to make an architecturally oriented official visit to Herod's kingdom.

Herod would have been particularly interested in Agrippa's hydraulic efforts. The hydraulic infrastructure of Rome had suffered through neglect and disinterest during the civil wars: by the 40's B.C. no new aqueduct had been built since the completion of the Aqua Tepula in 125 B.C.[30] Much of Agrippa's early career was spent in restoration of this crucial element of the city.[31] Perhaps as early as the year of Herod's visit, Agrippa had begun to repair various aqueducts,[32] and in 33 B.C. he undertook work on the sewers, making his famous voyage through them.[33] His repair of aqueducts[34] was complemented by building two new ones, the Julia and the Virgo.[35] Agrippa was interested in hydraulics during much of his life, becoming perpetual curator of water for the city of Rome. At his death he was succeeded by Messalla, and eventually, nearly a century later, by Frontinus, who recorded the history of the aqueducts.[36] Herod himself had more than a passing interest in hydraulics, as he was to bring this particularly Roman art[37] to the

26. Reinhold, 169–70; Magie, *RR*, 468–69.

27. Dio 53.23.

28. Shipley, *Agrippa* (supra, n. 7), 37–72.

29. Glanville Downey, *A History of Antioch in Syria from Seleucus to the Arab Conquest* (Princeton, 1961), 170–74. See also infra, pp. 214–16.

30. Pliny, *Natural History* 36.121; Frontinus, *De aquis* 8–9. See, generally, Christer Bruun, *The Water Supply of Ancient Rome: A Study of Roman Imperial Administration* (Commentationes Humanarum Litterarum, 93 [Helsinki, 1991]). On the Tepula, see Harry B. Evans, *Water Distribution in Ancient Rome: The Evidence of Frontinus* (Ann Arbor, 1994), 95–98.

31. Reinhold, 46; Shipley, *Agrippa* (supra, n. 7), 19; Roddaz, 145–47; Harry B. Evans, "Agrippa's Water Plan," *AJA* 86 (1982): 401–11.

32. Dio 48.32.

33. Pliny, *Natural History* 36.104–8; Dio 49.43; Shipley (supra, n. 7), 21–24.

34. Shipley (supra, n. 7), 24–28; Evans, *Water Distribution* (supra, n. 30), 99–110.

35. Frontinus, *De aquis* 9–10; Platner-Ashby, 28–29.

36. Frontinus, *De aquis* 98–102.

37. Strabo 5.3.8.

East. Within a year he began construction of a notable sewer system at Caesarea, and he was eventually to build Roman-style aqueducts throughout Judaea and Syria.

The sources do not tell how long Herod and Agrippa spent together at Mytilene. Agrippa remained in the East until 21 B.C., when he was recalled by Augustus,[38] and there is no further record of contact until Agrippa made his tour of Herod's dominions in 15 B.C. Agrippa spent 21–20 B.C. in Rome and married Julia,[39] but before the end of 20 B.C. he began a series of campaigns in the west.[40] He did not return to Rome until 18 B.C.[41] It is possible that Herod made his second trip to Rome,[42] generally dated to 18 or 17 B.C., to coincide with Agrippa's presence, but this is by no means certain or even probable.[43]

In late 17 B.C. or early 16 B.C., Agrippa was again sent from Rome, this time to spend over three years in the East. A significant portion of these years he spent in the company of Herod. After a leisurely progression through Greece and Asia Minor, Agrippa arrived in Syria, probably in the autumn of 15 B.C.,[44] where he was involved in founding the new Roman *colonia* at Berytos, for which Herod provided the major public buildings.[45] Throughout this journey Agrippa indulged in the expected architectural constructions.[46]

At some point Herod came to meet him. The locale of this meeting is unknown, although it may again have been Mytilene.[47] Herod extended an invitation to come to Judaea, and Agrippa did so late in 15 B.C.[48] Herod spared no effort to entertain him and provided a thorough and lavishly catered tour of his kingdom, beginning at Sebastos, the recently completed harbor of Caesarea. Caesarea itself was still under construction, having been founded seven years previously at a ruined Hellenistic anchorage. Herod

---

38. Dio 54.6.

39. Ibid.

40. Dio 54.11; Reinhold, 88–94; Roddaz, 637–638.

41. Dio 54.12.

42. *AJ* 16.6.

43. See infra, ch. 5.

44. Reinhold, 106, 112–13; Magie, *RR*, 476–79; Roddaz, 422.

45. Strabo 16.2.19; *BJ* 1.422. For other sources, see Reinhold, 110–11; Roddaz, 431–33; see also Halfmann (supra, n. 23), 163. Schalit, *KH*, 547, preferred early 14 B.C., after the Judaean trip. On Berytos as a Roman *colonia*, see Fergus Millar, "The Roman *Coloniae* of the Near East: A Study of Cultural Relations," in *Roman Eastern Policy and Other Studies in Roman History*, ed. Heikki Solin and Mika Kajava (Commentationes Humanarum Litterarum, 91 [Helsinki, 1990]), 10–23.

46. Reinhold, 108–11.

47. *AJ* 16.12–15. The only hint that it might have been at Mytilene is Josephus's mention of Asia and Ionia in the context of the visit.

48. Otto, *RE, Zeittafel;* Reinhold, 112–13; Roddaz, 451–52.

and Agrippa progressed inland to Sebaste (ancient Samaria), now fully rebuilt as a Hellenistic-Roman city. There followed a tour of three of Herod's fortresses, Alexandreion, Hyrkania, and Herodeion, the last also designed as Herod's tomb.[49] Finally, Agrippa was brought to Jerusalem, where he was greeted festively. He saw the ceremonies in the Temple and was deeply impressed, repeatedly visiting the structure and watching the sacrifices, especially noting the High Priest in his ritual garments, perhaps at the Feast of Tabernacles and Day of Atonement.[50] Agrippa then responded as fully as Jewish law allowed, sacrificing a hecatomb to the God of Israel and providing a feast for the population.[51] His religious piety and friendship toward the people were recorded by Nikolaos of Damaskos.[52]

Agrippa presumably entered the Temple precinct in Jerusalem by the gate that had been named after him,[53] and saw the structures in Herod's palace named the Agrippeion and the Kaisareion.[54] He also would have noticed that the two cities Herod had built were named after Augustus, one in Latin, the other in Greek. All these honors would have been duly reported to Rome: Agrippa and Augustus often discussed Herod.[55] But Agrippa would also have seen the more subtle romanizing that filled Herod's realm: the theaters, Italian-style temples, porticoes, and hydraulic systems, and even Herod's imitation of Augustus's Mausoleum, forms that were familiar in Rome but unknown in Judaea until Herod introduced them. One would suspect that Agrippa's repeated visits to the Temple in Jerusalem were more to admire its architecture than an interest in the local religious practices.

---

49. There were two fortresses named Herodeion built by Herod (see infra, pp. 164–69). One was his mausoleum: the account makes it clear that this is modern Jebel Fureidis, 12 km south of Jerusalem. The other Herodeion was east of the Jordan on the Arabian frontier. It is unlikely that Agrippa went this far east. His route can easily be traced: from Caesarea he proceeded southeast to Sebaste, and then to Alexandreion, then south through Jericho to Hyrkania, and finally southwest to Herodeion and north to Jerusalem.

50. Philon, *Embassy to Gaius* 294–97; Philon, ed. Smallwood (supra, n. 4), 299.

51. *AJ* 16.14–15.

52. *AJ* 16.54–56. As early as the time of the dedication of the original Temple by Solomon, non-Jews were allowed to make sacrifices under certain conditions, one of which was if they had come from far away (1 Kings 8.41–43). Withdrawal of this privilege was one of the events leading to the Jewish revolt of A.D. 66, since it allowed rejection of long-established official Roman sacrifices (*BJ* 2.409). Among the notable Gentiles who had sacrificed in the Temple were (according to dubious tradition) Alexander the Great (*AJ* 11.336: there is no other record of his having been in Jerusalem) and the Seleukid king Antiochos VII (*AJ* 13.243); C. Sosius dedicated a gold crown after capturing Jerusalem for Herod (*BJ* 1.357; *AJ* 14.488).

53. *BJ* 1.416.

54. *BJ* 1.402; *AJ* 15.318 refers to such-named *klisiai*, which although commonly "couches," can also mean a small structure (*LSJ*: see Homer, *Iliad* 9.663; Sophokles, *Aias* 191, 1408); perhaps "pavilion" best translates the concept. There were also identically named structures at Herod's palace in Jericho (*BJ* 1.402).

55. *AJ* 16.141.

Agrippa was so impressed with what he saw that he was reluctant to leave Judaea, but since winter was approaching, he felt it necessary to hasten his departure, presumably around November of 15 B.C. He left laden with gifts from Herod and with a great multitude escorting him to the coast and showering him with leaves as though he were a victor in the games.[56]

The following spring Agrippa mounted an expedition to the Kimmerian Bosporos in order to settle an uncertain situation that had resulted from a usurpation of the throne and the eventual murder of the usurper.[57] The problem had been festering for a number of years, and direct intervention was deemed necessary.[58] Agrippa would already have known about the Bosporan crisis when he was in Judaea, and presumably Herod's assistance had been volunteered or requested at that time.[59] Herod may have been eager to join Agrippa both for political reasons and because he had learned from Strabo the benefits of geographical knowledge to a ruler.[60] Thus, in the spring of 14 B.C., Herod and a fleet departed for Mytilene to join Agrippa. Agrippa had already left when the fleet arrived, and Herod was delayed on Chios, unable to proceed because of a north wind, but he utilized the time to arrange for the rebuilding of a stoa that had been in ruins since the war with Mithradates.[61] Eventually, the wind was favorable and Herod continued his pursuit, not catching up with Agrippa until Sinope. Agrippa was impressed that Herod had undergone such a lengthy journey. According to Josephus, Herod was Agrippa's loyal advisor and colleague on this campaign and the only one on whom he could rely. The crisis was settled diplomatically; in time, a Bosporan city was renamed Agrippias and Bosporan coins were struck with portraits of Augustus and Agrippa.[62]

While on this campaign, Herod and his entourage had an opportunity to demonstrate diplomatic skill of their own. Agrippa's wife Julia had nearly drowned in the Skamandros near Troy, and Agrippa fined the city of Ilion a large sum for negligence. The citizens of Ilion, not daring to approach Agrippa directly, appealed to Herod through Nikolaos of Damaskos for remission. Nikolaos pointed out to Herod both the essential unfairness of

---

56. Philon, *Embassy to Gaius* 297.

57. Lucian (?), *Makrobioi* 17; Dio 54.24; Reinhold, 113–14; Magie, *RR*, 477–478; Roddaz, 465–67.

58. M. Rostovzeff, "Queen Dynamis of Bosporus," *JHS* 39 (1919): 88–109.

59. On the military obligations of Herod's client kingship, see E. Mary Smallwood, *The Jews under Roman Rule* (Studies in Judaism in Late Antiquity, 20 [Leiden, 1976]), 85–86.

60. Strabo 1.1.1–2. Herod may also have seen the opportunity to demonstrate his legitimacy among the extensive Jewish population of Asia Minor, which had long been contributing to the Temple in Jerusalem (*AJ* 14.110–13). He certainly gave the impression upon his return to Jerusalem that the welfare of Asian Jews had been a primary concern (*AJ* 16.63).

61. *AJ* 16.16–20.

62. The honoring of Agrippa probably did not occur until after his death, perhaps as late as 8 B.C. See Rostovzeff (supra, n. 58), 100–101.

the fine and the unique historical status of the city of Ilion, both as the site of the Trojan War and the home of Julia's ancestors. Herod then persuaded Agrippa to cancel the fine, and Nikolaos personally delivered Agrippa's message to the citizens of Ilion. In return, they honored Agrippa[63]—as a member of the Julian family, if only by marriage, he was considered a descendant of the Trojans—but they honored Herod even more. The incident is revealing in terms not only of the influence Herod had on Agrippa but of the respect in which he was held in Asia Minor. It is also illustrative of the status of Nikolaos both among the Greeks of Asia Minor and with Herod.[64]

Evidently Herod's services had been substantial and impressive enough that Agrippa asked the king to join him on an overland journey from Sinope back to Ionia, an event considered the peak of Herod's career.[65] The entourage passed through Paphlagonia, Kappadokia, and Great Phrygia to Ephesos and eventually to Samos. Throughout, Herod advised Agrippa regarding appropriate actions toward the cities of Asia Minor, served as a go-between for those petitioning Agrippa, and made liberal and repeated benefactions in all the cities he visited: presumably some of this liberality was architecturally oriented.[66]

When they arrived on Samos, Herod and Agrippa remained together until the autumn. During this time they received petitions from the Jewish communities of Asia Minor and elsewhere, which took advantage of this collegiality between the most powerful Jewish leader and the second most powerful Roman. Complaints were made regarding an inability of the Jews to practice their religion freely, especially in Ephesos and Kyrene. Nikolaos was again the conduit by which these petitions were eventually submitted to Agrippa.[67] Herod persuaded Agrippa to give the Jews a hearing, and Nikolaos was chosen to speak on their behalf. In a lengthy speech, Nikolaos persuasively made the case to Agrippa, noting in particular Herod's continued good will, honor, and assistance to Rome. References were also made to the help Herod's father had given to Julius Caesar, and the Roman citizenship that had been the reward for this aid. Finally, Nikolaos recalled Agrippa's reception in Judaea and his sacrifices in the Temple. Thus, in reminding Agrippa of the services of Herod and his father to Rome, he implied that it was now a Roman obligation to uphold Jewish rights (perhaps thus giving an insight into some of the reasons for Herod's philoromanity). And Agrip-

63. *SIG*[3], 776.

64. Nikolaos (*FGrHist*, # 90), fr. 134; see also *AJ* 16.26; Wacholder, *Nicolaus*, 27–28; Reinhold, 116.

65. Otto, *RE* 73.

66. *BJ* 1.425.

67. *AJ* 16.31–65.

pa was persuaded, largely because of his friendship with Herod, although his official reason for supporting the Jews was that he was merely upholding established policy.[68] He thus confirmed the right of the Jews to observe their own customs, and sent letters of rebuke to the archons, *boulai*, and people of Ephesos and Kyrene.[69] Despite the strongly pro-Herodian sources for these events, it seems Agrippa's actions throughout were motivated largely by his friendship with Herod rather than any strong sensitivity about religious freedom. Nevertheless, Agrippa's policy toward the Jews was to be remembered and cited by both Romans and Jews thereafter. When M. Antonius's son Iullus Antonius (cos. 10 B.C.) was proconsul in Asia, he wrote the Ephesians that he had been reminded of Agrippa's ruling and upheld it.[70] In Rome a synagogue was named after Agrippa,[71] and in A.D. 40 King Agrippa I of Judaea was to remind the emperor Gaius of his grandfather's policy.[72] Regardless of how upholding Jewish rights fit into Roman provincial policy, it seems unlikely that Agrippa could have failed to be influenced by his close association with Herod.[73]

When Agrippa made his ruling, Herod was deeply touched by what Agrippa had said about him. Herod then embraced Agrippa, and Agrippa in response embraced Herod, "treating him like an equal."[74] They then went their separate ways: Herod to Judaea and Agrippa to Mytilene for the winter of 14/13 B.C.[75] The two had one final meeting, the following spring.[76] Agrippa was on the verge of returning to Rome, and Herod brought his son Antipatros to be sent to Rome. Herod had become embroiled in family disputes as soon as he had returned to Judaea the previous autumn. These resulted in the reinstating of Antipatros and his mother Doris, who had been banished when Herod had become king and married Mariamme.[77] Hence Antipatros, who would have been nearly thirty,

---

68. *AJ* 12.127.

69. *AJ* 16.167–70; Kathleen M. T. Atkinson, "The Governors of the Province Asia in the Reign of Augustus," *Historia* 7 (1958): 318–22.

70. *AJ* 16.172; on Antonius, who was to commit suicide after adultery with Agrippa's widow Julia (who had remarried, to Tiberius), see Syme, *RR*, 426–27; Ronald Syme, *The Augustan Aristocracy* (Oxford, 1986), passim.

71. Smallwood, *Jews* (supra, n. 59), 138; Harry J. Leon, *The Jews of Ancient Rome* (Philadelphia, 1960), 140–41.

72. Philon, *Embassy to Gaius* 294–97.

73. *AJ* 16.157.

74. *AJ* 16.60–61; Reinhold, 120–21; Smallwood, *Jews* (supra, n. 59), 140–41; Schalit, *KH*, 426; Roddaz, 456–63.

75. *AJ* 16.62–66.

76. *AJ* 16.86.

77. *BJ* 1.432–33, 448.

had not shared in the Roman residency accorded his half brothers Alexandros and Aristoboulos. Antipatros took many gifts to Augustus, and soon he was living under the Princeps's care.[78]

With their departure for Rome, Herod returned to Judaea, never to see Agrippa again. Although Herod came to Rome the following year, largely for reasons connected with his own domestic and dynastic problems,[79] Agrippa was probably already dead. He died in Campania in late March of 12 B.C. and became the second of Augustus's prospective heirs to be buried in his Mausoleum.[80] It is unlikely that Herod's journey to Rome was connected with Agrippa's funeral,[81] although the trip may have been in part due to Herod's realization that his strongest advocate in Rome was now dead, and that he needed to assert his power with those surviving. Nevertheless, Agrippa's influence on Herod continued. A city in the kingdom was renamed in his honor.[82] Agrippa became a dynastic name in Herod's family, beginning with his grandson born two years later in 10 B.C.[83] The name Agrippa (or variants thereof) is documented six times in the family of Herod. As late as A.D. 79, a great-great-grandson of Herod's was still alive, bearing the name Antonius Agrippa, a neat summation of the two Roman patrons of the family, and the name even passed into the royal family of Armenia through Herod's great-grandson Tigranes V, whose grandson was C. Julius Agrippa, quaestor of the province of Asia in the Flavian period.[84] These namesakes of M. Vipsanius Agrippa's survived after his own family became extinct with the death of his great-grandson Nero in A.D. 68. People in Judaea unrelated to the royal family were also named Agrippa.[85]

One cannot overemphasize the influence that Agrippa had on Herod. Even if their friendship was at its most intense only during the last decade of Agrippa's life, this was when Herod was at his peak.[86] The relationship between Agrippa's architectural interests and those of Herod is clear, as is their repeated and almost competitive architectural largesse in Asia Minor and Syria. In the last decade of his life, Agrippa spent almost as much time with Herod as with Augustus: this more than anything supports Josephus's statement about mutual esteem. Throughout this decade Herod was using Agrippa as his model for the architectural and cultural responsibilities of

78. *AJ* 16.273.

79. *BJ* 1.452–66.

80. Velleius 2.96; Dio 54.28; Reinhold, 125–26; Roddaz, 485–86.

81. But see Reinhold, 133.

82. Anthedon was renamed Agrippias: see infra, pp. 128–29.

83. *BJ* 1.552: see Stemma 4.

84. See Stemma 13; E. Groag, "C. Julius Agrippa" (# 50), in *RE*, 19 (1917): 143.

85. *CIG*, 4539, 4594.

86. Otto, *RE*, 80.

dynasts. Clearly. Nikolaos, already favored in both Rome and Judaea, and serving as the official recorder of the actions of both Augustus and Herod, was also a major factor in Herod's romanization. But it was Agrippa who was always the model: no cities or descendants were named after Nikolaos. Through Agrippa, Herod learned how a Roman should act, and Agrippa saw a dynast of the Hellenistic east at the peak of his powers. It was in large part owing to Agrippa that Herod modeled his architecture on Rome, and not on the Greek world, and that his architectural benefactions extended beyond Judaea throughout the Greek world and perhaps to Rome itself.

CHAPTER FOUR

The Herodian Intellectual Circle

Herod's desire to structure his kingdom in a proper fashion included encouragement to scholars, artists, and other intellectuals. One can only guess at the innumerable unknown architects, sculptors, painters, and mosaicists who implemented his artistic program: early in his career, he had a substantial personal art collection, mostly objects of gold and silver.[1] But Herod also persuaded Greek scholars and intellectuals to take up residence at his court. The Hellenism implicit in such an attitude may have been as much a personal trait as a political one, since Herod was believed to prefer the company of Greeks to that of Jews.[2] More important, he was also imitating the patronage of scholars and artists of late Republican and Augustan Rome, a phenomenon he had seen as early as 40 B.C. Thus Herod's support of an intellectual circle was another way in which he placed himself within the mainstream of Augustan Rome. In addition, this coterie of talent at his court was an important source of information about the latest trends in architecture.

Royal patronage of intellectuals was an ancient Greek tradition, at least as old as the honor given Demodokos by King Alkinoos at the Phaiakian court. In post-Homeric times there were numerous famous examples, including Solon at the court of Kroisos of Lydia, Euripides with Archelaos of Makedonia, Plato at the Syracusian court, and Aristotle with Hermias of Assos and Philip II of Makedonia, as well as countless others in the Hellenistic period, especially at Pella, Pergamon, and Alexandria. The many casual references in Greek and Roman literature indicate the extensiveness of the phenomenon.

---

1. *AJ* 15.306–7.

2. *AJ* 19.329; Nikolaos, fr. 136. See also fr. 135; David M. Jacobson, "King Herod's 'Heroic' Public Image," *RBibl* 95 (1988): 386–91.

In Rome a similar trend developed as early as the third century B.C., as Greek intellectuals became attached to Roman aristocrats. The first documented example is Andronikos of Taras, who was the slave of M. Livius Salinator and took the name L. Livius Andronicus, becoming famous as the first Roman playwright.[3] Many of the prominent personalities of the last generation of the Republic encouraged Greek scholars: the circle around M. Antonius that Herod infiltrated was one of many.[4] All in all, Herod had ample evidence from both Greek and Roman culture about the role a ruler was expected to play in encouraging artists and scholars, and one would expect him to have been an active part of this tradition. Moreover, the court at Alexandria provided Herod with a particularly notable example of royal patronage. Some of the intellectuals Herod had met in Rome in 40 B.C. had moved to the Egyptian court. At least one of these, Nikolaos of Damaskos, had gone to Alexandria to tutor the royal children and then, after the collapse of the dynasty, went to Herod's court. Others also came from Egypt to Judaea, both before and after 30 B.C., and association of the two lands as an outlet for intellectual talent became proverbial.[5]

Herod may have encouraged intellectual achievement by founding a library.[6] The recent history of libraries in the East had been particularly unfortunate. Although the modest library at Antioch built around 100 B.C. by the merchant Maron continued to flourish,[7] the Library at Alexandria had suffered at the hands of Julius Caesar in late 48 B.C., when perhaps as many as 400,000 scrolls had burned.[8] Antonius had attempted to replenish the Library by removing 200,000 scrolls, evidently the bulk of the collection, from Pergamon.[9] Thus the two great libraries of the Hellenistic world were seriously damaged in Herod's day. Herod, knowing that a library was an essential part of a dynamic royal state of his era,[10] and essential for the work of the scholars he was trying to attract to his court, would attempt to found his own. The library may have emphasized Herod's own interests in

3. Eduard Fraenkel, "Livius" (# 10a), *RE*, suppl. 5 (1931): 598–607.

4. On the Antonian circle, see supra, pp. 19–28. On other circles in Late Republican Rome, see J. P. D. V. Balsdon, *Romans and Aliens* (London, 1979), 54–58; Bowersock, *Augustus*, 30–32, 75.

5. Krinagoras of Mytilene, 20 (= *Greek Anthology* 7.645).

6. Otto, *RE*, 105; Schalit, *KH*, 413.

7. Malalas 235–36; Glanville Downey, *A History of Antioch in Syria from Selecus to the Arab Conquest* (Princeton, 1961), 132–33.

8. Plutarch, *Caesar* 49; Dio 42.38. Accounts of the loss range from 400,000 (Seneca, *On the Tranquility of the Mind* 9.5, quoting Livy) to 700,000 (Aulus Gellius, *Attic Nights* 7.17.3). Caesar himself was discreetly silent about the fire (*Civil War* 3.111–13).

9. Plutarch, *Antonius* 58.

10. Inge Nielsen, *Hellenistic Palaces: Tradition and Renewal* (Studies in Hellenistic Civilization, 5 [Aarhus, 1994]), 26. Private libraries had also become common in the elaborate homes of Late Republican Rome (Nielsen, 235–36).

philosophy, rhetoric, and history.[11] In creating a library he was fulfilling an interrupted vision of Julius Caesar's—always a strong motivation for Herod—since Caesar (despite his unfortunate role at Alexandria) had planned to create the first public library in Rome, with Varro as librarian.[12]

Mostly from the evidence of Josephus and Nikolaos, it is possible to reconstruct a picture of the Herodian intellectual circle that flourished in Judaea. The picture is vague, but a few personalities stand out, and others can be dimly seen. Many of the names are Alexandrian. The circle began to develop by 30 B.C., when the deaths of Antonius and Cleopatra meant unemployment for their scholars, and it was still active at the time of Herod's death a quarter-century later. The most famous member was Nikolaos himself, who came to Judaea after the death of his patrons in Alexandria, remained with Herod until the king's death, and was of service to the next generation of the dynasty. Another prominent personality who may have been at Herod's court was the historian and geographer Strabo of Amaseia. Others included the rhetorician Eirenaios; the royal tutors Gemellus and Andromachos; Herod's secretary Diophantos; a priest of Apollo from Kos named Euaratos; the adventurer Eurykles of Sparta; Nikolaos's brother Ptolemaios; another Ptolemaios, who was Herod's chief minister; and other refugees from Egypt, including the physician Olympos and the historian Philostratos. Additional personalities were described by Josephus as particular friends or companions of Herod. Since Friend (*philos*) is a technical term in the structure of Hellenistic monarchy, referring to a circle of talented advisors and confidants who served the king,[13] Josephus's citation of a particular person as a Friend of Herod's indicates more than personal intimacy or companionship. In the ideal sense, only Greeks could be Friends, and given Herod's obsessive Hellenism, it is likely that he adhered as much as possible to this principle, although some of his Friends had Semitic names. Regardless of their training or talents, Friends could be used by the king in any role, as the career of Nikolaos makes clear.[14] Many

11. For Herod's intellectual interests, see Nikolaos, fr. 135. An attempt to reconstruct the shelf list of Herod's Greek library has been made by Ben Zion Wacholder (*Nicolaus*, 81–86), based on works known to Nikolaos and Alexandros Polyhistor, as well as others associated with Herod's court. Wacholder's list includes forty-four authors, to which one would certainly add Strabo of Amaseia's *History*, completed just before he was at Herod's court. For an objection to Wacholder's shelf list, see Louis H. Feldman, *Jew and Gentile in the Ancient World* (Princeton, 1993), 472.

12. Suetonius, *Divine Julius* 44. Like so many of Caesar's plans, this was only implemented after his death, by Asinius Pollio (supra, p. 42).

13. See, e.g., the manner in which the citizens of Hierapolis Kastabala in Kilikia honored "the Friends of the King" (*OGIS*, 754)

14. On the *philoi* in Hellenistic monarchy, see F. W. Walbank, "Monarchies and Monarchic Ideals," in *CAH*, 2d ed. (Cambridge, 1984), 7.1: 68–71; on *philoi* at Herod's court, see Otto, *RE*, 83–85.

of the Friends are little more than names in the historic record, often ones common in the Hellenistic world, so it can be difficult further to identify those around Herod.[15] A consistent element, obvious from the biographical details outlined in the following catalogue, is the number of Friends involved in plots against Herod, an insight into the turbulent life at the Herodian court.

Examination of the Herodian intellectual circle assists in understanding the building program. Many of Herod's associates influenced his architectural endeavors. Most obvious are Nikolaos and Strabo, who commuted regularly between Rome and the East, providing Herod with a steady source of information about Augustan Rome. Earlier, before 30 B.C., contacts between Alexandria and Judaea were steady and strong (although not always positive), and those who visited both the court of Cleopatra and that of Herod would have been informative to Herod about Alexandria and its innovative architecture. After 30 B.C. there was a general movement from Alexandria to Judaea. In addition, citizens of Damaskos, Kos, and Sparta all resided at the Herodian court, and it seems no accident that Herodian architectural patronage extended to those cities.

APPENDIX: CATALOGUE

The following catalogue lists those at Herod's court who seem to have been members of the intellectual circle, or who were Greeks especially close to Herod, although having a Greek name does not inevitably mean that a person was ethnically Greek.[16]

1. *Alexas* (*RE*, # 1b), one of Herod's Friends, was married to his sister Salome,[17] who was persuaded by Livia to consent to the marriage.[18] He announced the news of Herod's death to the army, assembled at Jericho;[19] this implies Alexas held a high post, perhaps chief of military staff, in Herod's government. He was probably the father of the Alexas Helkias who married Salome's granddaughter Kypros.[20] It is possible that he was the son of Alexas of Laodikeia, the intimate of M. Antonius's and protégé of Timagenes whom Herod tried unsuccessfully to save in 30 B.C., but it is more likely that he was Jewish. The family seems to have owned land in the vicinity of Gezer, which

---

15. Otto, *RE*, 81–87; Schalit, *KH*, 412–13.
16. Otto, *RE*, 85–86.
17. *BJ* 1.566.
18. *AJ* 17.10; but see *BJ* 1.566.
19. *BJ* 1.666; *AJ* 17.193–94.
20. *AJ* 18.138; Stemma 2.

was probably given to them by Herod, who had acquired it from the Hasmoneans; Alexas's family retained these lands until at least the second century A.C.[21]

2. *Andromachos* was the tutor of Herod's sons as well as an advisor to the king. He was eventually dismissed for involvement in plots by Herod's sons against the king.[22] As a tutor to royal children, he would have been a scholar, perhaps the sons' tutor in Greek culture, but he is otherwise unknown. He may have been from Alexandria: the name was known at the Ptolemaic court from the third century B.C.[23]

3. *Antipatros Gadia* (*RE*, # 20b), one of Herod's closest Friends,[24] was executed after complicity in a revolt led by Kostobaros, governor of Idumaea.[25] It is unlikely that he was related to any of the numerous literary figures named Antipatros, and the Semitic surname indicates that he was probably Jewish.

4. *Antiphilos* was also involved in a plot against Herod.[26] His brother was a physician in Alexandria, which implies that Antiphilos himself was an educated man, and he had contacts with the imperial family in Rome.[27] Perhaps a descendant of the Alexandrian painter of the same name,[28] he came to Herod from the Alexandrian court.

5. *Demetrios* (*RE*, # 48), son of Andromachos (supra, # 2) was a close friend of Herod's son Alexandros, but is otherwise unknown.[29]

6. *Diophantos* (*RE*, # 11), one of Herod's secretaries, gained notoriety as a forger and was eventually executed for the crime.[30]

7. *Dositheos* (*RE*, # 5), son of Kleopatrides of Alexandria, was one of Herod's closest Friends, but he was eventually executed along with Lysimachos and Antipatros Gadia for involvement in the revolt of

---

21. Greek inscriptions with the names Alexas and Helkios have been found south and east of Gezer; they seem to be stones to mark the boundary between the town and private estates: see Ben Zion Rosenfeld, "The 'Boundary of Gezer' Inscriptions and the History of Gezer at the End of the Second Temple Period," *IEJ* 38 (1988): 235–45.

22. *AJ* 16.241–45.

23. Polybios 33.8.4; P. M. Fraser, *Ptolemaic Alexandria* (Oxford, 1972), 2: 121.

24. *AJ* 15.252.

25. For the revolt, see *AJ* 15.252–66.

26. *BJ* 1.592; *AJ* 17.70–77.

27. *BJ* 1.641.

28. Pliny, *Natural History* 35.114, 138; O. Rossbach, "Antiphilos" (# 6), in *RE*, 2 (1894): 2525.

29. *AJ* 16.243. The name existed in the Jewish community in Alexandria as early as the third century B.C., in the person of a Jewish historian of that name (*RE* # 79; Fraser [supra, n. 23], 1: 690–93).

30. *BJ* 1.529; *AJ* 16.319. The name existed at Alexandria; those bearing it included a famous mathematician (Fraser [supra, n. 23], 1: 391, 400, 549, 812).

Kostobaros.[31] In his *Memoirs*, Herod credited him with a major role in the betrayal and execution of Hyrkanos II.[32] Dositheos had also petitioned L. Cornelius Lentulus Crus (*cos.* 49 B.C.) regarding military exemption for Jews.[33] He may have been Jewish rather than Greek, given his involvement in Jewish causes; Dositheos is a common Jewish name in Hellenistic Judaea.[34]

8. *Eirenaios* (*RE,* # 6) was a brilliant rhetorician. Although only known as an advocate for Antipas in the succession struggle after Herod's death,[35] his prominence at this time indicates that his reputation had already been established, perhaps coming from Alexandria in 30 B.C. The name was common in the Alexandrian scholarly community,[36] and Eirenaios may have been a relative of the grammarian of the same name, also known as Minucius Pacatus, of the following century.[37]

9. *Euaratos*[38] of Kos visited Judaea and was a friend of Herod's son Alexandros's. This is probably the priest of Apollo at Halasarna in 12 B.C., C. Julius Euaratos.[39] Euaratos's visit may have been connected with the largesse Herod bestowed on Kos.[40]

10. *Eurykles* of Sparta (*RE,* # 5) visited Herod around 8 B.C.,[41] in need of money, and ingratiated himself, bringing Herod presents and soon becoming knowledgeable about Herod's character. The two may have known each other twenty years previously, as both were involved in the development of the city of Nikopolis. Eurykles soon became active in the palace intrigues, implicating Herod's secretary Diophantos, and playing Herod's sons Alexandros and Antipatros

31. *AJ* 15.252–60.

32. Herod (*FGrHist,* # 236), fr. 1.

33. *AJ* 14.236–37; E. Mary Smallwood, *The Jews under Roman Rule* (Studies in Judaism in Late Antiquity, 20 [Leiden, 1976]), 127–28.

34. Hugo Willrich, "Dositheos" (## 3–5), in *RE* 10 (1905): 1605–6; see also 2 Macc. 12.19–24, 35. Herod's advisor may have been a descendant of the Jewish general of the same name (*RE,* # 4) who served Ptolemaios VI Philometer in the second century B.C. (*Apion* 2.49; Fraser [supra, n. 23], 1: 83, 222). But Dositheos was also the name of an Alexandrian astronomer, a pupil of Konon's and associate of Archimedes, active in the latter third century B.C. (F. Hultsch, "Dositheos" [# 9], in *RE,* 10 [1905]: 1607–8).

35. *BJ* 2.21; *AJ* 17.226.

36. See the entries in *RE,* 10 (1905): 2120.

37. L. Cohn, "Eirenaios" (# 6), in *RE,* 10 (1905): 2120–24.

38. The name is spelled Euarestos at *BJ* 1.532 and Euaratos at *AJ* 16.312.

39. *IGRR* 4.1101, although the name is common on Kos (Susan M. Sherwin-White, *Ancient Cos* (Hypomnemata 51 [Göttingen, 1978]), 445; see also infra, pp. 226–28.

40. Hugo Willrich, "Euaratos," in *RE,* 11 (1907): 847–48.

41. The date is shortly before the execution of Alexandros and Aristoboulos in 7 B.C.: see G. W. Bowersock, "Eurycles of Sparta," *JRS* 51 (1961): 112–18; Hugh Lindsay, "Augustus and Eurycles," *RhM* 135 (1992): 293.

against each other, convincing Herod of the loyalty of the latter and treachery of the former. He gave Eurykles fifty talents for his services, feeling that he had been saved from Alexandros's treason, whereupon Eurykles promptly left for Kappadokia, whose king, Archelaos, was Alexandros's father-in-law. Eurykles extorted further funds from Archelaos, alleging that he had reconciled Alexandros with his father.[42] This was particularly inventive, since Eurykles' intrigues were a major reason for Herod's eventual execution of Alexandros.

This was but one incident in the turbulent career of this Spartan, who has been called "the most notable personality in the history of Augustan Greece."[43] His first known act was to appear flamboyantly at Actium, leading a Spartan contingent in support of Octavian, and becoming instrumental in the naval defeat of Antonius.[44] In reward Octavian made him ruler of Sparta, although the legalities of his position remain unclear.[45] It was while in power at Sparta and enjoying the patronage of Augustus that he visited Judaea and Kappadokia.[46] He may have decided to visit Herod because of benefits that Herod had previously bestowed on the Spartans[47] as well as the tradition that Spartans and Jews had a common ancestry.[48] After the Kappadokian episode, Eurykles returned to Greece and became notorious through further intrigues,[49] although he may also have become a patron of architecture.[50] His plots only came to an end with his death.[51]

11. *Gemellus* (*RE*, # 6), also a tutor of the royal children and an advisor

---

42. *BJ* 1.513–31; *AJ* 16.301–10.

43. Bowersock, "Eurycles" (supra, n. 41), 112.

44. Plutarch, *Antonius* 67.

45. Bowersock, "Eurycles" (supra, n. 41), 112. Octavian also gave him—or at least the government of Sparta—management of the Aktian games at Nikopolis: see infra, pp. 228–29.

46. *BJ* 1.531.

47. *BJ* 1.425.

48. 1 Macc. 12.6–23; *AJ* 12.226–27, 13.166–67; Michael S. Ginsburg, "Sparta and Judaea," *CP* 29 (1934): 117–22; Burkhard Cardauns, "Juden und Spartaner zur hellenistisch-jüdischen Literatur," *Hermes* 95 (1967): 317–24.

49. Strabo 8.5.5.

50. According to Pausanias, Eurykles built a gymnasium at Sparta (3.14.6), and was responsible for the most notable baths at Corinth (2.3.5), generally identified with the prominent remains on the Lechaion Road. Recent evidence has suggested, however, that these were built by C. Julius Eurykles Herculanus, a senator of the early second century A.C. and probably the great-great-grandson of Herod's acquaintance (Bowersock, "Eurycles" [supra, n. 41], 118). See Jane C. Biers, *Corinth*, vol. 17: *The Great Bath on the Lechaion Road* (Princeton, 1985), 63.

51. Bowersock, "Eurycles" (supra, n. 41), 112–14 (bibliography, p. 112); see also Niese, "Eurykles" (# 5), in *RE* 11 (1907): 1330–31 (called "inaccurate" by Bowersock). His death was

to Herod, was an associate of the royal family's for many years. Like Andromachos, he was dismissed by the king for alleged involvement in a conspiracy.[52] Gemellus had accompanied Herod's son Alexandros to Rome, which meant that he probably lived in the household of Asinius Pollio along with Timagenes.[53] As a royal tutor in this exalted company, he presumably had scholarly interests himself. It has been suggested that he was actually a Roman, giving the royal family one Greek and one Roman tutor,[54] although he may have been a Greek with Roman citizenship.

12. *Lysimachos* (*RE*, # 11) was another close Friend of Herod's who was involved in the revolt of Kostobaros and executed along with Antipatros and Dositheos.[55] He was probably Jewish.

13. *Nikolaos* of Damaskos (*RE*, # 20) was the best-known scholar at Herod's court.[56] Extensive fragments of his writings are extant.[57] He was frequently mentioned by Josephus as Herod's daily companion,[58] teaching the king philosophy, rhetoric, and the value of history.[59] Little is known about his early life, but he may have met Herod in Damaskos in 43 B.C. and again in Rome in 40 B.C. while studying with Timagenes as a fellow-pupil of Strabo's. He then became attached to the court of Antonius and Cleopatra as tutor to their children, and eventually ended up at Herod's court some time after 30 B.C., although his early years with Herod are scantily documented. He also had the respect of Augustus, and repeatedly served as an intermediary between Princeps and king,[60] spending much time in Rome and writing the earliest known biography of Augustus, which helped Herod win favor with the Princeps.[61] Herod may have suggested the topic to Nikolaos and have sent him to Rome to do the research (and to watch over Herod's interests). The biography also served Augustus in helping to make him and his policies known in the East and among Greek-speaking populations. Augus-

---

after 7 B.C. (the date of his Judaean and Kappadokian intrigues) but before A.D. 15: see Lindsay (supra, n. 41), 296–97.

52. *AJ* 16.242–43.

53. Supra, p. 20.

54. Otto, *RE*, 87.

55. *AJ* 15.252, 260.

56. There are numerous modern studies of Nikolaos; see the commentary on *FGrHist*, # 90; Richard Laqueur, "Nikolaos" (# 20), in *RE* 33 (1936): 326–424; Wacholder, *Nicolaus*; Bowersock, *Augustus*, 134–38. His early contacts with Herod are discussed supra, pp. 22–23.

57. *FGrHist*, # 90 consists of 143 fragments, some lengthy.

58. *AJ* 17.99.

59. Nikolaos, fr. 135.

60. Nikolaos, fr. 136; *BJ* 1.574; *AJ* 16.299, 333–44.

61. Wacholder, *Nicolaus*, 25–26.

tus responded by naming a species of date palm native to the region of Jericho the *nikolai*.[62]

In the last two decades of Herod's life, Nikolaos was his constant companion; his role as advisor during the Bosporan expedition has already been discussed.[63] When Herod died, he was briefly involved in supporting Archelaos in the succession.[64] He then seems to have retired from politics,[65] writing copiously on history,[66] as well as an autobiography. Although Josephus believed Nikolaos wrote merely to please Herod and only about his triumphs and successes,[67] he used his works extensively for material from the Flood[68] to the succession struggle after the death of Herod. Despite their fragmentary and eulogistic nature, the writings of Nikolaos are essential to an understanding of Herod.

14. *Olympos* was sent by Herod to Augustus to report his arrest of his sons Alexandros and Aristoboulos.[69] He also went to Sebaste in Kilikia and reported the news to Archelaos of Kappadokia (Alexandros's father-in-law), who was also suspect at this time.[70] Olympos is otherwise unknown, but it has been suggested[71] that he was another Alexandrian refugee: Cleopatra's former physician, who had assisted in her death and then wrote an account of it.[72]

15. *Philostratos*, a historian, was the author of an *Indika* (or *Ioudaika*) and a *Phoinikika*.[73] Josephus, Krinagoras of Mytilene, and Plutarch all refer to a Philostratos of this period, and it is probable that in each case it is the same person. According to Krinagoras,[74]

---

62. Athenaios 14.66; Wacholder, *Nicolaus*, 26.

63. Supra, pp. 49–51.

64. Nikolaos, fr. 136; *BJ* 2.14, 34–37, 92; *AJ* 17.219, 240–48, 315–16.

65. Nikolaos, fr. 138.

66. A project Herod had suggested to him: Nikolaos, fr. 135.

67. *AJ* 16.183–85.

68. *AJ* 1.94–95.

69. *BJ* 1.535; *AJ* 16.354.

70. *AJ* 16.332.

71. Conrad Cichorius, *Römische Studien* (Leipzig, 1922), 317.

72. Plutarch, *Antonius* 82; *FGrHist*, # 198; Fraser (supra, n. 23), 2: 543.

73. *AJ* 10.228; *Apion* 1.144; *FGrHist*, # 789.

74. *Greek Anthology* 7.645 = Krinagoras # 20. Krinagoras of Mytilene himself may have been a member of the Herodian circle. Roughly the same age as Herod, he participated in several Mytilenian embassies to Rome, beginning with one to Caesar in 45 B.C., when he may have met Cleopatra. He wrote a number of epigrams in honor of the imperial family, and one (# 25) on the occasion of the marriage of Cleopatra's daughter to Juba II of Mauretania. He seems to have known Strabo (13.2.3) and at least one other member of the Herodian circle, Philostratos. Herod was in Mytilene several times and may have made the acquaintance of Krinagoras there. Krinagoras may have come to Judaea after participating in an embassy to Augustus in 26/25 B.C., perhaps first visiting Egypt at the time Strabo was there. At the very least, Krinagoras functioned in the same circles and places as did Herod and some of his cultural and

Philostratos received royal patronage both on the Nile and in Judaea but eventually was exiled to the remote Egyptian town of Ostrakina.[75] Plutarch noted he was an outstanding speaker at the court of Antonius and Cleopatra and was eventually pardoned by Octavian.[76] Presumably, he then migrated to Herod's court and continued to write his histories there, but eventually lost his position (perhaps, like so many, accused of treason) and ended up at Ostrakina.[77]

16. *Ptolemaios* (*RE*, # 55) was an important associate of Herod's, the most honored of his Friends.[78] He knew Herod before he became king, and was on Rhodes in 40 B.C. as Herod made his way to Rome.[79] He was the royal treasurer,[80] and was given lands within the kingdom.[81] Active in putting down the civil disturbances during Herod's reign,[82] he nonetheless did not escape the accusations Herod eventually made against most of his Friends,[83] but survived to become the executor of Herod's will and to announce the king's death to the people.[84] He then became a proponent of Archelaos's in the succession, joining Nikolaos in the delegation to Augustus.[85] He enlisted the aid of Quinctilius Varus, legate of Syria (who was to become infamous some years later when he lost three legions and then killed himself in Germany), to put down the disturbances that broke out after Herod's death.[86] His prominence at the court, especially at Herod's death, and his early friendship with the king has led to the conclusion that he was Herod's prime minister.[87] The name Ptolemaios implies an Alexandrian origin, and it is quite pos-

---

intellectual associates. See J. S. Phillimore, "Crinagoras of Mytilene," *Dublin Review* 139 (1906): 74–86; J. Geffcken, "Krinagoras," in *RE*, 22 (1922): 1859–64; Cichorius (supra, n. 71), 308–23.

75. Cichorius (supra, n. 71). 314–17.

76. Plutarch, *Antonius* 80. Philostratos was also in Sicily: see Plutarch, *Cato the Younger* 57.

77. See *The Greek Anthology: The Garland of Philip*, ed. A. S. F. Gow and D. L. Page (Cambridge, 1968), 2: 227–28; K. von Fritz, "Philostratos" (# 7), in *RE*, 19 (1941): 123–24. Elizabeth Rawson (*Intellectual Life in the Late Roman Republic* [London, 1985]) believed that he was the court philosopher first of Cleopatra and then of Herod (p. 36); see also Fraser (supra, n. 23), 1: 490, 494.

78. *BJ* 1.473.

79. *BJ* 1.280; *AJ* 14.377.

80. *AJ* 16.191; Otto, *RE*, 60–61.

81. *BJ* 2.69; *AJ* 17.289. They were at the village of Arous, northwest of Sebaste: see *TIR-IP*, 68.

82. *AJ* 16.321.

83. *AJ* 16.257.

84. *BJ* 1.667–69; *AJ* 17.195.

85. *BJ* 2.14–24; *AJ* 17.219–28.

86. *BJ* 2.16; *AJ* 17.221.

87. Menahem Stern, "The Reign of Herod," *HP* 94.

sible that such an experienced talent was sent to Herod from the court of Cleopatra. Whether this Ptolemaios is the same as the historian (# 18) is unknown.

17. *Ptolemaios* of Damaskos (*RE*, # 54), brother of Nikolaos, is only documented in the succession struggles after Herod's death, when (unlike his brother) he supported Antipas,[88] but he had been one of Herod's best Friends, and his family background indicates that he was an educated man.

18. *Ptolemaios* the historian (*RE*, # 75) wrote a work on Herod. He is only known through a citation by the obscure lexicographer Ammonios.[89] Whether he was actually at Herod's court, or whether he was one of the two men of that name known at the court (# 16, # 17), cannot be determined.

19. *Sappinos*[90] was with Ptolemaios (# 16), Herod's future minister, on Rhodes to meet Herod on his journey to Rome in 40 B.C.[91] He was accused by Herod of involvement in a plot,[92] but is otherwise unknown. He may have been Egyptian, and thus, like Ptolemaios, from the court of Cleopatra.

20. *Strabo* of Amaseia, the historian and geographer, is not explicitly placed at Herod's court.[93] To Josephus he was merely a source for Hellenistic and Roman history.[94] But it is probable that he spent some time with Herod in the 20's B.C. He had been in Rome as a protégé of Timagenes when Herod first visited and had developed an early interest in Judaea. Around 26 B.C., after completing his historical work, Strabo joined the staff of Aelius Gallus, prefect of Egypt, accompanying him on an expedition up the Nile, but not on the disastrous Arabian campaign that followed, to which Herod sent assistance.[95] Herod's involvement with Gallus's efforts and the presence of Strabo's classmate Nikolaos at Herod's court may have led Strabo to a new interest in Judaea and perhaps an invitation to visit.

88. *BJ* 2.21; *AJ* 17.225; *Souda*, s.v. "Antipatros" (# 2705) (Ptolemaios's father).

89. *FGrHist*, # 199. Ammonios probably lived in the late first or early second century A.C.: see L. Cohn, "Ammonios" (# 17), in *RE*, 1 (1894): 1866–67. For other possible identifications of Ptolemaios, as well as places he might have been quoted by Josephus (all highly speculative), see commentary on *FGrHist* # 199.

90. The name is Samphinios at *BJ* 1.280 and Sapinnios at *AJ* 16.257.

91. *AJ* 14.377.

92. *AJ* 16.257.

93. Judaea, however, was within the area of his travels, which extended from the Euxeinos to Ethiopia (2.5.11).

94. *AJ* 13.286–87, 319, 347; 14.35, 68, 104, 111, 114, 118, 138–39, 15.9–10.

95. Strabo 2.5.12; Shelagh Jameson, "Chronology of the Campaigns of Aelius Gallus and C. Petronius," *JRS* 58 (1968): 71–84.

With the termination of Gallus's prefecture in late 25 B.C., Strabo would have been free to visit Judaea. Detailed personal knowledge is revealed in the Judaean sections of Strabo's geography, especially the passages on plants, Lake Sirbonis, and Tarichaiai.[96] Although certain details about the life of Herod were added later,[97] Strabo's eyewitness description of Judaean topography cannot have been based on material collected after 22 B.C., the year Herod began the construction of Caesarea. Strabo's account reveals no knowledge of Caesarea but refers only to Straton's Tower, the ruined Hellenistic anchorage that Caesarea replaced.[98] On the other hand, Strabo knew that Herod had rebuilt ancient Samaria and renamed it Sebaste,[99] an event of the early 20's B.C. Since Strabo was still in Egypt with Gallus until late 25 B.C., the information in this section of the *Geography* was collected between 25 and 22 B.C. Its final revision, however, was not until after A.D. 6, since it refers to the deposing of Archelaos.[100] Strabo may have told Herod about recent architectural developments in Rome and have taught him the value of geography to a ruler.[101] Since Strabo spent his later years at the court of Pythodoris I of Pontos (fig. 43), he may for his part have learned the value of a royal patron from Herod and Nikolaos.[102]

21. *Tryphon* (*RE*, # 3) was the court barber, who became involved in one of the palace intrigues late in Herod's reign.[103]

96. Strabo 16.2.25–46. Plants: 16.2.41; Lake Sirbonis: 16.2.42; Tarichaiai: 16.2.45.

97. For example, 16.2.46 is awkwardly attached to the previous chapters.

98. Strabo 16.2.27.

99. Strabo 16.2.34.

100. The date of composition of the *Geography* has long been disputed. As noted, parts were complete by the 20's B.C. but revisions continued for over forty years. The latest datable event mentioned seems to be the death of Juba II of Mauretania (17.3.7, 25), around A.D. 23. The *Geography* may never have been published, and Strabo may have added details for years after its "completion." It seems to have been unknown to Pliny and emerged only in Byzantine times. On this problem, see J. G. C. Anderson, "Some Questions Bearing on the Date and Place of Composition of Strabo's *Geography*," in *Anatolian Studies Presented to Sir William Mitchell Ramsay*, ed. W. H. Buckler and W. M. Calder (Manchester, 1923), 1–13; Ronald Syme, *Anatolica: Studies in Strabo*, ed. Anthony R. Birley (Oxford, 1995), 356–67.

101. Strabo 1.1.16.

102. Anderson (supra, n. 100), 11–12. This is one of several connections Herod seems to have had with Pontos and Amaseia. Pythodoris's husband was Herod's in-law Archelaos of Kappadokia, and Herod's erratic general Machairas, perhaps the eponym of Machairous, was probably a member of the Pontic royal family (see infra, p. 185).

103. *BJ* 1.547; *AJ* 16.387. This name is also Alexandrian, most notably belonging to a grammarian of the Augustan period (*RE*, # 25; Fraser [supra, n. 23], 1: 474).

CHAPTER FIVE

Herod's Second
and Third Trips to Rome

After an absence of over twenty years, Herod returned between 19 and 16 B.C. for a second visit to Rome. In the intervening two decades, he had done much for the architectural adornment of his kingdom: Samaria had been rebuilt and dedicated in Augustus's name, Caesarea had been started, and the new Temple in Jerusalem dedicated (although it was far from completed). Thus Herod's second visit to Rome was not as influential architecturally as the first. But much remained for Herod to build, and regardless of his political agenda in Rome, he would have eagerly absorbed the changes in the physical city since 40 B.C.

Documentation for this second trip is scant, resting on a single notice by Josephus,[1] which explains that Herod went to Rome to meet with Augustus and to see his sons. These were Alexandros and Aristoboulos, who had begun their stay in Rome several years earlier at the house of Pollio, but who had eventually gone to live with Augustus himself.[2] According to Josephus, Augustus received Herod cordially and sent the sons home with him, inasmuch as they had finished their education. No other information is provided.

The date of this visit cannot be determined with precision. Josephus's dating is "at the same time," either as certain theft legislation,[3] or, more likely, the dedication of the Temple in Jerusalem.[4] The visit must coincide

---

1. *AJ* 16.6; see also Schalit, *KH*, 588–89.
2. *AJ* 15.342–43.
3. *AJ* 16.1–5.
4. *AJ* 15.421–23.

with residency in Italy by Augustus: he was in the East through 19 B.C. and left for Gaul in 16 B.C.[5]

The dedication of the Temple followed a construction period of seventeen or eighteen months.[6] It had been started in the eighteenth year of Herod's reign, just after a visit of Augustus to Syria;[7] this would be the one dated by Dio to 20 B.C.[8] This simple synchronism avoids the convoluted and uncertain arguments about how to reckon Herod's regnal years.[9] Herod had come to see Augustus in Syria, accompanied him to the coast upon his departure from the province,[10] and returned home to begin the Temple. Thus the earliest Temple construction could have been initiated was late 20 B.C. or perhaps early 19 B.C., and the 17- or 18-month construction period (obviously not enough time to complete the entire structure) provides a date in the summer or autumn of 18 B.C. Dedicatory festivities were held on Herod's accession day, which seems to have been in the autumn.[11] In light of Josephus's explicit comments about the construction period and the speed with which the Temple was dedicated, it seems unlikely that the dedication waited another year until the autumn of 17 B.C.; thus the autumn of 18 B.C. seems the only possible time for the ceremony. Herod was then free to go to Rome. Most commentators have therefore decided on the 18–17 B.C. period for the trip.[12] Herod may have departed promptly in the latter

5. For Augustus's periods away from Rome at this time, see Helmut Halfmann, *Itinera principum* (Heidelberger Althistorische Beiträge und Epigraphische Studien, 2 [Stuttgart, 1986]), 158.

6. *AJ* 15.421. What the seventeen or eighteen months refers to cannot be determined and may be little more than initial surveying or groundbreaking, or perhaps the time to extend the platform to the necessary size for the new construction. The outer courts and stoas took eight years to build (*AJ* 15.420), and construction on the complex was still in progress forty-six years later (John 2.20) and lasted for nearly a century (*AJ* 20.219).

7. *AJ* 15.380. *BJ* 1.401 gives the fifteenth year, but this is generally considered an error or a confusion of de jure and de facto accession (Otto, *RE*, 84; Schalit, *KH*, 372).

8. Dio 54.7 (during the consulship of M. Apuleius and Publius Silius [Nerva]); see Ronald Syme, *RR*, 528; Halfmann (supra, n. 5), 158.

9. See, e.g., the complex uncertainties of W. E. Filmer, "The Chronology of the Reign of Herod the Great," *JThS*, n. s., 17 (1966): 295–96, yet the date conforms to the chronology constructed by Ormond Edwards (Herodian Chronology," *PEQ* 114 [1982]: 29–42); see also Thomas Corbishley, "The Chronology of the Reign of Herod the Great," *JThS* 36 (1935): 25–27. Uwe Baumann, *Rom und die Juden* (Studia Philosophica et Historica, 4 [Frankfurt a/M, 1983], 217) preferred the too-early date of 23/22 B.C.

10. *AJ* 15.357–63.

11. The date of Herod's accession day has long been argued; see Filmer (supra, n. 9), 285–91.

12. Schürer (NEV), 1.292; Otto, *RE, Zeittafel;* Schalit, *KH,* 588–89. It has also been suggested (Corbishley [supra, n. 9], 28; E. Mary Smallwood, *The Jews under Roman Rule* [Studies in Judaism in Late Antiquity, 20 (Leiden, 1976), 81, 89]) that the voyage was not until 16 B.C., because at some time in his career, Herod made a trip to Rome that included a stopover at

part of 18 B.C. or, more likely, have waited until the propitious sailing weather of spring 17 B.C., spending the winter of 18–17 B.C. on the theft legislation. This would have put Herod in Rome for the *ludi saeculares* in June of 17 B.C., the greatest celebration of the new Augustan era of which he was so much a part.

Herod's return to Rome was under quite different circumstances than his hurried and desperate trip of 40 B.C. Then he had been a refugee seeking Roman protection from eastern dynastic wars; now he was a respected client king who had come unscathed through the last years of the Roman civil disturbances and had upheld Roman policy along the eastern frontier for over twenty years. In 40 B.C. he had been seeking contacts with the Roman leaders; now access to the highest levels of government was automatic and his sons were housed with the Princeps himself. Herod had received a good reception twenty years before; now he would receive an outstanding one.

Unfortunately, nothing is known about the details of this visit. The paragraph by Josephus does not describe what Herod saw, although one may presume that it included the house of Augustus on the Palatine. Yet in the past twenty years, both the Augustan and Herodian building programs had been implemented. Herod had become an intimate of Augustus's closest advisor and the director of his architectural program. Thus the king would have been intensely curious about architectural developments in Rome.

Visible from Augustus's house was the new temple of Apollo Palatinus, where fourteen years later Augustus would hear testimony regarding the succession after Herod's death.[13] Nikolaos of Damaskos, who was present at that time, is probably Josephus's source for a comment on the impressive ornamentation of the structure. It had been dedicated in 28 B.C.,[14] Horace writing a poem for the occasion.[15] The temple was famous for its rich decoration,[16] and it contained a particularly impressive collection of Greek sculpture, including works by Kephisodotos, Skopas, and Timotheos.[17] The temple complex included a portico[18] and a double library.[19] Few buildings

---

Olympia to serve as president of the Olympic Games (*BJ* 1.427). On the improbability of this, see further infra, p. 74.

13. *BJ* 2.81.

14. Dio 49.15; Suetonius, *Augustus* 29; Richardson, *NTD*, 14; Pierre Gros, "Apollo Palatinus," in *LTUR*, 1: 54–57.

15. Horace, *Odes* 1.31.

16. Propertius 2.31; Velleius 2.81.

17. Pliny, *Natural History* 36.24–32.

18. Augustus, *Res gestae* 19.

19. Suetonius, *Augustus* 29; Dio 53.1. For the current state of the remains, see Coarelli, *Guida*, 133–34.

better expressed the transformation of Rome and of Herod's fortunes in the previous quarter century. Herod was constructing his own spectacular temple and portico in Jerusalem, and was thus part of the contemporary architectural revolution, rather than merely a bystander. Previously, Herod had come to Rome as an unemployed petty dynast seeking Roman protection: now his program equaled that of Rome itself. Rather than admire wishfully the urbanization of the late Republican city, he could now feel that his own architectural creations rivaled those of Rome, although if he made this point to Augustus, he probably did so discreetly.

In 40 B.C., the Forum Romanum had been a major construction zone. Now, in 17 B.C., buildings were taking shape throughout the area. Some that Herod had previously seen under construction were not yet finished, such as the Basilica Julia, whose completion had been delayed by a fire. On the other hand, the controversy regarding a suitable memorial for Julius Caesar had abated, and the well-known temple in his honor had finally been dedicated at the east end of the Forum.[20] Immediately to the south, between this temple and the ancient Temple of Castor, was the triumphal arch in honor of Augustus, erected in 19 B.C. to commemorate the return of the legionary standards the Parthians had captured from Crassus thirty-five years previously.[21] Carved on the arch were the Fasti Consulares and Triumphales, the record of Roman achievement. Thus the monument was a piece of integrated historical propaganda that would have been of special relevance to Herod, in a political as well as an architectural sense, since the very reason for his existence as Roman client king of Judaea was to be a balance to the Parthian threat, as Antonius and Messalla had pointed out long before. The returned standards were to be housed in the Temple of Mars Ultor, which was under construction behind the Basilica Paulli.[22] Moreover, the return of the standards would be commemorated on official Augustan art, of which a surviving remnant is the scene on the breastplate of the Prima Porta statue of the Princeps.[23] Thus after two decades on the throne of Judaea, Herod could see physical evidence of the political power of his kingship in preserving peace on the eastern frontier. He probably took much of the credit for the diplomatic rapprochement between Rome and Parthia.

20. Augustus, *Res gestae* 19; Dio 51.22.

21. Dio 54.8; Coarelli, *Guida*, 76–77.

22. Suetonius, *Augustus* 29, although it was not dedicated until 2 B.C.: Velleius 2.100; Dio 55.10. Richardson, *NTD*, 160, has suggested that the project began "in earnest about 25 or 24 B.C."

23. Donald Strong, *Roman Art*, 2d ed. (Harmondsworth, 1988), 85–87; Diana E. E. Kleiner, *Roman Sculpture* (New Haven, 1992), 63–67; on the Parthians as a symbolic and mythic motif in Roman art of the Augustan period, see Paul Zanker, *The Power of Images in the Age of Augustus*, trans. Alan Shapiro (Ann Arbor, 1988), 187–92.

It was in the Campus Martius that the greatest changes had occurred since Herod's previous visit. There was new construction to the northwest of the Saepta and Theater of Pompey, and the area between the theater and the river was also the site of many new buildings. Marcus Agrippa's Pantheon had been completed, probably in 27 B.C., west of the Saepta.[24] Here was another strange memory from Herod's past: the statue of Venus within had earrings made from pearls that had belonged to Cleopatra.[25] Immediately to the south, and part of the same construction project, were a basilica dedicated to Neptune[26] and baths. These Agrippa had originally constructed as a Greek-style hot-air bath,[27] but when the Aqua Virgo was brought into the area in 19 B.C.,[28] they were expanded into the first of the great Roman baths,[29] adorned with major works of art by sculptors such as Lysippos.[30]

Of particular interest to Herod was an amphitheater built in the northern Campus Martius in 29 B.C. by T. Statilius Taurus,[31] who had triumphed five years earlier for his reconstruction of the province of Africa. Although built in stone, it may not have been a large or particularly substantial structure, and seems to have become despised for its smallness.[32] Nevertheless, it was the first permanent example of this new architectural form, which does not appear in the Roman architectural repertory before the late Republic: the word *amphitheatrum* is not known before the Augustan period.[33] No other permanent amphitheater existed in Rome until the great

---

24. *ILS*, 129 (the inscription visible today on the façade of the Hadrianic building); Dio (53.27) placed it two years later. For the scanty remains, almost totally eliminated by the famous Hadrianic structure, see Coarelli, *Guida*, 292.

25. Pliny, *Natural History* 9.121; Macrobius 3.17.17–18.

26. Dio 53.27; Nash 1.196; Coarelli, *Guida*, 295.

27. A. W. Lawrence, *Greek Architecture*, 4th ed., rev. R. E. Tomlinson (Harmondsworth, 1983), 349–50.

28. Ovid, *Fasti* 1.464; Dio 54.11.

29. Platner-Ashby, 518; Ward-Perkins, *RIA*, 25; Coarelli, *Guida*, 291–92; Richardson, *NTD*, 386–87. Recent analysis, however, has brought into question the novelty of these baths: see Christopher J. Simpson and Nadine Brundrett, "Innovation and the Baths of Agrippa: An Exaggerated Claim?" *AJA* 100 (1996): 391–92.

30. Pliny. *Natural History* 34.62.

31. Suetonius, *Augustus* 29; Dio 51.23. For its probable location, see Coarelli, *Guida*, 278; Richardson, *NTD*, 11; Alessandro Viscogliosi, "Amphitheatrum Statilii Taurii," in *LTUR*, 1: 36–37.

32. Dio 59.10.

33. The earliest citation is probably Vitruvius 1.7.1; the word appeared shortly thereafter in Greek (Dionysios of Halikarnassos, *Roman Antiquities* 3.68, 4.44 [where it is still used descriptively, rather than as a technical term referring to a specific building type]; Strabo 14.1.43). There is also epigraphic evidence from the Augustan period (*IGRR*, 1.1024.27), and Augustus himself used the term in the *Res gestae* (22), to refer to Statilius Taurus's structure.

Flavian Amphitheater of a century later.[34] Yet Herod was immediately to build one at Caesarea.[35]

When Herod first visited Rome, the city had only a single theater, the unusual one built by Pompey in the Campus Martius. By the time of his second visit, two more were under construction. One had actually been started by Julius Caesar, but construction had probably lapsed until Augustus purchased more land[36] and created a memorial to his nephew M. Claudius Marcellus, who had died suddenly in 23 B.C.[37] Although the theater was not dedicated until at least 13 B.C.,[38] it was probably the "theatrum quod est in circo Flaminio" used in the *ludi saeculares* of 17 B.C.[39] The other theater, the work of L. Cornelius Balbus after his African triumph of 19 B.C., was not far away.[40] It, too, was to be dedicated in 13 B.C.[41]

There were many continuing building projects in and about Rome. The hydraulic efforts of Marcus Agrippa would have been of particular interest to Herod. Aqueducts had been constructed regularly over the previous twenty years, with the Virgo the most recent, completed in the summer of 19 B.C.,[42] allowing the full development of the Baths of Agrippa. Various temples had also been built or restored over the years, such as that to Hercules Musarum in the southern Campus Martius next to the Theater of Balbus. It had originally been erected by M. Fulvius Nobilior after his conquest of Ambrakia in 189 B.C.,[43] and had been restored by L. Marcius Philippus in 29 B.C.[44] A few years later, in 22 B.C., the Temple of Juppiter Tonans was built on the Capitol,[45] vowed by Augustus four years earlier when he had been nearly struck by lightning. There is no reason to believe that Herod was particularly interested in these minor Roman temples—he had introduced the Italian temple to Judaea at Sebaste a decade previously—but he

34. For possible construction by Gaius and Nero, see infra, pp. 258–59.

35. Duane W. Roller, "The Wilfrid Laurier University Survey of Northeastern Caesarea Maritima," *Levant* 14 (1982): 100–102. But see infra, pp. 140–41.

36. Augustus, *Res gestae* 21.

37. Dio 53.30; Coarelli, *Guida*, 272–74; Richardson, *NTD*, 382–83.

38. Dio 54.26.

39. *CIL* 6.32323.157–58.

40. Frederick W. Shipley, "Chronology of the Building Operations in Rome from the Death of Caesar to the Death of Augustus," *MAAR* 9 (1931): 37–38; Richardson, *NTD*, 381–82.

41. Dio 54.25; Coarelli, *Guida*, 286–87.

42. Ovid, *Fasti* 1.464.

43. Platner-Ashby, 255.

44. Ovid, *Fasti* 6.801–2; Suetonius, *Augustus* 29; Richardson, *NTD*, 187. This Philippus may have been the stepfather of Augustus, but it was more likely his son, also L. Marcius Philippus (cos. suff. 38 B.C.: Broughton, 2: 390), since the elder Philippus is otherwise unknown after 43 B.C. (Broughton, 2: 588). But see Richardson, *NTD*, 187. For further on the elder Philippus, see infra, pp. 79–80.

45. Augustus, *Res gestae* 19; Suetonius, *Augustus* 29; Dio 54.4.

might have taken a personal interest in the Temple of Apollo in the Campus Martius. Although it was ancient, dating to the fifth century B.C.,[46] it had been restored by C. Sosius after his triumph of 34 B.C.,[47] the triumph *ex Judaea* following the military assistance that had implemented Herod's kingship. The structure itself became noted as an art gallery, including works by Aristeides of Thebes, Philiskos of Rhodes, Timarchides, and a famous Niobid group by either Skopas or Praxiteles.[48] Sosius himself was still politically active when Herod visited, a prime example of an adaptable survivor of the civil wars. Although having been with Antonius at Actium,[49] he lived to assist in the celebration of the *ludi saeculares* of 17 B.C.[50] If the festival did not lead Herod to renew acquaintance with his benefactor, he may nonetheless have visited the monument that honored his service.

Of the remaining constructions that had come to adorn Rome since Herod's last visit, one in particular was worthy of interest. In the northern part of the Campus Martius, well away from the existing monumental constructions, Augustus had built a dynastic tomb for himself and his family (fig. 3). It represented his thinking in the period immediately after Actium and the deaths of Antonius and Cleopatra.[51] Antonius had not been buried in Rome—and would not have been, even if he had died there[52]—but the victorious Julio-Claudian dynasty would be buried in the city.[53] Octavian had

---

46. Livy 4.25, 29.

47. Shipley (supra, n. 40), 25–28. Some have associated the temple with Sosius's consulship of 32 B.C., or even dated it later. But, as Shipley has cogently pointed out, the realities of the last phase of the civil war would hardly have allowed such a prominent Antonian to reconstruct a Temple of Apollo in competition with the one Octavian was building on the Palatine. Moreover, Sosius left Rome to join Antonius in January of the year of his consulship (Dio 50.2), not to return until after Actium. It is difficult to assume reconstruction of a temple at the very time the political point of view he represented was collapsing and when he was out of the city: see Alessandro Viscogliosi, "Apollo, Aedes in Circo," in *LTUR*, 1: 50–51. For the remains, see Coarelli, *Guida*, 275; Richardson, *NTD*, 12–13.

48. Pliny, *Natural History* 35.99–100, 36.28, 34–35.

49. Dio 50.14.

50. *ILS* 5050.150. On the festival, see J. Gagé, *Recherches sur les jeux séculaires* (Collection d'études latines, 11 [Paris, 1934]).

51. Suetonius, *Augustus* 100; Nash, 2: 38; Coarelli, *Guida*, 308–9; Richardson, *NTD*, 247–49; John R. Patterson, "The City of Rome: From Republic to Empire," *JRS* 82 (1992): 198. The exact chronology of its construction is unclear: Suetonius (*Augustus* 100) wrote that it was built ("exstruxerat") during Octavian's sixth consulship, or 28 B.C., but according to Dio (53.30) it seems to have been still in progress when Marcellus was buried there five years later.

52. Plutarch, *Antonius* 58.

53. Zvi Yavetz, "The *Res Gestae* and Augustus' Public Image," in *Caesar Augustus: Seven Aspects*, ed. Fergus Millar and Erich Segal (Oxford, 1984), 1–36, esp. 6–7; see also Konrad Kraft, "Der Sinn des Mausoleum des Augustus," *Historia* 16 (1967): 189–206. The most recent and thorough study of the structure is Henner von Hesberg and Silvio Panciera, *Das Mausoleum des Augustus: Der Bau und Seine Inschriften* (Bayerische Akademie der Wissenschaften, Philosophisch-Historische Klasse, Abhandlungen, n.s., 108 [Munich 1994]).

still been in the East in the summer of 29 B.C.[54] and had seen the tomb of Antonius and Cleopatra: in fact, he was responsible for assuring their burial in their royal mausoleum.[55] Within two years Octavian would begin his own dynastic mausoleum in Rome.

While this mausoleum was under construction, Strabo of Amaseia returned to Rome from several years in the East.[56] In a possibly contemporary description, he was the first to call it a *mausoleion*.[57] Although this may not have been the official name (which was probably Tumulus Iuliorum), this term aptly described both the physical aspect and the concept of the tomb.[58] Moreover, it was a term associated in the Roman mind with eastern dynasts, especially Egyptian ones.[59] Even before Herod had had an opportunity to see the tomb on his next Roman visit—by then holding its first occupant, Marcellus[60]—he was planning his own imitation of it.

Herod's tomb, Herodeion, was begun a few years after the Mausoleum of Augustus. Josephus placed the initiation of its construction between Gallus's Arabian campaign and the beginning of Caesarea, or in the late 20's B.C.[61] This is exactly the time when Strabo may have been at Herod's court.[62] Herodeion was completed by the time of Agrippa's visit of 15 B.C.[63] Thus the sequence of events is as follows: in 28 B.C., after returning from the East and authorizing the burial of Antonius and Cleopatra in a royal mausoleum, Octavian built his own analogous tomb, which came to be described in terms the Romans associated with eastern dynasts. Strabo may have witnessed the initial stages of construction and reported details to Herod, who then began his own version of the mausoleum. Soon after the Roman structure was completed, Herod visited the city and saw it. By 15 B.C. he could show his own mausoleum to Agrippa as one of several constructions with parallels in Augustan Rome.[64]

---

54. Syme, *RR*, 303.

55. Plutarch, *Antonius* 78–86; Dio 51.11–15.

56. Strabo 10.5.3.

57. Strabo 5.3.8. The earliest extant citation of the word is Vitruvius 2.8.11, referring to the tomb of Maussolos of Karia. Strabo was the first extant author to use it in Greek; see also Suetonius, *Augustus* 100.

58. Zanker (supra, n. 23), 72–77.

59. Lucan 8.697; see Jane Clark Reeder, "Typology and Ideology in the Mausoleum of Augustus: Tumulus and Tholos," *ClAnt* 11 (1992): 265–307, on the issue of the contemporary context of the Mausoleum.

60. Dio 53.30.

61. *BJ* 1.419; *AJ* 15.317–33: these references, however, do not refer to Herodeion as Herod's tomb, but this function is made clear at *BJ* 1.673 and *AJ* 17.199, both of which indicate that Herod left instructions to be buried at Herodeion.

62. Supra, pp. 64–65.

63. *AJ* 16.13.

64. See Arthur Segal, "Herodium," *IEJ* 23 (1973): 27–29, who suggested that the Mausoleum of Augustus was the inspiration for Herodeion, but who unfortunately wrote that

The second visit of Herod to Rome was more transitional than profound. Much of his building program was already being implemented. Nevertheless, he was able to see changes in the city, especially the development of particularly Roman forms such as the Italian theater and amphitheater, and the concepts of dynastic architecture that Augustus was creating, typified by the Mausoleum. Herod returned to Judaea no later than the autumn of 17 B.C., and within two years he was able to show Agrippa the products of his own architectural efforts.

Herod made a third and last trip to Rome, in late summer of 12 B.C.[65] The date is certain because the trip must fall in an Olympiad and when Augustus was in Aquileia.[66] The following Olympiad, 8 B.C., is too late in Herod's career—less than four years before his death—whereas the previous one, 16 B.C., was when Augustus was away from Italy from midsummer on. Moreover, Augustus's presence in Aquileia arose out of the political situation in Illyricum in 12 B.C. and the change of the province from senatorial to imperial control.[67]

The reason for this third trip was totally dynastic: to accuse his sons Alexandros and Aristoboulos of conspiracy. Herod may also have wanted to assert his presence before the Roman leadership in the months after the death of his patron Marcus Agrippa; a new visit to the Mausoleum of Augustus to view the grave of its second occupant, Herod's closest associate among the Romans, would have been appropriate. But there is no significant architectural component to this third Roman trip: Herod's building era was already virtually over. Since Augustus was not in Rome, Herod's time in the city was brief; he seems to have continued on to Aquileia to meet with the Princeps there. Augustus exonerated the sons and rebuked all for their suspicions, whereupon Herod returned to Judaea. He did make a present to Augustus of 300 talents for public spectacles in Rome,[68] which may have

---

Herod "saw the mausoleum [of Augustus] during his many visits to Rome" (p. 29), none of which occurred between the initiation of construction of the two mausolea. For this Segal was rightly taken to task by E. Jerry Vardaman in "Herodium: A Brief Assessment of Recent Suggestions," *IEJ* 25 (1975): 45–46; unfortunately, Vardaman compounded the error by using his correction of Segal's error as a reason for rejecting any relationship between the two structures.

65. *BJ* 1.426, 452–55, 481; *AJ* 16.90–130; Schürer (NEV), 1: 293; Otto, *RE*, 122–24; Corbishley (supra, n. 9), 30–31; Schalit, *KH*, 613; Arnoldo Momigliano, "Herod of Judaea," in *CAH*, 1st ed., corrected (1952), 10: 333–34; Halfmann (supra, n. 5), 159. *AJ* 16.271 may refer to another trip, but this is probably a reference to the third trip of 12 B.C. For the suggestion that it is a fourth trip (third as king), see Schürer (NEV), 1: 293.

66. According to *AJ* 16.91, Herod actually went to Aquileia to meet Augustus, but *AJ* 16.106 and *BJ* 1.452 imply that the meeting was in Rome. On the date of Augustus's trip, see Halfman (supra, n. 5), 159.

67. Syme, *RR*, 394.

68. *AJ* 16.128. This perhaps helped finance Augustus's donation of 400 sesterces per man during his twelfth year of tribunician power (*Res gestae* 15); see also Schürer (NEV), 1: 293.

included some necessary architectural constructions, and he may also have endowed a synagogue in the city.[69]

69. Jean-Baptiste Frey, *Corpus of Jewish Inscriptions* (New York, 1975), no. 173; Harry J. Leon, *The Jews of Ancient Rome* (Philadelphia, 1960), 159–62. The synagogue, if it is of the Herodians and not of the island of Rhodes or an individual named Rhodion (since the inscription reads merely ρωδιο: see Harry J. Leon, "The Synagogue of the Herodians," *JAOS* 49 [1929], 318–21), may have been organized without any personal patronage by Herod, although this seems unlikely given Herod's interest in Jewish communities in the Greek and Roman world. There seem to have been four synagogues in Augustan Rome named after famous people, all of whom had been favorable toward the Jews. Those honored were Herod, Marcus Agrippa, Augustus, and Volumnius, who was probably the Roman official mentioned several times by Josephus as governor of Syria and a liaison between Herod and Augustus (*BJ* 1.535–42; *AJ* 16.277–83, 332, 344, 354, 369; see Schürer (NEV), 1: 257, who felt that Volumnius was merely an equestrian subordinate during C. Sentius Saturninus's governorship, ca. 10–7 B.C.). It was typical to place synagogues under the patronage of influential people, who were often not Jewish, but who contributed financially (see Luke 7.5). For the Synagogue of Augustus, see Leon, *Jews* (supra), 412.

CHAPTER SIX

Early Roman Building in the Southern Levant

Although Herod was the first to execute a large-scale Roman building program in the southern Levant, Roman magistrates had been architecturally active in the region for a quarter century previous to Herod's first efforts (map 4). Their work had been scattered and limited, and often fulfilled personal needs rather than Roman policy, but it nonetheless provided the groundwork for the Herodian program. The instability of the final years of the Seleukid kingdom, and the civil wars that afflicted Judaea thereafter, had caused economic decay and decline. There were localities where only the names remained to show they had once been cities.[1] The first Roman officials in the area sought to rectify this by occasional building, and by doing so, they legitimized Roman architecture in the area. Physical evidence for these constructions is almost nonexistent, but the historical record provides a consistent picture of an emergent Roman architectural interest in the region.

The increasing Roman presence in the decaying Seleukid world of the 60's B.C. resulted in Roman building in Syria even before it became a Roman province. During the reign of the next to last Seleukid king, Philippos II (67–65 B.C.), Q. Marcius Rex (cos. 68 B.C.), governor of Kilikia,[2] came to Antioch and allegedly built a palace and a hippodrome.[3] Both were

1. Strabo 16.2.27.
2. Broughton 2: 146, 154.
3. Malalas 225. The chronicle of John Malalas must be treated with extreme caution, but it is nonetheless an invaluable source for the building history of Antioch, and indeed the only source for a number of details, in particular the specifics of early Roman and Herodian construction in the city. Analysis of Malalas's work is not assisted by its preservation merely in a single incomplete manuscript (Baroccianus 182 in the Bodleian Library, Oxford).

probably repairs rather than new constructions. Marcius paid for the work himself,[4] and he perhaps rebuilt structures damaged in an earthquake a few years previously. His motives were varied and serve as a paradigm both for future Roman building in Syria and the Levant and for Herod's projects. First, he desired to show that the Romans respected the venerable traditions of the East, in particular those of the great city of Antioch. Second, he demonstrated support for the existing Roman and Italian commercial interests in the region. And, finally, he was soliciting Seleukid financial assistance for his own operations against the Kilikian pirates.[5] All of these motives, in their appropriate contexts, were used by Herod in his own building program: respect for ancient institutions (Roman as well as Greek), demonstration of encouragement of compatriots (in his case, Jewish populations in the Greek and Roman world), and establishment of financial and moral support for his policies.[6]

Three years later, in 64 B.C., Pompey arrived in Syria, and by the following summer, he had come to Judaea. The circumstances that brought him to the area, and his activities there, are well known, as is his complex and extensive Roman reorganization of the region.[7] One result was the Dekapolis, a loose grouping of ten cities east of the Sea of Galilee and the Jordan, serving as a buffer between the new Roman province of Syria and the unstable kingdoms to the south.[8] Lists of the ten cities vary slightly, but one

---

Malalas lived and wrote in the late sixth century A.C. As might be expected, his descriptions of events of half a millennium before are imperfect, even though Antioch was his home and he may have had access to the official city building records (Glanville Downey, "Imperial Building Records in Malalas," *BZ* 38 [1938]: 1–15, 299–311). Many of his errors are chronological, minor to him, but frustrating to the modern scholar. In addition, he seems to have believed that the emperor (or a senior member of the Roman government) needed to be personally present in the city for construction to have occurred. These errors can generally be rectified by the modern critic and are not a serious detriment to interpreting the evidence. The most recent study of Malalas's work found it "a fundamental and generally reliable source for the construction of Antioch." (Brian Croke, "Malalas, the Man and His Work," in *Studies in John Malalas*, ed. Elizabeth Jeffreys, Brian Croke, and Roger Scott [Byzantina Australiensia, 6 (Sydney 1990)], 1–25, esp. 6–8).

4. Downey (supra, n. 3), 13–14.

5. Glanville Downey, "Q. Marcius Rex at Antioch," *CP* 32 (1937): 144–51.

6. The location or nature of the palace is unknown, and given the ultimate collapse of the Seleukid monarchy within three years, it was unlikely to have been completed as a major project: it may merely have been a repair of the existing palace. The hippodrome was located on the Orontes island at the north edge of the city, and continued in use for some time: see W. A. Campbell, "The Circus," in *Antioch-on-the-Orontes*, vol. 1, *The Excavations of 1932*, ed. George W. Elderkin (Princeton, 1934), 40.

7. See, most recently, A. N. Sherwin-White, "Lucullus, Pompey, and the East," in *CAH*, 2d ed. (1994), 9: 258–62.

8. Hans Bietenhard, "Die syrische Dekapolis von Pompey bis Traian," *ANRW* 2.8 (1977): 221–38; Robert Wenning, "Die Dekapolis und die Nabatäer," *ZDPV* 110 (1994): 6–8. On

consistent member was Gadara, which lay just southeast of the Sea of Galilee. Gadara was the home of Demetrios, a freedman of Pompey's, presumably an important member of his staff, perhaps his secretary, who would have been an invaluable local contact. Demetrios was to return to Rome so enriched that he was able to purchase an estate, which came to be known as the Horti Demetriou.[9] Pompey paid Demetrios the unique compliment of rebuilding his home town.[10] In such a way was the era of Roman building in the southern Levant introduced.[11]

The site of Gadara had been settled by the seventh century B.C.[12] By the third century B.C., it was a noteworthy city,[13] but it was destroyed in the early first century B.C.[14] Pompey's rebuilding of the city would have been commissioned during the summer of 63 B.C., since this was the only time he was in the area. The city used the Pompeian era of 64 B.C. for its chronology, and it was the only Dekapolis city to mention Pompey on its coins.[15] It was added to Herod's territory after the death of Cleopatra,[16] but he did not build there.[17]

The rebuilding of Gadara was at the beginning of Pompey's fame as a builder. His theater in Rome was dedicated eight years later.[18] His extended tour of the East in the 60's B.C. provided much of the inspiration for his

---

whether the Dekapolis was a political or territorial concept, and Pompey's role in its formation, see David F. Graf, "Hellenisation and the Decapolis," *ARAM* 4 (1992): 2–3, 23–25. Pompey also came to realize that client kingship was the best way to deal with Judaea (G. W. Bowersock, *Roman Arabia* [Cambridge, Mass., 1983], 36).

    9. Plutarch, *Pompey* 40. Its location is unknown: Richardson, *NTD*, 198; Susan Treggiari, *Roman Freedman during the Late Republic* (Oxford, 1969), 184–85. Demetrios was perhaps Pompey's secretary (Peter Greenhalgh, *Pompey: The Roman Alexander* [London, 1980], 164).

    10. *BJ* 1.155; *AJ* 14.75.

    11. Pompey may also have begun, or planned, the restoration of Gaza and Raphia, work implemented a few years later by Gabinius (BMC Palestine, lxviii, lxxxii).

    12. Ute Wagner-Lux et al., "Bericht über die Oberflächenforschung in Gadara (Umm Qēs) in Jordanien im Jahre 1974," *ZDPV* 94 (1978): 144.

    13. Polybios 5.71.

    14. *BJ* 1.155; *AJ* 13.356, 14.75.

    15. Barclay V. Head, *Historia Numorum: A Manual of Greek Numismatics* (Oxford, 1911), 787.

    16. *AJ* 15.217.

    17. Gadara is at modern Umm Qeis, which is rich in remains. Virtually all of them, however, date to after the first century B.C. (Bert De Vries, "Archaeology in Jordan," *AJA* 96 [1992]: 535). Although an understanding of the chronology is made difficult by the excavators' placing everything from Pompey through the Flavian period into one phase (Peter Cornelius Bol et al., "Gadara in der Dekapolis," *AA* 1990: 197), it seems clear that none of the visible monuments, which include a hippodrome, theaters, baths, walls and gates, colonnaded streets, and tombs, dates from Pompey's restoration, the extent of which remains at present unknown (Ute Wagner-Lux et al., "Vorläufiger Bericht über Ausgrabungs- und Vermessungsarbeiten in Gadara [Umm Qēs] in Jordanien in Jahre 1992," *ZDPV* 109 [1993]: 70–72).

    18. For the sources, see Richardson, *NTD*, 383–85.

future architectural successes, as is shown by the often-quoted, if improbable, tale about the theater of Mytilene.[19] Elsewhere in the East, he indulged in other building programs, founding perhaps as many as forty cities and rebuilding others.[20] He continued Roman interest in the architecture of Antioch by repairing its bouleuterion,[21] probably the structure built by Antiochos IV Epiphanes, which had recently suffered earthquake damage.[22] Another famous city Pompey rebuilt was Soloi, on the south coast of Asia Minor, an Argive and Rhodian foundation that had become a notable cultural center (Chrysippos and Aratos were among its citizens), despite giving the world the term *solecism*.[23] After it had suffered during the Mithradatic wars, Pompey resettled the city, presumably rebuilding it, and it was renamed Pompeiopolis.[24]

In late 63 B.C., Pompey withdrew from Syria, leaving M. Aemilius Scaurus in command.[25] Scaurus remained until 61 B.C. There is no evidence that he continued Pompey's policy of restoring and building cities. Sometime in 61 B.C., however, he was replaced by L. Marcius Philippus, the future stepfather of Octavian, who spent the remainder of 61 B.C. and all of 60 B.C. as governor of Syria.[26] During his command he rebuilt the city of Gabae and named it Philippeis.

The rebuilding of Gabae is not documented in any literary or epigraphical source, but only by coins of the city, which indicate an era beginning in 61 or 60 B.C. and refer to Philippus by name.[27] This scanty yet definite evidence is of little assistance, however, in locating the town. The toponym Gaba or Gabae is frequent in the southern Levant, especially in the area around Mount Carmel, and it may be a regional name. Philippus's Gabae is probably not the Gaba that Herod was to rebuild as a military settlement, which itself cannot be located with certainty.[28]

The most probable location for Philippus's Gabae is one of the two sites, et-Harritiyeh and Tel Shosh, that are the best candidates for Herod's Gaba. The former seems to have fallen into disrepair early in the first century B.C.,[29] and it thus would have been a ripe candidate for rebuilding, but no

19. Plutarch, *Pompey* 42.

20. Alois Dreizehnter, "Pompey als Städtegründer," *Chiron* 5 (1975); 213–45.

21. Malalas 211.

22. Downey, *CP* (supra, n. 5), 150.

23. Strabo 14.2.28.

24. *IGRR* 3.869; Strabo 14.3.3, 14.5.8; Plutarch, *Pompey* 28; Dio 36.37; W. Ruge, "Soloi" (# 1), in *RE*, 2d ser., 5 (1927): 935–38; Magie, *RR*, 273–74.

25. *BJ* 1.157; Schürer (NEV), 1: 244–45.

26. Broughton, 2: 180, 185. On Philippus's career, see J. van Ooteghen, *Lucius Marcius Philippus et sa famille* (Académie royale de Belgique, *Mémoires*, 55.3 [Brussels, 1961]), 171–81, which, however, passes over his time in Syria and the Levant.

27. Head (supra, n. 15), 786; Avi-Yonah, *Holy Land*, 80; Jones, *Cities*, 258; *TIR-IP*, 125–26.

28. See infra, pp. 161–62.

29. Arthur Segal and Yehuda Naor, "Sha'ar ha-'Amaqim," in *NEAEHL*, 1339–40.

evidence of such a rebuilding has been found, and remains, particularly coins, are "noticeably absent" from the first century B.C. Tel Shosh, a few kilometers to the southeast, has recently been favored as Philippus's town,[30] but on no particularly strong evidence. Virtually all the arguments advanced for locating Herod's Gaba at a particular site can also be applied to Philippus's Gabae, and the abundance of Gaba toponyms in the area, as well as the limited evidence for Philippus's foundation, makes exact attribution impossible.

Philippus may also have been involved in the refounding of Pella, in the Jordan valley. The city had Bronze Age origins but is first attested as Pella in the third century B.C.[31] It was destroyed by Alexandros Jannaios in 83 B.C.[32] Although its restoration was attributed to Pompey,[33] by the late second and early third centuries A.C., it seems to have been known as the city of the Philippeans, as is shown on coins of Commodus and Elagabalus.[34] Unfortunately, these coin legends raise more questions than they answer, most notably, why should the name appear so late, and indeed who is the eponymous Philippus or Philippos. Augustus's stepfather is not the only candidate. Herod's son Philippos, whose territory was just to the south of Pella, is another possibility. It may be that in the late second century A.C., when Syrians had been implicated in a revolt against Rome, certain cities wished to demonstrate their ancient loyalty.[35] Archaeological evidence is no help, as it provides no support to Marcius Philippus as founder, and suggests that the city was not rebuilt until late in the first century B.C. or later.[36]

Philippus's governorship ended in 60 B.C., and he was succeeded by Cn. Cornelius Lentulus Marcellinus, who was in office for two years,[37] to be followed by Aulus Gabinius, the greatest Roman builder in the southern Levant previous to Herod. Gabinius was in office for three years, 57–55 B.C. He had long familiarity with the region, having arrived with Pompey in 64 B.C.[38] He had also had vast experience in the Roman government, having

30. *TIR-IP*, 126.

31. Polybios 5.70.12.

32. *AJ* 13.397.

33. *AJ* 14.75.

34. Hélène Nicolet, "Une monnaie de bronze frappée à Pella (Décapole) sous Commode," in *Coins, Culture, and History in the Ancient World: Numismatic and Other Studies in Honor of Bluma L. Trell,* ed. Lionel Casson and Martin Price (Detroit, 1981), 51–55; Augustus Spijkerman, *The Coins of the Decapolis and Provincia Arabia,* ed. Michele Piccirillo (Studi Biblici Francisciani Collectio Maior, 25 [Jerusalem, 1978]), 215, 217.

35. Glen Bowersock, review of *The Coins of the Decapolis and Provincia Arabia,* by A. Spijkerman, *JRS* 72 (1982): 197–98.

36. Robert Houston Smith, "Pella," in *NEAEHL,* 1174–80.

37. Broughton, 2: 190, 197.

38. Ibid., 164.

been praetor probably in 61 B.C.[39] and consul in 58 B.C.[40] After his consulship, he went to Syria; his staff included M. Antonius, in his first overseas post. During this period he instituted a wide-ranging building and reconstruction program, rebuilding at least ten cities throughout the southern Levant,[41] thus laying the groundwork for the Herodian projects of the following generation.

The cities Gabinius rebuilt included Samaria, Azotos, Skythopolis, Anthedon, Raphia, Adora, Marisa, Gaza, Apollonia, Iamneia, and Gamala, as well as others unspecified by Josephus.[42] Of these, only Samaria and Anthedon were the beneficiaries of any further rebuilding by Herod, perhaps a testimony to the quality of Gabinius's work. Little can be identified at any of these sites that might be due to Gabinius: only Samaria, Azotos (Ashdod), Skythopolis (Beth Shean), Marisa, Gaza, and Apollonia have received any systematic excavation.

Samaria had extensive Herodian construction, and the excavators of the site found examples of relatively new residential structures, which seem to have been demolished for Herod's temple at the summit: these have been dated to the period of Gabinius.[43] Other examples of supposed Gabinian construction were found elsewhere, some of which continued in use after Herod's rebuilding.[44] All of the assumed Gabinian material was domestic, but it is possible that some of the monumental constructions attributed to Herod may be Gabinius's work of thirty years earlier.

At Azotos, Stratum III, identified as Herodian, seems to include earlier material and may be Gabinian.[45] At Skythopolis, the temple on the northwest part of the summit was identified as Early Roman,[46] and the city seems to have begun to expand in late Hellenistic times.[47] At Marisa, a small temple in Block I was originally identified as Gabinian without strong evidence,[48] but this attribution has recently been rejected,[49] and it has been

39. Ibid., 179.

40. Ibid., 193.

41. *BJ* 1.166; *AJ* 14.87–88.

42. Coins of Kanatha in Syria, dated to the time of Commodus, call the city Gabinia, but like the use of the name of Philippus at Pella, there is no further evidence of a Republican foundation, and the reason for remembering a Late Republican governor of Syria may be the same in both cases: to prove an ancient loyalty to Rome (Bowersock [supra, n. 35], 198).

43. J. W. Crowfoot, Kathleen M. Kenyon, and E. L. Sukenik, *Samaria-Sebaste*, vol. 1: *The Buildings at Samaria* (London, 1942), 31–32.

44. Ibid., 122.

45. Moshe Dothan, "Ashdod," in *NEAEHL*, 102.

46. Amihai Mazar, "Beth Shean: Tell Beth Shean and the Northern Cemetery," in *NEAEHL*, 222.

47. Gideon Foerster, "Beth Shean at the Foot of the Mound," in *NEAEHL*, 223.

48. Michael Avi-Yonah, "Mareshah (Marisa)," in *EAEHL*, 783.

49. The attribution to Gabinius was removed from the reprinting of Avi-Yonah's *EAEHL* article in *NEAEHL* (p. 949).

rather implausibly suggested that Gabinius's work never took place.[50] At Gaza, no definite conclusions have been reached regarding Gabinius's constructions,[51] although they may only have been implementations of work started by Pompey.[52] No material has been found at Apollonia that can be associated with Gabinius.[53]

The remaining cities at which Gabinius is known to have built are today even more obscure. But it is clear that repopulation was an important element of Gabinius's policy, and many of the towns are in the southwest frontier zone at the borders of Ptolemaic Egypt, so one of his purposes was to secure the southern limits of the new Roman sphere of influence. Herod too was to follow this policy and assure favorable populations along the borders of his kingdom.[54]

A final note on early building in the area of Herod's future architectural endeavors again concerns Antioch, the nexus of Roman architectural policy in this region. Julius Caesar built extensively there, work presumably commissioned after his brief and only visit to the city in April of 47 B.C. The construction, known almost entirely from the *Chronicle* of Malalas,[55] was noteworthy, including the first known Roman basilica in the East, the Kaisareion, located in the center of the city, not far from where Herod would build a street. It contained an open courtyard and an apse with statues of Caesar himself and the Tyche of Rome.[56] Caesar also built or rebuilt the theater, Pantheon, an amphitheater, aqueducts, and baths.[57] The

50. Rami Arav, *Hellenistic Palestine: Settlement Patterns and City Planning, 337–31 B.C.E.* (*BAR-IS* 485 [London, 1989]), 57.

51. Carol A. M. Glucker, *The City of Gaza in the Roman and Byzantine Periods* (*BAR-IS* 325 [London, 1987]), 16–18, 38–39.

52. BMC Palestine, lxviii.

53. Israel Roll and Etan Avalon, "Apollonia-Arsuf," in *NEAEHL*, 72–75.

54. Gabinius's immediate successors as governors of Syria do not seem to have done any building. Gabinius was followed by M. Licinius Crassus (54–53 B.C.), who soon died at Carrhae, and then by C. Cassius Longinus (53–51 B.C.). As Rome slipped further into civil war, governors' tenure of office became shorter and the office was vacant on occasion. Many of these latest Republican governors built at Rome and were close associates of Herod's, but they had no real opportunity to build in Syria: thus Roman construction in the province did not continue until Herod began his own projects there, probably no earlier than the late 30's B.C. Among the later governors with whom Herod was closely associated were Sextus Caesar (47–46 B.C.), C. Cassius Longinus (who was again governor 44–42 B.C.), C. Sosius (38–37 B.C.), L. Munatius Plancus (35 B.C.), and of course Messalla (ca. 30–28 B.C.) and Marcus Agrippa (after 23 B.C.). Sosius, Plancus, and Agrippa all built in Rome. For a list of the governors and the evidence for their tenure of office, see Schürer (NEV), 1: 246–57.

55. Malalas 216–17, 287, 338. See also map 6.

56. Glanville Downey, "The Architectural Significance of the Use of the Words *Stoa* and *Basilike* in Classical Literature," *AJA* 41 (1937): 197–99; Erik Sjöqvist, "Kaisareion: A Study in Architectural Iconography," *OpRom* 1 (1954): 94–95.

57. Glanville Downey, *A History of Antioch in Syria from Seleucus to the Arab Conquest* (Princeton, 1961), 154–57.

amphitheater may have been a slight or temporary structure, something not realized by Malalas from his perspective, hundreds of years later, in a world filled with stone amphitheaters.[58] The Kaisareion was largely demolished by Valens in the late fourth century A.C., but the theater was renovated a number of times and is still visible east of Herod's street. Nothing remains of the other structures except aqueduct fragments, many times rebuilt. Caesar's work in Antioch was no less innovative than his constructions in Rome and was an important part of the western transmission of Hellenistic architectural forms,[59] which would return to the East in their new Italian guise through the architecture of Herod. The Kaisareion continued the style and affected the building of the contemporary Forum Julium in Rome (fig. 2).[60] The amphitheater, however temporary, was the first in the East, and probably the first outside Italy, and it would have been a major influence on Herod's amphitheater at Caesarea, built thirty years later. Herod was in Antioch frequently, and nowhere else in the East could he have seen such examples of contemporary Roman architecture at its best. Always anxious to honor Caesar, Herod, too, was to be at his most innovative in Antioch.

The frustrating scantiness of the physical evidence for Roman building in the southern Levant during the period 67–40 B.C. should not cause one to lose sight of the underlying process, which was crucial to Herod's intellectual formation and maturation as a royal builder. This period of early Roman architectural endeavors in the region from Antioch to the Egyptian frontier was exactly contemporary with the first twenty-five years of Herod's life, and his father was a close associate of the three major builders (Pompey, Gabinius, and Julius Caesar). Young Herod was inspired by this environment, in which Roman architecture became the symbol of

58. Caesar may have been responsible for two early amphitheaters in Spain, at Carmo and Ucubi, and perhaps one at Corinth in Greece. These too would have been modest and probably temporary structures. Regardless, the supposed Spanish amphitheaters had no influence on Herod, who was never west of Italy; he might have seen the one in Corinth, although there is no specific information that he ever was in that city. There are serious attribution and dating problems with respect to all these Caesarian amphitheaters, as well as uncertainty as to the nature of the structures. An example is the situation at Ucubi (modern Espejo) in Spain. In the confrontation between Pompey the Younger and Caesar in 45 B.C., Ucubi was burned by the former during his retreat (*De bello hispaniensi* 7–10, 20, 27). A large rock-cut amphitheater that is visible today has been assumed on no strong evidence to be part of an otherwise unknown rebuilding of the city by Caesar (Jean-Claude Golvin, *L'amphithéâtre romain: Essai sur la théorisation de sa forme et des ses functions* [Paris, 1988], 42; see also R. Thouvenot, *Essai sur la province romaine de Bétique* [BEFAR, 189 (Paris, 1940)], 457). It seems unlikely: no rebuilding is documented, a stone amphitheater outside Italy, even in a major center, would be unprecented (none existed in Rome at this time), and Caesar, who was dead within the year, is unlikely to have had the time or inclination to give special honor to the obscure city of Ucubi.

59. Downey, *AJA* (supra, n. 56), 211.

60. Sjöqvist (supra, n. 56), 105–7.

the changing world. Before the time of Herod's birth, virtually no Roman—certainly none with architectural ambitions—had set foot in the area of Herod's future dominions. But by the time Herod was thirty years old and struggling for his personal and political survival in an increasingly unstable world, Roman architecture had become a symbol of the new order that would replace the decadent one represented by the decayed Seleukid and Ptolemaic empires. Inevitably, Herod was swept into this renewal, making contact with the Romans who came to the southern Levant and even beginning his own architectural attempts when he rebuilt Rhodes in late 40 B.C. And when he fled to Rome that winter, his alliance was formed with two men who not only represented the new Roman era but had close ties with the Roman builders of the southern Levant: Antonius, the protégé of Gabinius, and Octavian, the stepson of Philippus. It seems impossible that Herod would have been anything else than a royal builder.

CHAPTER SEVEN

The Building Program
of Herod the Great

The building program of Herod the Great was in progress for approximately thirty years. It began on Rhodes in late 40 B.C., and the last specifically dated construction is the city of Antipatris, shortly after 9 B.C. It is unlikely that much was initiated in the stormy last years of Herod's life; he was in his last illness and acting increasingly erratically, arresting the best and brightest of his kingdom and locking them into the Jericho hippodrome, and executing three of his sons. Nevertheless, as was inevitable, many of the projects that were under construction continued for years, even after his death: the Temple in Jerusalem became proverbial for its lengthy building period, continuing into the time of Herod's great-grandchildren.

A synthetic organic analysis of the Herodian building program is made difficult by both ancient and modern limitations. Archaeological scholarship within the area of Herod's kingdom has generally not been sensitive to an understanding of Herod's needs, goals, and antecedents, especially in his relations with Rome. There are problems caused by selective excavation, ignoring or even disposing of "unimportant" strata, and inadequate analysis of Greek and Latin sources. Chronological schemes may be obsolete, and historical, textual, and field evidence are seen as contradictory, competing, and mutually exclusive, rather than as differing parts of the same puzzle. Academic training in the classics is often not seen as a necessity for excavating in Greek and Roman levels. Unnecessary competition between excavations can be detrimental to true understanding, and methodology may be seen as more important than interpretation. Far too much material is never published, or published only in brief, uninformative summaries.[1]

In addition, the literary source material is often baffling in its chronological contradictions, largely because of Josephus's failure to blend sources consistently. Many chronological problems in Josephus's text have already been noted, although these are not as contradictory or confusing as they often have been made out to be. Josephus, like all historians during the Hellenistic and Roman periods, was afflicted with the problem of the lack of a universal chronological era and the different starting dates for years, so that even when a synchronism could be created, as between Athenian archons and Roman consuls, the overlap was significantly less than an entire year.

Moreover, the quality and precision of Josephus's information varies, from detailed descriptions of Herod's major city foundations to brief notices that provide no information other than a site name. Thus Caesarea is described in detail, but Athens is mentioned only as the location of many of Herod's *anathemata*, which can mean practically anything from a votive tripod to a building. Most of Josephus's catalogue seems to have been based on literary sources rather than autopsy; this is especially true of the list of sixteen cities outside Herod's kingdom mentioned at *BJ* 1.422–25. Moreover, Josephus's catalogue was incomplete, as he himself acknowledged.[2]

Nevertheless, it is possible to create a chronological framework of the major components of the Herodian building program. Herod's efforts as a builder began late in 40 B.C. on the island of Rhodes.[3] He was not yet king—his official title was tetrarch, awarded by Antonius the previous year at Daphne,[4] and it is not clear what, if any, authority this title conferred—yet Herod already had some sense of the use of architectural patronage as an implement of political power. He had grown up in an environment that had

---

1. On this problem, see James F. Strange, "The Capernaum and Herodium Publications," *BASOR* 226 (1977): 65–67.

2. *AJ* 16.146. As an example of how little is known, and how tantalizing the fragmentary information can be, consider *IGRR* 1.1024, an inscription erected in the amphitheater at Berenike in Kyrenaika sometime between the 30's B.C. and the late Augustan period. It is perhaps the earliest Greek citation of the amphitheater as a building type. Berenike was a Herodian family name; there was a Jewish community in the city; and the inscription honored M. Titius, who may have been the *consul suffectus* of 31 B.C. and the governor of Syria whom Herod knew (*AJ* 16.270), perhaps the successor of Marcus Agrippa in 13 B.C. Thus the inscription, and therefore the Berenike amphitheater, cuts into Herod's world on several levels, and one is left with the question as to whether it records an otherwise unknown piece of the Herodian building program. On the career of Titius, see Thomas Corbishley, "A Note on the Date of the Syrian Governorship of M. Titius," *JRS* 24 (1934): 43–49; Rudolf Hanslik, "M. Titius" (#18), in *RE*, 2d ser., 6 (1937): 1559–62; Broughton, 2: 420; Ronald Syme, "Problems about Janus," *AJP* 100 (1979): 191–92; Schürer (NEV), 1: 257.

3. *AJ* 14.378.

4. *BJ* 1.245; *AJ* 14.326.

repeatedly seen the political use of architecture. His father, Antipatros, had been an associate of several great Roman builders, particularly Pompey, Gabinius, and Caesar,[5] and had even engaged in some modest building himself, reconstructing the walls of Jerusalem, which had been destroyed by Pompey.[6] Gabinius's building program, implemented during Herod's adolescence, was the first example of extensive Roman architectural works in Judaea. Herod's innate astuteness and political sense recognized the importance of architectural largesse, especially to one trying to make his mark on the world.

The Herodian building program began slowly, in part a reflection of the turmoil both in Judaea and in the Roman world generally. The documented constructions of Herod's first decade as a builder are heavily military: fortresses such as Alexandreion (fig. 18) and Machairous (fig. 16), and fortified palaces such as those at Jerusalem and Masada. All these seem to have been built within the first few years after Herod's return from Rome. Alexandreion is securely dated to 39–38 B.C.,[7] and Machairous was constructed about the same time.[8] Both were ostensibly an attempt to defend Judaea and Rome against the Parthians.[9]

Herod's two fortified palaces were respectively at the symbolic center of his kingdom, Jerusalem, and at Masada, near his alleged ancestral homeland of Idumaea. The fortress of Masada may be slightly earlier, because of its strategic position,[10] and because of Herod's possession of the site as early as 39 B.C. Jerusalem, on the other hand, was a center of anti-Herodian activity. It did not come under his control until 37 B.C. and then only because of the assistance of Antonius in the shape of the troops of C. Sosius. Herod promptly rewarded Antonius's role in legitimizing his kingdom by naming the new fortified palace the Antonia. This was the first example of a tradition that would last throughout the Herodian dynasty: the naming of constructions, parts of constructions, and even whole cities after Roman leaders.

In these early years of Herod's reign, there does not seem to have been any purely civil building, or any building outside his kingdom, except the initial work at Rhodes. Given the political instability in the kingdom and the deterioration of eastern Roman politics as a result of the intrigues of Antonius and Cleopatra, there was little opportunity for city foundation or civic

---

5. *BJ* 1.131, 162, 194; *AJ* 14.37, 127–39.

6. *BJ* 1.201; at *AJ* 14.143, the Hasmonean Hyrkanos II is credited with the rebuilding.

7. *BJ* 1.308; *AJ* 14.419. Herod's brother Pheroras supervised at least the initial stages of construction, perhaps a glimpse of building talent among Herod's siblings.

8. *BJ* 7.171.

9. On the Herodian frontier system, see M. Gihon, "Idumea and the Herodian Limes," *IEJ* 17 (1967): 27–42.

10. This was well known both to Herod and his enemies: *BJ* 1.238, 293.

building. But additional fortresses, such as Kypros and the frontier fort of Herodeion, in Peraia, probably date from this period.

The political balance changed drastically in 30 B.C. Antonius and Cleopatra were dead. Herod, fortunately, had not joined them at the debacle of Actium and had made his peace with Octavian. A political vacuum now existed in the eastern Roman sphere, which Herod, already a builder of some note in both Judaea and Greece, could fill in a variety of ways, including architecturally. Moreover, at almost the same time as the battle of Actium, the worst earthquake in memory devastated Judaea: Herod's involvement in the disaster relief was a major reason (or a convenient excuse) why he had not appeared at Actium. Some 30,000 people and countless livestock were killed, and numerous buildings were destroyed, in a cataclysm so great that it was rumored that all of Judaea lay in ruins. Some cities had to be abandoned.[11] Thus, by coincidence, just as a new era that would result in an extensive architectural program began in Roman history, Judaea lay devastated, in desperate need of rebuilding.

Yet Herod's first opportunity to demonstrate his role as a builder in the new Augustan world came not at home but in Greece. In 30 B.C., Octavian established a victory city, Nikopolis (in Latin, Actia Nicopolis), at Actium. The building of this city was a dramatic way for Herod to demonstrate the security of the East and his role in the renovation of the new era. In a gesture typical of the pragmatic symbolism of the Augustan world, Herod, formerly the client of Antonius and Cleopatra, but now a supporter of Octavian's, would construct the city memorializing the defeat of his former patrons, showing both his loyalty to the new regime and his architectural expertise. Whether Octavian invited Herod to build Nikopolis or Herod volunteered is not known.[12]

As an internal counterpart to Nikopolis, Herod soon founded his first city within his kingdom, taking the ancient town and religious center of Samaria and reestablishing it as Sebaste, with a temple to Augustus, the first Italian-style temple in the East, as its centerpiece. Octavian had acquired the name Augustus early in 27 B.C., and its Greek version, Sebastos, was soon known in the East. Construction of Sebaste was promptly initiated. The city would be dedicated in 22 B.C. as two of Herod's sons were on their way to Rome, eventually to live with Augustus.[13] Within the same year, a new city was started: Caesarea was to be a great seaport able to rival Alexandria (and

---

11. *BJ* 1.370–72, 408; *AJ* 15.121–23. See D. H. K. Amiran et al., "Earthquakes in Israel and Adjacent Areas: Macroseismic Observations since 100 B.C.E.," *IEJ* 44 (1994): 260–305.

12. *AJ* 16.147. Herod's role as an implementor of Augustan policy is reflected, without naming him, by Suetonius, *Augustus* 59–60.

13. *AJ* 15.342–43. Herod's Sebaste was probably the first use of the new toponym, although within a generation it had become common, especially in Asia Minor. Archelaos of Kappadokia established his Sebaste at Elaioussa around 20 B.C. (infra, pp. 251–53), and his wife Pythodoris founded a Sebaste at Kabeira in Pontos (modern Niksar), which Pompey had

presumably would remain loyal to Rome, as Alexandria had not), honoring the new Alexander, Augustus Caesar.[14]

Throughout the decade of the 20's B.C., there were other constructions, which cannot be precisely dated, including the fortress of Hyrkania, the military colonies of Gaba and Esebonitas, the palaces at Jericho and Askalon, and the palace-mausoleum at Herodeion, near Bethlehem, inspired in part by Augustus's recently constructed mausoleum in Rome.[15] The Temple of Augustus at the Paneion resulted when Augustus gave the area to Herod in 20 B.C.[16]

Herod's extensive constructions in Syria entirely lack any definite chronology. The literary evidence for these buildings rests almost entirely on a single, although detailed, passage at *BJ* 1.422, which lists eight Syrian cities and the specific buildings Herod constructed in them. A ninth Syrian city, Antioch, is described slightly later at *BJ* 1.425 and again at *AJ* 16.148, using another source. The list of eight cities seems derived from a catalogue of Herodian buildings—Greek cities are also included at this point—not linked chronologically to other events. It is clear that Herod built extensively in Syria, a region with which he had been associated since his youth: Syria was the closest Roman province to his kingdom, and it was where he had met many of the Romans who were to influence his life. Thus it was a

---

renamed Diospolis (Strabo 12.3.31). The date of her foundation is uncertain, but was probably between 20 and 1 B.C. For other early cities named Sebaste, see Magie, *RR*, 1334.

14. Like Sebaste, the toponym Caesarea became so commonplace in the Roman provinces that it is difficult to remember that in the 20's B.C. it was a striking novelty. Nevertheless, it gained favor quickly, especially after Augustus's visit to Asia and Syria in 20 B.C., when a number of existing cities, such as Tralleis, seem to have adopted the name. Yet few new cities named Caesarea were built in the last quarter of the first century B.C. Roughly contemporary with Herod's Caesarea were Caesarea in Mauretania, built by Juba II, who was married to the daughter of Antonius and Cleopatra, and Caesarea in Kappadokia, founded by Archelaos, the father-in-law of Herod's son Alexandros. Shortly thereafter, Herod's son Philippos would build his Caesarea near the Paneion. A strange family relationship runs through these cities: Archelaos's daughter Glaphyra was married first to Alexandros and then to Juba II. Thus most of these early towns named Caesarea were founded by Herod, his family, or his in-laws. The only exception seems to be Caesarea Anazarbos, founded around 19 B.C. by the Kilikian king Tarkonditimos II, but even it comes close to Herod's world, and the Herodian and Kilikian dynasties were intermingled at more than one time. Herod's Caesarea may be the earliest use of the toponym—certainly the earliest use applied to a newly founded city—although it is possible that Antioch-in-Pisidia was renamed Colonia Caesarea just after the creation of the province of Galatia in 25 B.C. This would be no more than three years before Herod's foundation (if the earliest possible date for Colonia Caesarea is used, not a certainty), and the name seems to have lasted for only about a century (Barbara Levick, *Roman Colonies in Southern Asia Minor* [Oxford, 1967], 34–35; Stephen Mitchell, *Anatolia: Land, Men, and Gods in Asia Minor* [Oxford, 1993], 1: 76). See further, infra, ch. 9. Some communities in Bithynia may have adopted the name of Julius Caesar at an earlier date, but this is by no means certain (Magie, *RR*, 1334).

15. *BJ* 2.98; *AJ* 15.295, 16.13, 17.321.

16. *BJ* 1.293–94.

good place to demonstrate his Romanness. One can only suppose that building in Syria began early and continued throughout his reign. Specific events may have encouraged Herod's efforts: his urban renewal at Berytos is almost certainly connected with Marcus Agrippa's establishment or expansion of the Roman *colonia* there in 15 B.C.

Herodian building in the traditional Greek world is also difficult to date. Although his efforts in Asia Minor and the eastern islands were undertaken during the years 14–13 B.C., when he was in the region with Marcus Agrippa,[17] the period of Herod's work on the Greek mainland other than at Nikopolis must remain uncertain. Herodian inscriptions from Athens and the intrigues of Eurykles of Sparta do not shed any particular light on the dates of Herod's buildings in those two cities. Olympia probably benefited from Herodian largesse while he was *agonothetes* of the games in 12 B.C.

The last years of Herod's life saw little additional construction. He was ill and embroiled in intense family disputes, which left little time for architectural innovation. Only Antipatris and Agrippias, both founded at about the time of the dedication of Caesarea, date from these years.[18] Even on his last trip to Rome in 12 B.C., Herod could do no more than give Augustus 300 talents for public spectacles.[19] Within a few years he was dead.

Yet his building program continued. The Temple of Jerusalem became proverbial for lengthy construction, as Jesus of Nazareth found out in the late 20's A.C.,[20] and was not officially completed until the time of Herod's great-grandson, or, in Roman terms, the reign of Nero. Its completion caused the immediate unemployment of 18,000 workmen, who unsuccessfully petitioned King Agrippa II to initiate renovations that would allow construction to continue.[21] Over half a century after the death of Herod the Great, his building program was complete.

The innovative quality of the Herodian program was profound. Often bypassing mainstream Hellenistic models, he went direct to Rome. Even when his inspiration was from Antioch and Alexandria, the sources tended to be the new Roman buildings in those cities rather than the traditional Greek structures. Much of Herod's interest in Roman architectural innovation was pragmatic: Romans, not Greeks, were providing the political and financial support for his livelihood, and, in some cases, for the buildings themselves. Although not adverse to using tested Hellenistic forms, especially where Roman types were unavailable or inappropriate, Herod was at his most creative when he brought indigenous Italian forms to the East,

---

17. One construction, a stoa on Chios, is specifically dated to the spring of 14 B.C. (*AJ* 16.18).

18. *BJ* 1.416; *AJ* 16.142–43.

19. *AJ* 16.128.

20. John 2.20.

21. *AJ* 20.219–21.

often for the first time. These included the theater, temple, amphitheater, and villa. In some cases, Herod completed a circle begun by the Romans: the enclosed portico, a Hellenistic creation, had reached Italy during the late Republic, only to be brought back east in a new italianized form by Herod. Baths followed a similar route.

The amphitheater provides a particularly strong example of the process of Herodian architectural thinking. He built at least three: at Caesarea, Jericho, and Jerusalem. The one at Jerusalem has not been located, and the one at Jericho may be part of the enigmatic constructions at Tell es-Samarat. The Caesarea amphitheater was probably the earliest, and if the well-known remains in the northeastern part of the city are those of Herod's structure, it is the earliest extant.

In the middle of the first century B.C., the amphitheater was still purely an Italian form. Although there had been a long tradition in Rome and its Italian colonies of temporary wooden structures that were amphitheatral in shape, the permanent amphitheater is a feature of the first century B.C.[22] and did not appear in Rome until 29 B.C., when Statilius Taurus built his well-documented, if little-known, stone structure.[23] It was a mere seven years old when Herod began Caesarea. Soon after Taurus built his amphitheater, Herod perhaps learned about it from Strabo, and he certainly would have seen it for himself in 17 B.C.

Herod may have been especially interested in the amphitheater because of its association with Julius Caesar. Knowing that honoring Caesar fulfilled both personal and political goals, Herod would hardly have missed the opportunity to include a Caesarean element in Caesarea. The evidence for Caesar's involvement in the early diffusion of the amphitheater is vague, but he was said to have built at least one, in Antioch.[24] Herod, whose own urban renewal of Antioch was a high point of his architectural career and who was in the city early and frequently, could not have failed to be aware of Caesar's structure.

Thus Herod's use of the amphitheater is a fine indication of the role architecture played in his personal and political fulfillment. It not only demonstrated his talent as a royal builder but allowed him to honor Rome, the innovations of the Augustan architectural and cultural program, and the memory of Julius Caesar, both in a national and in a personal sense, as the one responsible for his Roman citizenship, who had laid the entire basis for his role as a client king of Rome's. Since the Caesarean amphithe-

22. On this topic generally, see Robert Étienne, "La naissance de l'amphithéâtre: Le mot et la chose," *REL* 43 (1966): 213–20; and Katherine Welch, "The Roman Arena in Late-Republican Italy: A New Interpretation," *JRA* 7 (1994): 65–67.

23. Richardson, *NTD*, 11.

24. Welch (supra, n. 22), 67. Other Caesarean amphitheaters may have existed in Spain and at Corinth, but the evidence is vague and dubious. See supra, p. 83.

aters are slight and ephemeral, Herod's use of the form remains the first substantial example outside Italy. Until the great Flavian Amphitheater was built in the 70's A.C., Judaea was better equipped with amphitheaters than Rome.

Another building type Herod brought to the East was the Italian temple.[25] The temples to Augustus at Sebaste (fig. 9), Caesarea (fig. 30), and the Paneion (fig. 32) initiated this form in the East and also inaugurated the imperial cult. The earliest, at Sebaste, was begun almost as soon as Octavian received his new title, and the others followed within the decade. Here, too, Herod was following a Caesarean precedent, the Kaisareion at Antioch, which was a functional prototype for the imperial cult temple, even containing statues of the honoree and the Tyche of Rome. It followed a slightly earlier construction of the same name at Alexandria,[26] which, although more influential in the general development of Roman provincial architecture, was probably less important to Herod, because of his lesser familiarity with that city. These Kaisareia seem to have been enclosed porticoes of a type that was to become familiar in the Roman world, perhaps Pergamene or Ptolemaic in origin, and appearing first in Rome in another and contemporary Caesarean structure that influenced Herod, the Forum Julium (fig. 2). As its name shows, the forum was less personal than dynastic, although it did include a statue of Caesar, set up during his lifetime, and many other personal touches.[27]

In establishing his version of the imperial cult, Herod was guided by the concept of the two Kaisareia and the Forum Julium, but not by their actual enclosed portico form, something he reserved for other structures, particularly the Temple in Jerusalem. Herod's temples to Augustus used the ancient Italian temple style, common in Rome, but as yet unknown outside Italy. Rejecting the Hellenistic Greek temple form (which was used both in his temple to Apollo on Rhodes and in what was probably the earliest non-Herodian temple to Augustus, that at Ankyra),[28] Herod made his buildings more Italian and innovative.

---

25. For examples of the Italian temple plan, with its frontal stairway, colonnade around three sides, and long, deep cella, see Axel Boëthius, *Etruscan and Early Roman Architecture*, 2d ed. (Harmondsworth, 1978)), 156–57.

26. Ward-Perkins, *RIA*, 366; Erik Sjöqvist, "Kaisareion: A Study in Architectural Iconography," *OpRom* 1 (1954): 86–108.

27. Pliny, *Natural History* 34.18.

28. In 29 B.C., according to Dio (51.20), Octavian built *temene* in Ephesos and Nikaia that honored Roma and Julius Caesar, but whether these included actual temples is not specified and there is no archaeological evidence. The same passage refers to *temene* in honor of Octavian at Pergamon and Bithynian Nikomedia, but it is not clear when these were established. See also Klaus Tuchelt, *Frühe Denkmäler Roms in Kleinasien, 1: Roma und Promagistrate (Ist-Mitt*, suppl. 23 [1979]) 32–33; Mitchell (supra, n. 14), 1: 100–102.

The enclosed portico—the form of the Kaisareia and the Forum Julium—was also an influence on Herod, not as a dynastic monument, but in the building of the Temple in Jerusalem. In this he was guided by another Caesarean structure, the Saepta Julia, which was the continuation of the monumental complex on the Campus Martius initiated, to some extent, by the Theater of Pompey. Caesar conceived the Saepta in 54 B.C., only months after Pompey's theater was completed, although it was not finished until thirty years later, when Marcus Agrippa further monumentalized the area and built his baths.[29] The Saepta was a massive enclosure, which Herod imitated and expanded upon in his Temple precinct. A more modest portico was in front of the Temple of Augustus at Sebaste, and one may assume similar constructions at the other temples to the imperial cult. Once again, Herod was able in his own way to fulfill the architectural vision of Julius Caesar.

Another Herodian importation of an Italian type is the theater. There were at least six, at Caesarea, Jerusalem, Damaskos, Sidon, and perhaps Jericho and Sebaste. The one at Caesarea is the best known. Again, Herod rejected an existing Greek format and chose the Roman style, although it was still a rarity. The Theater of Pompey (fig. 1) was only fifteen years old when Herod made his first trip to Rome, and it was a major tourist attraction in the city. Another Roman theater had been started by Caesar, but like so many Caesarean projects, it languished at his death, and it was only continued twenty years later by Augustus, as a memorial to his nephew Marcellus.[30] The construction of Caesarea began only a few months after Marcellus's death: thus Herod again both honored the memory of Caesar and built in the latest Augustan fashion.

Although it was a new architectural form, the Italian theater,[31] unlike the amphitheater, had already begun to spread beyond Italy in Herod's day. Several theaters were built outside Italy during the Augustan period, but precise dates are lacking, and it cannot be determined how they relate chronologically to the Herodian constructions; all are essentially contemporary. By the end of the Augustan period, Italian theaters were common in the West, including one built by Juba II of Mauretania at his Caesarea,[32] but Herod's at his own Caesarea remains the first example in the East, since Caesar's at Antioch seems to have been merely a reconstruction. Whether

29. Richardson, *NTD*, 340–41.

30. Ibid., 382–83. Caesar was also credited with a theater at Antioch, but this was probably a rebuilding of an existing Hellenistic structure.

31. The Italian theater, freestanding, with its semicircular orchestra and elaborate stage building, seems to have developed in Sicily and South Italy during the late second and early first century B.C.: the Pompeii theater, probably from the 70's B.C., is the purest early example (Boëthius [supra, n. 25], 198–206).

32. Gibert Picard, "La date du théâtre de Cherchel et les débuts de l'architecture théâtrale dans les provinces romaines d'occident," *CRAI* 1975: 394–95; David B. Small, "Studies in Roman Theater Design," *AJA* 87 (1983): 55–68.

the Herodian theaters at Damaskos and Sidon were Greek or Roman in form remains to be determined; the one at Damaskos, at least, may have been a rebuilding of an existing Hellenistic structure. The Italian theater was a physical definition of the spread of Roman culture and institutions: to Vitruvius it was second only to the forum as the most important architectural element of a Roman city.[33] Vitruvius was active as a practicing architect at the time of the early years of the Herodian building program, but whether or not Herod was personally acquainted with Vitruvius or his writings, he aggressively followed Vitruvius's principles in order to leave no doubt that he was building in the accepted Roman fashion.

As noted, Vitruvius felt that the most important element of a proper Roman city was its forum. Herod's awareness of this concept is demonstrated by the care he gave to the urban centers of his cities, particularly Caesarea (whose central area appears more lavish with each season of excavation), Sebaste, and Nikopolis.[34] Even in the hellenized cities on the perimeter of his kingdom, such as Askalon, Berytos, and Tyre, he paid special attention to the center. Berytos is a particularly notable example, as the city was intensively romanized under Herod's direction after it became a Roman *colonia* around 15 B.C., including the laying out of a complete Roman forum. All Herod's cities had the temples, porticoes, and basilicas that characterized the Roman Forum and became the epitome of Roman urban architecture.[35]

In the construction of his residences, Herod had to be cautiously adaptive. There was no strong Roman precedent for the royal palace, since kingship and its trappings were anathema to the Roman mind. Despite the increase in his personal power, Augustus pointedly did not change his lifestyle and lived for nearly half a century in a house noted for its austerity and modest size, which had originally belonged to the famous orator Q. Hortensius Hortalus.[36] Other aristocratic houses on the Palatine, such as that of Antonius,[37] may have been more lavish but were hardly in the tradition of a king's palace.

---

33. Vitruvius 5.3.1.

34. Although Josephus used the word *agora* to describe the civic centers of Herod's cities, it is clear he was translating the Latin word *forum* rather than using the term in its original Greek sense. This trait is clearest when the Roman Forum is meant (e.g., *BJ* 4.494, where the emperor Galba is killed in the agora of Rome), but the word *agora* as used by Josephus means forum in any Roman context (such as the agora of Caesarea, *BJ* 1.415, 2.270), although it can mean agora in a Greek context (such as at Antioch, *BJ* 7.55, 61). Similarly, Vitruvius used *forum* even when describing the agora of a Greek city (e. g., 5.1.1).

35. His street in Antioch, although lacking the public buildings characterizing a forum, is another example of the care given to urban planning.

36. Suetonius, *Augustus* 72.

37. Dio 53.27.

As many as eight Herodian residences are known, at Jerusalem (fig. 37), Masada, Caesarea, Jericho (fig. 7), Herodeion (fig. 8), Askalon, and perhaps Livias and Sepphoris. The best understood are the most elaborate, at Masada, Jericho, and Herodeion, with current excavation adding much information about the seaside villa at Caesarea. Yet they varied greatly in size, from the massive complex at Herodeion to the modest country residence at Livias.[38]

The Herodian residential structure is one form where the evolution of Herodian thought—and its impact on Roman architectural forms—can be clearly seen.[39] Lacking a strong Roman precedent, Herod first turned to existing Hellenistic models within and near his territory. These mixed Seleukid and Ptolemaic elements, with some features even drawn from Persian governors' palaces, particularly the use of parks and gardens. Towers, used by Herod especially at Herodeion and Jerusalem, may ultimately have been Makedonian in inspiration, but they had closer precedents in Alexandria and had become prevalent in late Hellenistic Judaea and its environs.

The palace of Tyros, built as a country manor by Hyrkanos of the Tobiah family early in the second century B.C., is the best early example of the Hellenistic palace form in the region of Herod's future dominions.[40] Lying east of Jericho at the site of Arak el-Emir, it combines Greek and Oriental elements in a simple and even primitive form, with, according to Josephus,[41] parks, gardens, and sophisticated hydraulics. Somewhat more elaborate was the first Hasmonean palace at Jericho, constructed by Hyrkanos I in the late second century B.C. and modified and enlarged over the following century. This was certainly a direct influence on Herod: Jericho was to have more Herodian palatial construction than anywhere else, and Herod may have lived in the Hasmonean structure in his early years. The palace was centered on a large banqueting hall and surrounded by gardens and pools. It is the most direct prototype for Herod's early palatial construction.

Herod's first residences were in this Hellenistic style of governor's palace, but eventually his tastes and inclinations outgrew the form of a dying era and became increasingly lavish. In addition, he moved from Hellenistic patterns to Roman ones, a transition conspicuously visible at Jericho. There was only the faintest precedent for a Roman palace, but it is significant: in 67 B.C. the aptly named Q. Marcius Rex had rebuilt, or perhaps remodeled,

---

38. Inge Nielsen, *Hellenistic Palaces: Tradition and Renewal* (Studies in Hellenistic Civilization, 5 [Aarhus, 1994]), 181–208.

39. On this topic generally, see Nielsen (supra, n. 38), who relies heavily on the evidence of Herod's residences and palaces in order to illuminate the Hellenistic palace tradition: six of her thirty-one catalogued examples of the form were built by Herod (pp. 298–305).

40. Nielsen (supra, n. 38), 138–46.

41. *AJ* 12.228–36.

the Seleukid palace in Antioch.[42] This provided Herod with the authority that palatial construction was a legitimate Roman activity, although he turned to a stronger Roman model for his later domestic architecture, the Italian country villa.

The Italian country villa was itself an evolution of the Hellenistic palace, especially in its use of peristyles.[43] It appeared in the second century B.C. and became common in the following century; by Augustan times it had become the epitome of Roman excess.[44] There were two distinct types. Rooms were constructed around a peristyle, such as the Villa of the Mysteries at Pompeii (fig. 4), which flourished from ca. 200 B.C. to A.D. 79,[45] or rooms were arranged along a row that had a court on one side, creating a porticus, of which there are also numerous examples around the Bay of Naples: some of the most accessible are at Herculaneum.[46] The porticus villa, not enclosed like the peristyle type, paid particular attention to its natural setting, as it could have large windows that brought in light and provided striking views.

Although most of the Republican evidence for villas comes from Campania, such constructions existed in the environs of Rome and in the city itself. As Vitruvius pointed out, important people needed elaborate houses because of their social and political obligations, and their houses needed to contain spacious peristyles and rooms, libraries, and even basilicas for holding meetings and trials.[47] The private homes that Herod visited in Rome were of this type: the modesty of Augustus's residence was perhaps an exception and was more than offset by the houses of Antonius: that on the Palatine, which was large enough to be divided eventually between two of Herod's intimates, Messalla and Marcus Agrippa, and Antonius's other home on the Carinae, the former home of Pompey, which became notorious as the scene of drunken parties.[48] The actual late Republican houses

---

42. Malalas 225.

43. Alexander G. McKay, *Houses, Villas and Palaces in the Roman World* (Ithaca, N.Y., 1975), 103–16.

44. See, e.g., Strabo's sardonic comment (5.2.5) that the timber once used to defend Rome (through shipbuilding) was now used to make villas suitable for a Persian. Pliny (*Natural History* 35.26) was equally cynical, noting that art was no longer visible to the public because it was hidden away in villas. Further contemporary criticisms are cited by McKay (supra, n. 43), 247.

45. McKay (supra, n. 43), 108–10.

46. Ibid., 117–24. A number of Herod's associates were among the many prominent personalities of the late Republic who had villas around the Bay of Naples, in particular, Marcus Antonius, Julius Caesar, and Marcus Agrippa: see the catalogue in John H. D'Arms, *Romans on the Bay of Naples: A Social and Cultural Study of the Villas and Their Owners from 150 B.C. to A.D. 400* (Cambridge, Mass., 1970), 171–232.

47. Vitruvius 6.5.2.

48. Plutarch, *Antonius* 21, 32.

whose remains still exist in Rome, such as the Casa di Livia, the house of Augustus, and the Casa dei Grifi, follow the peristyle and porticus plans of the Campanian villas.

Herod's familiarity with the houses of those who entertained him in 40 B.C. and again in 17 B.C. provided much of the inspiration for his own residential structures. At Jericho, in particular, he demonstrated his knowledge of the villa form: his modification of the original Hasmonean palace created both a peristyle court and an adjoining porticus with an excellent view to the south. The later palace, completely Herod's creation and totally Roman in form, was centered on two basilicas or audience halls, peristyle courts, and baths. The northern palace at Masada, although affected by the unusual topography of the site, has the same combination of peristyle court and magnificent view, with ornamental decoration in a distinctly Italian style, and the palace at Caesarea used the porticus form to create a seaside retreat remindful of the villas of Campania. At Jerusalem, he created a Roman town house. But it was at Herodeion that Herod's imagination reached its peak, in a sprawling complex that may have been the largest palatial structure in the Roman world of its day and was a direct forerunner of the elaborate palaces built in Rome in the late first century A.C.[49]

Another particularly Roman feature in Herodian architecture is the Campanian private bath of the late Republic.[50] Although modest private baths had existed in the areas of Herod's future kingdom since the second century B.C.,[51] Herod, as usual, went to Italian models, using hypocausts, a technical refinement of the early first century B.C., later modified to include hollow walls (tubulation): some of the earliest known tubulation is at Masada,[52] striking proof that Herod was at the forefront of technology. In fact, he may have been ahead of contemporary Roman use in his baths, since Rome did not have a public bathing establishment until the completion of the one begun by Marcus Agrippa around 25 B.C.[53] Herod's association with Agrippa influenced his general interest in hydraulics and baths and perhaps

49. Herodeion even foreshadows Hadrianic construction: see William L. MacDonald and John A. Pinto, *Hadrian's Villa and Its Legacy* (New Haven, 1995), 85–88.

50. Fikret Yegül, *Baths and Bathing in Classical Antiquity* (New York, 1992), 64; Gideon Foerster, "Hellenistic Baths in Israel," in *Akten*, 164. For a contrary view, which, however, does not seem to take into account the evidence of contemporary Italian bath technology, see David B. Small, "Late Hellenistic Baths in Palestine," *BASOR* 266 (1987): 59–74.

51. Foerster (supra, n. 50), 164. The best-preserved and most elaborate are those at Tel Anafa, which were constructed shortly after 125 B.C. and remained in use for somewhat over half a century (Sharon Herbert, "Tel Anafa," in *NEAEHL*, 59–60).

52. Vitruvius (5.10.2) was the first to define the system, although he did not use the term; see Inge Nielsen, *Thermae et Balnea: The Architecture and Cultural History of Roman Public Baths* (Aarhus, 1990), 1: 14–15.

53. Dio 53.27; Richardson, *NTD*, 386–87.

allowed him access to the latest technological developments. Agrippa and his aqueduct constructions played a major role in the development of the Roman bath: his extension of the Serino aqueduct to Pompeii in the 30's B.C. provided the necessary water supply for the rebuilding of the Stabian and Forum Baths, including the addition of tubulation.[54] Likewise, in Rome, Agrippa's Aqua Virgo created a water supply for his baths.[55] The need for more and better aqueducts was not merely to supply baths, for as Frontinus noted, monumental architecture required water for its extensive pools and fountains.[56]

Baths are one of the most common elements of the Herodian program. He followed the precepts outlined by Vitruvius, constructing them at least at Jerusalem, Herodeion, Masada, Machairous, Kypros, and Askalon. All except the last are on Herod's own territory, although the gymnasia he built in Greek cities almost certainly included baths. In providing water for his baths, and the hydraulic constructions of his own monumental architecture, such as the great pools at Caesarea and Herodeion, Herod faced a problem that Agrippa did not: the aridity of Judaea. Herod first tackled this problem in supplying water to his fortresses in the Jordan valley, one of the driest parts of his kingdom. As noted by the experts on ancient water supply in the region, "Precipitation is minimal and very unevenly distributed throughout the year. . . . The mean annual precipitation . . . is 50 to 200 mm, [but this] can be misleading, since there are years in which only a few millimeters of rain falls, and such years can occur consecutively."[57] Hence it is not astonishing that Herod was at his most innovative in this matter of survival, the bringing of water into his desert fortresses, thus laying the basis for the sophisticated hydraulics that watered his baths. His hydraulic astuteness was not limited to the acquisition of water, but also extended to its removal, as shown by the notable sewer system at Caesarea, presumably not the only example. His reputation was such that he provided the water supply to at least one Syrian city, Laodikeia.

Herod's adaption of Roman forms was not limited to the buildings themselves, but included their actual construction materials and technology. Great barrel-vaulted platforms in the style of the late Republican sanctuaries of Italy supported many a Herodian structure, particularly at Caesarea, Herodeion, and Jerusalem.[58] He made use of contemporary Augustan tech-

---

54. Nielsen, *Thermae* (supra, n. 52), 1: 32–34.

55. Frontinus, *De aquis* 9; Dio 54.11.

56. Frontinus, *De aquis* 23.1; see Propertius's description of the pools and fountains of monumental architecture (2.32.11–16).

57. Gunther Garbrecht and Yehuda Peleg, "The Water Supply of the Desert Fortresses in the Jordan Valley," *BiblArch* 57 (1994): 161, 162.

58. Similar vaults may have existed at Sebaste, as part of the platform of the Temple of Augustus and even the substructures of the forum. Such vaults seem to be depicted on a mosaic in the church of St. Stephen at Umm al-Rasas, 30 km southeast of Madaba, dating to

niques such as *opus reticulatum* (fig. 27), *opus incertum*, and marble decoration, all essentially alien both to the indigenous tradition and (with the exception of marble decoration) to the neighboring traditions of Hellenistic Syria and Egypt.[59] *Opus reticulatum* was a product of the last years of the Republic,[60] and it would thus have been the most modern Roman construction technique when Herod first toured Rome: it was commonplace to Vitruvius, but recent enough that he was suspicious of it.[61] *Opus incertum*, the other type of walling recognized by Vitruvius, was a variant of *opus caementicium*, concrete, which was dependent on the unique cementing properties of the Italian *pozzolana* and had been in existence since at least the third century B.C.,[62] becoming one of the most visible and enduring elements of Roman architectural technology. Marble decoration, although Greek in origin, came to be particularly associated with the Augustan rebuilding of Rome.[63]

Herod specifically chose these Roman techniques for his program. Josephus remarked on the marble decoration at the Paneion,[64] and presumably other temples to Augustus were similarly built. *Opus reticulatum* is known from Jericho (fig. 27), Jerusalem, and perhaps the Paneion: concrete was used in the harbors of Caesarea, even to the point of importing Italian *pozzolana*. The role played by Italian architects and engineers remains uncertain, although it has been suggested that a Roman team was sent by Marcus Agrippa to assist in constructing Herod's later palace at Jericho, and that Roman architects and decorators were also at Masada and Herodeion.[65]

A.D. 756. The floor contains a number of city views: the one of Sebaste shows eight barrel vaults supporting a church. See Michele Piccirillo, *The Mosaics of Jordan* (Amman, 1993), 224 (pl. 350), 238. The technique of the barrel-vaulted platform, perhaps Etruscan in origin, reached its Late Republican peak during the period of Sulla, when the great sanctuaries of Praeneste and Terracina were constructed (Boëthius [supra, n. 25], 169–78).

59. On these Roman techniques and their use in the East, see Hazel Dodge, "The Architectural Impact of Rome in the East," in *Architecture and Architectural Sculpture in the Roman Empire* (Oxford University Committee for Archaeology, Monograph 29, ed. Martin Henig (Oxford, 1990), 108–20. Nevertheless, Herod—like Augustus—was not adverse also to making frequent use of Hellenistic-style ashlar masonry with marked anathyrosis, which is conspicuous at many a Herodian site (figs. 11, 28).

60. Marion Elizabeth Blake, *Ancient Roman Construction in Italy from the Prehistoric Period to Augustus* (Washington, D.C., 1947), 254. See also Jean-Pierre Adam, *Roman Building: Materials and Techniques*, trans. Anthony Mathews (Bloomington, Ind., 1994), 129–34.

61. Vitruvius 2.8.1.

62. Boëthius (supra, n. 25), 126–29; Adam (supra, n. 60), 79–80.

63. Suetonius, *Augustus* 28. For a good study of the marble quarrying and transportation in the Roman period, see *Marble in Antiquity: Collected Papers of John Bryan Ward-Perkins*, ed. Hazel Dodge and Bryan Ward-Perkins (Archaeological Monographs of the British School at Rome, 6 [London, 1992]), 13–30.

64. *BJ* 1.404.

65. Ehud Netzer, "Architecture in Palaestina prior to and during the Days of Herod the Great," in *Akten*, 45; Roger Ling, *Roman Painting* (Cambridge, 1991), 169. Regardless, the

There is no specific evidence for this assumption, although it is plausible simply because Herod, however great his personal interest, could not have been familiar with all the details of the immense Roman repertory his architects used. At the very least there was close coordination between those implementing the Augustan and Herodian programs.[66]

Other aspects of the Herodian program had purer Greek antecedents, or so mix Greek and Roman elements that it is difficult to determine exactly where the inspiration originated. In some cases Herodian architecture was an important transition between Hellenistic and Roman Imperial forms. This is true not only of Herod's residences but of the great harbor at Caesarea and the street at Antioch. The Caesarea harbor drew its inspiration from Alexandria and perhaps other Greek harbors, used Roman technology, and was the forerunner of the imperial harbors at Ostia and Lechaion. A Herodian harbor, little known, also existed at Nikopolis, and Herod's contribution to the Rhodian shipbuilding industry may have included some harbor works. The street at Antioch took Hellenistic porticoes of the Pergamene or Alexandrian type, a form already known in Rome, but joined them with the street as an longitudinal architectural unit, facilitating the Imperial development of the colonnaded street. The urban cores of other Herodian cities, particularly in Syria and Greece, as yet little known archaeologically, may have represented other stages of this process. Yet Herod was not adverse to using that ancestor of the portico, the Greek stoa, particularly on Chios and at Berytos and Tyre: those at the last two cities may have been similar to the porticoed street of Antioch.

Herodian artistic program laid the groundwork for "a vigorous native art" style that lasted for centuries: see Michael Avi-Yonah, "Oriental Elements in the Art of Palestine in the Roman and Byzantine Periods," *QDAP* 10 (1944): 106.

66. One element of the Augustan architectural repertory conspicuously ignored by Herod is the triumphal arch. Arches had been a part of Roman architecture since the early second century B.C. (Livy 33.27, 37.3.7), and Octavian had been honored after Actium with an arch in the Forum (Dio 51.19; Elizabeth Nedergaard, "Arcus Augusti [a. 29 a. C.]," in *LTUR*, 1: 80–81). Augustus also erected one in the Forum in 19 B.C. next to the Temple of Divine Julius (Dio 54.8; Richardson, *NTD*, 23; Elizabeth Nedergaard, "Arcus Augusti [a. 19 a. C.]," in *LTUR*, 1: 81–85). There was every reason for Herod to make use of the arch, since it was an existing yet recent form in the city of Rome, an element of the Augustan program, and the two honoring Augustus commemorated events important in Herod's career. But there were good reasons discreetly to ignore the arch and not to erect any in Judaea. First, it was as conspicuous a Roman symbol as possible, and Herod's difficulties with the Jerusalem eagle (*BJ* 1.648–55) demonstrated that Roman symbols needed to be subtle. Moreover, an arch commemorated the vanquishing of enemies, not as obvious and straightforward in the turbulent politics of Judaea as at Rome. It seems that the triumphal arch was not a feature of the architecture of the early imperial Levant: the earliest in the East is perhaps one at Antioch-in-Pisidia, from the Augustan period, but even it is dubious and no longer extant. Arches were not common even in Syria until the second century A.C. (Maurice H. Chéhab, "Fouilles de Tyr: La nécropole, I. L'arc de triomphe," *BMusBeyr* 33 [1983]: 69).

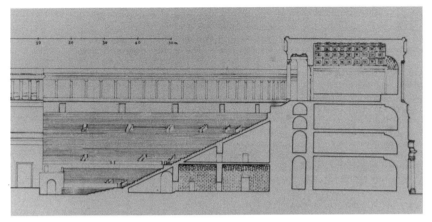

Fig. 1. The Theater of Pompey, Rome, section view. Courtesy Department of Classics, the Ohio State University.

Fig. 2. The Forum Julium, Rome: excavated area from the west. Courtesy Department of Classics, the Ohio State University.

Fig. 3. The Mausoleum of Augustus, from the southeast. Courtesy Department of Classics, the Ohio State University.

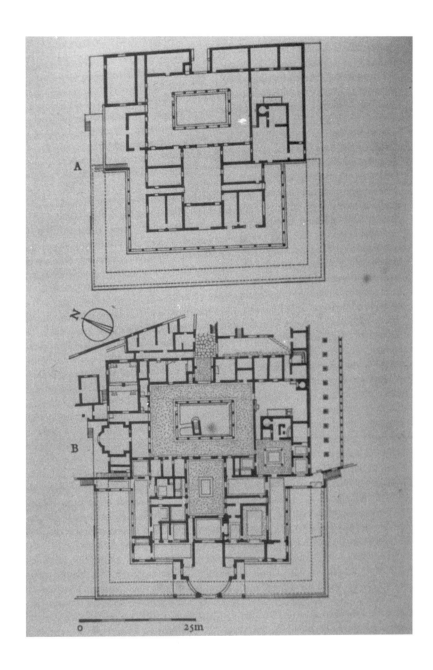

Fig. 4. The Villa of the Mysteries, Pompeii. *A*. Early phase, ca. 150–100 B.C.
B. Last phase, before A.D. 62. From J. B. Ward-Perkins, *Roman Imperial
Architecture*, 2d ed. (Harmondsworth, 1981), fig. 123. Courtesy Yale Univer-
sity Press Pelican History of Art.

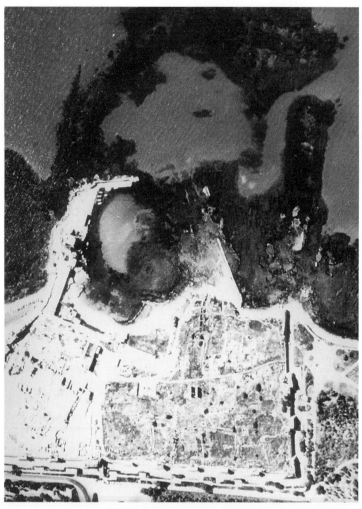

Fig. 5. Caesarea, aerial view of the harbor and city center. Courtesy R. L. Hohlfelder.

Fig. 6. Phasaelis: view north to Alexandreion. Photograph by Duane W. Roller.

Fig. 7. Jericho, the second palace from the south; first palace, Herod's palm groves, and Tell es-Samarat beyond. Photograph by Duane W. Roller.

Fig. 8. Herodeion, the lower palace from the southeast. Photograph by Duane W. Roller.

Fig. 9. Sebaste, the Temple of Augustus from the northeast. Photograph by Duane W. Roller.

Fig. 10. Paneion, the Grotto of Pan from the south. Herod's Temple of Augustus stood before the grotto. Photograph by Duane W. Roller.

Fig. 11. Hebron: the southeast corner of the Herodian enclosure. Photograph by Duane W. Roller.

Fig. 12. Mamre from the east. Photograph by Duane W. Roller.

Fig. 13. Herodeion, summit structure (Herod's tomb?) from the east. Photograph by Duane W. Roller.

Fig. 14. Jerusalem, the Nikophorieh Tomb, perhaps the tomb of Herod's family, from the east. Photograph by Duane W. Roller.

Fig. 15. Kypros, from the west. Photograph by Duane W. Roller.

Fig. 16. Machairous, from the east. Photograph by Duane W. Roller.

Fig. 17. Hippos, from the southeast. Photograph by Duane W. Roller.

Fig. 18. Alexandreion (high point on central skyline), from the northeast. Photograph by Duane W. Roller.

Fig. 19. Kypros (l.) and Dagon (r.) from the east, just south of Jericho. Photograph by Duane W. Roller.

Fig. 20. Jericho: view south from Tell es-Samarat along the hippodrome to palaces. Kypros on skyline. Photograph by Duane W. Roller.

Fig. 21. Rhodes, the Temple of Apollo from the east. Courtesy Marjorie W. Roller.

Fig. 22. Antioch, view south along Herod's street. Photograph by Duane W. Roller.

Fig. 23. Nikopolis (theater). Photograph by Duane W. Roller.

Fig. 24. Chios town, where Herod built a stoa. Courtesy Duane H. D. Roller.

Hellenistic lighthouse technology, little known today, was also an influence. Josephus compared the Phasael tower in Jerusalem to the Pharos of Alexandria,[67] and the Drousion tower at Caesarea would have had similar antecedents, as, perhaps, did the towers at Herodeion and on the Antonia. The Pharos, which Herod saw as early as 40 B.C., was built in the early third century B.C. by Sostratos of Knidos. It is only known through literary descriptions, particularly that of Strabo, who saw it just before he may have come to Judaea,[68] but a close—if much more modest—relative is the extant Tower of the Winds in Athens, constructed ca. 50–37 B.C. and thus new in Herod's day. Although octagonal, as was one level of the Pharos but as the extant Herodian tower ("David's Tower") in Jerusalem is not, and decorated with reliefs, a Corinthian porch and an internal Doric colonnade, the Tower of the Winds nevertheless provides a glimpse of contemporary tower building and thus perhaps of the nature of Herod's constructions.[69] The lighthouse form—whether used directly or in other tower construction—is another example of an innovative architectural element utilized in Herodian buildings. Significantly, the first monumental lighthouse at the port of Rome was not constructed until more than half a century later, when Claudius created his great harbor at Ostia, inspired not only by forgotten plans of Julius Caesar (who himself was quite familiar with Alexandria) but by the existing structure at Caesarea.

As a proper dynast, Herod was a founder of cities. This was a traditionally Greek talent but had recently been adopted by the Romans, especially those who spent time in the East. Herod is known to have founded eight cities, from the modest Phasaelis to the grandiose Caesarea. All but one are within his territory, and the exception, Nikopolis, fulfilled a specific requirement of Augustan policy. As was common in the art of Hellenistic city foundation, some (Agrippias, Antipatris, and Sebaste) were merely renaming and reconstructing of ancient cities. Phasaelis, probably the earliest and most modest, fulfilled the best qualities of the tradition, attempting to bring economic prosperity to a remote and little-populated region. Caesarea had a similar role, with the additional element of assisting the recovery from the devastation of the earthquake of 31 B.C. The most enigmatic is Herodeion, called a city by Josephus but never seeming actually to be one: it may have originally been established with the same goals as Phasaelis. Another aspect of city foundation was the providing of names

67. *BJ* 5.619; *AJ* 16.144.

68. Strabo 17.1.6.

69. For the Pharos and Tower of the Winds, see A. W. Lawrence, *Greek Architecture*, 4th ed., rev. R. E. Tomlinson (Harmondsworth, 1983), 310–14. Tower-like constructions were not unknown in Roman architecture: the structure known as the Tabularium in Rome is perhaps the most visible example. These too may have influenced Herod. See Nicolas Purcell, "*Atrium Libertatis*," *BSR* 61 (1993): 147.

that could make political statements, and here Herod was at his most astute, using the names of Augustus (in both Greek and Latin), Livia, Marcus Agrippa, his father Antipatros, his brother Phasael, and himself.[70]

Less important than cities but in a similar tradition of concern for demographics were the Herodian military colonies at Bathyra, Gaba, and in the Esebonitis region. Here Herod had both Seleukid and Roman precedents but was probably guided by the former; the Seleukid military organization of the southern Levant had inspired his early residences and also influenced the numerous forts, especially in the eastern parts of his kingdom, that both protected himself and secured the Roman frontier. Many of these had long been in existence—the names Hyrkania and Alexandreion betray their Hasmonean origins—and were simply rebuilt, although with the particular care for water supply that typified Herodian construction. Masada and the Antonia are the best known and largest; others include Kypros, the lesser Herodeion, and Machairous, and there are several other sites, not mentioned in literature, whose archaeological remains suggest the existence of a Herodian fortress.

A particularly important influence on the Herodian program, more Greek than Roman, was his interest in athletics. Athletic construction forms the single largest class of Herodian buildings, and his position as *agonothetes* in perpetuity at Olympia, his endowment of the office of *gymnasiarchos* on Kos, also in perpetuity, his donation of funds for festivals in Rome in 12 B.C., and the games he established in various of his cities all indicate that he was a major patron of athletics and devoted substantial financial resources to this interest.

Gymnasia and stadia were frequent Herodian constructions. Many of these were built to house the various Herodian games: the Aktia at Nikopolis, and the Kaisareia at Caesarea and at Jerusalem (which included music and drama).[71] There were probably also games at Herodeion and the Paneion. Although amphitheaters were used for these games, by and large,

70. Nikopolis, whose name was probably chosen by Octavian, honored the victory at Actium. Other personal names were used at forts: those of his mother, Kypros, his father-in-law, Alexandros, and Marcus Antonius.

71. The Aktian games were considered equal in status to the Olympic games (Strabo 7.7.6; see also the allusion by Vergil, *Aeneid* 3.278–80). On the games generally, see Manfred Lämmer, "Die Aktischen Spiele von Nikopolis," *Stadion* 12–13 (1986–87): 27–38; Robert Alan Gurval, *Actium and Augustus: The Politics and Emotions of Civil War* (Ann Arbor, 1995), 74–81; on those at Jerusalem, see Lämmer, "The Introduction of Greek Contests into Jerusalem through Herod the Great and Its Political Significance," in *Physical Education and Sports in the Jewish History and Culture*, ed. Uriel Simri (n.p., 1973), 18–38; and his "Griechische Wettkämpfe in Jerusalem und ihre politischen Hintergründe," *Kölner Beiträge zur Sportwissenschaft* 2 (1974): 182–227, where he perhaps assumed more elaborate architectural constructions than necessary: see John H. Humphrey, *Roman Circuses: Arenas for Chariot Racing* (London, 1986), 528–33.

the athletic architectural repertory was Greek: the Romans were as yet little accustomed to and still suspicious of Greek-style athletic festivals. Rome does not seem to have had a permanent gymnasium until the time of that other hellenophilic athlete, Nero,[72] or a permanent stadium until the one built by Domitian.[73]

Gymnasia were the most common Herodian athletic constructions, but they seem to have been built only in Syria. Although a gymnasium had been built in Jerusalem as early as the second century B.C., such a construction was still seen as a conspicuous example of excessive hellenization,[74] something Herod would have sought to avoid. But he constructed gymnasia in the more appropriate environment of the hellenized cities of Syria, particularly Damaskos, Tripolis, and Ptolemais. None of these is known archaeologically: the only extant gymasium that may be Herodian is at Nikopolis. Baths would have been part of these structures,[75] and it is probable that the Herodian gymnasium was little different from the standard Greek type, which had been established in the fourth century B.C. and changed little, although its bathing component became more elaborate, until independent, Roman-style public baths became the dominant form.[76]

The hippodrome and stadium were also traditional Greek forms little changed since Classical times.[77] No Roman models existed in Herod's day, but Greek precedents were numerous. Herodian hippodromes may have existed at Jericho, Jerusalem, and Nikopolis, but these may merely have been open areas for racing rather than monumental constructions.[78] Although no stadium is specifically attributed to Herod in the literary sources, one existed at Caesarea at the time of Pontius Pilate[79] and known structures at Nikopolis and Sebaste are probably Herodian in origin. There

---

72. Suetonius, *Nero* 12; Tacitus, *Annals* 15.22; Richardson, *NTD*, 183; Giuseppina Ghini, "Gymnasium Neronis," in *LTUR*, 2: 374. Although Vitruvius referred to the gymnasium as a building type (calling it a palaestra, 5.11.1), he noted that it was not part of the standard Italian architectural repertory. See also Friedrich Rakob, "Hellenismus in Mittelitalien: Bautypen und Bautechnik," in *Hellenismus in Mittelitalien*, ed. Paul Zanker (*AbhGött* 97 [1976]), 369–70.

73. Suetonius, *Domitian* 5; Richardson, *NTD*, 366–67. Both Caesar (Suetonius, *Divine Julius* 39) and Augustus (Dio 53.1) built temporary ones.

74. *AJ* 17.240–41; 1 Macc. 1.15; 2 Macc. 4.9; see also Jean Delorme, *Gymnasion: Étude sur les monuments consacrés à l'éducation en Grèce* (BEFAR, 186 [Paris, 1960]), 198–99. According to Pausanias (10.4.1), a gymnasium was one of the defining elements of a Greek city.

75. Nielsen, *Thermae* (supra, n. 52), 103–4.

76. Lawrence (supra, n. 69), 349–50.

77. Ibid., 362.

78. Humphrey (supra, n. 71), 528–33.

79. *BJ* 2.172. Current excavation at Caesarea is revealing a stadium near the theater, which may be this structure: see Yosef Porath, "Herod's 'amphitheatre' at Caesarea: A Multi-Purpose Entertainment Building," in *The Roman and Byzantine Near East: Some Recent Archaeological Research* (*JRA*, suppl. 14 [1995]), 15–27.

is no evidence that Herod was particularly innovative in his use of these ancient Greek forms.

In addition to the buildings themselves, Herod's use of architectural decoration also demonstrated his interest in the latest Roman styles. Particularly important in the Herodian scheme were painting and mosaic. Mural painting is known from a number of sites, especially Caesarea, Jericho, Masada (fig. 33), and Herodeion. At the latter, the baths were decorated in colored panels and painted columns on projecting pedestals remindful of the Casa dei Grifi in Rome. The mural decoration of the palace at Masada, although simple, mixes colors in a particularly Italian visual style and includes garden scenes that seem to have been derived direct from specific Augustan paintings in Rome.[80] The theater paintings at Caesarea, if in fact Herodian, are in the same tradition. As usual, Herodian painting was in the forefront of contemporary technique, since full-fledged Second Style decoration appears at Herodeion and Masada. This is some of the first outside Italy, although it had existed at Rome and around Naples since early in the first century B.C., as evidence at the Casa dei Grifi, Boscoreale, and the Villa of the Mysteries attests.[81] Since these structures influenced Herodian residential construction, it is no surprise that their mural painting was also of importance to Herod.

Floor decoration was also a major element of the Herodian repertory. Most Herodian structures had mosaics, and numerous examples are known from the major sites, particularly Caesarea, Machairous,[82] and Masada (fig. 34).[83] Private houses in Jerusalem preserve mosaics that reflect the contemporary Herodian decoration. Figured scenes were avoided, but a large number of geometric and vegetal patterns were used. Many of the geometric patterns are quite ancient and generic in design, and some, such as the honeycomb pattern found at Masada, come not from Greco-Roman sources but from Babylonia and Assyria.[84] Yet the vegetal designs seem particularly Italian (although with Greek antecedents) and have affinities with Augustan vegetal decoration such as that found on the Ara Pacis.

Sculpture presented a problem, as it might be considered a graven image. Yet Herodian monumental and architectural sculpture did exist:[85]

80. Ling (supra, n. 65), 169; Gideon Foerster, *Masada*, vol 5: *Art and Architecture* (Jerusalem, 1995), xvii–xviii.

81. Klaus Fittschen, "Zur Herkunft und Entstehung des 2. Stils—Probleme und Argumente," in *Hellenismus in Mittelitalien*, ed. Paul Zanker (*AbhGött* 97 [1976]), 539–63.

82. Michele Piccirillo, *I mosaici di Giordania* (Rome, 1986) 31; Piccirillo, *Mosaics* (supra, n. 58), 245.

83. Asher Ovadiah, *Geometric and Floral Patterns in Ancient Mosaics* (Rome, 1980), 38–39; Asher Ovadiah, "Mosaic Pavements of the Herodian Period in Israel," *Mediterranean Historical Review* 5 (1990): 207–21; Foerster (supra, n. 80), xx–xxi.

84. Ovadiah, *Geometric and Floral Patterns* (supra, n. 83), 139.

85. *AJ* 15.329.

examples include the cult and harbor statues at Caesarea, and perhaps the decoration of the theater at Jerusalem and the sculpted panels (fig. 35) and Aphrodite at Askalon. Cult statues existed in the other temples to Augustus, and there were statues of Herod on the Athenian Akropolis and at Seia in Syria, and probably elsewhere in Greece, such as at Olympia. And it is hard to imagine that Herod's gymnasia, theaters, and other public buildings in the Greek world did not have a proper amount of statuary. Of all these, none is extant, except the dubious material from Askalon, which is anomalous and uncertain enough to be of little value in understanding the stylistic trends of putative Herodian sculpture.

According to Josephus,[86] the cult statues at Caesarea were modeled (προσείκασται) after the Zeus at Olympia and the Hera at Argos. What this word means is unclear: its basic definition is "to make or look like,"[87] but whether this implies a conscious effort or merely a general resemblance cannot be determined. Nor is it certain whether Josephus referred to the statues as a whole, or to specific elements of their technique, materials, pose, or decoration. It may simply have been an attempt to glorify Caesarea and Herod by exalting the art of the city, placing it in the mainstream of the best Classical tradition. The Pheidian statue of Zeus at Olympia was still renowned well into the Roman period as one of the great works of Greek art.[88] If Josephus intended to make a considered art-historical criticism, it means that the Herodian cult statues were based on models several hundred years old, and thus quite old-fashioned. This is improbable, and it is far more likely that Herod sought his inspiration for statuary from a familiar and well-used source, the buildings of Julius Caesar that contained statues of the Dictator himself.

Founding seven cities and creating major architectural constructions was an expensive undertaking. Although commentators have had difficulty in explaining the sources of the immense revenue required,[89] despite unusually detailed information about the finances of Judaea in the late first century B.C., the problem is not inscrutable and it is possible to reconstruct a clear pattern of Herod's income and expenditures. He inherited a great deal of wealth.[90] His father was a major landowner who had loaned money to the Nabataeans.[91] His mother, a Nabataean princess, would have had a

86. *BJ* 1.414.

87. See the entries in *LSJ*.

88. Pliny, *Natural History* 7.127; 36.18.

89. Jones, *Herods*, 86; the most complete discussion of the finances of Herod's kingdom is by Schalit, *KH*, 256–98; see also Shimon Applebaum, "Judaea as a Roman Province: The Countryside as a Political and Economic Factor," *ANRW* 2.8 (1977): 367–79, and Emilio Gabba, "The Finances of King Herod," in *Greece and Rome in Eretz Israel: Collected Essays*, ed. A. Kasher, U. Rappaport, and G. Fuks (Jerusalem, 1990), 160–68.

90. Schalit, *KH*, 257–60.

91. *AJ* 14.372; Gabba (supra, n. 89), 162.

substantial dowry, probably also in land: Herod thus would have obtained extensive revenue-producing lands from his parents.[92] He was able repeatedly to spend money with ease, lavishing financial donations on individuals, both compatriots and Romans, and on cities throughout the Greek world. Before he was king, he was able to pay for the restoration of Rhodes, although Josephus noted that he was not particularly wealthy at the time and spent beyond his means:[93] only a few weeks previously he had attempted unsuccessfully to borrow money from the Nabataean king Malichos (perhaps his uncle) in order to ransom his brother Phasael, who had been captured by the Hasmoneans and their Parthian allies.[94] But just after his return to Judaea in early 39 B.C., Herod was able to give each of his soldiers 150 drachmas each (and larger sums to his officers).[95] So it seems that in his early years he was wealthy, but not so rich that unexpected expenses were easy to meet.

In the early years of his kingship, his financial situation seems to have been steadily improving. He reluctantly paid the tribute Cleopatra assessed him,[96] entertained Octavian lavishly after Actium,[97] and began the construction of Sebaste a few years later. But the outlook was still precarious, since when a famine struck Judaea shortly afterward, he had to liquidate his personal art collection and purchase grain from Petronius, the prefect of Egypt.[98] It is probable that the cost of building Sebaste became a severe strain on his resources, although it was paid back in time because of the agricultural benefits produced by the revitalized city.

Yet this seems to have been the last financial problem Herod had. Judaea was steadily becoming more prosperous, largely through his own economic reforms, as the region made the transition from nomadism to pastoralism.[99] Like Sebaste, Phasaelis was founded with an economic purpose, the cultivation of previously unfarmed areas. Herodeion may originally have had the same intent.[100] Phasaelis eventually became the center of a wealthy agricultural zone and so rich that it was bequeathed to Livia by Herod's sister Salome, who had inherited it. Herod's personal prosperity was also augmented by confiscation of the lands of political opponents, particularly Has-

---

92. *AJ* 16.291.

93. *AJ* 14.378.

94. *AJ* 17.370–71; Jones, *Herods*, 91.

95. *BJ* 1.308.

96. *AJ* 15.106.

97. *BJ* 1.394; *AJ* 15.199.

98. *AJ* 15.299–316.

99. M. Rostovtzeff, *The Social and Economic History of the Roman Empire*, 2d ed. (Oxford, 1957), 271. For a more negative view of the effects of Herod's urbanization, see A. H. M. Jones, "The Urbanization of Palestine," *JRS* 31 (1931): 79–81.

100. Jones, *Herods*, 89.

moneans:[101] if this involved any redistribution, it would have aided in improving the economy of the country. An innovative sales tax, perhaps a Ptolemaic idea, also increased the revenue of the Herodian government.[102] By 20 B.C., Herod was able to reduce taxes by one-third,[103] even though construction of Caesarea had just begun and that of the Temple at Jerusalem was about to start. Josephus specifically noted that the Temple was built at Herod's own expense,[104] indicating an astonishing amassing of personal wealth in the few years since he had had to sell off his possessions to relieve the famine. He was also able to lend money to other area dynasts, particularly the Nabataeans,[105] to lighten the taxes of a number of towns in Kilikia,[106] and to pay the taxes of Chios.[107] When he spoke at the initiation of construction of the Temple in Jerusalem, in the autumn of 18 B.C., he specifically drew attention to the peace and prosperity Judaea now enjoyed.[108]

Rome also contributed to Herod's revenue. In 12 B.C., Augustus gave Herod the profits from half the Cypriot copper mines (and management of the other half, which implies certain additional revenues):[109] even if this were in return for the 300 talents Herod gave Augustus that year, it made a profitable investment.[110] And Rome may have made direct grants of funds for specific building projects: although none is documented in the case of Herod, this was standard imperial procedure, especially for rebuilding after natural disasters.[111]

101. *AJ* 17.305; Jones, *Herods*, 87.

102. *AJ* 17.205; Jones, *Herods*, 86–87.

103. *AJ* 15.365; Jones, *Herods*, 88. Herod may have also begun to receive revenue from Syria at this time: see Gabba (supra, n. 89), 163.

104. *AJ* 15.380.

105. *AJ* 16.279–91.

106. *BJ* 1.428.

107. *AJ* 16.26.

108. *AJ* 15.380–88.

109. The mines on Cyprus were royal property from an early date, eventually becoming part of the income of the Ptolemies (M. Rostovtzeff, *The Social and Economic History of the Hellenistic World* [Oxford, 1941], 339, 1173). When the island became a Roman province in 58 B.C., such revenue probably passed to the Roman government, but Caesar seems to have returned it to Egyptian control (Dio 42.35). The mines were presumably still under Ptolemaic control when Egypt became a Roman possession, and thus Octavian could claim them as his own, making the later donation to Herod possible.

110. *AJ* 16.128.

111. Stephen Mitchell, "Imperial Building in the Eastern Roman Provinces," *HSCP* 91 (1987): 343–52. See, e.g., the case of Tralleis in Asia Minor, which had suffered an earthquake, probably in 26 B.C. Its citizens appealed to Augustus, and the city was rebuilt at imperial expense (Strabo 12.8.18) and seems to have assumed the name Kaisareia, probably at the time of Augustus's trip to Asia Minor in 20 B.C. (BMC Lydia, cxl–cxli). Somewhat later, in A.D. 17, when an earthquake struck Sardis and other Asian cities, not only were financial benefits provided by Tiberius but the Senate sent one of its own, Marcus Ateius, as a commissioner to super-

Herod's will provides particularly detailed information about the state of his finances at the time of his death. He left 500,000 pieces of coined silver to his sister Salome, 10,000,000 to Augustus, and 5,000,000 to Livia, as well as other unspecified amounts to all his other relatives.[112] Since the kings of Judaea did not coin silver,[113] this must have been either Greek or Roman currency. Although Josephus regularly used drachmas as his standard of currency, even when totally inappropriate,[114] he scrupulously avoided mentioning any standard in describing the terms of Herod's will. It is thus likely that Josephus was quoting from the original document, and that the will itself (or the copy Josephus saw) was a Latin version, perhaps that made available to the imperial family in Rome,[115] and the currency used was Roman. The words *denarii* and *sestertii* were not commonly used in the Greek literature of Josephus's day,[116] and so Josephus wrote "coined silver." Thus the inheritance was at least 15,500,000 pieces of silver in either sestertii or denarii; if the latter, a total of 62,000,000 sestertii. By comparison, Augustus left an estate of 150,000,000 sestertii.[117] Thus Herod's estate might have been over one-third that of Augustus, not an inconsiderable sum for the king of a small territory who had spent vast amounts on royal building and other donations.

---

vise the reconstruction of the city (Tacitus, *Annals* 2.47): one would expect professional architects to have been on his staff. The excavations at Sardis have revealed evidence of his efforts (George M. A. Hanfmann, *Sardis from Prehistoric to Roman Times: Results of the Archaeological Exploration of Sardis, 1958–1975* [Cambridge, Mass., 1983], 141). For other similar examples, see Magie, *RR*, 469, and for the issue of professional architects and builders sent out from Rome, see Robert L. Hohlfelder, "Caesarea's Master Harbor Builders: Lessons Learned, Lessons Applied?" in *CMR*, 78–80.

112. *AJ* 17.189–90, 321; there were also nonmonetary donations. At *AJ* 17.146, other amounts are listed, but this is from an earlier and revoked will.

113. Menahem Stern, "The Herodian Dynasty and the Province of Judea at the End of the Period of the Second Temple," in *HP*, 169.

114. For example, *AJ* 8.189, a purchase of King Solomon, which Josephus converted from shekels (see 1 Kings 10.29), probably at a rate of four drachmas to one shekel (*AJ* 3.195); see also *AJ* 9.233. Another later but equally inappropriate use has the emperor Claudius using drachmas to pay off the Praetorian Guard who made him emperor (*AJ* 19.247).

115. Since the will was filed under Roman law—hence Augustus's involvement in the disputes regarding it—there was certainly a Latin copy in Rome at some time. See Harold W. Hoehner, *Herod Antipas* (Cambridge, 1972), 18–19.

116. Δηνάριον is rare until the second century A.C.: an early epigraphical use is *SEG* 16.490 (late first century B.C.: infra, p. 224). The author of the *Periplous of the Erythraian Sea*, writing around the middle of the first century after Christ, may have been one of the first to use it in literature (6, 8, 49), although he was hardly in the mainstream and used the term to mean "currency" rather than a specific amount. Σηστέρτιον seems primarily to be used in Greek epigraphically, never entering the literature, and only from the second century A.C. See the references in *LSJ*.

117. Suetonius, *Augustus* 101.

Nevertheless there were constant complaints about Herod's profligate nature. He was seen as a spendthrift who bankrupted his own citizens in order to enrich foreigners:[118] this was the point of view adopted by a Jewish embassy to Augustus at the time of Herod's death. Much of this was probably the traditional complaint of people everywhere: that their leaders overtax them and then misspend the money, coupled, in this case, with a substantial dose of xenophobia. It also probably represents the view of the old Hasmonean nobility, now dispossessed (if still alive), with their wealth confiscated.[119] Significantly, the complaints made no impression on Augustus, himself an astute fiscal manager. He ignored them and actually gave substantial funds to Herod's heirs, particularly dowries for his daughters Roxane and Salome,[120] demonstrating that Augustus saw himself in virtually a familial relationship with Herod.

It seems that Herod left Judaea substantially more prosperous than he found it, making significant steps toward its modernization and urbanization. In doing so, he replaced the old Hasmonean aristocracy with his new one, creating a source of discontent. After the famine of the mid-20's B.C., Herod's financial system seems to have been stable, with occasional donations from Rome assisting in making this possible. His reign was largely peaceful and followed nearly a century of intermittent civil war: this, if nothing else, would have stabilized the economy. His enormous building program caused financial problems at first—midway through the construction of Sebaste, he had clearly used up all his capital—but after the completion of the city, no further problems arose, and the building program became a major source of employment for many years: 18,000 were employed on the Jerusalem Temple alone.[121] Under the watchful eye of Augustus—who never seems to have objected to Herod's fiscal policy, although frequently criticizing his relationships with surrounding states and his family—Herod and Judaea prospered. Although Augustus made major adjustments to the political organization of the region, he left Herod's fiscal arrangements untouched, beyond remitting some of the taxes of Samaria,[122] a political decision rather than a financial one, and one that would nevertheless not have been possible if the economy had not been stable.

No substantial changes were made in the tax structure during the remaining years of the Herodian dynasty, yet by the time of the death of

118. *BJ* 2.85–86; *AJ* 16.150–59; 17.304–7.
119. *AJ* 17.305; Martin Goodman, *The Ruling Class of Judaea* (Cambridge, 1987), 38.
120. *BJ* 2.99; *AJ* 17.321–23.
121. The construction of the Temple may have been the principal industry of Jerusalem for nearly a century, and thus, as a local reinvestment of revenue, a major stimulus to the economy. See Gabba (supra, n. 89), 166.
122. *AJ* 17.317–21.

Herod's grandson Agrippa I, fifty years later, and despite substantial further income, the family's wealth was exhausted, and Agrippa died in debt.[123] Although he too was an extensive builder, his constructions were nowhere near the magnitude of those of his grandfather, and his ability to exhaust the money of his family with minimal building in a short reign indicates that building programs were not a major expenditure of any of the Herodian kings.

123. *AJ* 19.352.

CHAPTER EIGHT

Catalogue of Herod's Building Program

INTRODUCTION

The following catalogues are divided geographically between Herod's king-dom and external areas. Any site that was ever within Herod's kingdom, regardless of the date of building, is listed in Part 1; all others are in Part 2. An attached bibliography for each place lists only those sources that illumi-nate the period of Herod the Great. Three different types of sites have been included:

1. The sites within Herod's kingdom that were the focus of major Herodian architectural endeavors (Caesarea, Jericho, Jerusalem, Masada, Sebaste). All these sites have been extensively excavated and published. Although there is a wide divergence of opinion regarding the relationship of visible and excavated remains to the Herodian building program, the entries in the following catalogue are of necessity brief and are not meant to replace the previously published material. Thorough summaries and varying points of view are available in the *New Encyclopedia of Archaeological Excava-tions in the Holy Land* (*NEAEHL*).

2. Other sites both inside and outside Herod's kingdom. Knowledge about these varies immensely: some sites, such as the fortresses around the Dead Sea and the Jordan, are well known, even if not excavated or published. In other cases (e.g., Bathyra), attribution of a statement by Josephus to a particular site is nearly impossible. Identification of Herodian material depends on the vicissitudes of later occupation and excavation. When the Herodian contribution was a minor part of a lengthy urban history, as in the Syrian and Phoenician cities, the remains are often difficult to find.

3. Sites where excavators have found "Herodian" material (e.g., Horbat Masad), or where historical tradition or architectural evidence gives a strong probability of building by Herod (e.g., Hebron). Vagueness of interpretation often causes uncertainty as to whether remains suggested to be "Herodian" actually belong to the period of Herod the Great, but other indicators, such as ceramics, can provide a clue. Excluded are casual and minor constructions that do not seem to fit the category of royal building, such as the possibly Herodian frontier forts on the south edge of the kingdom, which are highly utilitarian and of uncertain date.[1]

Obviously, Herod was not responsible for all building in his kingdom during his reign, and only those sites that seem to be indicative of royal patronage are included. Moreover, there is no guarantee that these catalogues include all the royal building done by Herod; in fact, there is every certainty that they do not. The literary and archaeological evidence used to create the catalogues is by nature incomplete, as excavation and surface surveys have not revealed all the Herodian remains, and Josephus's interest in the Herodian building program was secondary to his larger purpose. He was no Pausanias. As an example of the unanswered quandaries regarding sites, one may consider Oresa (or Rhesa, or even Thresa: not even the exact form of its name is known with certainty). It was mentioned by Josephus in two pairs of repeated references to a fortress between Herodeion and Masada at which Herod briefly stayed ca. 42 B.C., and that he eventually captured in 39 or 38 B.C.[2] The pattern is similar to Herod's early relationship with other Hasmonean fortresses that he eventually made his own. Although the site has been identified with biblical Horesa, where David hid in the wilderness, perhaps modern Khirbet Khoreisa, southeast of Hebron, it is essentially unknown, and no further information is forthcoming.[3] Equally enigmatic is Drousias, mentioned only by Ptolemy,[4] whose name is perhaps preserved in Khirbet Drousia, north of Beit Guvrin,[5] or it may be located at et-Majdal in the Plain of Sharon.[6] Such a site would have been named after a Drusus, such as Nero Claudius Drusus, brother of the emperor Tiberius, who was the eponym for the large tower at the Caesarea harbor, but there were several

---

1. M. Gihon, "Idumea and the Herodian Limes," *IEJ* 17 (1967): 27–42.

2. *BJ* 1.266, 294; *AJ* 14.361, 400.

3. 1 Sam. 23.15; F.-M. Abel, *Géographie de la Palestine* (Paris, 1938), 2: 349–50; Michael Avi-Yonah, *Gazetteer of Roman Palestine* (*Qedem* 5 [Jerusalem, 1976]), 85; *TIR-IP*, 98 (Caphar Orsa).

4. Ptolemy 5.15.

5. Abel (supra, n. 3) 2.309; *TIR-IP*, 114.

6. Avi-Yonah (supra, n. 3), 52.

other men named Drusus who are possible candidates, including a great-grandson of Herod's who died before adolescence.[7]

Moreover, there are certain vague indications in the text of Josephus and elsewhere of additional building by Herod. Josephus wrote repeatedly that Herod made *euergesiai* or *doreai*. *Doreai* are gifts. *Euergesia* is a word used frequently by Josephus in regard to royal patronage: it described to the Roman Senate the actions of Herod's father.[8] Although originally meaning "good deeds,"[9] by the Hellenistic period it had come to mean services, especially public ones, and had even become the name of a royal festival on Delos.[10] To Josephus, the term is generally vague, with the predilection for services simply a character trait of the person involved. Clearly, neither *doreai* nor *euergesiai* need to have been architecture, and they were in many cases probably financial, but given Herod's attitudes and Josephus's more than occasional mentions of *euergesia* in an architectural context, constructions should not be ruled out. Often these are credited to a region, in particular Asia,[11] Ionia,[12], Kilikia,[13] and Syria.[14] No towns are specified in these districts, although sites within them may be mentioned in other contexts,

7. *AJ* 18.132.

8. *AJ* 14.384.

9. *Odyssey* 22.235.

10. *SEG* 2.588.43.

11. *AJ* 16.24. The context is Herod's return from the Bosporos with Marcus Agrippa in the late summer of 14 B.C., when they traveled from Pontos through Paphlagonia, Kappadokia, and Great Phrygia to Ephesos. Herod was particularly interested in the local Jewish populations (*AJ* 14.111), and he and Agrippa could ensure that their donations to the Temple in Jerusalem would never again be appropriated by a Roman official, as had happened with L. Valerius Flaccus in 62 B.C. (Cicero, *Pro Flacco* 68–69).

12. *BJ* 1.425. The term used is *doreai*, and may imply financial donations rather than architecture, but the passage is in the midst of a discussion of the Herodian building program. Again the chronological context may be the late summer of 14 B.C.

13. Herod lightened the taxes of a number of Kilikian towns (*BJ* 1.428), which presumably meant a direct payment to Roman officials, as he did in the case of Chios (*AJ* 16.26). He was in Kilikia frequently, since it was in the territory of the Kappadokian king Archelaos, father-in-law of Herod's son Alexandros. But it is unlikely that Herod would have impinged on the territory of another client king who was himself a notable builder (infra, pp. 251–53).

14. Herod gave *euergasiai* to unspecified Syrian cities (*AJ* 16.146). Most of the major Syrian cities of Herod's day are cited elsewhere (*BJ* 1.422–27) as recipients of architectural patronage: the only omission is the obscure but prosperous city of Chalkis (Diodoros 33.4a), which was to become the capital of a territory ruled by Herod's grandson, also named Herod, in A.D. 41 (*BJ* 2.217–23; *AJ* 19.277). The interest of Herod's grandson in this city may indicate it had been favored by the founder of the dynasty, but the site has never been excavated. See Paul Monceaux and Léonce Brossé, "Chalcis ad Belum: Note sur l'histoire et les ruines de la ville," *Syria* 6 (1925): 339–50; Miller, *RNE*, 87–88, 238, 260, 270–71; M. C. A. MacDonald, "Herodian Echoes in the Syrian Desert," in *Trade, Contact, and the Movement of Peoples in the Eastern Mediterranean: Studies in Honour of J. Basil Hennessy*, ed. Stephen Bourke and Jean-Paul Descoeudres (*MeditArch*, suppl. 3 [Sydney, 1995]), 285–90.

such as Phaselis or Balaneia.[15] None of these places has enough evidence, either literary or archaeological, to justify being included in the catalogue, and for some, particularly Lykia and Kilikia, there are good arguments that Herod did not build there.[16]

Three other sites may have been the recipients of Herodian building, but the evidence is highly speculative. Herod seems to have spent a fair amount of time on Mytilene, whose theater is said to have been the prototype for that of Pompey in Rome.[17] Syrian Seia had a statue of Herod in its sanctuary of Ba'al Shamin (fig. 26), and was eventually within Herod's kingdom.[18] And the island of Syros has yielded an inscription mentioning Herod, but it is probably from Delos.[19] In none of these cases is there any solid evidence of royal patronage. There are many gaps in the topographical history of the Roman east, some of which may hide unknown parts of the Herodian building program.[20]

PART 1: SITES WITHIN HEROD'S KINGDOM

Agrippias

The coastal city of Anthedon, near Gaza, has a vague history. It is not documented before Hellenistic times, but its name indicates that it was founded

---

15. Herod remitted the taxes of these cities (*BJ* 1.428). Phaselis, in Lykia, seems to have been in a state of poverty (Lucan, *Pharsalia* 8.251–54), and despite Herod's largesse, showed few signs of recovery until the second century A.D. (Helmut Schläger and Jörg Schäfer, "Phaselis: Zur Topographie der Stadt und des Hafengebietes," *AA* 86 [1971]: 542–61). Balaneia ("baths") is a common toponym, but Herod probably assisted the one in the district of Arados in Syria (Strabo 16.2.12; see also Pliny, *Natural History* 5.79): modern Banijas may preserve the name. See I. Benzinger, "Balanaia," in *RE*, 2 (1896): 2816–17; René Dussaud, *Topographie historique de la Syrie antique et médiévale* (Paris, 1927): 128–29; Millar, *RNE*, 260.

16. As noted (supra, n. 13), Kilikia was within the sphere of interest of Archelaos of Kappadokia; Lykia was essentially an independent state in Herod's day, neither a client kingdom nor a province, and thus perhaps of marginal interest. On Lykia in the first century B.C., see Magie, *RR*, 516–39.

17. *AJ* 15.350; 16.17. On Roman Mytilene, see Hector Williams, "Notes on Roman Mytilene," in *The Greek Renaissance in the Roman Empire*, ed. Susan Walker and Averil Cameron (*BICS*, suppl. 55 [1989]), 163–68.

18. Infra, pp. 272–73.

19. *IG* 12.5.713.6; Ersie Mantzoulinou-Richards, "From Syros: A Dedicatory Inscription of Herodes the Great from an Unknown Building," *AncW* 18 (1988): 87–99. Despite the inscription, the total obscurity of Syros in any period makes it an unlikely candidate for royal patronage, and material from Delos has regularly ended up on Syros.

20. One also wonders about the obscure Syrian city of Mariamme or Mariammia (the form used by Pausanias of Damaskos in his *Founding of Antioch* of the fourth century A.C. [*FGrHist*, #854, fr. 8]), a city with the same name as two of Herod's wives. Although mentioned by Arrian (*Anabasis* 2.13.8) in the context of Alexander the Great, the citation may reflect a more Roman perspective, as Pliny is the earliest extant source (*Natural History* 5.81–82; E. Honigmann, "Mariame" [#3], in *RE*, 14 [1930]: 1745–46).

much earlier: its mother city was probably Boiotian Anthedon, already old when mentioned by Homer (*Iliad* 2.508), which was one of Boiotia's few seaports and thus a center for external contacts. Palestinian Anthedon was incorporated into Jewish territory at the time of Alexandros Jannaios (*AJ* 13.395), perhaps resulting in a decline in importance, because it was rebuilt by Gabinius in the 50's B.C. (*BJ* 1.166; *AJ* 14.88). Yet its renewed prosperity was short, for it was destroyed in the warfare surrounding Herod's accession (*BJ* 1.416), and it may also have suffered in the earthquake of 31 B.C. It became part of Herod's kingdom after the death of Antonius and Cleopatra, along with other depopulated coastal towns (*BJ* 1.396; *AJ* 15.217). Herod eventually rebuilt it and renamed it Agrippias (*BJ* 1.87, 118; *AJ* 13.357; *BJ* 1.416 has Agrippeion, but the feminine form is the proper one, since the word *polis* is also feminine). Herod's city-name did not last long—hence Josephus's confusion as to the exact orthography—for it had reverted to Anthedon by the 30's A.C. (*AJ* 18.158). It was only the second time Herod had built where Gabinius had (the other was Samaria): perhaps, late in life, Herod was not as sensitive to the political subtleties that had led him to rebuild a major Gabinian site early in his career and then to avoid all others.

The date of Herod's construction is not documented, but it was probably after Marcus Agrippa's death in 12 B.C. Herod's work at the city may have been slight, since Josephus provided no details, and the city soon reverted to its pre-Herodian name. Its construction may simply have been repair after the disruptions of the 30's B.C., but if Herod did not build at the city until after 12 B.C., the damage of twenty years previously could not have been great, and a project so late in Herod's life would have been modest.

Despite Pliny's curious statement that Anthedon was an inland city (*Natural History* 5.68), its Greek name, the nature of its donation by Octavian to Herod, and its listed position in Ptolemy's *Geography* (5.15) make it clear that it was a coastal town. Except for W. M. Flinders Petrie, topographers have consistently located Anthedon at the site of Khirbet Teda, on the coast north of Gaza. The site is unexcavated, however, and there are no visible remains that shed light on Herod's constructions.

Gatt, *ZDPV* 7 (1884): 1–14; Phythian-Adams, *PEFQ* 1923: 11–17; Petrie, *Anthedon (Sinai)* (*BSAE* 58 [1937]); Abel, *Géographie* (1938), 2: 244–45; Fossey, *Topography and Population of Ancient Boiotia* (1988), 252–57 (Boiotian Anthedon); *TIR-IP*, 63.

Alexandreion

The site of Alexandreion lies north of Jericho on the west side of the Jordan, at the northern edge of Herod's original kingdom (figs. 6, 18). It had presumably existed as a fortress since Hellenistic times and was perhaps originally built by Alexandros Jannaios, but nothing is known about its history before the time of Pompey. At that time, it was already noted for its beauty (*AJ* 14.49; see also *BJ* 1.134) and may have served as a treasury (Strabo 16.2.40). The Hasmonean Aristoboulos II hid there from Pompey, and his son Alexandros rebuilt or fortified the site in his defense against Gabinius in the 50's B.C. (*BJ* 1.161; *AJ* 14.83) and may have named it at that time. Gabinius eventually destroyed the fortress (*BJ* 1.168, *AJ* 14.89–90), and it was abandoned for nearly twenty years until Herod ordered his brother Pheroras to rebuild it (*BJ* 1.308; *AJ* 14.419). This was probably early in 38 B.C., during the first winter Herod spent in Judaea after his return from Rome (*BJ* 1.290, 302, 304). It was thus one of Herod's earliest constructions, part of a chain of fortresses across the northern and eastern perimeter of Judaea. Although there is no specific information as to why Herod chose this site, its previous history as a fortress showed its value. It may have been considered particularly useful because of the imminent war against Parthia; one suspects that Herod may also have had in mind potential defense against Roman Syria.

The site, location of a Herodian treasury (*AJ* 16.317), figured variously in the politics of Herod's career. He entertained Marcus Agrippa there in 15 B.C. (*AJ* 16.13). It was where his wife Mariamme was incarcerated (*AJ* 15.184–185) and where his sons Alexandros and Aristoboulos were buried after their execution (*BJ* 1.551, *AJ* 16.394), a particular irony, since they were the daughter and grandsons of Alexandros the builder of the fortress, who was also buried there. Herod's contributions to the architecture of the site may have been minimal. His failure to rename it is unusual among Herodian sites (although he may have wished to continue to honor his father-in-law), and the scarcity of remains and short history of occupation implies a modest construction. When Herod's kingdom was expanded to the northeast in the 20's B.C., its role as a frontier fortress diminished. Herod would have renamed it if it had remained important after Alexandros ceased to be his father-in-law, since it is hardly likely that he would have continued to honor the father of a discredited and executed spouse. Alexandreion is not mentioned after the burials of Herod's sons there in 7 B.C., and it may already have fallen into disuse, to be completely abandoned and destroyed soon after. It seems to have ceased to exist by the time of Vespasian.

Alexandreion is located at modern Qarn Sartabeh, a promontory at 380 m elevation rising some 700 m above the Jordan valley. It lies directly north of Herod's city of Phasaelis and is conspicuous from that site (fig. 6). Although attribution as Herodian Alexandreion is not in dispute, there are few visible remains. Early visitors saw an artificial platform on the summit and fragments of ashlar masonry whose blocks seemed Herodian in origin but that had more recently been piled into a crude fortress. A cursory examination of the surface pottery in 1935 revealed only Late Hellenistic and

Early Roman wares, consistent with the brief history of the site. Limited excavations in the early 1980's yielded a peristyle attributed to Herod, a square building 19.2 m on a side, with colonnades forming an interior square of 9.6 m. The columns, of the Corinthian order, were plastered with stucco; a mosaic floor, hardly preserved, was in the center. Particularly sophisticated are the complex hydraulic installations, which include an aqueduct 5 km long, leading to a number of cisterns.

Abel, *RBibl* 10 (1913): 227–34; Moulton, *BASOR* 62 (April 1936): 14–18; Plöger, *ZDPV* 71 (1955): 142–48; Tsafrir, *JC* 2 (1982): 120–25; Garbrecht and Peleg, *AntW* 20.2 (1989): 2–20; Tsafrir and Magen, *NEAEHL*, 1318–20; *TIR-IP*, 60–61.

Antipatris

On the most beautiful plain of his kingdom, Herod founded the city of Antipatris, named after his father. The district was noted for its fertility, with a river flowing around the city, a rich and lush plain, and particularly large trees (*BJ* 1.417; *AJ* 16.142–43; Sextus Julius Africanus, *Chronography* 17.4; Stephanos s.v.; Synkellos 581, 594). Antipatris was in the vicinity of biblical Aphek (*BJ* 2.513) and may have been the city of Arethousa that Pompey liberated (*BJ* 1.156; *AJ* 14.75). Hellenistic Pegai was also nearby (*AJ* 13.261): the area was notorious for its numerous name changes. Although the city figured in events of the later Herodian dynasty (*BJ* 2.513–14, 554, 4.443), no details regarding Herod's construction are extant. Josephus implied that it was not founded until after the dedication of Caesarea, ca. 10 B.C. (*AJ* 16.142); this would make Antipatris the last dated Herodian construction.

Herod's Antipatris has long been identified with the site of Ras el-'Ain, a mound that was surrounded in the late nineteenth century by swamps, perhaps a remnant of the river that once flowed around the city. The site had been occupied since the Bronze Age, so Antipatris does not seem to have been a new foundation. Extensive amounts of Hellenistic pottery may indicate that the town of Pegai, perhaps renamed Arethousa by Pompey, was rebuilt by Herod as Antipatris. Pegai/Arethousa may have been damaged in the earthquake of 31 B.C.

Archaeological excavation at Ras el-'Ain since the 1930's has revealed various remnants of the Roman city, although most of the remains are later than the Herodian period—the city lasted until the fifth century A.C.—and attribution of particular elements to Herod's constructions is not certain. Evidence has been found of the main street, flanked by colonnades and shops, and a large building built of ashlar masonry. Few obviously Herodian details have been found, but it has been suggested that the street was part of Herod's reconstruction. As is often the case, the most conspicuous Roman remains are from the Severan period.

Albright, *JPOS* 3 (1923): 50–53; Netzer, *Nikopolis* 1 (1987): 126–27; Kochavi, *BiblArch* 44 (1981): 75–86; *TIR-IP*, 63.

Bathyra

In the last years of his reign, Herod established a military colony named Bathyra at the northeast corner of his kingdom. In the late 20's B.C., Augustus gave Herod lands northeast of the Sea of Galilee that had been subject to brigandage and general civil disorder, causing the local inhabitants to appeal for help to the governor of Syria (*AJ* 15.343–48). But the situation did not stabilize over the next decade, and when Herod was in Italy in 12 B.C., open rebellion broke out, in part fomented by the Nabataean Syllaios, still ill disposed to Herod because of the latter's breaking up of his relationship with Salome. Herod was given permission by the Roman authorities in Syria to invade Nabataea. Although Herod scrupulously did not act before he had permission and made a full report about his successful invasion, Syllaios had gone to Rome to plead his case and was at the imperial court when news of Herod's invasion arrived. Thus Augustus heard Syllaios's version before he heard about it from either Herod or the Roman officials in Syria. Augustus was particularly offended at Herod's actions and wrote to him that their friendship was at an end (*AJ* 16.271–92). Despite the military success of Herod's invasion, Syllaios's intrigues in Rome incited further rebellion. It was only when Nikolaos of Damaskos presented Herod's side of things to Augustus—and, presumably, when Augustus had also received field reports from his personnel in Syria—that Herod and Augustus were reconciled (*AJ* 17.52–57); Syllaios was then condemned to death (*AJ* 16.351–53; Strabo 16.4.24).

In light of these problems, which almost destroyed his relationship with Augustus, Herod decided that a strong local presence in the unstable northeastern areas of his kingdom was necessary. Accordingly, he gave land in the district of Batanaia to a group of 600 Babylonian Jews, including 500 cavalry, who were staying near Antioch. Their leader was a certain Zamaris. Fortresses and a settlement were built, and the colony was named Bathyra, a name of unknown specific origin but perhaps indicating that the site lay in a valley. The inhabitants obtained the land free of charge and were exempt from taxation, although this changed under Herod's successors (*AJ* 17.26–28).

The precedent for the establishment of this colony was Hellenistic, following Seleukid patterns of giving land to supporters of the king, modified to some extent by the Roman concept of veterans' colonies and the realities of Roman policy, which discouraged offensive military expeditions by a client king. Augustus's intense displeasure at what seemed to be an unauthorized military expedition by Herod outside his kingdom—even if the facts were not yet clear and the strategic concerns obvious—was a lesson to

Herod about the limitations of client kingship. He astutely responded by creating Bathyra on generous terms, leaving the responsibility of defense to the new landowner, Zamaris, and exonerating himself from any future charges of aggressiveness unbecoming to a client king. Eventually, Zamaris and his descendants became one of the most important families in southern Syria and Galilee.

The physical nature of Bathyra and its location cannot be determined with precision. The details provided by Josephus are slight: that Zamaris built on the land a *kome* and *phrouria* (*AJ* 17.26). The latter is Josephus's standard word for a fortress, whether a massive structure like the Antonia in Jerusalem (*BJ* 1.118) or Masada (*BJ* 1.264), or a temporary hilltop fortification used in a military engagement (*BJ* 1.380). *Kome* is contrasted with *polis* and is often a dependency of the latter (*AJ* 20.159), with less population and less well fortified (*AJ* 18.28). Josephus wrote that Bathyra was a *kome* no smaller than a *polis* (*AJ* 17.23), so the distinction was a political rather than a demographic or physical one, but Bathrya had only one-tenth as many settlers as Sebaste (*BJ* 1.403). If the toponym Bathyra has any literal force, one might imagine a small valley town, perhaps without fortifications, with small garrisons in the surrounding hills. Since it was virtually an independent state (*AJ* 17.28), it presumably had appropriate civic institutions, perhaps with some sort of legal and constitutional system as at Sebaste (*BJ* 1.403). Yet there is no indication as to what sort of civic buildings Bathyra had, or whether there was any monumental architecture. One might expect at least a bouleuterion, agora, and subordinate structures, but they would have been modest.

The location of Bathyra is also uncertain. The only information provided by Josephus is that it was in eastern Batanaia on the frontier between Trachonitis and Jewish territory (*AJ* 17.25–26). Various suggestions that have been made are all onomastic. The most common location is in the vicinity of Basir or Nawa, some 60 km east-northeast of the Sea of Galilee, first proposed in the 1920's, when René Dussaud noted that Basir was a particularly favorable location for observation of the surrounding territory.

Dussaud, *Topographie historique* (1927), 330–31; Klein, *BJPES* 4 (1936): 33–34; Abel, *Géographie* (1938), 2: 261; Cohen, *TAPA* 103 (1972): 83–95; Stern, *HP*, 115–16; Avi-Yonah, *Gazetteer* (1976), 35; MacAdam, *BAR-IS* 295 (1986): 65.

Caesarea

In the early years of Herod's reign, his kingdom lacked a major port city. It was only to be expected that eventually his building efforts would create the seaport that any major state was expected to have. Athens, Seleukid Syria, and, perhaps most significant, Ptolemaic Egypt, possessed the great seaports of the eastern Mediterranean, and Herod's own building program had begun at the famous Hellenistic port city of Rhodes.

Building a harbor was not one of Herod's initial priorities. He used existing seaports on the fringes of his kingdom, especially Ptolemais and Askalon, for nearly twenty years before construction of his own. Although a seaport was crucial in establishing the identity of his kingdom, and would have had a military function as well (*AJ* 15.293), it was not the vital political necessity that fortresses, palaces, and religious structures were. And because there was no major port within the confines of the kingdom, such a construction would be a totally new endeavor, not simply a rebuilding. A desire to complete the project in the most expert way would have led Herod to postpone it as long as possible (as the Temple in Jerusalem was postponed even longer).

Conversion of Samaria to Sebaste may be seen as a trial effort at Herodian city-foundation. Completion of Sebaste around 22 B.C. led naturally to the initiation of the greatest urban construction of the Herodian program. The coast of Herod's kingdom, the long smooth eastern edge of the Mediterranean, was notorious for its lack of harbors (*AJ* 15.333). For the site of his seaport, Herod chose the Hellenistic town of Straton's Tower (*BJ* 1.408; *AJ* 15.331), which had been prominent in its day, but had suffered in the earthquake of 31 B.C. and was now destroyed, or at best dilapidated and decayed. There was no constructed harbor at Straton's Tower (Strabo 16.2.27), only an anchorage and roadstead, but its location at the northern edge of Herod's seacoast meant that it was closest to Rome and Greece. The droughts and famine that afflicted Judaea in the mid-20's B.C., when Herod had to convert his personal treasures into coinage to send to Egypt to pay for emergency shipments of grain (*AJ* 15.299–316), may have catalyzed the beginning of construction. He realized at this time that whatever the political benefits of a major port city, the economic security of the kingdom depended on a good harbor and its associated warehouses.

He named the city Caesarea (map 8), as a counterpart to Sebaste, thus honoring Augustus in both Latin and Greek forms, although the name was quickly, if not originally, hellenized into Kaisareia. Those knowledgeable about the latest in contemporary architecture would also have been reminded of the name Kaisareion, innovative structures built at Alexandria and Antioch by Julius Caesar. Thus by implication Herod also honored Caesar, whose bestowal of Roman citizenship on Herod's father had eased Herod's future career. Clearly, the town was named just Caesarea, with no qualifying second name. But the eventual commonness of the toponym led to Herod's Caesarea being called Caesarea Maritima or even Caesarea Palaestinae, both names that are anachronistic to the Herodian era.

Josephus was fairly precise about the date of founding and constructing of Caesarea. The city was completed during Ol. 192 (12–9 B.C.), or the twenty-eighth year of Herod's reign, probably 10 B.C. (*AJ* 16.136–37), although it is possible that the official foundation ceremonies were held in 13 B.C. to coincide with Augustus's fiftieth birthday. It took either 10 (*AJ* 16.136) or 12 (*AJ* 15.341) years to complete, which would mean construction began in either 22 or 20 B.C. The earlier date is when Marcus Agrippa was at Mytilene—Herod visited him there during the winter of 23/22 B.C.— and it has been assumed that this contact might have prompted Herod to begin construction the following year, although Josephus's text gives no hint of this. Herod's trip to Rome and presence at the *ludi saeculares* in 17 B.C. may further have provided inspiration for the city and the festivals that accompanied its dedication. Various parts of the city were functioning by late 15 B.C., since Agrippa was entertained there and Josephus implied that the harbor was completed by then (*AJ* 16.13). By 14 B.C., Caesarea had become the principal port of entry into Judaea, replacing Ptolemais (*AJ* 16.62).

The showplace of the city was its port, named Sebastos Harbor (*BJ* 1.613; *AJ* 17.87; fig. 5), to which Josephus devoted some of his most lavish description (*BJ* 1.408–14; *AJ* 15.331–41). It was one of the largest harbors in the Roman world, bigger than Peiraieus. Particularly difficult of construction, because of the currents and siltation of the area, the harbor contained multiple inner anchorages and a massive breakwater 200 feet across. According to Josephus, the blocks for these constructions were 50 feet long and up to 18 feet wide and were sunk into 20 *orgyai* (the interval between the outstretched arms) of water. There were towers along the breakwater, of which the largest was the Drousion, built in imitation of the Pharos of Alexandria. It was named after Nero Claudius Drusus, the younger son of Livia and brother of the future emperor Tiberius. Why a construction was named after a young (and to Herod, obscure) member of the imperial family who spent all his career in the north and seems never to have been in the East (if Herod ever met him, it would have been in Rome in 17 B.C.) is not a matter of particular curiosity. Drusus died in Germany in 9 B.C., shortly after the lavish festivities and spectacles for the dedication of Caesarea, which were largely financed by Livia, Drusus's mother. When he died a few months later, it must have seemed only natural to name a structure in the city after him, even if he did not fit the standard criterion of having benefited Herod personally.

A second breakwater, to the north of the first, created an enclosed harbor with an opening to the north (the direction of the most favorable winds); a lighthouse stood at the end of this breakwater. The harbor itself had numerous docks and piers and a broad quay on the landward side, which became popular as a promenade. There were also numerous (or narrow) *psalides* along the quay for the use of ships entering the harbor, built into the breakwater as shelter for seamen. The basic meaning of *psalis* is "scissors" (*LSJ*), which implies a cutting or clipping: hence the most appropriate connotation is docks cut into the quay. Although in Hellenistic times the word was occasionally used to mean a vault, Josephus's description makes it clear that maritime installations for the convenience of sailors are meant.

The city proper was laid out on a regular orthogonal grid. Prominent from the harbor—and from some distance out to sea—was the Temple of Augustus, raised on a high platform. It contained cult statues of both Augustus and Roma, which were compared, perhaps with some exaggeration, to the Zeus at Olympia and the Hera at Argos. The Temple of Augustus was one of several temples in the city, but no details of the others were provided.

After describing the harbor and quayside in some detail, Josephus passed briefly over the other components of the city: the theater (in a seaside location), amphitheater (where some of the dedicatory festivities of the city may have been held), agoras, and public buildings. Herod's palace was particularly lavish. The building material was all imported, with extensive use of "white stone" (Josephus's common term for marble). Of note was the sophisticated sewer system in the city, which was self-flushing by the action of the sea. That the city had aqueducts leading into it may be assumed, even though this was not recorded by Josephus. He did not mention a hippodrome either, but circus entertainments occurred at the dedication of the city, and it is inconceivable that the Kaisareia, the quinquennial games of the city, did not require some sort of a racecourse or circus. The Kaisareia survived at least into the second century A.C., when M. Aelius Aurelius Menander of Aphrodisias, a notable athlete of his day, won the pankration. Josephus also ignored the city walls, perhaps because they were purely functional and undecorative, and because his description is based on a seaward rather than a landward approach to the city. Yet walls were a necessary component of a great city, even if not needed for defense, and Caesarea was conceptually completed by its simple wall circuit, which defined its limits. The city was a particularly rich repository of art, especially public statues: six colossai stood at the mouth of the harbor, in direct (and hyperbolic) imitation of the Kolossos of Rhodes at the site of Herod's first building effort. Josephus called the plan on which the city as a whole was laid out μεγαλοπρεπής (magnificent), a word consistently used by Herodotos [5.18] and others to describe the grandiose actions of great men.

The Physical Remains of Caesarea.   The rich and expansive site of Caesarea, whose name has never been lost, has been the scene of major excavations for many years, especially since the 1940's. Unfortunately, a series of uncoordinated and unnecessarily competitive field projects has left an excavation history that is far less than the sum of its parts. Caesarea has tended to overwhelm the field archaeologist, and meticulous excavation of a few square meters of a city often tells nothing about broader questions of history or culture. Fieldwork has gravitated toward the spectacular (and touristically acceptable) rather than an overall understanding of what is both the last of the great Hellenistic city foundations and the first newly built eastern Roman provincial capital. In addition, recent development of the site as a resort and industrial area has meant that since the early 1980's much of the city has been irrevocably lost to the archaeologist. Nevertheless, most of the urban components mentioned by Josephus, as well as others of the Herodian period, have been revealed in the excavations, although the lack of a comprehensive urban survey (which it is no longer possible to make) has meant that these discoveries have stood in isolation rather than integrating into an overall understanding of the history of urbanization.

The Harbors.   The harbors of Caesarea have been the focus of a great deal of archaeological activity, especially since the late 1970's (fig. 5). Josephus's description is largely accurate, although exaggerated and short on technical understanding. There was no harbor at the site in Hellenistic times, but a seawall or quay existed where small ships could dock, in water less than 2 m deep, with a roadstead further out for larger ships. The Herodian builders constructed two massive breakwaters, much as Josephus described, which today have largely sunk beneath the sea level because of subsidence of as much as 7 m. The southern breakwater begins at a natural promontory and runs west for 200 m, then northwest for 300 m, eventually turning back east to create an entrance to the harbor. It is substantially wider than Josephus reported. A structure 15 by 40 m lying against the inside of the breakwater may be the ruins of one of the towers. In addition, remnants of a northward-leading mole mark the separation of the harbor into a large outer harbor and two smaller inner harbors.

At the end of the breakwater, massive piles of ashlars up to 5 m across are presumably the remains of the lighthouse that stood at the entrance. This may be the Drousion, although Josephus implied that it was not at the end of the breakwater. The enclosure of the harbor area was completed by a northern breakwater, which extended west for 180 m from another natural outcrop. Although the remains are largely from a Byzantine rebuilding of ca. A.D. 500, the original construction is Herodian. Rectangular blocks north of the breakwater may have been the bases for the statues Josephus described as adorning the entrance to the harbor: one pair of blocks, 4 m apart and 6–7 m north of the eastward turn of the southern breakwater, may have supported the legs of a colossus in the Rhodian style, a reminder of where the Herodian building program had begun.

The harbor proper was divided into three basins, with the outer substantially larger than both the inner two. There is evidence of shipyards to the north of the middle basin and channels on the south, with floodgates that seem to have ensured an adequate flow of water through the harbor, minimizing the enormous siltation, which hundreds of years later was nevertheless to become uncontrollable and cause the final decay and decline of Caesarea as a port city. The inner harbor is lined with a quay, which may be a remnant of the port of Straton's Tower.

It is clear that the technology of Sebastos Harbor was the most modern available. Rome did not as yet have the great Claudian and Trajanic harbors of the Imperial period and was still functioning in the fashion of the Republic, based largely on Tiber-side moorages. Other great Roman provincial harbors, such as at Lechaion and Leptis Magna, were yet to be built. Kenchreai at Corinth, contemporary with or slightly later than Sebastos at Caesarea, shows none of the latter's innovation. As usual, Herod stood in the forefront, actually creating the transition between Hellenistic Greece and Imperial Rome.

Perhaps the most innovative element at Sebastos was the extensive use of hydraulic concrete. Although concrete had been developed in Italy in the second century B.C., and was perhaps first used hydraulically at Cosa, its extent at Caesarea is remarkable. Since the unique bonding and hydraulic properties of Italian concrete are related to the chemical qualities of the *pozzolana* found in the vicinity of the Bay of Naples, the question arises of whether Herod imported not only the concept of hydraulic concrete but the raw material for the actual concrete itself, and analysis has demonstrated that the *pozzolana* used at Caesarea was indeed imported from quarries near Puteoli. Although this might seem predictable, given Herod's desire to imitate Roman architectural technology as fully as possible, it is still remarkable that he imported materials over a distance of 1,250 miles in order to be totally Roman, even surpassing Roman technology in the process. The use of Italian *pozzolana* is striking confirmation of Josephus's statement (*AJ* 15.332) that the city of Caesarea was constructed with materials imported at great expense: the large expanses of concrete may have led Josephus to believe that the quays were constructed of 50-foot ashlars.

In addition to their use of materials, Herod's engineers were also technically innovative. They developed a new type of wooden form for pouring the concrete, using a unique double-walled construction that could be floated into position. This allowed expeditious progress in the building, because the forms could be prepared on land rather than in the treacherous waters of the harbor.

The Capitolium and Warehouses.   Immediately inland from the port was an artificial platform, built by creating a series of vaulted constructions (which cannot be Josephus's *psalidas*). This was presumably the Capitolium of the city, rising 13 m above present sea level and extending for 105 m along the shore and nearly 100 m inland. It has long been reasonably assumed that the Temple of Augustus and Roma stood here, on a platform as at Sebaste and the Paneion, although the temple is marked only by foundations. It may appear on coins of King Agrippa I, struck at Caesarea in A.D. 43/44 (fig. 30). These show a simple pedimental structure with two statues within; the obverse has a bust of the emperor Claudius. A monumental stairway ascended to the summit of the platform from the harbor quay, and the seaward face of the platform consisted of twelve barrel vaults built of ashlars in local stone. There was also a stairway on the south, which joined the platform to the street grid in the southern district of the city. Recent excavation has revealed portions of the southeastern corner and west side of the temple foundation. Architectural fragments, probably of the Corinthian order, in local kurkar (sandstone) have long been visible on the site. Although it has been suggested that these are remnants of the Temple of Augustus, they do not conform to Josephus's implication that the temple decoration was in marble. If Herod could import Italian *pozzolana* for the harbor, it is improbable that he would have resorted to the local stone for his Temple of Augustus, and the visible fragments may be Severan in date.

Further to the south, and perhaps architecturally connected with the Capitolium, is a series of barrel-vaulted warehouses. Thirteen are known, but the area is deeply buried under sand dunes and there may have been many more. The northernmost was excavated in the 1970's and was found to be 31 m long, 5 m wide, and 5 m high, constructed of ashlars in local stone. Entrance was on the west, or harbor, side. The floor of the vault was bedrock, and ceramics found at this level are from the Augustan period, indicating that this vault was part of the Herodian city. Many amphora fragments indicate the wide trade in commodities of the Herodian city, with imports from throughout the Roman world. Although some of the warehouses are post-Herodian, at least the northernmost are those of Herodian Caesarea, designed both to avoid a repeat of the famines of the 20's B.C. and to create an emporium of the eastern Mediterranean at Caesarea, perhaps in substitution for Alexandria, which was by then somewhat discredited.

The Urban Plan and the Theater.   The city seems to have been laid out mathematically, with certain important points, such as the Drousion, on arcs of a circle centering on the Temple of Augustus. Little is known about the street grid of Herodian Caesarea, since the visible street levels, and even the sewers beneath them, are Late Roman or Byzantine. By Severan times, and perhaps earlier, an insula in the northern part of the city was 415 by 237 Roman feet. The warehouses probably fronted on what might be called First Street (assuming a Harbor Street to the west); behind the warehouses, Second Street ran south from the east side of the Capitolium several hundred meters to the theater of Caesarea. In all probability, this was the earliest Italian-style theater in the East, but since it was several times rebuilt, little remains of its original Herodian construction other than the cavea and its substructures, and the style seems a peculiar mixture of Hellenistic and Roman elements. Of particular interest are paintings in the orchestra in an imitation of marble panels, with circle, diamond, and rectangle patterns.

It is not known to whom the theater was dedicated. Since construction at Caesarea began shortly after Augustus named Caesar's theater in Rome after his late nephew Marcellus, and since Herod tended to name structures after members of his family, one might easily assume that the theater at Caesarea was dedicated to a Herodian family member. The most likely candidate is his brother Joseph, who was a consistent supporter of Herod's policies (*BJ* 1.266, *AJ* 14.413) until he was killed at Jericho around 38 B.C. (*AJ* 14.448–50), and whose name is conspicuously absent from the Herodian building list.

Herod's Palace.   Remains seaward and slightly northwest of the theater are believed, based on recent and current excavation, to be Herod's palace. Situated on a natural promontory—an Alexandrian element—the structure was dominated by a large central freshwater pool, itself a technical tour de force, 18 by 35 m in extent, bounded by colonnaded porticoes and rooms beyond, including a dining area and the inevitable bathing establishment. Gardens and flower boxes were throughout. On the east side, there was a series of rooms with mosaic floors. The central dining room, 8.5 by 12 m, contains a striking mosaic imitation of a carpet, 2.6 by 5.2 m, with borders and a central design of interlocking polygons. A similar pattern is known from Jericho. Hypocausts on the north provided the luxury of heat on the colder side. West of the central pool was a large semicircular colonnade, like an open exedra, creating a seaside loggia. Entrance to the complex seems to have been at the northeast corner. An eastern wing at a higher level, the focus of more recent excavation, seems to have been the public area of the palace, perhaps the Praetorium of Herod of Acts 23.35.

Although much has been destroyed by wave action, the pool and its associated structures were part of a complex as large as 60 by 110 m, thus supporting Josephus's assertion that Herod's palace at Caesarea was particularly lavish: in the words of the excavator, it seems "to flout nature" (as do Herodian palaces generally), with its freshwater pool surrounded by the sea and its gardens on the desert seashore. Recent excavation has begun to indicate that the palace and nearby theater, as well as other structures as yet little understood, perhaps including a stadium or hippodrome, are part of a monumental urban complex remindful of the southern Campus Martius in Rome.

The Amphitheater.   The hollow of an amphitheater is visible northeast of the city, 750 m from the present shoreline, and outside the Herodian wall circuit. Today, it is marked by an oval of brush-covered rubble, 60 by 95 m, in extent, oriented with the long axis north-south and parallel to the street grid. Few actual constructional elements are visible. It is set against the west side of a ridge, and there may have been a platform or upper seating area on the ridge. According to Josephus (AJ 15.341), Herod built both a stone theater and an amphitheater at Caesarea. The amphitheater was said to have been south of the harbor, to have been able to hold a large number of people, and to have had a view of the sea. This strange passage makes two obvious points—that the theater was of stone and that the amphitheater could hold a large number of people—and places the amphitheater by the sea, which is not the location of the known structure. It is possible that the two structures have been reversed in the text, and that the amphitheater was noteworthy because it was of stone, a rarity in the first century B.C. Rome did not have a stone amphitheater until seven years before the founding of Caesarea, the one built by Statilius Taurus, which Herod would have seen in 17 B.C., while Caesarea was under construction. Herod would also have been familiar with Caesar's amphitheater at Antioch, however modest and temporary it had been. Yet Herod's Caesarea structure was in all probability the first permanent amphitheater outside Italy. A difficulty with Josephus's reference is that the visible amphitheater is well outside the city walls and would be the only Herodian structure so located. There are no strong diagnostic controls for the date of the extant amphitheater, and it is thus quite possible that it is post-Herodian. But this leaves the question of the location of Josephus's Herodian amphitheater unresolved. Josephus may actually have been referring to a structure on the waterfront south of the harbor, currently under excavation, which would be a stadium or hippodrome, rather than an amphitheater. This seems an unusual slip for Josephus to have made, but it is possible if he were using an earlier source (rather than relying on autopsy), perhaps Nikolaos or Herod's memoirs, written at a time when the word *amphitheatron* was still new, and was descriptive of form rather than defining a specific building type. The structure now under excavation has a theatral curved southern end, but also seems to have long parallel sides like a stadium. The excavators have dated it to the period of Herod the Great, but without any strong evidence other than the reference by Josephus. In fact, the excavators have also noted that the structure was built on land deposited by sediments from Herod's harbor construction, which would seem to preclude it as part of the original Herodian city plan, even given the rapid rate of siltation on this stretch of coast. It seems more likely that it is from a later phase of the city, after siltation had created new land in the urban center of Caesarea, and it is probably the stadium that existed in the time of Pontius Pilate (BJ 2.172; AJ 18.57). Only further excavation can determine the true nature of the monumental southern quarter of Caesarea and resolve the textual difficulties at AJ 15.341.

Hydraulic Installations.   Herod's interest in water supply and hydraulics is well documented, and there is hardly a Herodian site that does not pay careful attention to the movement and storage of water. The water sources for Caesarea were springs on Mount Carmel and the damming of the Krokodeilon River (modern Nahal Tanninim) north of the city. The Mount Carmel springs are around the site of Maiumas (Shuni), 9 km northeast of Caesarea, from where an aqueduct carried the water into the city. Portions are elevated on arches, and there is one tunnel, 400 m long. The graceful ashlar arcades along the seashore north of Caesarea have long been a familiar visual element of the city and its region. Aqueducts commonly approached Roman cities in such a fashion, and Herod's architects were consciously imitating the endless arcades at the southern approaches to Rome, another way in which Caesarea could mirror that city's greatness. The southernmost several hundred meters have been destroyed by wave action. The aqueduct underwent almost continuous repair and rebuilding, with a doubling of its width on the western side shortly after the original construction. Inscriptions on the existing structure date a number of the repairs to the second century A.C. A second aqueduct, less monumental than the first, leads 5 km from the Krokodeilon dam to the city, crossing the Mount Carmel aqueduct 3 km north of Caesarea and then paralleling it on the east. The original period of the Mount Carmel aqueduct is Herodian; the date of the Krokodeilon aqueduct is uncertain, but it is probably substantially later. It is possible that the former was for drinking water and the latter an addition purely for irrigation.

Virtually nothing is known about the water distribution system within the city or the elaborate sewer system Josephus described. Some sewers that appear Herodian in date are visible in the eroded coastal cliffs in the northern part of the city, but these have not been stratigraphically examined. Sewers excavated in the central area, especially south of the Capitolium, seem to be post-Herodian.

Other Structures.   Throughout the ancient city are scattered remains ascribable to Herod's day, especially structures at the northern edge of the site that seem to have originated in the Hellenistic period, and that were rebuilt or reused in Herodian times. In particular, there are remains of a building 9 m square in ashlar masonry standing several meters high. By the fourth century A.C., parts of the structure had been incorporated into a synagogue, leading the excavators to assume that it may have served as such as early as the Herodian period, although the evidence is scanty. Nevertheless, it is clear that this district of the city, just south of the northern limit of the Herodian city walls, was predominately a residential quarter, perhaps occupied since Hellenistic times.

In addition, excavations south of the Capitolium and east of the Herodian warehouses have uncovered the imperial offices of the Late Roman and Byzantine period (fourth through seventh centuries A.C.), and although nothing Herodian has been found in this area, it is probable that this was the administrative center of the city even in his day.

The City Walls.   Remnants of the Herodian wall of Caesarea have been discovered at several points. In some places it may have incorporated Hellenistic fortifications of uncertain date. Only the extremities of the Herodian wall have seen any excavation, especially at the north end, where over 100 m of wall has been exposed, but it can be traced for much of its length, creating a polygonal circuit with perhaps five gates: two at the ends of the cardo and three equidistant on the eastern side. The wall was perhaps no more than 2.3 m across, with few towers, only visible at the seaward ends, which may be reused Hellenistic structures, and it served no defensive purpose. Rather, it was the simple yet impressive circuit that any major city was required to have, as noted by authors as diverse as Herodotos (1.178–81) and Vergil (*Aeneid* 1.418–80), creating a pomerium that divided the city from its hinterland. In this Herod was more Hellenistic than Roman, since by the late first century B.C., the decaying city walls of Rome were hundreds of years old and had long since failed to enclose the urbanized area, making them only marginally functional.

The Hinterland.   The establishment of Caesarea created a renewal of its hinterland, which had been in a period of decline during much of the first century B.C. The decay of Straton's Tower, perhaps accelerated by the earthquake of 31 B.C., affected the surrounding area. Yet the creation of Caesarea immediately caused an economic resurgence in the region: the numerous warehouses in the city would not only have stored imports but have collected the produce of the northern Plain of Sharon for distribution and export. Moreover, the robbery and brigandage that had characterized the region in late Hellenistic times (Strabo 16.2.28, 37) diminished with the increase in economic fortunes, making rural settlement more propitious. Typical is the large estate at Khirbet Mansur el-'Aqab, virtually a small fortified village, which was established (with no prior history) at roughly the time of the founding of Caesarea, 6 km northeast on the southern ridges of Mount Carmel. A small rural bathhouse existed 2.5 km away at Horvat 'Eleq. The wealthy villa, which prospered for over a century, and the bathhouse are demonstrative of the emergence of Caesarea as a great city where none had existed previously: it tapped a potentially wealthy hinterland that had languished because of the political instability and natural disasters of the previous century.

Conclusions.   Most of Caesarea will remain unexcavated, although there is physical evidence for practically all the civic elements listed by Josephus, with the agora or forum and secondary temples the only exceptions. There is little doubt that the agora was located east of the Capitolium, perhaps to the southeast, where government offices existed by the fourth century A.C., or to the northeast and thus more in line with the harbor. Both areas are deeply buried under extensive later habitation. In addition, there is a vast range of elements of urbanization not described by Josephus, such as markets, gymnasia, and residential quarters, which are hardly known.

BMC Palestine, 238; Otto, *RE*, 70; Avi-Yonah, *IEJ* 1 (1950–51): 169; Reifenberg, *IEJ* 1 (1950–51): 20–32; Moretti, *Iscrizioni agonistiche greche* (1953), # 72; Albricci, *BdA* 47 (1962): 289–304; Avi-Yonah and Negev, *IEJ* 13 (1963): 146–48; Negev, *IEJ* 14 (1964): 237–39; Frova et al., *Scavi di Caesarea Maritima* (1966); Negev, *Caesarea* (1967), 7–13; Levine, *Caesarea under Roman Rule* (1975) 149–50; Levine, *Roman Caesarea* (1975); Olami and Peleg, *IEJ* 27 (1977): 127–37; Ward-Perkins, *RIA*, 310–13; Roller, *BASOR* 247 (1982): 50; Roller, *Levant* 14 (1982): 90–103; Beebe, *JNES* 42 (1983): 195–207; Blakely, *The Answers Lie Below* (1984), 3–38; Hohlfelder, *BAR-IS* 257 (1985): 81–86; Oleson, 257 (1985): 165–72; Levine and Netzer, *Excavations* (1986); Blakely, *CaesMarit* 4 (1987): 25–59; Peleg, *Die Wasserversorgung Antiker Städte* (1987), 176–78; Holum et al., *King Herod's Dream* (1988); Arav, *PEQ* 121 (1989): 144–48; Raban, *BAR-IS* 491 (1989); Hirschfeld and Birger-Calderon, *IEJ* 41 (1991): 81–111; Vann, *IJNA* 20 (1991): 123–39; Hodge, *Roman Aqueducts* (1992), 170; Everman, *JRA*, suppl. 5 (1992): 181–93; Oleson and Branton, *JRA*, suppl. 5 (1992): 49–67; Roller, *JRA*, suppl. 5 (1992): 23–25; Burrell, Gleason, and Netzer, *BAR* (1993): 50–57, 76; Negev et al., *NEAEHL*, 275; Bull et al., *AASOR* 51 (1994): 63–65; Nielsen, *Hellenistic Palaces* (1994), 183–84; Burrell and Gleason, *AJA* 99 (1995): 306–7; Hirschfeld, *JRA*, suppl. 14 (1995): 28–55; Porath, *JRA* suppl. 14 (1995): 15–27; Segal, *Theatres* (1995), 64–69; Bull, *AJA* 100 (1996): 370; Burrell, *CMR*, 228–47; Gleason, *CMR*, 208–27; Holfelder, *CMR*, 77–101; Kahn, *CMR*, 130–45; Netzer, *CMR*, 193–207; Oleson, *CMR*, 359–77; Porath, *CMR*, 105–20.

Dagon (Doq)

The fortress of Dagon, or Doq, was mentioned by Josephus only in the context of events of the second century B.C. (*BJ* 1.56; *AJ* 13.230; see also 1 Macc. 16.11–16): thus it is one of the Hasmonean fortresses. Josephus located it above Jericho, and it has been identified with the ruins on Jebel Qarantal, the promontory northwest of Jericho, where the springs of 'Ein Doq seem to preserve the ancient name (fig. 19). Although unexcavated, the site reveals the typical assemblage of a Jordan valley fortress: an artificial raised summit with cisterns and other hydraulic paraphernalia, monumental walls, and remnants of Ionic columns. An aqueduct lies to the north of the site, and there are a number of cisterns to the east, although the hydraulic installations are relatively primitive.

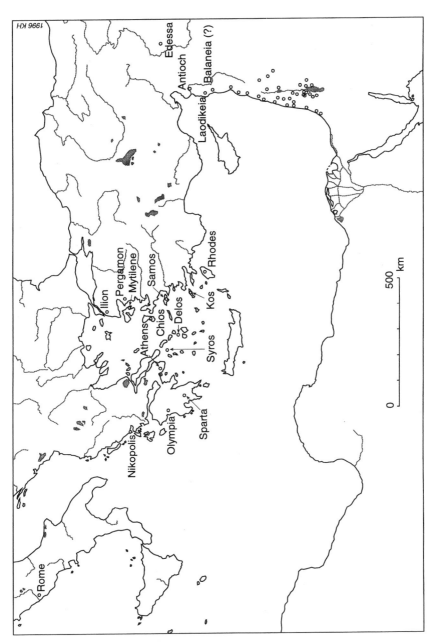

Map 1. The building program of Herod the Great.

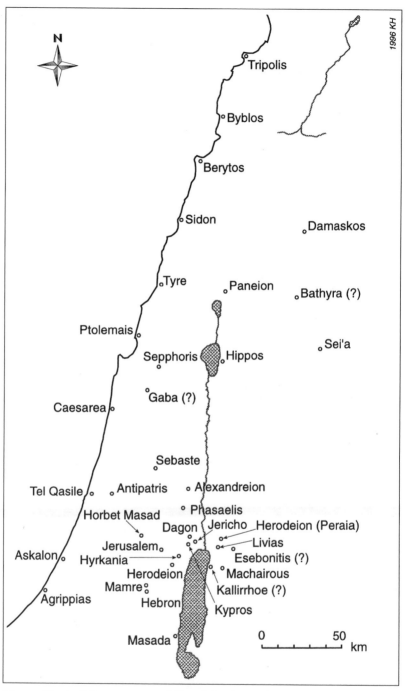

Map 2. The building program of Herod the Great: sites in or near his kingdom.

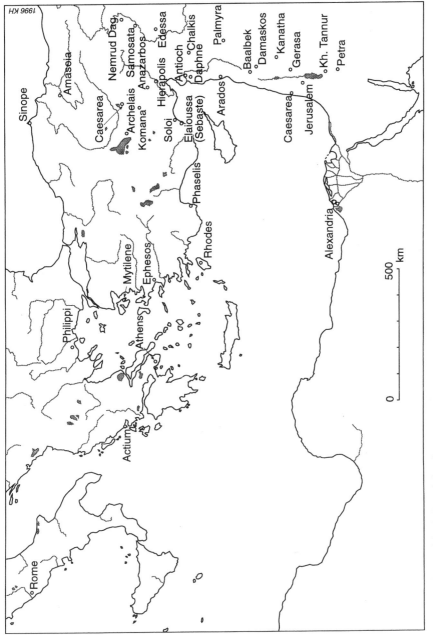

Map 3. The world of Herod the Great.

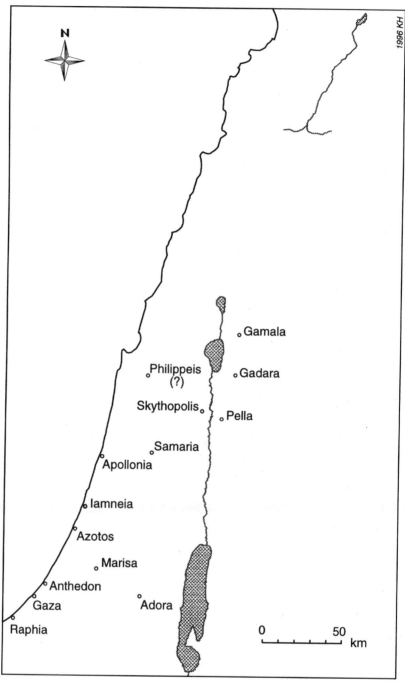

Map 4. Roman building in the southern Levant before Herod the Great.

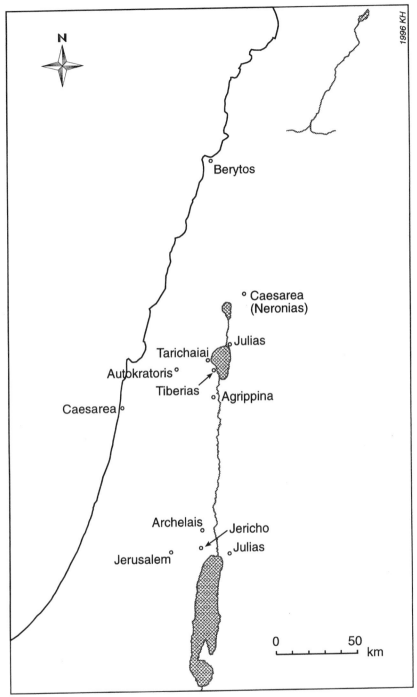

Map 5. Building sites of the descendants of Herod the Great.

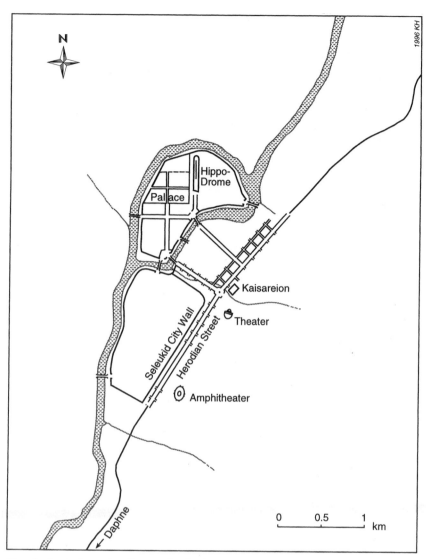

Map 6. Antioch-on-the-Orontes in the first century B.C. Adapted from Glanville Downey, *Ancient Antioch* (Princeton, 1963), ill. 5.

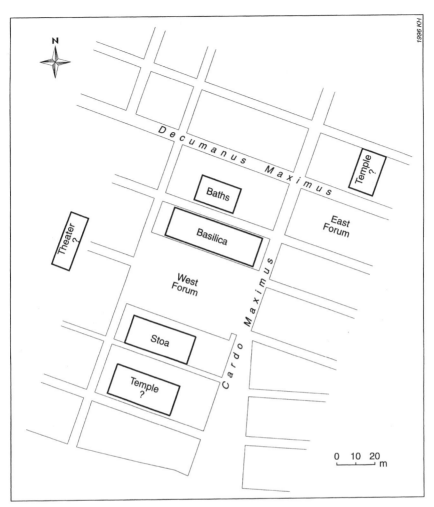

Map 7. Berytos. Adapted from René Mouterde and Jean Lauffray, *Beyrouth ville romaine: Histoire et monuments* (Beirut, n.d.).

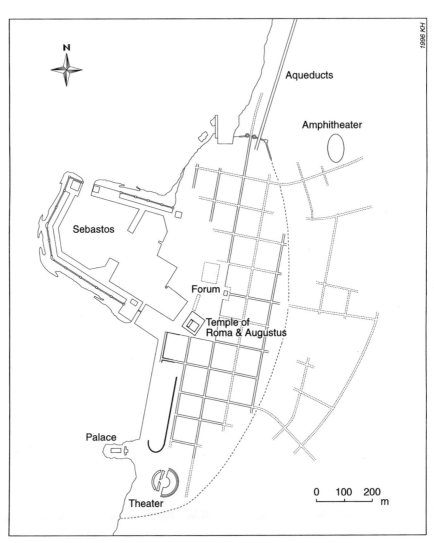

N

Aqueducts

Amphitheater

Sebastos

Forum

Temple of
Roma & Augustus

Palace

Theater

0   100   200
                m

Map 8. Caesarea.

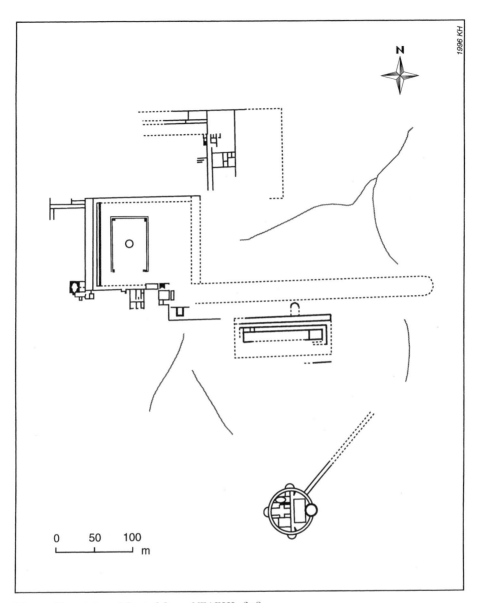

0 50 100
m

Map 9. Herodeion. Adapted from *NEAEHL*, 618.

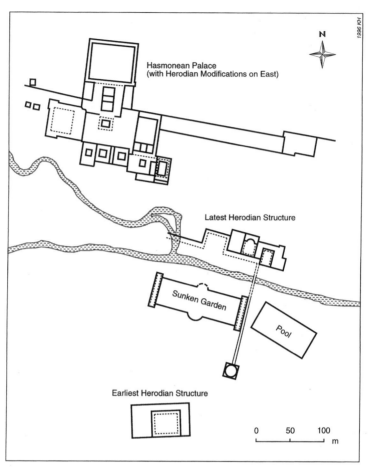

1996 KH

N

Hasmonean Palace
(with Herodian Modifications on East)

Latest Herodian Structure

Sunken Garden

Pool

Earliest Herodian Structure

0   50   100
                    m

Map 10. Jericho: the palace area. Adapted from *NEAEHL*, 682.

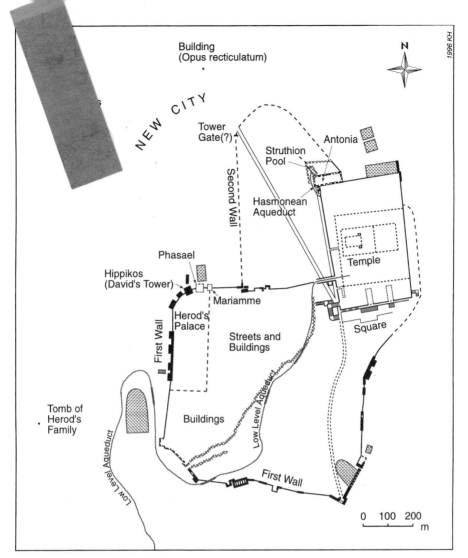

Map 11. Jerusalem in the early first century A.C. Adapted from *NEAEHL*, 718.

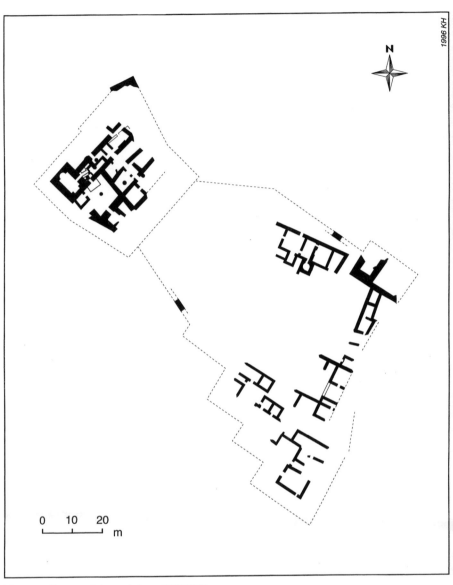

Map 12. Kypros. Adapted from *NEAEHL*, 315.

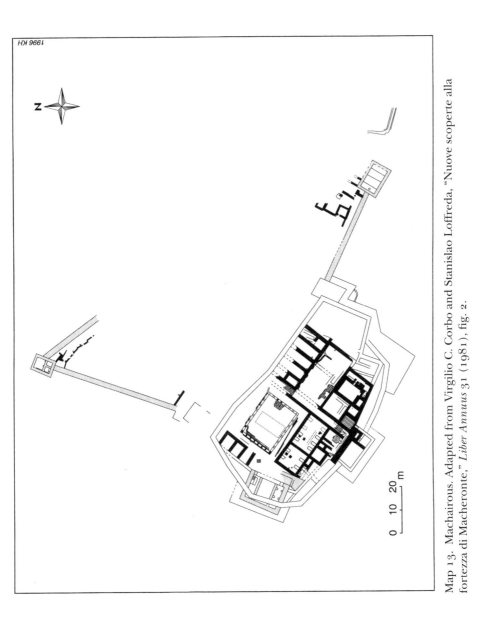

Map 13. Machairous. Adapted from Virgilio C. Corbo and Stanislao Loffreda, "Nuove scoperte alla fortezza di Macheronte," *Liber Annuus* 31 (1981), fig. 2.

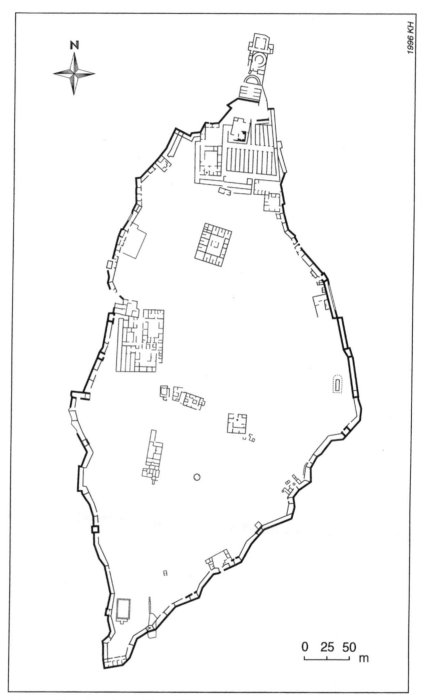

0 25 50
m

Map 14. Masada. Adapted from *NEAEHL*, 974.

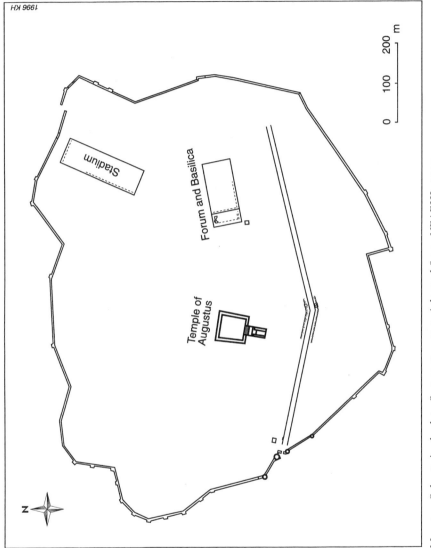

N

Stadium

Forum and Basilica

Temple of
Augustus

0   100   200
m

Map 15. Sebaste in the late first century B.C. Adapted from *NEAEHL*, 1301.

No association of Herod with Dagon has been preserved in the literary sources. Yet its position immediately north of Kypros, across the gorge of the Wadi Qelt, its Hasmonean origin, and its location protecting Jericho make it highly probable that Herod was interested in it. The lack of a known Greek toponym and the limited hydraulic components indicate, however, that Herodian involvement may have been minimal, perhaps merely renovation of the existing fortress.

Tsafrir, *JC* 2 (1982): 120–25; Amit, *AAP*, 223–28; Garbrecht and Peleg, *AntW* 20.2 (1989): 11–14; Garbrecht and Peleg, *BiblArch* 57 (1994): 164–65; *TIR-IP*, 112–13.

Esebonitis

Herod rebuilt Esebonitis, in which he settled a number of his cavalry (*AJ* 15.295). Yet the name, with its *-itis* ending, is more appropriate to a territory (such as Trachonitis, the territory around Trachon), than a town. The town name would be Esebon or Essebon, which was part of the Jewish territory at the time of Alexandros Jannaios (*AJ* 13.397) and is usually equated with biblical Heshbon, 12 km north of Madaba.

Josephus provided no information about the settlement in the district of Esebonitis. The text is vague and the verb *rebuilt* must be carried over from the previous entry, describing Gaba. Elsewhere (*BJ* 2.458), Josephus used the name Esebonitis in a list of cities; thus this may be an instance where district name replaced town name. Yet it is difficult to assume that this was as structured a settlement as Bathyra and other Herodian military colonies, and it may simply be that a detachment of cavalry was stationed in the area, perhaps after Herod's defeat of the Nabataeans near Philadelphia in 31 B.C. (*BJ* 1.364–85; *AJ* 15.108–60).

Excavation at Heshbon in the 1970's revealed little that could be dated to Herod's putative settlement, although various Roman-period remains were found. But rather than being interpretive documents, the published "reports" are logs of the excavation process, based on which reconstruction of the history of human habitation and relation of events at Heshbon to the wider world are problematic. There seems to have been a major rebuilding of public spaces on the south side of the site after 37 B.C., but the excavators assigned the entire period from 37 B.C. to A.D. 73 to a single subphase, making identification of any Herodian contribution impossible. Defensive towers located on the western edge of the site may be part of the Herodian fortifications, but the excavators were unable to provide any date more precise than between 63 B.C. and A.D. 135. The only evidence that the excavators attempted to link directly with Herod, although very dubiously, was a courtyard—perhaps part of a fortress—on the southern side of the site. Yet none of these pieces of questionable evidence sheds any light on Herodian construction at Heshbon.

Abel, *Géographie* (1938), 2: 348–49; Sauer, *Hesbon, 1971* (1973), 53, 55; Boraas and Horn, *Heshbon, 1973* (1975), 109–10; Boraas and Geraty, *Heshbon, 1974* (1976), 10–11; Horn, *EAEHL*, 510–14; Schürer (NEV), 2: 165–66.

Gaba

One of several military settlements established by Herod was at Gaba in Galilee (*AJ* 15.294; Synkellos 594), which was populated by discharged cavalry (*BJ* 3.36), somewhat on the model of a Roman *colonia*. It is probably not the site of Gabae renamed Philippeis by Marcius Philippus in 61/60 B.C.: if Herod had built there, he would have used the Roman toponym, which honored Augustus's stepfather. Josephus located Gaba in western Galilee near Mount Carmel, south of Ptolemais (*BJ* 2.459), sixty stadia from Simonias and twenty from Besara (*Life* 115–18). Despite these topographical details, it is one of the most difficult Herodian sites to locate with precision. A Geba mentioned by Pliny, a coastal city near the Carmel promontory, may be the same site, but there was also a Gaba in the area of the Syrian Dekapolis, and Pliny listed in succession three linguistically similar toponyms, Egbatana, Getta, and Gaba (*Natural History* 5.74). Adding to the confusion is a corrupt name at *BJ* 1.166, Gamala, Gabala, or Gadera, one of the cities Gabinius repopulated, and, in fact, there were numerous toponyms beginning with *Gab-* or *Geb-* in the southern Levant.

A number of sites have been suggested as the location of Herod's settlement. Although the village of Jebata, 25 km southeast of Haifa, seems to preserve the name, it is generally equated with Gabatha. Another candidate is the Gaba north of Caesarea, which was destroyed in the 60's A.C. (*BJ* 2.459) and is identified with modern Jaba, on the west slope of Mount Carmel, probably one of the towns mentioned by Pliny.

More probable, however, is either et-Haritiyye or Tell Shosh. These lie only a few kilometers apart, in the same vicinity as Jebata, on the east side of Mount Carmel. At et-Haritiyye, northwest of Beth She'arim (ancient Besara), remains no earlier than the Roman period were discovered, including "a long wall of small ashlars." The site is defensively located at an important road junction, controlling the route from southern Phoenicia to the interior, and there seems a strong possibility that this was Herod's settlement. Yet a lead weight with "Gaba" in Greek on it found at Tell Shosh, thirteen kilometers to the southeast, has led the discoverers to suggest that this is Gaba. Coins of Gaba have long been found in this area and are more common than at et-Haritiyye. Against this argument one may note that Tell Shosh is less strategically located and that small portable objects move around easily. In fact, two inscriptions with the name Gaba were discovered near Khirbet Gidru just south of Akko (Ptolemais), a location nearer where Pliny seems to have placed Gaba.

Locating Gaba is probably impossible with the present confusing and uncertain evidence, an indication of the difficulties topographers face when there is no strong literary or archaeological information. The frequency of similar names in the region suggests that Gaba may have been as much a district as city toponym. There is no question that Herod's Gaba was located in the general vicinity of Mount Carmel, probably on its east side near Besara. But the scattered location of finds and the toponymic problems make certainty impossible. If one had to choose between et-Haritiyye and Tell Shosh, which are only three hours' walk apart, the former seems more probable because of its location nearer Besara and the coast.

Dussaud, *Topographie historique* (1927), xxi; Alt, *ZDPV* 62 (1939): 3–21; Maisler, *HUCA* 24 (1952–53): 76–80; Avi-Yonah, *Gazetteer* (1976), 57–60; Ward-Perkins, *RIA*, 309; Siegelmann, *PEQ* 116 (1984): 89–93; Schürer (NEV), 2: 164–65; Schmitt, *ZDPV* 103 (1987): 22–48; *TIR-IP*, 125–26.

Hebron

The ancient city of Hebron (fig. 11), renowned as the home and burial place of Abraham (Gen. 23), is somewhat of a puzzle for the student of Herod's building program. It was described by Josephus (*BJ* 4.529–31), with particular emphasis on its fine marble tombs, but there is no mention of Herod. One might argue that Herod's architectural endowment of traditional Jewish cult was limited to Jerusalem, and that at other cities within his kingdom, even those of ancient significance, such as Samaria, his focus was on hellenizing and Roman influences. Yet at the same time it is inconceivable that Herod would have done nothing at the second most important Jewish site, which stood in the heart of Judaea and had been part of his kingdom from the beginning. Even if the archaeological evidence did not give strong support to Herodian construction at Hebron, in this case the lack of a literary citation cannot be used to exclude Herod's activity at the site.

Josephus's reason for not including this important place, as well as its companion Mamre (infra, pp. 186–87), six stadia to the north, where Abraham actually lived, provides some insight into the nature of Josephus's information regarding the Herodian building program. With the exception of the Temple at Jerusalem, which could hardly be ignored, all the constructions documented by Josephus are either secular or, if religious, Greek or Roman. Judaism did not have the tradition of elaborate architecture—at least outside of Jerusalem—that Greco-Roman cult did, but Herod's own survival demanded a sensitivity to Jewish needs. His efforts in that direction were by and large not accepted by religious elements in Judaea, and his extensive assumption of Greek and Roman cultural paraphernalia negated (in the minds of many) any efforts he made toward Judaism. Yet evidence of his support—for whatever reason—of Jewish principles can be seen not only in his reconstruction of the Temple in Jerusalem, but also in his extensive efforts on behalf of Jewish populations in the Greek and Roman world, his incorporating of prominent Jews into his court circle, and his interest in the various Jewish sects, especially the Essenes (*AJ* 15.378). Thus it is inconceivable that he would have ignored the city of Hebron, with its ancient religious associations.

Nevertheless, Josephus did not mention any Jewish religious construction by Herod other than the Temple at Jerusalem. Josephus's literary sources (other than Herod himself, exclusively Greek and Roman) probably emphasized the Greco-Roman aspects of the building program rather than any cult places outside of Jerusalem. The main sources were Nikolaos, Strabo, and Herod's own memoirs. Nikolaos, although he spent many profitable years at Herod's court, and then at that of Archelaos, was nevertheless a product and frequenter of a wider world: native of Damaskos, student in the hellenized circle of late Republican Rome, intimate at the court of Antonius and Cleopatra, and scholar in Rome during his last years. His perspective on the Herodian building program would always have been from the standpoint of Rome and Alexandria, not of Judaea. Strabo had even fewer ties to Judaea. Herod's memoirs would have emphasized his western outlook: like Nikolaos and Strabo, he wrote for a Greek and Roman audience, not a Jewish one. Thus it is in no way astonishing that Josephus, whose information on the Herodian building program was, outside the two political centers of Jerusalem and Caesarea, essentially derivative and not by autopsy, has little to say about Herod's architectural support of Jewish cult, except at the one site familiar to him.

Hebron had been destroyed, at least in part, in the second century B.C. (*AJ* 12.353). At some later date a precinct was built around the Cave of Machpelah, the traditional burial place of Abraham, Sarah, and their descendants. This enclosure, 34 by 59 m with its axis northwest to southeast, consists of well-laid ashlar blocks with flat pilasters on the exterior. The walls, still almost perfectly preserved despite the varied history of the site, are remindful of visible Herodian masonry in Jerusalem, particularly the western wall of the Temple precinct. They enclose a platform, raised above ground level on the southeast because of the slope of the surface. Regularly spaced within the enclosure are six cenotaphs, of Abraham, Isaac, Jacob, Sarah, Leah, and Rebecca, each within its own enclosure. These were laid out in two parallel rows and in strict symmetrical pattern, although two seem to have been moved slightly to accommodate later construction. Josephus (*BJ* 4.532) comments on their high-quality marble and fine workmanship, terminology normally used to describe Herodian construction. The cenotaphs seem to have been points of reference in the laying out of the entire construction, which is strong evidence, in the absence of solid proof, that cenotaphs, platform, and exterior wall were all part of the same construction phase. An almost identical enclosure was built at the same time at nearby Mamre. It was probably the enclosure at Hebron that Jesus of Nazareth mentioned a quarter-century after Herod's death (Luke 11.48), an indirect *terminus ante quem.* Since the Hasmonean destruction of Hebron in the second century B.C., there had been no one other than Herod who could have built such a structure: Herod's son Archelaos, who ruled the territory from 4 B.C. to A.D. 6, was a modest builder and is credited only with secular constructions. Thus on the basis of architectural style, approximate date, the intuitive conclusions outlined above, and even the diction of Josephus, the structure at Hebron is universally attributed to Herod.

Vincent, Mackay, and Abel, *Hébron* (1923), 142–44; Mader, *Mambre*(1957), 69–74; Jacobson, *PEQ* 113 (1981): 73–80.

Herodeion (in Judaea)

South of Jerusalem, at Herodeion, Herod built a fortress, palace, and associated structures (map 9, figs. 8, 13). This was one of two places he named after himself, the other being a fortress northeast of the mouth of the Jordan river (infra, pp. 168–69). Josephus seems to have been confused as to whether the more prominent place, the one in Judaea, was named Herodeion (*BJ* 1.265, 419, 673; 7.163; *AJ* 16.13, 17.199) or Herodia (*AJ* 14.360). The feminine form, although cited only once, is more likely to be correct, since Josephus called the site a *polis*, not a *phrourion.* Nevertheless, usage since the time of Josephus has preferred the neuter form.

Herod chose the site of his future Herodeion to commemorate a skirmish he had had there with his opponents in 40 B.C. He was in the process of retreating from Jerusalem, beginning the journey that would take him first to Egypt and then to Rome, when he was attacked sixty stadia south of the city by supporters of the Hasmoneans, whom he defeated. He thus established Herodeion as his victory city (*BJ* 1.265; *AJ* 14.359–360). Josephus's implied date for the foundation, 25–22 B.C. (*AJ* 15.317–33; see supra, p. 73), seems unusually late, as it would create a victory city commemorating events of fifteen years previously, although it does allow Herod's victory city to be founded shortly after Augustus's Nikopolis. It is possible that Josephus's date reflects when it was designed to be Herod's tomb. A date of the mid-30's B.C. for the original construction, contemporary with the other early palaces and fortresses in the area, seems more probable. Although not a city-foundation in the technical sense—there was no provision made for population or government—Herodeion demonstrates both Herod's early thinking as a founder of cities and the economic purpose of urbanization and bringing agriculture to a relatively unpopulated area. He probably named it Herodia, but its elaborate nature pushed into obscurity the slightly earlier fortress of Herodeion in the Jordan valley, and even by the time of Josephus, Herodia had usurped the name of Herodeion. Herod took a natural hill and leveled its summit, creating a platform on which vaults were constructed in the style of Late Republican terraces in Italy. He also seems to have reduced the height of another hill nearby, making the hill of Herodeion more prominent. He then built a fortified palace on the summit, whose access was via a marble stairway. With difficulty, an aqueduct was constructed, producing a particularly notable lavishness of water for this barren region, and in the urbanized area around the base of the mountain there were *diatribai*—places to pass the time—presumably gardens and fountains (*BJ* 1.419–21; *AJ* 15.323–25). It was either so elaborate as to resemble a city, or, with its outbuildings, an actual city (*AJ* 14.360).

Little is known about Herodeion during Herod's reign, except that Marcus Agrippa was entertained there in 15 B.C. (*AJ* 16.13). The city to which Josephus referred, which is below the summit palace, may have been a court city, a place for Herod to carry out the secular business of his court in a location away from the religious intensity of Jerusalem. As a created town with no previous history, Herodeion may have been a more comfortable place than Jerusalem for the Greek scholars who frequented the royal court; Caesarea may have served a similar function in later years.

Herodeion played a final dramatic role in the career of Herod: it became his tomb. When Herod died at Jericho, probably in 4 B.C., his son Archelaos supervised the funeral, which as might be expected was elaborate. A procession consisting of Herod's few surviving sons, other relatives, bodyguard, household, and troops marched the nearly 200 stadia to Herodeion (the distance makes it clear that the other Herodeion is not meant), and buried him (*BJ* 1.670–73; *AJ* 17.196–99). Herod seems to have conceived of the idea of being buried at Herodeion in the years 25–22 B.C., when reports of Augustus's mausoleum in Rome (fig. 3) reached him. He would not see the Roman structure until his trip of 17 B.C., but the long-noted physical resemblance between the two indicates the influence. Even if there were no architectural resemblance, Herod's concept of a dynastic tomb would require adherence to the Augustan model, as was the case with everything else in the Herodian architectural program. Augustus began his mausoleum in 28 B.C., and within two or three years at most, reports of it had reached the Herodian court (probably via Strabo) and the process of turning Herodeion into the royal tomb was under way. As usual, Herod was among the first to imitate an Augustan model, since most of the familiar cylindrical mausolea still visible today throughout central Italy—the tomb of Caecilia Metella on the Via Appia south of Rome is perhaps the most familiar example—are later than Herodeion. Many followers of Augustus, especially the late Republican aristocrats in his inner circle during his early years, followed his example and built similar cylindrical tombs: these included close associates of Herod's such as Messalla and L. Munatius Plancus. Another influence may have been the Tumulus Iuliae, the tomb of the Julian family, located in the Campus Martius.

Herodeion has long been identified without question with Jebel Fureidis, twelve kilometers south of Jerusalem, which seems to have preserved the name. The complex at Jebel Fureidis has two distinct parts: the construction at the summit of the mound, and the lower structures. The upper fortification, excavated in the 1960's, was an unusual circular building, 63 m in diameter, built over barrel vaulting. There were four symmetrically placed towers, with the eastern one, facing the Dead Sea, the most elaborate, being taller and circular (perhaps 45 m high), whereas the other three were semicircular. The double circular wall of the fortress created an enclosed area, which was carefully designed as a geometric unit, with all parts of the structure being multiples of the radius of the fortress. In fact, the modules used in the construction indicate that it was probably designed by the same architect who had built Masada, using a Roman foot of 0.2957 m. The entire circular structure is particularly innovative architecturally and foreshadows the curved forms of Roman architecture of the late first century A.C.

The interior of the fortress was in the style of a royal villa. Access was by a stairway that led up the hill from the northeast, and there was a double gateway at the northeast point of the circular structure. On the east side, there was a peristyle court, with the round tower intersecting this court at the center of the eastern side: the eastern side of the courtyard was actually a façade with attached pilasters, creating a monumental forecourt to the round tower, which may have been the actual tomb chamber. The peristyle seems to have been a garden. Exedrae were at the north and south margins of the peristyle. West of the peristyle court was the residential area proper: a passageway led beyond two columns into a cross-shaped courtyard. To the right (north) was a bath, and to the left (south) a triclinium. The ground plan is similar to that at Machairous. Mosaics and wall painting decorated the baths: the painting is in the Pompeian First Style, creating flat panels in red, green, brown, and yellow, with some additional Second Style architectural forms. Cisterns lie to the northeast, under the stairway, and an aqueduct leads seven kilometers from the Wadi Artas on the west, originating at the same point as two serving Jerusalem.

The lower structures, which lie directly north of the hill (fig. 8) and west of the lower end of the access stairway to the summit, were excavated in the 1970's. At the west end is a large garden complex, 110 by 145 m, on an artificial terrace, with a pool 46 by 70 m, oriented north-south, in the center. A round structure 13.5 m across in the center of the pool created an artificial island. Colonnades surrounded the garden on all sides except the east, where there was a north-south wall creating a long passageway, with halls 9 by 110 m on two levels. Southeast of the garden, on the slopes of the hill, is a large rectangular structure, 55 by 130 m, which was probably the central wing of the lower city complex: a small apsidal projection on its north side may have served as a loggia overlooking the valley below. Large storerooms seem to have been on the basement level of this structure.

Two baths were also part of the lower complex: one, southwest of the garden, is the largest Herodian bath so far known. Mosaics and paintings in the traditional Herodian style decorated these structures; a washbasin sculptured with a Silenos figure was also part of the ornamentation. Faint traces of structures to the north of the garden are probably the remnants of a northern wing of the complex.

A peculiar feature is a terrace ca. 350 m long, yet only 30 m wide, which runs to the east from the southeast corner of the garden, extending past the central wing. At its west end was a rectangular structure, 14 by 15 m, entered from the terrace, with attached columns on all four sides. Other structures, including a ritual pool, were part of this complex. The terrace seems almost circus-like in form, and perhaps it was used for games. Another building of uncertain function stood in the vicinity, because drafted and decorated ashlars, as well as fragments of a Doric frieze, were found in a nearby Byzantine church. The excavators believed that these were the paraphernalia of Herod's tomb, with the long terrace a monumental processional way, but the exact details are not yet understood, and the entire question of the location of the tomb remains disputable and depends, in part, on how closely Herod's burial arrangements adhered either to Jewish law or to Greco-Roman custom, the former prohibiting burial in a structure attached to a residence. On the other hand, this argument would evaporate if the upper structure (fig. 13) were seen as the tomb, not a residence, with its peristyle, baths, and triclinia part of the ritual of the burial and cult. In fact, it seems inconceivable that the upper structure should be anything other than Herod's tomb. Although constructed in the style of a royal villa, the large round tower on the east—which intersects the villa peristyle—dominates the structure. It is strikingly remindful of cylindrical tombs in Rome. The "villa" is enclosed by a high external circular wall, which excludes it from its environment and landscape, as well as from significant ventilation. It is impossible to imagine that Herod, whose attention to physical situation, landscape, and environment is legendary, would have created such an airless enclosure as a residence. As a tomb, however, it is eminently sensible.

The entire complex of Herodeion, whatever the exact function of its parts, was probably the largest palatial structure of its day in the Greco-Roman world, surpassed only when Nero built his Domus Aurea. Although inspired by Hellenistic palaces, the Herodeion complex drew more on Late Republican villas in Italy, especially the luxury dwellings around the Bay of Naples. The construction is highly innovative, and looks ahead to later

Roman palaces and villas, where long subterranean halls, pools, and round structures dominate.

Vardaman, in *The Teacher's Yoke* (1964), 58–81; Holloway, *AJA* 70 (1966): 173; Segal, *Qadmoniyot* 7 (1974): 54–61; Segal, *ErIsr* 12 (1975): 109–15; Vardaman, *IEJ* 25 (1975): 45–46; Busink, *Der Tempel von Jerusalem, vol.* 2 (1980), 1025–27; Chen, *BASOR* 239 (1980): 37–40; Netzer, *Greater Herodeion* (1981); Netzer, *JC* 1 (1981): 48–61, 73–80; Tsafrir, *JC* 1 (1981): 68–72; Jacobson, *ZDPV* 100 (1984): 127–36; Netzer, Επιστημονικη επετηρις της Φιλοσοφικης σχολης του Πανεπιστημίου Αθηνων 28 (1979–85): 524–27; Netzer, *Herodium: An Archaeological Guide* (1987); Netzer, in *Nikopolis* 1 (1987): 121–28; Ovadiah and Ovadiah, *Hellenistic, Roman and Early Byzantine Mosaic Pavements* (1987), 69 (## 94–96); Corbo, *Herodion* 1 (1989); Garbrecht and Peleg, *AntW* 20.2 (1989): 2–20; Netzer, *Akten*, 37–50; Colvin, *Architecture and the After-Life* (1991), 66–71; Richardson, *NTD*, 402; Foerster, in *NEAEHL*, 619–20; Netzer, in *NEAEHL*, 621–24; Amit, *Liber Annuus* 44 (1994): 561–78; Nielsen, *Hellenistic Palaces* (1994), 201–3.

Herodeion (in Peraia)

One of the more confusing elements of the Herodian building program is the existence of two sites named Herodeion. Josephus specifically mentioned that one was a fortress on the Arabian frontier and that the other, sixty stadia from Jerusalem, was more elaborate (*BJ* 1.419–20). The famous palace that was to become Herod's tomb (supra, pp. 164–68) was the latter place and was probably actually called Herodia. The former Herodeion is little known and has often been ignored or confused with the latter by modern commentators.

Because of this problem, the lesser Herodeion has not received much topographical inquiry. It was mentioned nowhere else by Josephus, leading one to surmise the possibility of a textual or source error. Yet the statement is specific, and for Herod to have had two sites named after himself would not be implausible. The famous Herodeion is nowhere near the Arabian frontier; in fact, it is quite centrally located, near major cities of Herod's realm. The text of Josephus must be read as is, that there were two sites named Herodeion, one Herod's tomb south of Jerusalem and the other in the eastern part of the kingdom, in southern Peraia.

The only site that has been proposed for this Herodeion is Khirbet es-Samra, or el-Hebbesa, an isolated hill approximately ten kilometers northeast of the mouth of the Jordan river. The location is similar to that of the fortress of Alexandreion, to the northwest, and the site has likewise been artificially terraced. A structure on the summit consists of a trapezoidal wall with a citadel in the northeast corner. Typically, water supply was a primary concern, with several cisterns located within the site. The pottery is of the

Roman period. The site commands an excellent view south and west, a counterpart to the fortress of Kypros, directly west. Although there is no definite evidence, there is a strong possibility that this is Herodeion. Its function may have been to protect the palace at Livias, just a few kilometers to the south, which eventually (but probably not until after Herod's death) replaced Herodeion as a fortress, being slightly more strategically located, near the road east from Jericho.

Mallon, *Biblica* 14 (1933): 400–405; Vardaman, in *The Teacher's Yoke* (1964), 60; Vardaman, *IEJ* 25 (1975): 46.

Hippos

Lying in a pleasant location east of the Sea of Galilee (Pliny, *Natural History* 5.71), the probably Seleukid foundation of Hippos (fig. 17) is first documented when Pompey took it from the Jewish territory and made it into a free city (*BJ* 1.156; *AJ* 14.75). It was added to Herod's kingdom by Octavian after Actium (*BJ* 1.396; *AJ* 15.217) and was always considered a Greek town (*BJ* 2.97; *AJ* 17.320). Although Josephus did not mention any Herodian building here, as a Greek city given to Herod by Octavian, it fits into a standard pattern of sites within his kingdom at which Herod built. It may have been the location of a Herodian customs station, perhaps similar to Capernaum during the reign of Antipas (Matt. 9.9–10; Mark 2.14–16; Luke 5.27–32). By at least the second century A.C., Hippos seems to have had a Nabataean merchant community. Since Herod was half Nabataean, this may be of more than passing interest.

Hippos is located 2 km east of the Sea of Galilee on a promontory that rises 350 m above the sea level. Although the limited excavation has generally revealed material of the Byzantine period, extensive Roman remains cover the site. Of interest are harbor works, fortifications that seem to have been initiated in the Roman period, and an aqueduct running 3.5 km across the saddle from the uplands to the east. This has a particularly Herodian quality, and the entire aspect of the site—on an isolated but connected promontory high above the water—is remindful of the Herodian fortresses around the lower Jordan and the Dead Sea.

Abel, *Géographie (1938)*, 2: 471–72; Schalit, *KH*, 296–97; Ovadiah, *PEQ* 113 (1981): 101–4; Ben David, *AAP*, 133–40; Epstein, in *NEAEHL*, 634–36.

Horbet Masad

The site of Horbet Masad lies sixteen kilometers west-northwest of Jerusalem on the road to the coast. It seems to have been established in the late Hellenistic period as a fortress. During the late first century B.C. and into the following century, a new fortress and watchtower, with a cistern, were superimposed on the ruins of the Hellenistic structure. The site was excavated in the late 1970's, but the excavators did not distinguish phases of occupation within the period of the entire Herodian dynasty, from 40 B.C. to A.D. 66, the most intensive and prosperous period of the site. Its Greco-Roman name is unknown. Although it has certain similarities with Herodian fortresses in the Jordan valley and around the Dead Sea, the lack of a contemporary toponym and literary information, as well as the vagueness of the interpretation of the excavated remains, makes attribution to Herod impossible.

Fischer, *ZDPV* 103 (1987): 117–36; *TIR-IP*, 185.

Hyrkania

Hyrkania, as its name implies, had existed since Hellenistic times. It was fortified by Alexandros Jannaios in the 50's B.C. and named after either his father or his son, Hyrkanos I or II (*BJ* 1.160–61). Gabinius demolished the fortress, as he did other Hasmonean fortresses around the north end of the Dead Sea (*BJ* 1.167; *AJ* 14.89–90: according to Strabo [16.2.40], it was Pompey who demolished it). Yet the territory remained under Hasmonean control until Herod captured it in 32 or 31 B.C. (*BJ* 1.364). Sometime in the next fifteen years, Herod rebuilt it, and soon it was used as a prison and place of execution for political dissidents (*AJ* 15.366), including, eventually, his son Antipatros (*BJ* 1.664; *AJ* 17.187). Since many of these dissidents would have been Hasmonean supporters, imprisoning them at a construction that bore the name of two prominent Hasmoneans was particularly ironic. This gloomy function did not keep Herod from entertaining Marcus Agrippa there in 15 B.C. (*AJ* 16.13).

Hyrkania has consistently been located at the site of Khirbet Mird, fourteen kilometers southeast of Jerusalem. The identification lacks any definitive evidence other than the general location and nature of the site, but has generally been upheld. Although the visible remains are largely of the Byzantine monastery of Kastellion, certain features typical of Herodian fortresses have been observed. Hyrkania is on a prominent, seemingly isolated peak at the edge of the hills overlooking the Jordan valley and Dead Sea. The usual cisterns and other hydraulic installations abound, especially an aqueduct built of ashlar masonry with the heavy rustication often seen as typical of Herodian work, which has been traced for several kilometers to the west. The hill was leveled with a large platform, 40 by 25 m, resting on masonry vaulting, with cisterns underneath it. The fortress itself consisted of rooms around three sides of a courtyard, similar to other Herodian fortresses. The pottery is of the late first century B.C. Of particular interest is an extensive cemetery 500 m to the east. These graves contained pottery of the period of the Herodian dynasty. Given the use of Hyrkania as a prison and place of execution, the cemetery is a notable witness to the realities of politics in Herodian Judaea.

Plöger, *ZDPV* 71 (1955): 148–51; Wright, *Biblica* 42 (1961): 1–21; Schalit, *KH*, 341; Negev, *PECS*, 401 (which, however, erroneously locates the site northeast of Jerusalem, a mistake also made in Ward-Perkins, *RIA*, 14, map); Garbreth and Peleg, *AntW* 20.2 (1989): 2–20; Patrich, *AAP* 243–60.

Jericho

Herod captured Jericho (map 10, figs. 7, 20, 27) during his early struggles with the Hasmoneans, but lost it to Cleopatra and did not regain it permanently until after Actium (*BJ* 1.361–62, 396; *AJ* 14.410). It was a center of Hasmonean strength well after Herod's accession, with a palace that Herod visited on a number of occasions (*BJ* 1.331), one of which was to effect the murder of the Hasmonean Aristoboulos III—his brother-in-law—around 35 B.C. by having him drowned in one of the palace pools (*BJ* 1.437; *AJ* 15.53–56). Jericho had long been a resort for the aristocracy, and Herod may have built a villa there even before the territory was part of his kingdom.

The Hasmonean palace may have suffered in the earthquake of 31 B.C., and Herod began to rebuild it after acquiring the territory. As with his palace in Jerusalem, he named parts of the edifice after Augustus and Marcus Agrippa (*BJ* 1.407). Josephus supplied no details except to note that the Herodian palace was better and more spacious than the Hasmonean one it replaced.

Other Herodian construction at Jericho included a hippodrome, an amphitheater, and possibly a theater. The theater is only mentioned at *AJ* 17.161, where the text is uncertain, and it is not clear whether an amphitheater or theater is meant. The hippodrome and amphitheater are known because of the roles they played in Herod's last days and death. During his terminal illness, he summoned numerous people of distinction to the city and first addressed them in the amphitheater, recounting all his efforts on their behalf, but eventually he began to rave and had them locked in the hippodrome, intending to have them killed at the moment of his death, so that it would be marked by a general mourning throughout the kingdom (*BJ* 1.659; *AJ* 17.161, 175). When Herod died, a few days later, his sister Salome released those in the hippodrome (*AJ* 17.193, 233) and then announced the king's death to the populace in the amphitheater (*BJ* 1.666). Shortly afterward, the palace was burned by a usurper, a slave named Simon (*BJ* 2.57; *AJ* 17.274). It was rebuilt by Archelaos during his brief reign (*AJ* 17.340).

The region of Jericho was internationally known for its fertility (*BJ* 4.459–75): Herod's palace and the surrounding gardens and rich fields were noted by Strabo (16.2.41). Pliny (*Natural History* 5.70) commented on the palm groves and abundant water, and Horace saw Jericho in the days of Herod as a metaphor for luxury and idleness (*Epistles* 2.2.184). The descendants of the palms still flourish and still produce their excellent dates, easily available today at roadside stands.

The Herodian palace at Jericho, as well as its Hasmonean predecessor, are to be sought at Tulul Abu el-'Alayiq, west of the modern city and south of the prehistoric site of Tell es-Sultan. At this point the Wadi Qelt enters the Jordan valley, and the Herodian fortress of Kypros lies on the bluffs a kilometer to the west. Excavations have occurred at various intervals since 1868, especially since the 1950's, and it is now possible to identify not only the original Hasmonean palace but its Herodian successors.

On the north side of the Wadi Qelt are the elaborate remains of the Hasmonean palace, built in several stages from the late second century to the early first century B.C. It remained in use until the 30's B.C., as the drowning of Aristoboulos demonstrates. Across the Wadi Qelt and about 300 m to the south is a rectangular peristyle 46 by 87 m, identified as the first stage of the new Herodian structure. Since it was a large peristyle court with a bath, yielding a large number of unguentaria, it was originally thought to be a gymnasium, but later excavation indicated that it was always a residential structure, perhaps built as a villa even before Herod officially possessed the territory and while the Hasmonean palace was still in use. When the region of Jericho passed permanently to Herod, he began to modify the now-abandoned Hasmonean structure, creating a garden over part of the Hasmonean ruins and building a new wing on the east. The central part of this new complex was a peristyle court 24 by 34 m, with an irrigated garden, surrounded by rooms on all sides except the west. On the east side there was a frescoed hall 7.5 by 10 m, adjoining a large portico with a fine view to the south. To the west the Hasmonean swimming pools—scene of Aristoboulos's demise—were remodeled and partially converted into gardens, and a bath was built on the south side.

At a later date another palatial structure was constructed southeast of the modified Hasmonean palace (fig. 7). This was primarily on the north side of the Wadi Qelt but extended over it to the south. The difference between this structure and its predecessor is striking. The earlier modified Hasmonean palace was built in the Hellenistic style of rectilinear patterns and ashlar masonry, but its successor used curved forms, brick, and *opus reticulatum*. There is no specific information on the date of construction, although the excavator has suggested it might have been at the time of Marcus Agrippa's visit of 15 B.C. The central part of this structure has two particularly noteworthy reception halls. The larger is at the west end of the complex and is 19 by 29 m, with an entrance on the south and an interior colonnade around three sides. There was a central mosaic carpet surrounded by *opus sectile*. Presumably, this was one of the halls Herod named after Augustus or Agrippa. It is remindful of Roman imperial audience halls, particularly that in the Domitianic palace in Rome (the so-called Domus Augustiana). To the east there was a peristyle court with a garden, 19 by 19 m, with an exedra at its north end. A number of rooms opened from this peristyle. East of it was a bathhouse, built in the contemporary Campanian style. Another peristyle court is to the south of the bath, with a second reception hall—presumably the other of the two named ones—to the east. A bridge (still standing as late as 1839, when David Roberts painted it) led south over the wadi to a walkway between a sunken garden on the west and a pool on the east to an enigmatic circular hall built on the summit of an artificial mound, perhaps a prototype for Herodeion. The sunken garden had a long façade on the south, with a central hemicycle, and stoas on the east and west sides. Numerous flowerpots have been discovered in the garden areas, especially in the west peristyle of Herod's first palace, southeast of the Hasmonean structure. This garden was planted in the Hellenistic fashion of straight rows, indicating a single plant, perhaps Judaean balsam. The large garden south of the Wadi Qelt may have been more Roman in form.

Considered as a whole, the palace complex at Jericho shows the same type of agglutination that was inspired by the Campanian villas of the late Republic and reached its peak in the Imperial period, especially in the Domus Aurea and the palatial complexes on the Palatine, and at Tivoli. Roman construction details abound at Jericho: *opus reticulatum* and *opus incertum*, fine frescoes in floral and geometric patterns, even including architectural representations, and indiscriminate use of the Ionic and Corinthian orders. The integration of the Wadi Qelt into the complex shows a typical Roman incorporation of available natural features; the sophisticated gardens and pools recreate the seaside villas of more luxuriant Italy. It is perhaps no accident that Jericho was the one place in Judaea that captured the imagination of Italian poets, as Italy had best been created here. The excavators of the complex believe that a team of builders from Rome, perhaps provided by Agrippa, supervised the construction. But it is difficult to untangle the various phases through which it grew, from the Hasmonean original through several Herodian versions, and one must take into account that some of the constructions are actually from the "splendid palace" of Archelaos, so that within little more than half a century there were five different construction periods.

North of the palace complex, at Tell es-Samarat, is the site of the hippodrome (fig. 20). The structure consists of a racecourse 320 m long and 85 m wide, surrounded by walls. Its long axis points toward the Herodian palace complex to the south. A theatral area is at the north, adjoining one of the narrow ends of the hippodrome. There seems to have been no scene building, so it appears that the "theater," the only evidence of seats at the hippodrome, was a viewing area for the races. Behind, or north, of this structure is a square (70 by 70 m) building on an artificial platform 8–12 m high, which perhaps supported a peristyle, possibly a gymnasium. The complex is dated to the Herodian period based on its short time of use and the architectural decoration. It may have been the locale for otherwise-unknown Jericho games. Since the amphitheater and hippodrome at Jericho are linked in Josephus's account, the theatral area may be what Josephus called the amphitheater, for which there is no other evidence. The complex is a unique and enigmatic collection of structures, and it is not astonishing that Josephus's account is unclear.

Kelso and Baramki, *Excavation at New Testament Jericho* (1949–51); Pritchard, *Excavations at Herodian Jericho* (1952–54); Netzer, *IEJ* 25 (1975): 89–100; Netzer, *BASOR* 228 (1977): 1–13; Netzer and Meyers, *BASOR* 228 (1977): 15–27; Busink, *Der Tempel von Jerusalem*, vol. 2 (1980), 1049–53; Ovadiah and Ovadian, *Hellenistic, Roman and Early Byzantine Mosaic Pavements* (1987), 76–77 (## 110–13); Gleason, *Bulletin of the Anglo-Israel Archaeological Society* 7 (1987–88) 21–39; Yellin and Gunneweg, *IEJ* 39 (1989): 84–90; Roberts, *The Holy Land* (1989), 61; Netzer, *Akten*, 37–50; Yegül, *Baths and Bathing in Classical Antiquity* (1992), 64; Nielsen, *Hellenistic Palaces* (1994), 193–201; Segal, *Theatres* (1995), 87–89; Netzer, *CMR* (1996): 202–7.

Jerusalem

It is not the intent of the present work to make a complete archaeological and topographical survey of Herodian Jerusalem (map 11, figs. 36, 37). Much has been written, and continues to be written, on this topic. Jerusalem is unique, not only for the vast amount of study it has received, but because nowhere else is there such a discrepancy between the amount of building Herod did and the amount of it that is preserved. Jerusalem is the only Herodian building site within his kingdom that has always been a major city, from the Iron Age until modern times. Its population during Herod's reign, estimated at between 35,000 and 70,000, was nearly half that of Classical Athens. Even without the unique religious status of the city, Herod would have lavished special attention to "longe clarissima urbium orientis" (Pliny, *Natural History* 5.70). Although it is possible from Josephus's precise descriptions, especially of the Temple, to make a detailed reconstruction—as is demonstrated not only by the famous model now visible on the grounds of a Jerusalem hotel but by other attempts through architectural drawings—much is still highly speculative. This summary thus confines itself to the literary evidence and a brief account of the archaeological remains that seem to relate to Herod's constructions; it is not intended to replace the extensive published material, most recently in *NEAEHL*, 719–47 (with bibliography).

Herod's building program in Jerusalem fitted into the existing Hellenistic city, rather than being a total reconstruction as at Sebaste or a new creation as at Caesarea. Although the focal point of the city was the Temple, which had been in varying states of disrepair for generations, its reconstruction was one of his last major building efforts. Herod did not wish to venture upon such a delicate project until he was certain of his abilities as a royal builder and had some assurance that the civil strife both within his kingdom and within the Roman world generally was diminishing. His earlier efforts in Jerusalem were similar to those in other cities: a fortress, a palace, and buildings demonstrative of Greco-Roman culture.

The Antonia.   Herod did not gain control of Jerusalem quickly: it took several years and Roman assistance. It was thus natural for his first building there, as elsewhere, to be military. Since at least the second century B.C., Jerusalem had contained a fortress called the Baris (*BJ* 1.75, 118), an Egyptian word that by Hellenistic times had come to mean (in Greek) a stronghold (*LSJ*). By Herod's day the Baris was probably dilapidated, and he lavishly and luxuriously restored it and renamed it the Antonia, after Marcus Antonius (*BJ* 1.401; Tacitus, *Histories* 5.11), which provides a *terminus ante quem* of the late 30's B.C. for its reconstruction. In all probability, it was built shortly after Herod's acquisition of Jerusalem in 37 B.C., although there was a second building phase twenty years later that integrated it into the adjacent Temple. It was the only structure in the Roman world to retain the name of Antonius after 30 B.C.: the Augustan cleansing of the record did not reach into interior Judaea, even at the time of Marcus Agrippa's visit of late 15 B.C. Herod implied that the reason for construction was to protect the adjacent Temple (*AJ* 15.292), an explanation more poetic than realistic, although the Antonia was the storehouse for priestly robes, a religious function continued from its Hellenistic predecessor (*AJ* 15.404; 18.91–95; 20.6).

The Antonia has variously been described as a tower or palace, perhaps indicating that from its original role as a fortified palace, an urban counterpart to Masada, it evolved into being purely a fortress when Herod built another palace in the city (*AJ* 20.6; *Life* 20). The Antonia lay at the northwest corner of the Temple and, after Herod began to restore the Temple twenty years later, was connected to it by stoas (*BJ* 2.330; 6.165). Herod was even said to have had a secret passage into the inner court of the Temple (*AJ* 15.424). Josephus described the Antonia as located on a precipitous rock, which had been made more precipitous by separating it from its surroundings, especially on the north (*BJ* 5.149, 238–46). The rock was paved over, both as an ornamental and defensive measure. The Antonia dominated the city, lying on virtually the highest land. There was a surrounding wall, with the Antonia itself constructed with towers at each corner, overlooking the Temple, and stairways on the south side leading down to the Temple stoas. The interior was like a palace, with residential areas, baths, and courtyards, all for the troops stationed in the city.

The Palace.   Although the Antonia originally served as a palace, it was eventually replaced as a royal residence by a new palace (fig. 37) in the western part of the city (*AJ* 17.255). According to the sequence of events described at *AJ* 15.317–18, the date of construction seems to have been immediately after 25 B.C., when Herod sent troops to assist Aelius Gallus on his Red Sea expedition, and thus probably during the period between the completion of Sebaste and the initiation of Caesarea.

The palace, enclosed by a wall, was noted for its many suites and rooms, arranged around a number of peristyles of varying orders: in fact, Josephus found it the ultimate in extravagance. There were extensive gardens, with fountains, pools, and streams (*BJ* 5.176–83). The interior decoration was particularly lavish, decorated in gold, stone (probably marble revetment), and περιαλείμματα (*AJ* 15.318). This rare word, used nowhere else by Josephus, is not clearly understood. He or his source was thinking of Plato (*Kritias* 116d), who (in perhaps the earliest instance of the word) also used it to describe decoration in a royal palace. Its root meaning is something smeared (Aristotle, *History of Animals* 624a), thus implying a fresco-like technique.

Portions of the structure were named after Augustus and Marcus Agrippa, a pattern followed at Jericho (*BJ* 1.402; *AJ* 15.318). Josephus's word is κλίσιαι, which is best translated as "pavilions." Particularly notable were the gardens, probably planted peristyles as at Jericho, with walkways, canals, and bronze sculptures (*BJ* 5.180–82): these were still renowned a century later (*BJ* 7.178). Just as the palace at Jericho imitated the Italian rural villa of the late Republic, that at Jerusalem was Herod's version of the Italian town house of the period, familiar today in the numerous examples from Pompeii and Herculaneum but known to Herod from the aristocratic houses on the Palatine that he had seen in 40 B.C.

The Temple Precinct.   In his speech at the inauguration of construction, Herod apologized for the delay in rebuilding the Temple (*AJ* 15.386–87). Josephus dated the beginning of the work to either Herod's fifteenth year (*BJ* 1.401) or his eighteenth year (*AJ* 15.380): the contradiction may not be an error, as there was probably ongoing preliminary surveying at the site for many years before the official initiation of work. Since construction seems to have begun immediately after Augustus's visit to Syria in 20 B.C., the work began late that year or early in 19 B.C. A dedication ceremony was held somewhat over a year later (*AJ* 15.421), but this was cosmetic and the Temple became proverbial for its lengthy construction (although the stoas were completed in eight years: *AJ* 15.420) and was not officially finished for over seventy years (*AJ* 20.219–21). Herod never set foot in the interior, since he was not a priest, and he seems to have been far more interested in the stoas, basilicas, and other Roman elements that surrounded the Temple proper (*AJ* 15.419–20), which were richer in construction details (Philon, *Special Laws* 71).

Josephus's detailed description of the reconstruction is well known (*BJ* 5.184–237; *AJ* 15.380–423), accompanied by information in other sources (Philon, *Special Laws* 1.71, 273–74; Philon, *Embassy to Gaius* 294–300; *Chronikon Paschale* 193), including the many rabbinical citations. There are numerous contradictions between the various sources, and even between *BJ* and *AJ*. Many of these problems, which tend to concern the number of gates, the size of the building site and the extent of construction, and the external decoration, are not errors but a reflection of the continuing activity at the site, both new construction and renovation, in the century between Herod's initial work and the time of Josephus's description. Representations of the Temple may appear on tetradrachms of the Bar-Kochba period (fig. 31), as well as on the frescoes of the Dura-Europos synagogue. The coins show a tetrastyle Ionic portico with possibly a stylized Ionic vegetal frieze above. At the synagogue, Panel WB3 shows a triple gateway, perhaps the temenos wall, and above, a Corinthian peristyle and a pedimental roof over a large double doorway. There are antefixes at each end, which seem to be winged victories. Within the colonnade is a plain ashlar cella wall. The stoas may appear on the Madaba map, but this is by no means certain.

There is little point in repeating a description that has been discussed and analyzed many times. Certain details are of particular interest, however, in a consideration of the Roman qualities of the Herodian construction. As usual, Herod's builders shaped nature to their needs, using a large amount of fill to build new foundations and to create a new precinct, which was double the size of the previous one (*BJ* 1.401): it may have been the completion of the foundations of the precinct that determined Josephus's construction period of 17–18 months (*AJ* 15.421). Bridges were built over the Tyropaion valley to the west of the temenos, and there were gates on the south side, one of which commemorated Marcus Agrippa (*BJ* 1.416). Stoas with marble columns surrounded the precinct: the one on the south, which Josephus found particularly notable, was called the *stoa basileia* (fig. 36), but it was probably more basilica than stoa. It had a precipitous view to the south, and consisted of four marble Corinthian colonnades, with a clerestory roof. The ceiling was of cedar, probably cedar of Lebanon as at Masada. There was little artistic adornment to the complex—Josephus said that the colonnades were impressive enough without it—but the Temple itself was decorated with golden vine clusters (*BJ* 5.210; *AJ* 15.395; Tacitus, *Histories* 5.5), in the contemporary Augustan style. Floor mosaics may also have existed. The Temple also had a golden eagle over its main gate, effectively a pedimental sculpture (*BJ* 1.648–55), whose removal became a symbol of opposition to Herod during his last days. The complex was integrated into existing Herodian buildings in Jerusalem, connecting to the Antonia on the north and to the palace on the west.

Other Structures. Jerusalem also contained the usual elements of a Hellenistic-Roman city, although the literary notices are scanty. There was a theater (*AJ* 15.268, 272, 279) adorned with inscriptions honoring Augustus and trophies commemorating his conquests and the expansion of Rome, which caused difficulty for Herod, since they were thought by some to be graven images. There was also an amphitheater (*AJ* 15.268), "in the plain," and so not in the city proper. The theater and amphitheater were the site of the quadrennial Kaisareia, the games in honor of Augustus, which included not only athletic contests but music and drama (*AJ* 15.268–71). Nothing further is known about the games, and they probably did not survive the destruction of the city in A.D. 70, if they lasted that long. Josephus also mentioned a hippodrome (*BJ* 2.44; *AJ* 17.255), but only in the context of events of the 60's A.C., and there is no specific evidence that Herod built it, although with his interest in athletics, he is a more probable builder than any of his successors. A bouleuterion, again of uncertain date, was near the temple (*BJ* 5.144), as was a *xystos* (*BJ* 2.344, 5.144), perhaps the Hellenistic gymnasium of the second century B.C. (2 Macc. 4.9). It is not clear what Josephus meant by the "Memorial of Herod" (*BJ* 5.108, 507), south of Mount Skopas, again cited only in the context of the 60's A.C., and with no specification as to which Herod was memorialized. Herod also built a marble monument at the Tomb of David, which he had opened and robbed (*AJ* 16.179–83: Josephus's source was Nikolaos [fr. 101], who, according to Josephus, ignored the matter of the robbery).

Josephus was particularly interested in the walls of Jerusalem, although Herod built little if any part of them (*BJ* 5.142–75). But Herod did build a number of towers, which were incorporated into existing fortifications. The first was named Hippikos, after an otherwise unknown friend (*BJ* 5.163). It was square and contained a cistern above a base of masonry. The second, named Phasael after his brother, was also square but nearly twice as large as Hippikos, and contained a residence, including a bath: it was said to resemble the Pharos of Alexandria (*BJ* 5.166–69; *AJ* 16.144). The third and smallest was named Mariamme; it too had residences. All three were constructed out of especially large blocks of marble (*BJ* 5.172–75). They adjoined Herod's palace, but the Mariamme tower must have been built before her death in 29 B.C. and so predates the palace construction. Since the towers contained living quarters, they may have served as Herod's Jerusalem residence before the palace itself was built. A fourth tower, Psephinos, "Rubble Tower" or "Stone Tower" (*BJ* 5.147, 159), lay to the north, but is only mentioned in the context of the 60's A.C. and may have been a rural watchtower of an earlier era.

The Extant Remains.   What has been written about Herodian Jerusalem far exceeds the visible remains, and what has been discovered has been continuously disputed and controversial. A brief summary of the evidence and its relationship to the Herodian building program is given below.

Little survives of the Antonia; most of the masonry and cuttings northwest of the Temple compound, in the vicinity of the convent of the Sisters of Zion, seem to date to the second century A.C. The only material that is probably part of the fortress is the platform itself. Although it is widely disputed exactly where the Antonia sat on this platform, and which of the various rock cuttings, water channels, and pools in the area represent the foundations and substructures of the building, it is clear that nothing of it is extant.

All that remains of the Herodian Temple are its platform and the exterior walls of the temenos. The location of the complex is not disputed, but none of the interior structures survives. The temenos is 485 m long on its longest side (the west), and 280 m on its shortest (the south). The site was rugged and required a great deal of leveling and filling, with walls up to 30 m high. The core was earth and rubble, except on the south, where there were barrel vaults. Large ashlar blocks, similar to those at Hebron, were used throughout, some up to 10 m long by 2.5 m, and approximately 1.0 m high. They reveal the marked drafting and anathyrosis typical of Herodian masonry. The western wall, built along the Tyropaion valley, is the most famous, and remnants of the bridges that spanned the valley and led west into the city are visible. The notorious construction delays and incomplete state of the project are perhaps seen in the unfinished northern portions of the western wall, accessible today only by tunnels.

Excavation in the 1970's revealed that Herod had made significant changes in the topography of the area around the southwest corner of the Temple precinct. He demolished many Hellenistic structures and incorporated others—especially elements of the water distribution system—into his urban plan. The area was a major focal point of the urban life of Jerusalem for the following century. The centerpiece was a monumental stairway that led up from an ancient street running north-south through the Tyropaion valley. This stairway began to the west of the street, turned north and then east—passing over the street—before entering the Temple *temenos*.

Virtually nothing of the north wall of the Temple precinct survives, but long stretches of the eastern wall are visible, including a join, 32 m north of the southeast corner, where Herodian masonry on the south seems to abut older masonry to the north, perhaps giving an indication of Herod's expansion of the site. The south wall is visible for much of its length and contains the remnants of the two gates described by Josephus. Medieval constructions along the south side of the Haram esh-Sharif—the successor to the Temple Mount that is visible today—seem in places to be based on the Herodian construction. In particular, the pillars of the "Women's Mosque" and the "Moslem Museum" reflect the columns of the basilica that Josephus (*AJ* 15.410–15) described as being along the south side of the Temple Mount. These medieval pillars are 5.36 m apart, which is exactly the intercolumniation of 17.3 feet that Josephus's calculations yield, using a foot of 0.3089 m that is known elsewhere in the area. Larger than the Roman foot of 0.2950 to 0.2963 m, this is perhaps a Seleukid foot, which was better known in the East. A stairway 64 m wide and consisting of thirty steps, seemingly leading up from a square south of the temenos, may be part of the access to the Temple precinct. In addition, architectural debris from the Temple destruction in A.D. 70 was found south of the temenos, along the south wall, including fragments of decorated reliefs in vegetal and geometric patterns, and architectural details in the Corinthian order. A goldleaf overlay was on some of the fragments. There was also an inscription recording the contribution of a certain Paris, son of Akestor of Rhodes, who around 18 or 17 B.C. helped pay for the Temple pavement, perhaps in return for the assistance Herod had provided his native island.

Remains of Herod's palace are also scant. The platform is 130 by 330 m, created by parallel retaining walls with earth placed between them: its shape is reflected in the outline of the present "Armenian Gardens" at the southwest corner of the Old City. In addition, some fragments of the superstructure, decorated in painted plaster, have been discovered. Standing at the north edge of the palace site is a structure long known as "David's Tower," which survives to 19 m It is 17 by 23 m at the base, constructed of ashlar masonry in the Herodian style (fig. 28). The interior is packed solid with masonry. There is little doubt that this is one of the three towers Josephus mentioned, which survived because it was incorporated into later fortification walls. It is normally identified with Phasael or Hippikos, but certainty is impossible, since its measurements fit none of Herod's towers. Its greatest significance is that it is the only piece of standing architecture in Jerusalem from Herod's royal building program.

Although none of the lavish interior decoration of the Herodian buildings of Jerusalem survives, insight may be obtained from the excavation of private houses in the Jewish Quarter, southwest of the Temple precinct. They represent the homes of the aristocracy of Herod's day, and their ornamentation is similar to Herodian decoration at Masada and Jericho. Mosaic floors in floral and geometric patterns, usually with a central rosette, are common, as are frescoes in the Pompeian First Style. In the "Peristyle Build-ing" is a fine *opus sectile* floor in an interlocking twelve-sided pattern of alter-nating squares and diamonds in gray-blue, burnt orange, and white. Also noteworthy are the remains of the "Palatial Mansion," a richly appointed two-story house, noted for its fresco depicting lotus buds. The decoration in these houses—those of the most prominent citizens of late-first-century B.C. Jerusalem—would have been little different from that in Herod's contem-porary palace and demonstrates that Herod's Roman tastes affected others in the city.

None of the other Herodian structures described by Josephus can be located, although the Memorial of Herod has been identified with the so-called "Tomb of Herod's Family" west of the ancient city. Remains known as the Nikophorieh tomb, near the present King David Hotel, have been iden-tified with this monument (fig. 14). A ledge of rock rising above the surface may have supported a monument such as is extant in other contemporary tombs in Jerusalem: fragments of architectural ornamentation are in the vicinity. But the evidence connecting it with Josephus's monument is hypo-thetical. Another possibility, conforming more to Josephus's location, is a structure in *opus reticulatum* found in the New City. Yet there are many pre-sumed Herodian remnants in and around the city, especially elements of the urban plan. The extensive hydraulic installations, most conspicuous in the vicinity of the Antonia, are also Herodian in date: a major aqueduct led into Jerusalem from the Wadi Artas, ten kilometers southwest, the same source as Herodeion's water supply. Portions of this aqueduct are visible in the southwest part of the city.

Schick, *PEFQ* 1892: 115–20; Macalister, *PEFQ* 1901: 397–402; BMC Palestine, 284–87; Abel, *RBibl* 35 (1926): 284–85; Aline de Sion, *La forter-esse Antonia* (1955); Kraeling, *Excavations at Dura-Europos* 8.1 (1956): 105–13; Maurer, *ZDPV* 80 (1964): 137–49; Ita of Sion, *PEQ* 100 (1968): 139–43; Grafman, *IEJ* 20 (1970): 60–66; Mazar, *BiblArch* 33 (1970): 47–60; Renov, *IEJ* 20 (1970): 67–74; Benoit, *HThR* 64 (1971): 135–67; Mazar, *The Excavations in the Old City of Jerusalem near the Temple Mount* (1971), 2–4; Amiran and Eitan, *IEJ* 22 (1972): 50–51; Lämmer, *Physical Education and Sports in the Jewish History and Culture* (1973), 18–38; Lämmer, *Kölner Beiträge zur Sportswissenschaft* 2 (1974): 182–227; Wilkinson, *PEQ* 106 (1974): 33–51; Mazar, *Dossiers de l'archéologie* 10 (May/June 1975): 34–39; Wilkinson, *Levant* 7 (1975): 118–36; Harris, *Greek Athletics and the Jews* (1976), 30–39; Mazar, *IEJ* 28 (1978): 230–37; Wilkinson, *Jerusalem as Jesus Knew It* (1978); Cohn, *PEQ* 111 (1979): 41–52; Busink, *Der Tempel von Jerusalem*, vol. 2 (1980), 1053–1251; Jacobson, *PEQ* 112 (1980): 33–40; Avigad, *Discovering Jerusalem* (1983); Geva, *IEJ* 31 (1981): 57–65; Geva, *IEJ* 33 (1983): 55–71; Isaac, *IEJ* 33 (1983): 86–92; Netzer and Ben-Arieh, *IEJ*

33 (1983): 163–75; *AEpigr* 1984, # 913; Ma'oz, *ErIsr* 18 (1985): 46–57; Mazar, *Die Wasserversorgung Antiker Städte* (1987), 185–88; Ovadiah and Ovadiah, *Hellenistic, Roman and Early Byzantine Mosaic Pavements* (1987), 85–87 (## 128, 129, 131, 134, 136); Patrich, *Bible Review* 4.5 (October 1988): 16–29; Garbrecht and Peleg, *AntW* 20.2 (1989): 2–20; Mazar, *AAP*, 169–95; Ritmeyer and Ritmeyer, *Reconstructing Herod's Temple Mount in Jerusalem* (1990); Jacobson, *Bulletin of the Anglo-Israel Archaeological Society* 10 (1990): 36–66; Wightman, ibid.: 7–35; Avigad, *The Herodian Quarter in Jerusalem* (1991); Wightman, *The Walls of Jerusalem* (1993), 84–87, 105–7, 125–26, 187–88; Avigad, *NEAEHL*, 750–53; Levine, *Josephus and the History of the Greco-Roman Period* (1994), 233–46; Nielsen, *Hellenistic Palaces* (1994), 182–83; Patrich, *Ancient Jerusalem Revealed* (1994), 260–71; Sivan and Solar ibid., 168–76; Jacobson and Gibson, *IEJ* 45 (1995): 162–70; Wightman, *Meditarch*, suppl. 3 (1995), 275–83.

Kallirrhoe

Shortly before his death, Herod, terminally ill, visited the warm baths at Kallirrhoe and participated in a cure prescribed by his doctors (*BJ* 1.657; *AJ* 17.171–72). The site was not otherwise mentioned by Josephus, but is presumably that located by Pliny (*Natural History* 5.72) near Machairous, and by Ptolemy (5.15) near Livias. In Pliny's day, and later, it was noted as a spa, and it appears on the Madaba mosaic map, where several pools, springs, a bathhouse, and palm trees are shown. The identification of the site is not certain, as hot springs are common along the eastern side of the Dead Sea, but remains in the vicinity of the mouth of the Wadi ez-Zara, especially a nymphaion, are probably part of the bathing complex. There also seems to have been a small constructed harbor.

There is no literary or archaeological evidence that Herod built at Kallirrhoe, although fieldwork that began in the 1980's may clarify this. But Kallirrhoe is in an area where Herod built extensively—Machairous is just above it, to the east—and it is probable that a spa visited by him during his last days (and surely at other times) was also a recipient of his architectural patronage.

Donner, *ZDPV* 79 (1963): 59–89; Schult, *ZDPV* 82 (1966): 139–48; Strobel, *ZDPV* 82 (1966): 149–62; Strobel, *ZDPV* 93 (1977): 247–67.

Kypros

Herod built a strong and attractive fortress in the hills above Jericho (map 12, figs. 15, 19, 29), perhaps enlarging a Hasmonean one, and named it Kypros after his mother (*BJ* 1.407, 417; *AJ* 16.143). Construction probably began after Herod permanently acquired the region of Jericho in 30 B.C. Its function was to defend both against internal and external threats, protecting not only the trans-Jordanian frontier but the palace at Jericho. The ruins of Kypros have been identified at Tell el-'Aqaba, on the south side of the Wadi Qelt, 3.5 km west-southwest of Jericho, near the old Jerusalem road. As usual, it is a prominent peak at the edge of the Jordan valley, rising ca. 250 m above the plain. There are the expected terracing and hydraulic installations. Cisterns seem to have been adequate in pre-Herodian days, but Herod's constructions required additional water, and a dramatically constructed aqueduct leads from springs at the west through precipitous terrain, curving around the north of the site, using ten bridges and five tunnels over its length of 14 km. The aqueduct continued below the fort to irrigate fields in the plain.

Excavations in the 1970's revealed remains on two levels: on the summit, there was a large building, whose preserved extent of 30 by 35 m is perhaps slightly more than half its original size. Prominent was a small bathhouse, with fragments of paintings preserved on the walls and some details of marble ornamentation. To the southeast of the summit structure, at a lower level ca. 70 m away, was a larger complex, with its own bathhouse, wall paintings, and a mosaic floor 6.2 m square in the apodyterium. Corinthian column fragments indicate that it may have been arranged around a peristyle. Mosaics are preserved in other rooms of the baths.

Harder, *ZDPV* 78 (1962): 49–54; Netzer, *Qadmoniyot* 8 (1975): 54–61; Ovadiah and Ovadiah, *Hellenistic, Roman and Early Byzantine Mosaic Pavements* (1987): 53 (# 70); Garbrecht and Peleg, *AntW* 20.2 (1989): 2–20; Meshel and Amit, *AAP*, 229–42; Netzer, in *NEAEHL*, 315–17; Garbrecht and Peleg, *BiblArch* 57 (1994): 165–67.

Livias

According to *BJ* 2.59, there was a palace at Betharamatha, a town of Iron Age or earlier origins, which was destroyed in the civil disorders at the time of Herod's death (see also *AJ* 17.277); Antipas fortified the site and named it Julias after Augustus's wife (*BJ* 2.168; *AJ* 18.27). Yet the *Topika* attributed to Eusebios (48.13–15, 49.12–13) records that Herod called Betharamatha Livias, a toponym unknown to Josephus. The name Julias would not have been appropriate to honor Livia until Augustus's death in A.D. 14 and Livia's official adoption into the Julian family. The suggestion that Antipas renamed the site is thus plausible, as is the assertion that the site was actually called Livias before A.D. 14. Yet it seems that there was always uncertainty between the two Roman names, and just as Julia was forgotten as a personal name for Livia, in late antiquity the site reverted to the name Livias. The information is confusing, especially because there is another

Julias, in Galilee, biblical Bethsaida (modern et-Tell), which Josephus recorded was founded by Philippos early in the reign of Tiberius (*BJ* 2.168), but that seems to have been occupied before that date. This Julias was allegedly named after Augustus's daughter (*AJ* 18.28), but such a name would hardly have been reasonable after her banishment in 2 B.C. and would have been highly improbable after her death in A.D. 14, a few weeks after Tiberius's accession (when a city named after Tiberius's mother, now renamed Julia, would have been appropriate). Nevertheless, it is likely that the two cities named Julias became confused—Josephus often mentioned them together—and that the use of the name Livias for one of them was an attempt to distinguish between them that only confused matters more.

Tell er-Ramah, which lies along the Jerusalem-Philadelphia road about eighteen kilometers east of Jericho at 220 m below sea level, has been equated with biblical Betharamatha, although the site does not appear to have any pre-Roman remains. The actual biblical site may be elsewhere in the immediate vicinity. Although early travelers saw Roman pottery at Tell er-Ramah, and there is a likelihood that it is Livias/Julias, no systematic examination of the site has been made.

Glueck, *BASOR* 91 (October 1943): 20–21; Harder, *ZDPV* 78 (1962): 60–63; Jones, *Cities*, 273–274; Schürer (NEV), 2: 176–78.

Machairous

The fortress of Machairous, whose origins were in Hellenistic times, lies on the eastern side of the Dead Sea, above the hot springs of Kallirrhoe (map 13, fig. 16). Founded by Alexandros Jannaios (*BJ* 7.171), it was demolished by Pompey (Strabo 16.2.40), refortified by the Hasmonean Alexandros, and destroyed again by Gabinius, in a campaign in which the young Marcus Antonius distinguished himself (*BJ* 1.160–63; *AJ* 14.83–84). Even after its second Roman destruction, there was another Hasmonean attempt to regain the place, when Aristoboulos II retreated to the site and was unsuccessful in refortifying it (*BJ* 1.172–73; *AJ* 14.95–97). It was this history that probably led Pliny to called it "secunda quondam arx Judaeae, ab Hierosolymis" (*Natural History* 5.72).

The origin of the name is uncertain. A *machaira* or *machairion* is a knife or a dagger (*Iliad* 11.844, Herodotos 6.75, etc.), a word used often by Josephus, perhaps most notably for the weapon of Goliath, with which he was killed (*AJ* 6.190). The term as a toponym could either be descriptive, indicating the dagger-like promontory on which Machairous is located, or metaphoric, indicating its defensive role. If so, Machairous is unusual among the Hasmonean and Herodian fortresses in that it was not named after a family member: only Masada, with which it shares many characteristics, also has a nonfamilial name. But it is possible that Machairous was named after Machairas, a commander whom Antonius sent to assist Herod in asserting control over his newly assigned kingdom (*BJ* 1.317–44; *AJ* 14.434–57). A problem with this interpretation is that Machairas seems to have been untrustworthy and somewhat of a problem for Herod, although they eventually settled their differences. It also requires the reference by Strabo (12.2.20) to Hasmonean Machairous to be anachronistic, but this is not a major problem since while in the region Strabo may have heard only the Herodian name.

Machairas is an enigmatic figure not known elsewhere. He seems not to have been Roman, but this was not unusual for commanders in the last years of the Republic. It is a Pontic royal name: a Machares was a son of Mithradates VI, the Great, who had been killed by his father in 63 B.C. after leading a revolt encouraged by the Romans (Plutarch, *Lucullus* 24; Appian, *Mithradatic War* 67, 78, 83, 102, 113; Dio 36.50): Herod's commander might have been Machares's son.

Predictably, Herod early showed great interest in the site. Because of its later role in the Jewish revolt of the 60's A.C., Josephus described it in greater detail than the other Herodian fortresses north and east of the Dead Sea (*BJ* 7.163–89). He noted its secure location, surrounded by deep ravines, and its virtually impregnable position. Herod fortified it because of its defensiveness and its position on the Nabataean frontier, virtually creating a city with a circuit wall and a palace at the summit. There were the usual hydraulic installations. The area was also noted for certain botanical, geological, and mineralogical phenomena. The date of Herod's construction is not known, although most of the fortresses in the vicinity belong to the first few years of his reign.

Some years after Herod's death, a famous event occurred at Machairous. It was here, in the late 20's A.C., that Antipas executed John the Baptist (*AJ* 18.117–19). The biblical tradition records that it was because of the entreaties of his stepdaughter, the daughter of his wife (and niece) Herodias, who had danced for him (Matt. 14.1–12; Mark 6.14–29). The daughter is not named, but the only daughter of Herodias known to Josephus was Herod the Great's granddaughter Salome (*AJ* 18.136). Despite the popular tradition that Salome herself was killed by Antipas after her dance and fateful request, as depicted by Oscar Wilde and Richard Strauss, she in fact survived to marry first her uncle Philippos (*AJ* 18.137) and then her cousin Aristoboulos, son of Herod of Chalkis. Nero made Aristoboulos king of Lesser Armenia in A.D. 54 (*AJ* 20.158); he and Salome had three children, Herod, Agrippa, and Aristoboulos, whose destinies are unknown.

There has been little question about the identification of Machairous: Mukawir, above Kallirrhoe, preserves the ancient name. Excavations in the 1970's and 1980's have extensively uncovered the site, which is being developed in the 1990's as a tourist location.

The basic plan conforms to that of other Herodian fortresses but is somewhat more elaborate than those north of the Dead Sea. The hill was artificially enlarged into the typical conical shape. An aqueduct brought water from the southeast. A circuit wall and tower enclosed both the lower city and the summit palace. At the southwest edge of the fortification is the palace proper, with its own walls. Towers at the southeast and northwest of this structure are probably remnants of one of the Hasmonean fortresses: at the southwest is a third tower, perhaps originally Herodian.

The palace consists of several units over an area of 4,000 m². It was spacious and attractive, virtually a city (*BJ* 7.173), elaborate enough for Antipas to use for a grandiose birthday party, probably his fiftieth (Matt. 14.6; Mark 6.21). The southeast corner is dominated by baths, south of a large courtyard with decorative plaster moldings and mosaics. A large mosaic in the tepidarium is preserved along its edges and reveals a spiral wave pattern in black on a white background. It may have been the work of the same mosaicists who decorated Masada. To the west of the baths, and separated from them by a long corridor, are two triclinia; north of these, in the northwest corner of the palace, is a peristyle courtyard. Living areas lie to the west and east. On the southwest, a tower, probably of Hasmonean origin, created a loggia overlooking the ravine. Machairous was second only to Masada as an elaborate Herodian country villa. Josephus used the term *polis* to describe the site, and based on the remains of the palace, the word seems an exaggeration, but it may refer to a village on the northeast slopes of the mound that existed by at least the latter part of the first century A.C.

Abel, *Géographie* (1938), 2; 371–72; Plöger, *ZDPV* 71 (1955): 151–55; Schottroff, *ZDPV* 82 (1966): 168–74; Strobel, *ADAJ* 17 (1972): 101–27; Strobel, *ZDPV* 93 (1977): 247–67; Corbo, *Liber Annuus* 29 (1979): 315–26; Loffreda, *Liber Annuus* 30 (1980): 377–402; Piccirillo, *Liber Annuus* 30 (1980): 403–14; Corbo and Loffreda, *Liber Annuus* 31 (1981): 257–86; De Vries and Bikai, *AJA* 97 (1993): 505–6; Piccirillo, *Mosaics of Jordan* (1993) 245.

Mamre

Six stadia north of Hebron is the site of Mamre, modern Ramat el-Khalil (fig. 12). Like Hebron, it was associated with Abraham: in Josephus's time, the tree under which Abraham settled and where he was warned about the destruction of Sodom and Gomorrah (Gen. 13.18, 14.13, 18.1) was still shown (*BJ* 4.533; *AJ* 1.196). Josephus mentioned no Herodian construction at Mamre, but there is compelling archaeological and intuitive evidence that Herod monumentalized this sacred site as he did that of Hebron.

An enclosure, 49 by 65 m, almost identical in technique to that at Hebron, but larger, was constructed at Mamre. Although much of it was rebuilt in the early second century A.C., probably at the time of Hadrian, the north wall is preserved in its earlier phase and is probably the best remnant of an original construction in the same type of ashlar masonry and pilasters as at Hebron. Thus the original phase is probably Herodian in date, a conclusion strengthened by the discovery of Herodian coins and fragments of decorative sculpture in the Herodian style. Josephus may unconsciously have described the structure when he placed Abraham sitting at the door of his courtyard.

Unlike that at Hebron, the Mamre structure continued to evolve and eventually became a Christian basilica, so the presumed Herodian material is only slightly preserved, and the version on the Madaba mosaic map may represent little of the Herodian work. The Herodian precinct seems to have been unfinished, which may indicate that it was constructed late in Herod's career: a legend concerning the lack of completion of the structure was still current among local villagers early in the twentieth century. Herod's precinct may have fallen into ruins by the latter first century A.C.

Dupont-Sommer, *Syria* 11 (1930): 16–32; Mader, *RBibl* 39 (1930): 84–117; Mader, *Mambre* (1957).

Masada

In the 40's B.C., when Herod was beginning to consolidate his power, Masada (map 14, figs. 33, 34) was renowned as the strongest of the Hasmonean fortresses (*BJ* 1.237; *AJ* 14.296). It was originally built by a certain Jonathan, perhaps the brother of Judas Maccabeus, implying original construction in the second half of the second century B.C. or (if another Jonathan were meant) as late as the first quarter of the following century. Jonathan was responsible for naming it Masada (*BJ* 4.399, 7.285). It is unusual among the Hasmonean-Herodian fortresses in that it does not seem to have had a Greek name.

Masada was of particular importance to Herod in his earliest days. He seized possession of it as early as 42 B.C. and used it as a stronghold and refuge for his followers and family, who stayed there while Herod went to Rome at the end of 40 B.C. But the Hasmoneans besieged the Herodians at Masada, and Herod's first goal upon returning was to rescue them (*BJ* 1.237–303; *AJ* 14.358–413).

Given its proven strength and recent turbulent history, Masada was thus, as might be expected, an early priority in the Herodian building program, probably the first fortified palace he built. It always served as a strong place of refuge at turning points in his career: for example, he placed his mother, sister, and children there when he went to meet Octavian after Actium (*AJ* 15.184). Its location near Herod's reputed homeland of Idumaea would have increased its attractiveness. Herod's greatest fear when he constructed the fortress was of Cleopatra, who coveted Judaea (*BJ* 7.300): this may date the original Herodian construction to around 36 B.C., when Antonius began giving parcels of Herod's kingdom to her (*BJ* 1.360; *AJ* 15.92).

The precipitous nature of Masada is well known and is the focal point of Josephus's description (*BJ* 7.275–303): the site was accessible only by two dangerous tracks, one 30 stadia long. Herod built an impressive circuit wall running 8 stadia around the summit, 12 *peches* high and 8 wide (about 7 by 5 m), with 37 towers, 50 *peches* high (about 30 m). Dwelling areas were attached to the wall throughout its circuit. There was a palace at a lower level than the summit, with peristyles and baths, mosaics on the floors, and four towers at the corners, 60 *peches* high. At the point where the rock of Masada connects with the uplands to the west, a tower defended the access. Numerous reservoirs were cut into the rock, and the modern visitor may be astonished to learn that in Herod's day, the site was noted for its tropical richness.

The site was intended to withstand a major siege: in fact, when it was defended against the Romans in the 60's A.C., the Herodian provisions of nearly a century earlier were found still usable, as well as arms and armor for 10,000 troops, and quantities of bulk metal for additional weapons. Herod also intended that the surface of the summit be cultivated so that the site would be as self-sustaining as possible.

The rock of Masada has been identified since the nineteenth century and was thoroughly excavated in the 1950's and 1960's. The site is surrounded by a wall of 1.4 km, as Josephus described it, in casemate style and covered with a white plaster, perhaps leading Josephus to believe it was of white stone. The width of 4 m also conforms to Josephus's measurement. Towers at irregular intervals are probably less than the height of 50 *peches* asserted by Josephus. There are four gates. Josephus's dwelling areas attached to the walls are in fact the casemates.

Josephus mentioned only the main palace, which is found at the northern extremity of the rock, on three levels. The uppermost consisted of a terrace holding a semicircular colonnaded exedra, similar to that in the palace at Caesarea, with a block of living quarters behind, surrounding an Ionic peristyle. An open area on the east side with a staircase leading up to the terrace was the method of entry. Approximately 20 m below this complex, on a ledge on the north face of Masada, is a middle terrace dominated by a circular building. Access is by a stairway leading from the upper terrace down the cliff to the west side of the middle complex, entering at a large room. A further 15 m below, on a constructed platform at the top of the talus slope, is the third level, also reached by a staircase down the west side. There is a central peristyle court in the Corinthian order, and, on the east side, a small bathhouse. All the elements of this multilevel palace were richly decorated with wall paintings, including floral motifs reflective of Augustan garden scenes. Imported wood, particularly cedar of Lebanon, was used in these and other residential structures. The function of this palace seems to have been purely recreational, in the style of the luxurious Italian villas of the late Republic.

Elsewhere there were other palatial structures, primarily a large (4,000 m²) western palace. It is essentially square, consisting of a residential area in the southeast built around an Ionic peristyle. The west side of the court contained the bedrooms and dining rooms, with a bath on the northeast side. Administrative and ceremonial rooms were also in this area. Other wings of the palace contained service areas and storerooms. The entire complex was richly paved with lavish mosaics (fig. 34), the finest known from the Herodian period. The mosaic patterns are both in geometric and floral styles, including rare examples of intersecting circles and fig-leaf patterns. Because of the presence of a throne room and the large size of this complex, the excavators assumed that it was the principal administrative structure on Masada.

There are three other residential structures southeast of the western palace, each of which seems to have been a small residence, perhaps for officials stationed on the site. An elaborate bathhouse stood south of the northern palace. The entrance was on the northeast side, from which one progressed through the usual bathing stages, leading to a caldarium on the east side. The bath is the best preserved of the numerous Herodian bathing structures and contains fine mosaics and wall paintings (fig. 33). The entire effect of the summit, given its lushness and scattered structures, was that of a Persian *paradeisos* and its pavilions, unique in the Herodian building program.

Josephus emphasized the storerooms and cisterns that made Masada impregnable. A large area of storehouses lies to the south of the northern palace, with long storerooms, generally 20 by 38 m. There are others scattered around the site and in the western palace. A dozen cisterns have been found, cut into bedrock, with a total capacity of 40,000 m³, and there are additional cisterns in the various residences. An aqueduct carried rainwater to the site from the west.

It seems that Masada was built in several phases during Herod's reign. It is not clear what Hasmonean structures may have existed when he began to build. The only certain Hasmonean constructions are cisterns (*BJ* 1.286–87; *AJ* 14.390), but there would have been other buildings to use the water collected. The initial Herodian work, around 36 B.C., which may have included repair or rebuilding of the Hasmonean structures, consisted of the beginnings of the western palace, some of the smaller residences, and some of the cisterns. The site was unwalled at this time, but there may have been a number of watchtowers. A few years later, perhaps between 26 and 22 B.C., the northern palace and the storehouses immediately to the south were constructed, the western palace was enlarged, and the large cisterns excavated. In a final phase, around 15 B.C., the fortification wall was built and the western palace enlarged to its final form.

Yadin, *Masada* (1966); Busink, *Der Tempel von Jerusalem*, vol. 2 (1980), 1027–34; Ovadiah, *Geometric and Floral Patterns in Ancient Mosaics* (1980), 38–39; Netzer, *Die Wasserversorgung Antiker Städte* (1987), 189–192; Ovadiah and Ovadiah, *Hellenistic, Roman and Early Byzantine Mosaic Pavements* (1987), 109–10 (## 181–83); Garbrecht and Peleg, *AntW* 20.2 (1989): 18–19; Lipschitz and Lev-Yadun, *BASOR* 274 (1989): 27–32; Netzer, in *AAP*, 261–71; Small, *Levant* 22 (1990): 139–47; Netzer, *Masada*, vol. 3: *The Buildings, Stratigraphy, and Architecture* (1991), 615–23; Nielsen, *Hellenistic Palaces* (1994), 184–93; Foerster, *Masada*, vol. 5: *Art and Architecture* (1995).

Paneion

At the sanctuary of Pan, immediately after Augustus's trip to Syria in 20 B.C. when he enlarged Herod's kingdom to the north, Herod built a temple to Augustus (*BJ* 1.404–6; *AJ* 15.363–64) of white (and thus imported) marble. At the Paneion there were a cave and a spring that was considered the source of the Jordan. It was a striking spot, suitable for Herod's second temple to the emperor, and allowed the ancient sanctity of the site to be transferred to the imperial cult (fig. 10).

In later years, Herod's descendants also favored the area: his son Philippos built his own Caesarea in the vicinity (*BJ* 2.168; *AJ* 18.28), and his greatgrandson Agrippa II further enhanced the natural beauty of the locality (*BJ* 3.514) and also enlarged Philippos's Caesarea and renamed it Neronias (*AJ* 20.211), a toponym that did not long survive. In Herod's day, a city called Paneas existed at the site, the predecessor of Caesarea, but there is a clear distinction in Josephus's text between the urban site of Caesarea and the natural cave of Pan where the temple of Augustus was located. It was a rare example, for the southern Levant, of a Hellenic rural shrine. Although it had non-Greek antecedents, it seems to have become hellenized by the second century B.C. (Polybios 16.18), and retained its simple character until Herod's construction. Games took place at the site in the second century A.C., but when they were established is uncertain.

Herod seems to have built his temple as a monumental entrance to the grotto of Pan. The use of white marble, an unusual specification, indicates the lavishness of the construction but is not enough to indicate the origin of the stone. Over twenty different types of marble were known in early Imperial times: the most common white ones were Pentelic and Parian, either of which could have been imported by Herod. Marble had been imported to Rome as early as 78 B.C. (Pliny, *Natural History* 36.49), and it would have been visible to Herod on his first trip to the city. Marcus Agrippa seems to have been involved in the marble trade, another reason for Herod's interest. There is no way of determining from the text of Josephus whether the temple was merely faced with marble (the more common technique at Rome in the Augustan period) or actually constructed of marble ashlars (a rare process at Rome, except in the Forum of Augustus, until the period of Domitian).

The Temple of Augustus at the Paneion is one of the few Herodian architectural monuments to appear on coins. A coin of Philippos's identifying him as a city founder was probably struck at a city that he founded (fig. 32). He is credited with two (*AJ* 18.28): Julias, a village with no strong Greco-Roman traditions, and Caesarea, whose grandiose name indicates both its importance and its role in Greco-Roman city foundation. This coin is therefore probably from his Caesarea. The date on the coin is the thirty-fourth year of his reign, probably A.D. 30/31. The emperor Tiberius is on the obverse, and on the reverse is the façade of a temple, which appears in the same form on almost all the known coins of Philippos. The earliest in the sequence has the date of year 9 or A.D. 5/6.

The façade represented is Ionic tetrastyle, with a pediment containing what appears to be a shield. The regnal dates usually appear between the columns. A high foundation, in the Italian style, appears on most of the coins. There is no reason to doubt that this is a numismatic representation of Herod's temple to Augustus, especially since the coin sequence began while Augustus was still reigning and the earlier ones bear his portrait on the obverse.

The question remains of how literal the temple representation is. The use of a shield on the pediment has precedents in late Republican Rome that would have been known to Herod: one is reminded of the trophies from the Piazza della Consolazione reliefs. The Ionic order is reasonable as an imitation of Augustan architecture: in examples too numerous to list, it was the preferred order in Augustan Rome, even as late as the Temple of Deified Augustus. As expected, the Ionic frieze course appears to be unsculpted. But the greatest problem is the tetrastyle format. If this is to be taken literally, it means that the structure was a shrine rather than a temple. This is not impossible: early eastern temples to Rome and the imperial cult were often mere chapels.

Josephus in both citations called the temple a *naos*, not a *naiskos*. But he never used the word *naiskos* in describing Greco-Roman architecture. The only Herodian Temple of Augustus whose plan is known is that at Sebaste, where the façade is 24 m across, implausible for tetrastyle, as it would give an intercolumniation half again as large as that of the Parthenon. Hexastyle or heptastyle is more reasonable for the Paneion, and one assumes that the coin representation was typical numismatic simplification. Herod would not have skimped on a Temple of Augustus, and his use of imported marble for the construction—an indulgence relatively uncommon even in Augustan Rome—indicates an elaborate building. But the limited space at the grotto, and the need to incorporate the temple into an existing area, may have meant this structure, however elaborate, was more modest in size than Herod's other temples. A structure near the Grotto of Pan in *opus quadratum* with walls 10.5 m apart may be the remains of the temple: 18 m of the west wall is visible.

To the west, a constructed terrace 20 by 120 m and 15 m above the nearby surface contains remnants of parallel vaults in *opus reticulatum*. The site is in a particularly attractive location, with a stairway approaching it from below. Recent excavation suggests, however, that this was a construction of the second century A.C. Other scattered remains in the vicinity may be those of the urban center that was developed by Herod and his successors.

BMC Palestine, 228; Hölscher, in *RE*, 36 (1949): 594–600; Ward-Perkins, *JRS* 41 (1951): 89–104; Moretti, *Iscrizioni agonistiche greche* (1953), # 72; Reifenberg, *Ancient Jewish Coins* (1965), ## 37–44; Rey-Coquais, in *PECS*, 670; Tuchelt, *IstMitt*, suppl. 23 (1979): 30–33; Ma'oz, in *NEAEHL*, 136–43; Wolff, *AJA* 97 (1993): 153–56: Strickert, *Bethsaida*, vol. 1 (1995), 165–89.

Phasaelis

In the Jordan valley north of Jericho (fig. 6), Herod built a modest yet important city, which he named after his brother Phasael (*BJ* 1.418; *AJ* 16.145), who had committed suicide during imprisonment by the Hasmoneans (*BJ* 1.271–72; *AJ* 14.367–69). The date of the foundation is unspecified, but since Phasael's death was one of the events that persuaded Herod to go to Rome in 40 B.C., and it had probably occurred in the autumn of that year, this may have been one of Herod's earliest civil building projects: he seems to have been particularly grieved at the death of his brother (*BJ* 1.278). The city seems to have been designed to bring agriculture and industry to a remote, unpopulated area, and it is thus a rare documentation of the Herodian economic program. It retained its agricultural prosperity for many years, perhaps one of the reasons Herod willed it to his sister Salome (*BJ* 2.98; *AJ* 17.189, 321), and she in turn willed it to Livia (*BJ* 2.167; *AJ* 18.31). Its date palms were noted by Pliny (*Natural History* 13.44) and perhaps Horace (*Epistles* 2.2.184) and seem to appear on the Madaba mosaic map. It was prominent enough to be mentioned by Ptolemy (*Geography* 5.15) and was one of only two Herodian foundations mentioned by Stephanos (q.v.)

Fig. 25. Askalon, bouleuterion from the south. Photograph by Duane W. Roller.

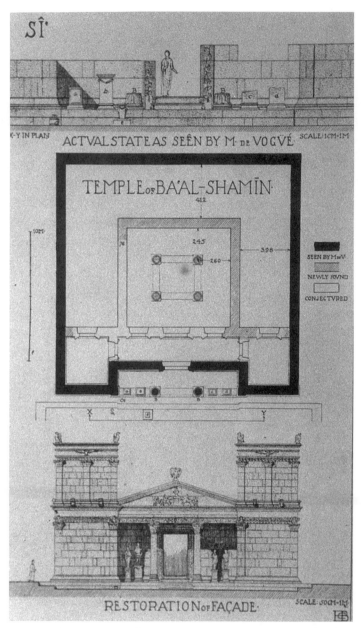

Fig. 26. Seia, Butler's plan and restoration of the Temple of Ba'al Shamin. The statue of Herod is to the right of the central door. From Howard Crosby Butler, *Publications of the Princeton University Archaeological Expeditions to Syria in 1904–1905 and 1909. Division II: Ancient Architecture in Syria. Section A: Southern Syria. Part 6: Si' (Seeia)* (Leiden, 1916), ill. 325.

Fig. 27. *Opus reticulatum* in baths at second palace, Jericho. Courtesy Letitia K. Roller.

Fig. 28. Ashlar masonry with anathyrosis (Jerusalem, "Tower of David"). Photograph by Duane W. Roller.

Fig. 29. Rubble masonry (Kypros). Photograph by Duane W. Roller.

Fig. 30. Façade of the Temple of Augustus and Roma, Caesarea, as depicted on the reverse of a coin of Agrippa I, A.D. 43/44 (BMC Palestine, p. 238, no. 23). Courtesy Trustees of the British Museum.

Fig. 31. Façade of the Jerusalem Temple, as depicted on the obverse of a Second Revolt tetradrachm, A.D. 132 (BMC Palestine, p. 284, no. 1). Courtesy Trustees of the British Museum.

Fig. 32. Façade of the Temple of Augustus, Paneion (?), as depicted on the reverse of a coin of Philippos, A.D. 8/9 (BMC Palestine, p. 228, no. 1). Courtesy Trustees of the British Museum.

Fig. 33. First Style wall decoration at Masada (apodyterium of the northern bathhouse). Photograph by Duane W. Roller.

Fig. 34. Mosaic at Masada (western palace). Photograph by Duane W. Roller.

Fig. 35. Sculpted Nike at Askalon, perhaps originally at the main doorway to the bouleuterion. Photograph by Duane W. Roller.

Fig. 36. Model of the *stoa basileia*, south edge of the Temple Precinct, Jerusalem. Courtesy Holyland Hotel.

Fig. 37. Model of Herod's Palace, Jerusalem. Courtesy Holyland Hotel.

Fig. 38. Archelais (?), at Khirbet el-Beiyudat, view from the southwest. Photograph by Duane W. Roller.

Fig. 39. Sepphoris (Autokratoris), theater, view from the southwest. Photograph by Duane W. Roller.

Fig. 40. Blocks from Philippos's Caesarea, now in the west gate of Qalat Nimrod. Photograph by Duane W. Roller.

Fig. 41. Drachm of Archelaos of Kappadokia, 22 B.C. (BMC Galatia, Cappadocia, and Syria, p. 44, no. 2). Courtesy Trustees of the British Museum.

Fig. 42. Elaioussa-Sebaste. Photograph by Duane W. Roller.

Fig. 43. Amaseia, where Strabo lived and worked. View southeast from the palace of Pythodoris. Photograph by Duane W. Roller.

Fig. 44. The Temple of Bel, Palmyra, the cella from the southwest. Photograph by Duane W. Roller.

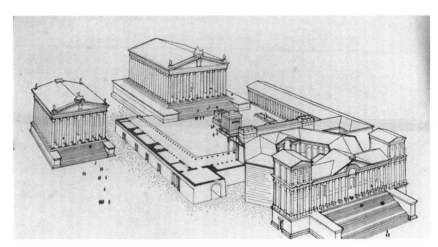

Fig. 45. The sanctuary, Baalbek. From J. B. Ward-Perkins, *Roman Imperial Architecture*, 2d ed. (Harmondsworth, 1981), fig. 156. Courtesy Yale University Press Pelican History of Art.

Fig. 46. Tivoli, Hadrian's Villa (the island villa known today as the Teatro maritti-mo). Photograph by Duane W. Roller.

Fig. 47. Ara Pacis, Rome, the south frieze of the screen, showing the group that may include Herod's son Antipatris. Photograph by Duane W. Roller.

Fig. 48. Head in the Museum of Fine Arts, Boston, displayed as "Hellenistic Ruler (A Ptolemy?)"; inventory number 59.51. Edwin E. Jack Fund. Courtesy Museum of Fine Arts, Boston.

The site of Phasaelis lies 22 km due north of Jericho at the western edge of the Jordan valley. The ancient name is preserved in the modern Khirbet Fasa'yil. To the north, and in alignment with the town, is Herod's fortress of Alexandreion. Northwest of the site is the Wadi Fasi'yil, where the spring of 'Ain Fasi'yil is the major water source for the region; an aqueduct leads 9 km to the city site. Ancient reservoirs and irrigation ditches are prominent in the area, perhaps, like the aqueduct, remnants of the Herodian hydraulics that fostered the agricultural productivity of the district. The town site is at the beginning of the slope, thus avoiding arable land. There are extensive ruins, which have not been excavated. Cursory examinations in the 1950's and again in the summer of 1996 revealed a town in a Greco-Roman orthogonal plan over an extent of approximately 4 km north to south. Several streets 3–5 m wide are visible, one running for 300 m north-east/southwest, with the foundations of several large buildings; it has been suggested that one of these, 65 by 70 m, was a palace. There are also a possible agora, 26.5 by 102 m, and the foundations of a temple. Remnants of baths are visible in the northeast part of the city. The town was not particularly endowed with major civic structures, and the visible construction is rubble and fieldstone, not ashlar, but its ruins give the impression of a prosperous agricultural community that was a significant factor in the economy of the Herodian state. There is immense potential for excavation at this untouched site, where the descendants of Herod's palms still flourish.

Abel, *Géographie* (1938), 2: 408–9; Glueck, *AASOR*, 25–28 (1945–49): 414; Mowry, *BiblArch* 15.2 (1952): 26–42; Harder, *ZDPV* 78 (1962): 54–60.

Sebaste

The ancient city of Samaria had been destroyed by Hyrkanos I in the late second century B.C. (*BJ* 1.64): Josephus described how the city was block-aded, besieged, and totally destroyed, with the inhabitants sold into slavery. Pompey included it in the original province of Syria (*BJ* 1.156), and Gabinius repopulated the site after some rebuilding (*BJ* 1.166). After Actium, Octavian placed it in Herod's kingdom (*AJ* 15.217), and very shortly thereafter Herod rebuilt it (map 15, fig. 9)

Herod had had a number of early associations with Samaria. It had been the scene of disturbances in 43 B.C., in the turbulent days after the murder of his father, Antipatros, and Herod had been instrumental in restoring order (*BJ* 1.229). Six years later, he left the siege of Jerusalem to marry Mari-amme at the city (*BJ* 1.344; *AJ* 14.467). Herod thus chose this site for his first city foundation for a combination of reasons: it was an ancient city whose fortunes had declined in recent years; the Romans had shown an interest in the place; it had figured in Herod's early career; and it was a place with a history of opposition to Herod, which might be neutralized by royal favor. Moreover, it was one of the several cities Gabinius had restored, so Herod could demonstrate his continuity with previous Roman building. In future years, his point made, he avoided building at Gabinian sites, until he rebuilt Anthedon as Agrippias late in life. Finally, Samaria had been given to the king by Octavian immediately after Actium, so a city foundation there would demonstrate support for the new regime at Rome.

In January of 27 B.C., Octavian announced to the Senate in Rome that he was resigning all extraordinary powers. It took the Senate three days to come up with a solution that would avoid a renewal of civil war. Part of the plan was a proposal put forth by L. Munatius Plancus, long an associate of Herod's, who had recently completed a term as governor of Syria. This was to give the *cognomen* "Augustus" to Octavian. Soon the title was known in the East in its Greek version, Sebastos; as is often the case, Strabo may have been the first to use the new term in literature (3.3.8; 12.8.16), if Nikolaos did not use it earlier in his biography of Augustus. The situation was thus perfect for Herod to found his first city within his kingdom, to honor the new regime, and to immortalize the new name of its leader by naming it Sebaste. By the end of the first century B.C., the eastern part of the Roman world was dotted with cities named Sebaste, or Sebasteia, or Sebastopolis; as usual, Herod's was the first.

Construction at Sebaste was initiated within the year of the conferring of the name Augustus, was well under way by the thirteenth year of Herod's reign, probably 25/24 B.C. (*AJ* 15.299), and was completed by the start of work on Caesarea and the sending of Alexandros and Aristoboulos to Rome, in 22 B.C. (*AJ* 15.342). Its chronological era seems to have begun in 27 or 26 B.C. By 15 B.C., the city was a showplace of the kingdom, and it was one of the major sights seen by Marcus Agrippa (*AJ* 16.13).

It was in an area of unusual agricultural fertility (*BJ* 1.403), and thus Kore seems to have been its major divinity. Inscriptions and a temple attest that the cult of Kore was well established at the time Sebaste became a Severan *colonia*. Evidence of the cult in the Herodian period is limited, but may be documented on a coin of the city probably dated to the nineteenth year of Herod's reign, ca. 19 B.C. The obverse has the legend "Sebaste" and a female figure facing right, perhaps a cult statue of the goddess.

Herod's Sebaste was enclosed by a circuit wall of twenty stadia and dominated by the Sebasteion, the Temple of Augustus. But Herod went beyond mere architectural construction at Sebaste, creating a constitution for the city and settling former allies in it. The particularly productive countryside was allotted to six thousand settlers: vestiges of the rural settlement and land use are visible even today. Since the city and region had a history of political disturbances, Herod's creation of a fortified and sympathetic population strengthened his own security. But, at the same time, he was careful to make his first major city visually attractive as a monument of his own aesthetic tastes (*BJ* 1.403; *AJ* 15.296–98): the landscaping of the city remained notable for many years. Thus, in the best tradition of city foundation, he was able to satisfy political, strategic, and cultural concerns, creating a city that was modern and attractive and yet fulfilled his own internal political needs. At the same time he demonstrated his loyalty to Rome and to the new regime by giving it a name honoring Augustus and by introducing the latest techniques of Roman architecture, already understood in Rome as a metaphor for the dynamic progressivism of the Augustan world. Both in its name and in its central positioning of the world's first Temple of Augustus, as well as the first Italian-style temple in the East, Herod established at Sebaste the pattern for city-foundation in the eastern Roman world that would last for the next three centuries.

Sebaste was largely excavated during the first third of the twentieth century. Much of the excavation was directed toward the Iron Age city, the capital of the Samaritan kingdom, and many questions remain about the excavated material, especially the later periods. Nevertheless, Sebaste remains the most visible of the three great Herodian cities within his kingdom, since Jerusalem and Caesarea are heavily encumbered with later material.

The city walls described by Josephus can be traced for most of their length, in many places incorporating Hellenistic walls and towers. Prominent are two round towers at the southwest that seem to be purely Herodian. The quality of the wall blocks, which show especially poor drafting, is not up to the usual Herodian standard, a reminder that this was Herod's first major urban project within his kingdom. Previous to this date, his work had been either in Greece or in Syria, where excellent local masons existed, or modest constructions such as fortresses, which did not have the monumentality required of a Hellenistic-Roman city foundation.

The centerpiece of the city was the temple of Augustus, built over the remains of the palace of the kings of Samaria and a Hellenistic fortress. Herod's builders constructed a terrace and extended a platform to the north. On this terrace and platform was built a large peristyle court, whose south side led to the temple proper. The temple and peristyle court rose high above the horizon and would have made an impressive central focus of the city, much as the temples of Pergamon created an urbanized skyline. The monumentalizing of the Capitolium in Rome was a more direct influence on Herod. The entire complex was a predecessor to the Temple at Jerusalem.

Access to the peristyle is not yet understood—the exact area is unexcavated—and the most recent suggestion is that it was from the north, with a stairway laid over arches. Still in question are the issues of whether the colonnade of the peristyle was single or double, and the nature of the columns of the temple. To the west of the temple, there seems to have been a villa, or perhaps a modest palace. It covered approximately 750 sq. m, centered on a peristyle. In the eastern section, the best preserved, were a number of rooms, including a bath. One room had a central mosaic floor, and First Style painting appeared in others. Also in the vicinity of the temple, especially to the east, were storerooms, offices, and other utilitarian structures. A gateway to the southeast seems to have provided access to the area. All these constructions, centering on the Temple of Augustus, seem to have formed a complex conceived as a unit, perhaps the fortified palace of Sebaste that Josephus mentioned as similar to the Antonia in Jerusalem (*AJ* 15.292–93).

The forum of Sebaste lay in the east-central part of the city. Although it, like many of the other monuments, reached its final form with the Severan establishment of a *colonia*, its origins were Herodian. The forum is on an artificial platform 28 by 128 m, raised up as much as 6 m. It was surrounded by porticoes, with a basilical structure on the west side, whose seven standing columns have long been the most visible remnant of ancient Sebaste. These columns are Severan, as is the final plan of the basilica, but Herodian masonry at the northwest corner indicates that the structure was originally of that period.

The only other visible construction from the Herodian period is the stadium, lying in the northeast part of the city. Its extent is 60 by 230 m, and it was surrounded by a colonnade, originally Doric, perhaps making it more of a gymnasium. Although it was rebuilt in later times, the earliest phase of the structure was Herodian. In the Severan period, the precinct became a center of the cult of Kore, but whether this was also the case in earlier times has not been established. The theater of Sebaste is also Severan in its latest form, but the substructures of the seats belonged to an earlier structure, perhaps in a different location, which may have been an otherwise-unknown theater of Herod's.

The extensive hydraulic installations, especially in the eastern part of the city, are almost certainly Herodian in origin, but there are no chronological controls to prove this. Other remains at Sebaste, such as the temple of Kore, are Severan in date, and there is no evidence of a Herodian phase.

Crowfoot, Kenyon, and Sukenik, *Samaria-Sebaste*, vol. 1: *The Buildings at Samaria* (1942), 41–50, 55–57, 62–67, 123–28; Smallwood, *The Jews under Roman Rule* (1976), 77–78; Busink, *Der Tempel von Jerusalem*, vol. 2 (1980): 1035–45; Fulco and Zayadine, *ADAJ* 25 (1981): 197–201; Kokkinos, *Liber Annuus* 35 (1985): 303–6; Dar, *BAR-IS* 308 (1986); Schürer (NEV), 2: 160–64; Netzer, *ErIsr* 19 (1987): 97–105; Frumkin, in *AAP*, 157–67; Barag, *ErIsr* 23 (1992): 293–301; Barag, *PEQ* 125 (1993): 3–17.

Sepphoris

There is no direct evidence that Herod built at the Galilean town of Sepphoris (fig. 39), but some hints indicate the possibility. The town is unknown before the late Hellenistic period (*AJ* 13.338), although scattered pottery indicates a settlement as early as Iron Age times. It was featured in Gabinius's administrative reorganization of the southern Levant (*BJ* 1.170; *AJ* 14.91), but not in his building program. Herod conquered the city early in his reign (*BJ* 1.304; *AJ* 14.404).

At Herod's death, Sepphoris contained a royal palace (*AJ* 17.271) and an arsenal (*BJ* 2.56). Whether these were the work of Herod or Hellenistic survivals is unknown. The site of Sepphoris has revealed extensive, if enigmatic, evidence from the late Hellenistic period onward, but it is difficult to attribute any specific remains to the period of Herod. The royal residence was probably on the summit of the site, and the area was occupied continuously from late Hellenistic into Roman times. On the northeast corner of the summit is the theater of Sepphoris, whose dating has remained controversial since it was excavated in the 1930's. Dates from the first century B.C. to the second or third century A.C. have been proposed. It seems unlikely that it was built by Herod, since Josephus did not mention it, but this negative evidence is by no means certain and Josephus was skimpy in discussing Herodian building in Galilee. Recent opinion has tended toward a date in the time of Antipas, but the archaeological evidence for this continues to be scanty.

Waterman et al., *Preliminary Report* (1937), 29; Albright, *Classical Weekly* 31 (1937–38) 148; Meyers et al., *IEJ* 35 (1985): 295–97; Schürer (NEV), 2: 172–76; Meyers et al., *IEJ* 37 (1987): 275–78; Meyers et al., *IEJ* 40 (1990): 219–33; Meyers, *The Galilee in Late Antiquity* (1992), 331–38; Weiss, in *NEAEHL*, 1325–26; Segal, *Theatres* (1995), 41–43.

Tel Qasile

The site of Tel Qasile lies about two kilometers inland on the north side of the Yarkon river. It was established in the Iron Age as a river port. Its Greco-Roman name is unknown. Excavations between 1948 and 1950 revealed a large structure with courtyard attributed to the Herodian period, which, according to the excavator, "resembles Herodian buildings at Samaria." Pottery from the Augustan period was found in association with the structure.

No indication of function was provided by the excavators. In earlier days, Tel Qasile had served as an important river port and agricultural and industrial center. There is no doubt that it continued to flourish at the time of Herod. As a port city, it may have benefited from royal patronage, and the structure in question may be a warehouse, but all interpretations are speculative.

Maisler, *IEJ* 1 (1950–1951): 214–215; Maisler, *BiblArch* 14.2 (1951) 43–49; Dothan and Dunayevsky, in *NEAEHL* 1204–1207.

PART 2: BUILDING SITES OUTSIDE HEROD'S KINGDOM

Antioch-on-the-Orontes

Herod played a limited but significant part in the building history of Antioch, the greatest Greek city of the Levant (map 6, fig. 22). Especially in his early years, he was often in Antioch (*BJ* 1.328, 512; *AJ* 14.440, 451), and it was there that he made his first official contacts with the Romans, Antonius in particular. In its suburb of Daphne, Messalla defended him against the complaints of the Jewish leaders (*BJ* 1.243), and after the deaths of Antonius and Cleopatra, he escorted Octavian to the city during the latter's return to Rome (*AJ* 15.218). Moreover, Antioch had seen some of the earliest Roman architecture in the East, beginning with that of Q. Marcius Rex in 67 B.C., and continuing with the work of Pompey a few years later and with Julius Caesar's numerous structures in the 40's B.C.

Herod might thus be expected to have adorned this distinguished city, which had figured so prominently in his early career. His efforts at Antioch are one of the few elements in his building program that are documented in sources in addition to Josephus. According to Josephus himself (*BJ* 1.425; *AJ* 16.148), there was a main or broad street twenty stadia long in Antioch that was avoided because of βόρβορος (mud, sewage, or general filth), which Herod paved with marble blocks and then provided with a stoa of equal length. At *BJ* 1.425, only one stoa is mentioned, but *AJ* 16.148 has stoas on both sides. The more modest single stoa is more likely, especially since colonnaded streets were not yet a feature of eastern cities, and *AJ* 16.148 may confuse Tiberius's reconstruction (which would have been the phase visible to Josephus) with Herod's original. The next comment is by the local historian John Malalas, writing in the sixth century A.C., but using official city building records, who recorded that to honor Augustus, Herod paved the streets outside Antioch with white stone (223). At first glance, Malalas's placement of the street outside the city is curious, but probably means outside the original Seleukid foundation and is proof that Malalas's source was a city building record contemporary with the construction. Malalas's detail of white stone, certainly marble, not in Josephus's account, may reflect an accurate memory of the richness of the Herodian workmanship. Finally, one may add the always untrustworthy but entertaining commentary of Moses Khorenats'i (2.25), who described how Herod asked the Armenian king Arsham for workmen to assist in the paving project. However, Moses' account, which is confused and based ultimately on Josephus, adds no information of value.

Marcus Agrippa, always an influence on Herodian building plans, also built at Antioch, creating an entire eponymous district of the city, constructing baths and the necessary hydraulic installations, and restoring the theater and hippodrome (Malalas, 222, 225). Malalas seemingly divided

Agrippa's work between Augustus's visit of 20 B.C. and Agrippa's own five years later. But the earlier date of 20 B.C. is more likely. Some of Agrippa's work may date to this time; Augustus himself was in the area, constructing buildings, and Malalas linked Herod's street with Augustus. Moreover, Malalas (232) wrote that Tiberius, seemingly while emperor (although the text is not clear) and on his return to Rome from a Parthian campaign, built a colonnaded street at Antioch. Although Tiberius never waged a Parthian campaign, or even left Italy, after he became emperor, it is possible that the campaign in question was that in 20 B.C., when he regained the standards lost to the Parthians by Crassus. It is plausible that Malalas confused and conflated Herod's and Tiberius's constructions, which were similar and (from Malalas's point of view of half a millennium later) virtually contemporary. Herod's street may thus be dated to the time Tiberius and Augustus were in the East in 20 B.C.

Regardless, Herod's work at Antioch did not survive long, as the city burned in A.D. 23/24 (Malalas, 235), and Tiberius commissioned a rebuilding, with colonnades along each side and tetrapyla at intersections (Malalas, 223, 232). In fact, Herod's street was rebuilt many times over the next few centuries, leading to both ancient and modern confusion about what belonged to any particular period. Certainly, Malalas, like the modern visitor to Antioch, could not have seen anything but the orientation of Herod's street (although local records provided construction details); the street Malalas walked on was probably originally Antonine and reconstructed by Justinian during Malalas's lifetime.

Nevertheless, there seems no doubt that Herod was the first to monumentalize the main street of Antioch, and that the street was the main north-south axis of the city, which presumably was modestly or even poorly constructed before Herod's day. It is still prominent today in the modern city as Vali Ürgen Bulvari (fig. 22), and, in a late antique version unspoiled by modern construction, appears in the ca. 1785 drawing of the Beroia gate by Louis-François Cassas.

Excavations in the street in the 1930's revealed some details of its construction, although attribution of visible remains to a particular period is difficult. It had pre-Herodian antecedents, and was probably last rebuilt by Justinian in the sixth century A.C. Probes in several places have revealed the modest shops that lined the street in the early Roman period, probably the Herodian phase. The first colonnade appears in the following phase, Tiberius's reconstruction. The street was 9.6 m wide at the time of Trajan, with porticoes 10 m wide, which may still have reflected the original Herodian dimensions (although with only a single portico in Herod's day). Previous to the Herodian constructions, the area was at the edges of the settlement, a poor district, with the Seleukid predecessor to the Herodian street either unpaved or badly drained.

It is important to keep in mind the modest yet profound nature of Herod's achievement. He did not create at Antioch the colonnaded street, so familiar from later Roman construction in the East. Columns as an architectural element of the street—rather than as part of the flanking shops—seem only to have been added by Tiberius. Rather, Herod was imitating the porticoes that, in varying degrees of monumentality, lined the streets of contemporary Rome, especially the shops around the Forum Julium, and the colonnades of the Saepta and the Theater of Pompey, also to be imitated by Herod, to some extent, in the stoas around the Temple at Jerusalem. Josephus's statement that the stoa was on only one side of the street is significant, because it indicates that the thinking of Herod and his architects was still in terms of a street with a portico along it, rather than a colonnaded street. Yet the street and portico were created as a unit, thereby differing from the practice at Rome, where a portico was built that incidentally produced a longitudinal axis and thus a street. Herod's street, located in one of the most important cities of the Greco-Roman world, is a crucial transition from portico to colonnaded street. Here Herod was at his most innovative, launching an architectural form that had not yet been produced at Rome but would become the epitome of eastern Roman architecture.

Cassas, *Voyage pittoresque de la Syrie* (1799), pl. 6; Weber, in *Festgabe für Adolf Deissmann* (1927), 20–66; Downey, *BZ* 38 (1938): 1–15, 299–311; *Antioch-on-the-Orontes, vol. 3* (1941), 12–18; Campbell, *AJA* 44 (1946): 417–19; Downey, *A History of Antioch in Syria from Seleucus to the Arab Conquest* (1961), 39–40, 170–79; Downey, *Ancient Antioch* (1963) 82–83; figs. 4, 10; Lassus, *ANRW* 2.8 (1977): 60–63, 69; Ward-Perkins, *RIA*, 313.

Armenia

For the peculiar problems regarding Herodian building in Armenia, see Appendix I.

Askalon

Askalon (figs. 25, 35) had existed since at least the Middle Bronze Age and seems to have been an independent city in Hellenistic and Roman times (Pliny, *Natural History* 5.68: see *BJ* 2.98, *AJ* 17.321, where, at Herod's death, Augustus gave Salome the palace at Askalon but there is no mention of the city itself). It lay at the southwestern corner of Herod's kingdom and is unique in that it is the only external building site that was not to the north or west of his territory. At Askalon he built baths, fountains, and peristyles that were notable architecturally (*BJ* 1.422), and a palace (*BJ* 2.98; *AJ* 17.321). A late source attributes a Temple of Apollo to Herod, perhaps at Askalon, dated to 30 B.C. (*Chronikon Paschale* [Migne, *PG*, 92] 186, 191).

The city had particularly strong walls at the time of Nero (*BJ* 3.12). It was also the site of a Herodian mint, at least in the early years of his kingship. Yet a mint need not be a particularly large or architecturally interesting structure, and Herod may have continued to use an existing mint, which had produced coins since the second century B.C. Herod's interest in the city may have been due to ancestral connections involving his father Antipatros, as there was a tradition that he came from Askalon and was of low birth. This was unknown to Josephus and Nikolaos: if true, one would not expect Herod's official historian to have recorded it. Mention of Herod's possible Askalonian origin first appears in the *Dialogue with Tryphon* (52) of the second-century A.C. author Justinus Martyr (Migne, *PL*, 6), and it may be merely a religious slander.

Archaeological work at Askalon has been limited. Excavations in the 1920's revealed a large basilical structure with a theatral area at the north end identified as the bouleuterion of Askalon and thus Josephus's peristyle (fig. 25). Attached to the south side was a structure 80 m long with exterior walls and an interior colonnade 6 by 24 m. The exterior walls had two entrances on the long (east and west) sides and three on the short south side; these entrances led to a covered portico approximately 6 m across. The interior side of the exterior wall was faced with shallow pilasters. The architectural order was Corinthian, with columns 6.20 m high standing on bases and pedestals 1.25 m high and with capitals 0.90 m high. Heart-shaped capitals were at the corners. Flooring was of Greek and Italian marble. The structure is remindful of the Basilica Aemilia in Rome, although differing in detail. Dating suggestions have ranged from the period of Herod the Great to the mid third century A.C.: the extant capitals seem to be Severan. Porticoes that appear on the Mabada map may have been remnants of the Herodian construction.

A bouleuterion was a defining feature of the Hellenistic city state and (through its relative the Senate House) of the ideal Rome of Augustus. At Askalon, where Hellenistic traditions were strong and there was no danger to Herod of free institutions running rampant—inasmuch as the place was safely outside his kingdom—a bouleuterion was an appropriate demonstration of Herodian adherence to the historic governmental traditions of the Hellenistic world and Rome.

Extensive remains of the sculptural adornment of the basilica were also found. Particularly interesting are three panels, each of which shows a woman in relief (fig. 35). Two show winged women, perhaps Nikai. One holds a palm branch and the other is standing on a sphere held by an Atlas-like figure. The third panel, less well preserved, shows a Tyche or Isis. The two Nikai were found at the door separating the peristyle proper from the bouleuterion and probably flanked that doorway; the Tyche was found near one of the western doors to the peristyle.

The panels were found deep against the foundations and had not been reused, perhaps having been buried when Askalon was destroyed in the 60's A.C. (*BJ* 2.460). They are difficult to date, because of lack of stratigraphic controls and the lack of comparanda from early Roman Judaea, given the local attitudes to graven images. The drapery is heavier and more rigid than Augustan drapery, which may indicate a later date or a provincial style. Drilling is limited. There are certain similarities to the sculptures of the Sebasteion at Aphrodisias, from the late Julio-Claudian period, and to Nabataean art of the same period, especially from Khirbet et-Tannur and its vicinity. There is a strong compulsion to consider the Askalon panels a remnant of Herodian sculpture, but this is impossible without a more precise knowledge of the sculptural traditions of the region, and the material may in fact be from the second century A.C. or later.

Among the finds within the basilica is what appears to be a copy of the Crouching Aphrodite. The sculpture, now in Jerusalem, is a version of the Hellenistic work attributed perhaps to Doidalsas (Pliny, *Natural History* 36.35: the text is corrupt, and neither the artist nor the location of the copy Pliny saw is certain). Copies of the work were common in the late Hellenistic East, and if Herod were not familiar with one of these, he might have seen a copy in Rome. The Askalon version is of poor quality, especially when compared to one in the National Museum in Rome. The former shows little understanding of anatomy and is rigid and awkward in pose. If it is derived from the same original as the Roman version, it seems that the sculptor at Askalon was working from a description rather than personal acquaintance with the original (or even a good copy), and was none too skilled as an artist, perhaps not unexpected in a region that objected to graven images. Although the dating of copies is particularly difficult, the most likely period for Askalon to have been adorned with copies of Greek sculpture would have been in Herod's time, and the Askalon Aphrodite may thus be a rare surviving example of Herod's imitation of the Greek and Roman tradition of placing famous works of art (or copies of them) in public buildings.

The baths, fountains, and palace mentioned by Josephus are not known. A small shrine, 4.5 by 7 m, found in the northern portion of the eastern covered portico of the peristyle may be the Temple of Apollo of the *Chronikon Paschale*. Yet it is not part of the original construction and is thus unlikely to be Herodian. It may rather date to around A.D. 200.

The only date for Herodian activity at Askalon is that in the *Chronikon Paschale*, 30 B.C. This was the year after the earthquake that devastated Judaea, and may indicate when Herodian work began. Although the basilica underwent a thorough rebuilding in the Severan period, in its original form it is Herodian, and it is the peristyle mentioned by Josephus, and thus one of the best preserved of Herod's architectural monuments outside his kingdom.

Garstang, *PEFQ* 1924: 24–29; Iliffe, *QDAP* 2 (1933): 110–12; Glueck, *Deities and Dolphins* (1965), pls. 32, 48, 136; Schalit, *KH*, 677–78; Richter, *The Sculpture and Sculptors of the Greeks* (1970), 44, 234; Diplock, in *PEQ* 103 (1971): 13–14; Rappaport, *PP* 36 (1981): 363–66; Ridgway, *Roman Copies of Greek Sculpture* (1984), 23, 34; Kleiner, *Roman Sculpture* (1992), 158–61; Stager, in *NEAEHL*, 111; Fischer, *JRA*, suppl. 14 (1995): 121–50.

Athens

Josephus wrote that Herod's *anathemata* were to be found throughout Athens (*BJ* 1.425). Although the word can mean merely a votive dedication, the passage appears in a list of Herodian architectural constructions and the same phrase is used of Nikopolis, which elsewhere (*AJ* 16.147) is described as one of Herod's greatest architectural efforts. Good relations had existed between the Athenians and the Jews since the second century B.C., when Hyrkanos I had established contact and his statue was set up in the precinct of Demos and the Charites (*AJ* 14.149–55). Josephus's text actually refers to Herod's elder contemporary (and grandfather-in-law) Hyrkanos II. The account of the Athenian decree is in the midst of a lengthy discussion of this Hyrkanos and the decree as quoted calls Hyrkanos "son of Alexandros," which would apply only to Hyrkanos II. But the archons of the decree are ones from the time of Hyrkanos I, grandfather of Hyrkanos II. It seems less likely that there is a mistake about the archons than that two personalities with the same name have been confused. The "son of Alexandros" could not have been the phrasing of the original decree. Josephus or his source confused the two Hyrkanoi, and then at some time the patronymic was added in an erroneous attempt at clarification.

The precinct of Demos and the Charites was on the north slope of Kolonaios Agoraios where the Athens-Peiraios railway line is today. It seems to have been a modest open-air shrine; interestingly, a cult of Roma was eventually added (*IG* 2.2.5047). The Athenian tradition of honoring Jewish leaders was perhaps precedent enough for Herod to show interest, although he would have needed little inducement to honor the most distinguished of Greek cities. Two Athenian inscriptions mention him by name. One (*OGIS*, 414 = *IG* 2.2.3440), a statue base of Eleusinian marble found on the Akropolis, honored Herod as Philoromaios, for his good deeds and favor toward the city. A second (*IG* 2.2.3441), also from the Akropolis, called Herod Philokaisar and honored his virtue and good deeds. A fragmentary inscription in Hymettian marble from the Agora, appears to be similar in form to *IG* 2.2.3441 and has been restored with Herod's name. No context for any of these inscriptions was found. It is clear that Herod was among those honored by the city, both for his policy as a supporter of Rome and for specific, although unnamed, benefactions.

There were many opportunities for Herod to assist Athens architecturally. The client kings of the Roman world all contributed financially to the completion of the Athenian Temple of Olympian Zeus, which was dedicated to the Genius of Augustus (Suetonius, *Augustus* 60; see also *AJ* 16.146, where it is noted in the context of Greece that Herod finished buildings left uncompleted by others). Since Suetonius's comment immediately follows a discussion of how all the client kings founded cities named Caesarea—the same subject (*reges amici*) is used in both clauses—it is hard to imagine that Herod was not one of those meant. But Josephus referred to plural *anathemata*, so there was more to Herod's activities in the city than a cooperative project involving all the client kings: it was hardly Herod's style to limit his work to a joint venture.

The flourishing period of Augustan architecture in Athens was after 17 B.C., when Marcus Agrippa, beginning his four-year sojourn in the East, commissioned the Odeion in the Agora. Another major building of Augustan Athens, the Market of Caesar and Augustus, was an unfinished Caesarean project completed by Augustus after 12 B.C. and dedicated between 11 and 9 B.C.; this may be one of the buildings left unfinished that Herod helped complete. One project whose donor is unknown and that would be typical of a Herodian construction is the small round Temple of Roma and Augustus on the Akropolis. The two inscriptions found on the Akropolis demonstrate that a Herodian dedication existed on the citadel. Herod was famous for his temples in honor of Augustus, and to have built one in Athens would have been particularly appropriate. Although the temple inscription survives (*IG* 2.2.3173), it does not name any donor, only priests and archon. Its date must be after 27 B.C., but it cannot otherwise be determined. Herodian interest in Athens might be dated to around or after 15 B.C., when Herod was particularly involved in the traditional Greek world, constructing a stoa on Chios and soon to serve as president of the Olympic games.

Meritt, *Hesperia* 21 (1952): 370, #14; Binder, *Der Roma-Augustus Monopteros auf der Akropolis in Athen* (1969); Travlos 28–29, 79–82, 494–97; Ward-Perkins, *RIA*, 265.

Berytos

In late 15 B.C., the ancient Phoenician city of Berytos became a Roman *colonia*, Colonia Julia Augusta Felix (map 7). This was a personal project of Marcus Agrippa's, who was about to visit Herod in Judaea and receive an architectural tour of his kingdom. Berytos had been of little importance and had languished, after a brief prominence in Hellenistic times, until the Roman restoration.

Herod was largely responsible for the Roman rebuilding. According to Josephus (*BJ* 1.422), he built exedras, stoas, temples, and agoras at both Berytos and Tyre; how many in each is not clear because of the textual coupling of the two cities. There is no evidence of personal association between Herod and Berytos, although it was to be the site of the trial of his sons Alexandros and Aristoboulos (*BJ* 1.538–51; *AJ* 16.356–72). But the chronological connection between the establishment of the *colonia* and Agrippa's visit to Judaea indicates that Herod may have volunteered to undertake the restoration, or it may have been suggested by Agrippa, who would have known about Herod's ability in restoring decayed cities. As one of only two Roman *coloniae* in Syria, it was an opportunity for Herod to demonstrate his capability to execute the eastern policy of Rome and to build the city in proper Roman style.

Roman Berytos is little known because it lies under modern Beirut, the materials that have been recovered are disputed, and little recent information is available. Yet various hints of the ancient town have been recovered, especially in a monumental quarter centering on the forum of Roman Berytos. Most interesting is an inscription of Herod's great-granddaughter Berenike (jointly with her brother Agrippa II) that recorded Herod's original construction of a building then under repair, probably the basilical structure in which the document was found. This inscription—the only one in Latin indubitably to mention Herod—is one of the most tangible pieces of evidence for Herodian building outside of Judaea (see further, infra, pp. 249–50).

Assuming that Herod built one exedra, stoa, temple, and agora at Berytos, one visualizes a single monumental quarter centered on the forum. On the north side of the forum and west of the presumed Cardo Maximus is the building that yielded the Berenike inscription; it may thus be a successor to a Herodian building. Although Josephus did not mention a basilica as a Herodian construction in Berytos, an exedra is only part of a structure and would be perfectly appropriate in a basilica. The basilica is a large structure, 99 m long, larger than any contemporary one in Rome. The excavators felt that the structure itself was Herodian, including the interior Ionic colonnade, whereas the exterior Corinthian embellishment was the work of Berenike. If the attribution to Herod is correct, it is the earliest known basilica in Syria and one of the earliest examples outside Italy.

Traces of a temple have been found near the forum, although the remains are limited and unclear. Following the Herodian pattern in other cities, the temple was probably dedicated to Augustus. A colossal statue found northeast of the basilica, thought to represent a member of the Julian family, may have come from the temple. Nothing of the stoa has been found, but it is not difficult to place it along the southern edge of the forum, thus completing Herod's monumental center of Berytos.

AEpigr 1928: 23; Lauffray, *BMusBeyr* 7 (1944–45): 13–80; Mouterde and Lauffray, *Beyrouth ville romaine* [n. d.]; Bowersock, *Augustus*, 1, 65–66;

Lauffray, *ANRW* 2.8 (1977): 135–63; Ward-Perkins, *RIA*, 325; Millar, *Commentationes Humanarum Litterarum* 91 (1990): 10–23; Millar, *RNE*, 279–85.

Byblos

The ancient city of Byblos was in decline in Herod's day. It had been settled since Neolithic times and had flourished in the Bronze Age and later eras, but after the period of Alexander the Great it began to fade in importance. When Pompey passed through the area, mountain tribes of Itouraians overran the city, a factor of the unstable last years of the Seleukid empire (Strabo 16.2.18).

About forty years later, Herod assisted Byblos in its urban renewal, building the city walls (*BJ* 1.422). The notice appears in Josephus's catalogue of Herod's constructions in Syrian cities, and no details are provided. This is the only documented example of Herod limiting his largesse to urban fortifications, and the sparseness of Josephus's information allows only speculation as to Herod's motive, and even as to whether the walling was fortification or rather landscaping or terracing, more typical of Herodian construction. If the walling were purely fortification, Herod's interest may have been to provide stability for the city after the Itouraian episode. He had had his own experience with the Itouraians, who continued to be a problem to the Roman government. In the early years of Herod's rule, Cleopatra had had their leader Lysanias executed for his pro-Parthian views (*BJ* 1.440; *AJ* 15.92). His successor, Zenodoros, terrorized the region northeast of the Sea of Galilee, whose inhabitants complained to the governor of Syria. When word reached Augustus, he gave Zenodoros's territory to Herod (perhaps initially only to stabilize or administer) but unfortunately did not deal with Zenodoros himself, who promptly showed up in Rome to complain, albeit fruitlessly, about his treatment. Zenodoros then stirred up anti-Herodian sentiment in his former territory, so that when Augustus came to Syria in 20 B.C., the locals complained to him about Herod. Herod defended himself successfully before Augustus, and the entire episode came to a unexpectedly quick end with the sudden yet natural death of Zenodoros at Antioch, whereupon Augustus formally gave his territory to Herod (*AJ* 15.344–60).

This may be the context in which Herod decided to fortify the city in Roman Syria that had specifically suffered at the hands of the Itouraians; if so, it might date his efforts to ca. 20 B.C. Yet most of the excavated Roman material at Byblos (including temples, a basilica, colonnaded street, and nymphaeum) dates from the second and third centuries A.C., as it seems to have been extensively developed as a Roman city only from the time of

Hadrian. Nothing that can be related definitely to Herod's construction has been found, although traces of Ionic capitals similar to those from the basilica at Berytos may be Herodian in date.

Lauffray, *BMusBeyr* 7 (1944–45): 50; Dunand, *Byblos* (1963), 36–39, 71–72; Jidejian, *Byblos through the Ages* (1968), 109–16; Rey-Coquais, in *PECS*, 176; Millar, *RNE*, 274–75.

Chios

In the spring of 14 B.C., Herod sailed to join Marcus Agrippa on the Bosporos expedition. Expecting to meet Agrippa at Mytilene, he was unable to move beyond Chios because of northerly winds, and remained there for several days. During this period, he was well received and decided to rebuild a stoa that had been in ruins since the Mithradatic Wars. Although Herod soon continued on his way, he left behind money for the reconstruction and instructions to complete the project quickly (*AJ* 16.17–19).

Josephus's account is unusually precise, the most detailed description of Herodian building outside Judaea and Syria, perhaps reflecting eyewitness information provided by Nikolaos of Damaskos. Josephus wrote that the stoa was in the city of Chios, and that it was especially large and beautiful, unlike other structures in the city. The implication is of a grandiose Hellenistic structure that could not be rebuilt in the more impoverished era of Herod's day, having remained a ruin for seventy years.

Although Roman remains have been found throughout Chios—some fifty sites have been identified, most of which also have Hellenistic material—it is clear that the Herodian stoa is to be sought in the modern town of Chios. Ancient Chios town underlies the modern town and is poorly known from any period (fig. 24). Aineias Taktikos (11.3) referred to the repair of a stoa on Chios that was near the harbor, probably in 357 B.C., the only other literary reference to a stoa on the island. The stoa Josephus described sounds more like a Hellenistic structure, however, and in any case a stoa that was already in need of repair by the mid fourth century B.C. is unlikely to have been the "large and beautiful" one Herod repaired. A brief salvage excavation in 1982 in the Bounaki district, some 400 m east of the modern harbor, uncovered a monumental quarter that included a portion of a stoa in a context of the third century A.C. or later, but the small building also seems too modest for the Herodian structure. Nevertheless, this may suggest where Herod's building is to be sought. It is most probable that, like other monumental public buildings of Chios town, it ended up in the medieval and modern harbor moles, which consist in part of numerous column, capital and base fragments.

There is further evidence of Herod's activity on Chios. He had a close relationship with the inhabitants, demonstrated by both his building activity and his contemporary payment of their taxes to Rome (*AJ* 16.26). Two Chian inscriptions may also be dedications by Herod. One (*SEG* 16.490), often attributed to Antiochos IV of Kommagene, refers to a donation by a Great King of 1,000 denarii, perhaps the annual payment for the Roman taxes. Another (*SEG* 16.488) mentions something repaired at the donor's own expense, under the supervision of one Apollonios son of Apollonios Philologos, and specifically refers to an athletic endowment. Since Herod was to be president of the Olympic Games in 12 B.C.—the next games after his visit to Chios—and endowed the office of *gymnasiarchos* on nearby Kos, as well as building numerous athletic constructions, it is not difficult to imagine that he endowed athletics on Chios. The Antipatros son of Herod who was an athletic victor on the island may also belong in this context (*SEG* 35.930B20).

Hunt, *BSA* 41 (1940–45): 29–52; Boardman, *BSA* 49 (1954): 123; Tsaravopoulos, *Chios* (1986): 305–15; Yalouris, *Chios* (1986): 166; Mantzoulinou-Richards, *AncW* 18 (1988): 97–98.

Damaskos

Herod constructed a gymnasium and theater in Damaskos (*BJ* 1.422). The vague reference by the always unreliable Moses Khorenat'si regarding Herodian building in Damaskos (2.25) is probably based on Josephus and does not imply any other projects. Herod had had a long association with Damaskos, and one might expect him to have assisted in its building programs. He had been in the city as early as 43 B.C., having fled there after the murder of his father (*BJ* 1.236; *AJ* 14.178, 295). In addition, Nikolaos, his advisor and court historian, came from one of the most prominent families of Damaskos. Nikolaos's father and Herod's father may have been acquainted as early as the 60's B.C. Pompey's rebuilding of Gadara had created the precedent for architecturally honoring the home town of a confidant.

Josephus provided no date for Herod's contributions: the source is the vague catalogue of Herodian building in Syrian cities at *BJ* 1.422. The Temple of Juppiter Damascenus seems to have been initiated by Augustus, and although Herod is not associated with this structure, his work may have been part of a general Augustan rebuilding of the city center, perhaps connected with or just after Augustus's visit to Syria in 20 B.C. Yet Damaskos's long history from prehistoric to modern times has meant that little is known of the Greek and Roman city, and as is often the case in Roman Syria, the few visible remains date from a later period.

No trace of a gymnasium has been found. Along the *decumanus*, the biblical "Street Called Straight," lie two unnatural hillocks, 200 m apart, south of the temenos of the Temple of Juppiter. Each is semicircular with its straight side toward the street. An examination of the two hills between 1924 and 1937 led to the conclusion that the westernmost conforms better to the profile of an unexcavated theater. A Hellenistic date and an early Imperial rebuilding have been proposed on little or no evidence; whether Herod modified an existing Hellenistic theater or built a new one, the Damaskos theater was in all likelihood the first in the Italian style in Syria. Its 100-meter size would make it similar to the one at Caesarea.

Sauvaget, *Syria*, 25–26 (1946–49) 350–58; Frézouls, *Syria* 36 (1959): 210–12; Freyberger, *Damaszener Mitteilungen* 4 (1989): 61–86; Millar, *RNE*, 310–19.

Delos

There is no specific information regarding Herodian construction on Delos, yet some tantalizing evidence raises the possibility that the island, although in a state of decline since the Mithradatic Wars and the commercial development of Italy during the late Republic, was a beneficiary of Herodian largesse.

Herod's interest in Delos may have been heightened because it was the home of a substantial Jewish community, which was active in assuring the religious freedom of neighboring Jewish populations (*AJ* 14.231–32; 1 Macc. 15.23). As he demonstrated during his Asia Minor trip with Marcus Agrippa, interest in local Jewish communities and their civic rights under the Roman government was always a priority with Herod.

There was also a Nabataean presence on Delos, since Herod's nemesis Syllaios seems to have made a dedication to Dushares on behalf of King Obodas in the twentieth year of his reign, ca. 9/8 B.C. Nabataean interest in the area may have stimulated the half-Nabataean but always wary Herod to show his own patronage: in turn, Syllaios, always eager to cause trouble for the family that had rejected him as an in-law, may have wished to assert his own presence—or that of his country—in Herodian spheres of interest.

An inscription discovered on Syros, perhaps of Delian origin, seems to be a fragment of a dedication by Herod: what remains is ΒΑΣΙΛ. . .ΡΟΔ. . .ΤΟΙ (*IG* 12.5.713.6). Although there is speculation as to what type of building Herod might have constructed, the evidence is so hypothetical as to be of little value. It has been suggested that it was the *xystos* next to the stadium, traditionally attributed to Ptolemaios IX, but perhaps another example of Herod's continuing interest in athletics.

Another tantalizing fragment is a Delian inscription honoring Antipas (*OGIS*, 417), dated to around A.D. 6, recording a statue erected in the precinct of Apollo. This is one of only two or three known inscriptions mentioning Antipas: the other certain one is from Kos (*OGIS*, 416), and more problematic is the Chian athletic victor Antipatros son of Herod (*SEG* 35.930B20). Herod's son might have been honored at Delos in part because his father had benefited the island.

Durrbach, *Choix d'inscriptions de Délos* (1921–22), 263–65; Bruneau, *Recherches sur les cultes de Délos* (1970), 244; Hoehner, *Herod Antipas* (1972), 106; Mantzoulinou-Richards, *AncW* 18 (1988): 93–95.

Ilion

Few places outside Judaea would have been more deserving of Herodian patronage than Ilion, the Hellenistic-Roman city that was believed to be built on the ruins of ancient Troy. Ever since Xerxes had visited the site in 480 B.C. (Herodotos 7.43), it had become the major tourist attraction of the eastern Greek world, favored by Hellenistic kings and Roman magistrates alike. By Roman times, a city far larger than the Bronze Age one spread to the east and south, containing all the paraphernalia of a Hellenistic-Roman town. C. Flavius Fimbria sacked it in 85 B.C., however, and by the late first century B.C., Ilion was thus in need of rebuilding. It was also of special interest as the ancestral home of the Julian family. Augustus seems to have reconstructed the theater, lying northeast of the Bronze Age mound, as well as the Sanctuary of Athene and the bouleuterion, and the city began to stress its importance to the Augustan family.

Josephus did not mention any Herodian building at Ilion. Herod was in the vicinity during the Bosporan expedition in 14 B.C., although it does not seem that he was actually at the site. The single incident involving Herod and Ilion was the successful attempt to placate Marcus Agrippa after his wife Julia fell into the Skamandros and to obtain remission of the fine Agrippa had assessed the city (supra, pp. 49–50). But Herod was not at Ilion at the time; he sent Nikolaos of Damaskos to reconcile the parties (*AJ* 16.26; Nikolaos, fr. 134).

Excavations reestablished in the late 1980's have been concentrating on the Hellenistic and Roman city of Ilion. An inscription in honor of Agrippa has long been known (*IGRR* 4.203). Herod was also honored by the Ilians, and it may be hoped that the current excavations will recover some evidence of his largesse.

Korfmann, *Studia Troica* 1 (1991): 17–26; Rose, ibid.: 69–77; Rose, ibid., 2 (1992): 43–60; Rose, ibid., 3 (1993): 97–116.

Kos

Like most of the eastern Greek islands, Kos suffered in the Mithradatic Wars and was in a state of decline in the Augustan period. It was in this context that Herod perpetually endowed the office of *gymnasiarchos* (*BJ* 1.423). The island had a Jewish community (*AJ* 14.112, 233), but Herod may have had a greater interest because of an early Nabataean presence. His patronage may have caused the friendship to develop between his son Alexandros and the priest of Apollo at Halasarna, C. Julius Euaratos, who eventually came to Judaea as a member of Herod's court circle (supra, p. 59). It was probably in memory of Herod's largesse that his son Antipas visited the island and was honored with a statue (*OGIS*, 416). In addition, Marcus Agrippa and Julia stopped here upon their return from visiting Herod in Judaea, and an Agrippea was established in Agrippa's honor.

The Nabataean community on Kos is documented by a number of inscriptions, especially a bilingual one recording that a certain Aswallah dedicated an altar to Aphrodite Ba'la, dated to the eighteenth year of King Aretas. The lettering of the inscription is no earlier than the first century B.C., and the king is probably Aretas III (87–62 B.C.) or IV (9 B.C.–A.D. 40): thus the date of Aswallah's dedication is either ca. 69 B.C. or ca. A.D. 9. The former seems more probable, as Nabataean trade in the Aegean—which also reached Delos—was more a late Hellenistic than Roman imperial phenomenon. Since Aretas III, who probably thus encouraged Nabataean merchants to establish themselves on Kos, may have been an ancestor of Herod's, this was reason for Herod himself to bestow patronage on the island.

Herod's endowment of the office of *gymnasiarchos* fits well with his interest in athletics. No date is possible for his patronage, and there is no evidence that he ever was on the island, although he must have passed it several times en route to Rome, Mytilene, or the Bosporos. Whether his endowment included building a gymnasium is not known, although he built several in his career. A Koan inscription honors an important person (whose name is lost) and mentions the "new gymnasium" and perhaps Halasarna, leading to the conclusion that Herod may have financed a new gymnasium at Halasarna, where his associate Euaratos was priest of Apollo: Herod had favored the cult of Apollo on neighboring Rhodes and perhaps at Askalon. The date of this inscription has never been established, and it now seems to be lost. Examination of the various transcriptions made in the late nineteenth century has led to the conclusion that it can be no earlier than 200 B.C. Certain elements of the dedication, especially the use of a gilded throne, suggest that it may be Ptolemaic. But there was a long history of patronage of the gymnasia on Kos since at least the days of Attalos I of Pergamon, and a Herodian date cannot be ruled out.

Of the various gymnasia known on Kos from literary and epigraphic sources, the best preserved is one found in the western part of the ancient city, dating originally to the second century B.C. It is not known whether this gymnasium or the one at Halasarna, or another, was the site of Herod's patronage.

Gardner, *JHS* 6 (1885): 248–60; Paton and Hicks, *The Inscriptions of Cos* (1891), # 8; Modona, *L'isola di Coo nell'antichità classica* (1933), 53, 77; Levi Della Vida, *ClRh* 9 (1938): 139–48; Moretti, *Iscrizioni agonistiche grechi* (1953), # 60; Delorme, *Gymnasion* (1960), 119–21; *AEpigr* 1971, # 461; S. Sherwin-White, *Ancient Kos* (1978), 135–36, 247, 249–50, 369.

Laodikeia

At Laodikeia in Syria, generally called Laodikeia-on-the-Sea, which had a substantial Jewish community (*BJ* 14.241), Herod is said to have provided the water supply (*BJ* 1.422), which, one presumes, means that he built an aqueduct. Herod was in Laodikeia in 35 or 34 B.C., summoned by Antonius (*AJ* 15.64–67) because of complaints against him by Cleopatra and by supporters of the Hasmonean Aristoboulos III, whom Herod recently had had murdered. Herod as usual cleared himself of all charges, although gifts from Jerusalem were also of assistance (*AJ* 15.75). This is the only time that Herod is known to have been in Laodikeia, but interest in the city may also have been stimulated by Herod's unfortunate association with a prominent local citizen, Alexas, the influential advisor to Antonius. Yet a more likely time for Herodian architectural benefaction is around 20 B.C., when Augustus was in Laodikeia, where he built a theater and a tetrapylon and established the imperial cult (Malalas, 222–23). Some years later. Strabo (16.2.9) called Laodikeia an unusually beautifully constructed city, although he did not mention its hydraulics. A gymnasium had existed since the second century B.C. (Appian, *Syrian War* 46; Cicero, *Philippic* 9.2.4), and Herod may have improved the water supply to this building.

Laodikeia was a Seleukid foundation. Although virtually destroyed during the Roman civil wars, it had clearly been rebuilt by Strabo's time. Herod's aqueduct would have been part of this rebuilding. Unfortunately, the city was destroyed again in the late second century A.C., and most of the known remains are Severan. Given the long life of Roman aqueducts, it is possible that remnants of Herod's installations still exist or are even in use, but none has been identified.

Sauvaget, *BEO* 4 (1934): 83–91, 106; Rey-Coquais, in *PECS*, 482.

Nikopolis (Actia Nicopolis)

Octavian founded Nikopolis as a free city after the battle of Actium, combining a number of existing cities and creating a new town near the location of his battlefield headquarters, where there was an ancient sanctuary of Apollo (fig. 23). Nikopolis is said by Josephus to have been a major recipient of Herod's largesse (*BJ* 1.425). He evidently erected most of its public buildings (*AJ* 16.147), but no further details are provided. The most contemporary description is that of Strabo (7.7.6), who did not mention Herod's role but noted that Nikopolis was founded largely to revitalize an area economically ravaged by the Makedonian-Roman wars. He particularly described the precinct of Apollo, including the gymnasium and stadium associated with the games of Aktian Apollo. The city was unusual because of its two harbors, since it was at the narrow point of the peninsula between the Ambrakian Gulf and the Ionian Sea (Strabo 10.2.2; Suetonius, *Augustus* 18; Pausanias 5.23.2; Dio 51.1.). which are about seven kilometers apart there.

The site of Nikopolis is dominated by a number of Byzantine churches, but recent archaeological activity has begun to define the visible element of the original Herodian city. The city walls enclosed a vast area of 1.6 km^2, but as at Caesarea, the wall had symbolic rather than defensive functions. It is significant that by Byzantine times the city covered less than 0.5 km^2. In fact, the whole Herodian city gives the impression of having been built at great expense. Other early remains include streets, the theater, stadium, hippodrome, and gymnasium, many of which were necessary components of the Aktian games Augustus established, probably in 27 B.C., perhaps enlarging an existing festival and games to Apollo, whose shrine had long been at the site.

The Aktian games, sacred to Aktian Apollo, were under the supervision of the Spartans, whose involvement raises the question of Sparta's most notorious contemporary citizen, Eurykles, who ended up at Herod's court (supra, pp. 59–60). With Herod building the facilities for the Aktian games and Eurykles or his designate managing them, and perhaps financing them, a picture emerges of the network of wealthy patrons Augustus came to rely upon to implement his plans: Augustus himself played little direct role in the development of the city and never seems to have visited the site after the time of the battle.

In addition to the necessities for the games, Nikopolis also contained sophisticated hydraulic installations and a bouleuterion and odeion, the last two forming an integrated structure in the center of the city, well south of the sports complex. Remnants of the sculptural decoration of the odeion have been dated to the early Augustan period.

It is significant that the visible Augustan structures at Nikopolis all reveal endeavors in which Herod had a particular interest. His favoring of athletics is demonstrated throughout the Greek world, culminating in his management of the Olympic games. Hydraulics were always a particular concern, as were the civic institutions of the traditional Greco-Roman world.

Andreou, *Nikopolis* 1 (1987), 145–52; Bokotopoulou, *Nikopolis* 1 (1987), 135–44; Hoepfner, *Nikopolis* 1 (1987), 129–33; Lämmer, *Stadion* 12–13 (1986–87): 27–38; Hoepfner, *Akten*, 275–85; Gurval, *Actium and Augustus* (1995), 65–86.

Olympia

In the first century B.C. the Olympic games were languishing. The general poverty that had affected Greece since 146 B.C. was particularly noticeable in its cults and festivals, and at Olympia events were discontinued and victor's statues failed to be erected. It was only in the Augustan period that a revival began, part of a general rejuvenation of athletics in Augustan Greece. Augustus himself led the way by establishing the Aktian Games at Nikopolis. Herod's own games at Jerusalem and Caesarea (*BJ* 1.415; *AJ* 15.268–76; 16.137–39) were a part of the pattern. Herod's interest in athletics is well documented: in addition to the games he founded, there are his endowment of the office of *gymnasiarchos* on Kos and the various athletic structures he built throughout the Greek world (*BJ* 1.422–23). It was only natural that his interest eventually turned toward Olympia.

He was especially concerned about the poverty of the Olympic Games, and in 12 B.C. he accepted the post of *agonothetes* (for the date, see supra, p. 74). That summer he was traveling to Rome for the last of his three trips, and he was thus able to be in attendance at Olympia during the games. His appointment as *agonothetes* may have been largely a honorary post, as it was in perpetuity, and may have been a result of Herod's perpetual endowment of the games (*BJ* 1.427), thus initiating a recovery that was to continue into the second century A.C. It is not clear what being *agonothetes* in perpetuity meant: perhaps it was only for Herod's lifetime, since a certain M. Cocceius Timasarchos, from Rhodes, also held the position ca. A.D. 200. He may also have been so honored because of a rich endowment.

The *agonothetes* was the manager or producer of the games, and the position often included a financial responsibility. An *agonothetes* might provide for catering and logistic support (Plutarch, *Symposiakon* 674f), prepare the program of the games, or assess fines against athletes. Herod not only gave his prestige to the games but probably financed the opening ceremony, official sacrifices and banquets (which took place on the third and fifth days), and possibly the cost of functionaries and even the victors' statues. Normally, the Olympic games did not have *agonothetai*: Pausanias's use (5.9.4) of the term for the manager of the games in his day may have been simple carelessness, since except at Olympia, the *agonothetes* was the common administrator of Greek games. Herod and Timasarchos (who had also been *agonothetes* at Rhodes) are the only two known from Olympia. It seems that using the precedent of games elsewhere in the Greek world, the managing committee of the Olympic Games created the office of Olympic *agonothetes* specifically for Herod.

Whether Herod's activities at Olympia included building or reconstruction is not documented, but it is probable. The long decline of the games would have affected their physical facilities as well as operations. The Augustan period saw a general repair and renovation of the structures at Olympia, and it is probable that Herod's endowment financed these. Two brick stamps refer to an *epimeletes* Herod, but this is probably not the king.

Earlier in his career, Herod might himself have participated in the games. He was a person of great physical prowess: an expert horseman, and a skilled fighter, javelin-thrower, and archer (*BJ* 1.429–30). There were many precedents for prominent citizens of the Roman world to take part in the games: the future emperor Tiberius would win at the four-horse chariot race a few years after Herod was named *agonothetes* (*SIG*⁴ 782). But Herod was past his prime in 12 B.C., in his sixties, and probably already affected by the debilitating disease that would kill him within a few years. It is unlikely that he took part.

Gardiner, *Athletics of the Ancient World* (1930), 46–48; Dittenberger and Purgold, *Die Inschriften von Olympia* (1960), ## 734, 735; Gardiner, *Olympia* (1973), 152–54; Lämmer, *Perspektiven der Sportwissenschaft* (1973), 160–73, Finley and Pleket, *The Olympic Games* (1976), 99; Pleket, *ZPE* 20 (1976): 6–7; Harris, *Greek Athletics and the Jews* (1976), 35–37; Miller, *Arete* (1991), 207, # 132, # 140.

Pergamon

Herod's *anathemata* were also bestowed on Pergamon, Josephus wrote (*BJ* 1.425), in a context alluding to Nikopolis, where Herod is known to have done significant building. At the time of Hyrkanos I, Pergamon had a Jewish community, or was sympathetic to Jewish concerns, and there were even claims of a friendship or common ancestry between the Pergamenes and the Jews from as early as the time of Abraham (*AJ* 14.247–55). Herod was in the vicinity of Pergamon when he visited Marcus Agrippa on Mytilene in 23/22 B.C., and again during the initial stages of the Bosporan expedition in 14 B.C., but no visit to Pergamon is recorded and no further details about his patronage are known.

Like much of western Asia and the Greek islands, Pergamon had suffered during the Mithradatic Wars, especially since it had served for a time as Mithradates' headquarters. Yet it became the regional seat of the imperial cult and the site of an early temple to Roma and Augustus. Both these were reasons for Herod's interest, as was the presence of a Jewish community or existence of pro-Jewish sympathies. Herod's architectural reconstructions were often bestowed on the victims of the instability of the earlier first century B.C., and he was particularly interested in the cult of Roma and Augustus.

No evidence linking anything at the site of Pergamon with Herod has been found. The site of the cult of Roma and Augustus is unknown, and there are no traces of Herod's *anathemata*, yet continuing excavation holds out the possibility of new discoveries.

Magie, *RR* (1950), 215–17, 447; Radt, *Pergamon* (1988).

Ptolemais

The ancient city of Akko had existed since the Middle Bronze Age on the Levantine coast at the southern limit of Phoenicia. It was refounded in the third century B.C. by Ptolemaios II Philadelphos and renamed Ptolemais, although a Hellenized form of the ancient name, Ake, persisted (Strabo 16.2.25), and eventually it reverted to Akko (see also Pliny, *Natural History* 5.75). Athenian merchants were in residence by the fourth century B.C. (Demosthenes, *Against Kallippos* 20), and in Hellenistic and Roman times, it was a flourishing port city. Glass-making was an early industry in this region and was a contributor to the local economy.

The town was important to Herod. It was here that he landed, probably early in 39 B.C., after his return from Rome (*BJ* 1.290; *AJ* 14.394). It was also at Ptolemais that he met Octavian after Actium while the latter was on his way to Egypt. Herod accompanied Octavian as he reviewed his troops, provided lodging and a banquet for him and his entourage, and supplied logistical assistance for his journey to Egypt (*BJ* 1.394; *AJ* 15.199). Thus it is not unexpected that Ptolemais benefited from Herod's building program and became one of several cities in which he erected a gymnasium (*BJ* 1.422).

There is no trace of Herod's gymnasium there now. The town has continued to flourish as one of the more picturesque Levantine cities, but most of the visible structures are medieval or later in date. A mound 1.5 km east of the medieval and modern city was the site of the Bronze Age town, and although there was some occupation in Hellenistic and Roman times, it is unlikely that Herod built a major public structure in what was already the "Old City." Yet scattered excavations in the "New City" to the west have been no more fruitful for evidence of the Roman period, although massive Hellenistic remains west of the modern Haifa-Nahariyah highway probably indicate the area of the Ptolemaic refoundation, and perhaps Herod's gymnasium is to be sought in this vicinity.

M. Dothan, *RBibl* 82 (1975): 566–68; M. Dothan, *BASOR* 224 (1976): 30–34, 37–41; Kindler, *BASOR* 231 (1978): 51–55; Kashtan, *Mediterranean Historical Review* 3 (1988): 37–53.

Rhodes

Rhodes occupied a unique place in the Herodian building program, for it was there that it began. Rhodes was the only place where Herod built before he was named king. Especially since the rise of Delos, Rhodes was no longer the power that it had once been. In Herod's day, it had suffered in the Roman civil wars: in early 42 B.C. the island was attacked, defeated, and pillaged by Cassius, ostensibly because the Rhodian navy had provided ships for P. Cornelius Dolabella, a protégé of Julius Caesar's who had been governor of Syria. Cassius's actual reason for the attack and plundering was more pecuniary than political, however; he profited to the sum of 8,500 talents.

Slightly less than three years later, Herod appeared on the island. Not yet king, he was on his way to Rome for the first time, having left the court of Cleopatra in Egypt. After a stormy journey, he arrived on Rhodes, where two of his associates, Sappinos and Ptolemaios, awaited him (*BJ* 1.280; *AJ* 14.377). Ptolemaios became Herod's royal treasurer and may have been at the court of Antonius and Cleopatra (supra, pp. 63–64). His presence on Rhodes was hardly accidental and provides some insight into the broad reach of Herod's thinking even at this early stage.

Noting that Rhodes was still suffering from the damage inflicted by Cassius, Herod paid for its restoration (*AJ* 14.378). He also rebuilt the temple of Pythian Apollo, which had burned down (*BJ* 1.424; *AJ* 16.147), although this was mentioned elsewhere by Josephus and may not have occurred on Herod's 40 B.C. trip.

The ship on which Herod had arrived from Egypt was evidently no longer serviceable (or its run did not take it west of Rhodes), so Herod commissioned the building of a large trireme and sailed on to Brundisium. He was not yet particularly wealthy, and both his reconstruction of the city and the building of the ship exceeded his funds: he may have received the ship on credit. At some later date, he virtually endowed the Rhodian ship-building industry, which had fallen on hard times given the general poverty of the city in recent years (*BJ* 1.424; *AJ* 16.147).

Even if some of Herod's efforts on Rhodes, especially the Pythian temple and the endowment of the shipbuilding industry, are from later than 40 B.C. and are representative of his typical technique of favoring localities that had been of assistance early in his career, one is nevertheless left with the bald fact that young Herod, not yet king, with no viable political standing, and not particularly rich, financed the reconstruction of a city in the traditional Greek world. The overriding question is, why should he have been disposed to do such a thing? Although young, he was neither untraveled nor inexperienced, having survived in the turmoil of late Hellenistic Judaea, and having already spent time in the two greatest Greek cities of the East. He had also seen a succession of Romans at work architecturally in the East. Some spark of enlightenment had told him that architectural reconstruction was a way for even an impoverished and unemployed potential petty dynast to make his mark on the world.

But why should those feelings have manifested themselves at Rhodes? It may simply be that for the first time in his life, Herod was in the traditional Greek world, in a city that was already old when Tleptolemos the son of Herakles led Rhodian warriors to Troy (*Iliad* 2.653–70): the awe Herod felt in such exalted surroundings—perhaps not unlike that felt by Americans on their first trip to Europe—may have resulted in his donation. But young Herod was already astute politically. Rhodes had been one of Rome's first eastern Greek allies, and what better way to impress Rome—upon whose mercy he was about to throw himself—than to assist its traditional allies. Rhodes was also a city that was particularly interested in its architecture and physical appearance (Strabo 14.2.5). Moreover, it was an unusually good place to begin a career of royal patronage, since it had a long history of such. In the 220's B.C., there had been the collective effort of nine kings, including Hieron II of Syracuse, Ptolemaios IV Philopator, and Seleukos II, who helped rebuild the city after a great earthquake that had toppled the famous Kolossos and generally devastated the city (Polybios 5.88–90). And there may have been subtle dynastic reasons for Herod's interest, as the city seems to have had a strong Nabataean community. There was a cult of Dushares (*IG* 12.1.963), and a Nabataean was a member of the guild of Aphrodisiastai as early as the second century B.C. (*SEG* 3.674.52–53). Herod's interest in Rhodes was in part repaid when a Rhodian named Paris son of Akestor made a donation for the paving of the courtyard of Herod's temple in Jerusalem, probably in 18/17 B.C.

The Rhodian sanctuary of Pythian Apollo lies in the northern part of the ancient city, near the akropolis (fig. 21). The temple is essentially Hellenistic in form, although earlier in conception. Four of its Doric columns and part of its architrave have been reerected. Nothing has been found that can be attributed to Herod's reconstruction, yet it is intriguing that the *temenos* is adjoined on the south by the gymnasium and stadium, an area in which Herod would have been particularly interested. The sanctuary of Apollo was placed on its own terrace above and to the north of the athletic complex. The Rhodian shipbuilding industry was in decline in Roman times—the Hellenistic shipyards at Mandraki were paved over—and Herod's donation may have kept a dying craft alive in its last days.

Magie, *RR* (1950), 423–25, 877–78, 1275; Kondis, *AM* 73 (1958): 146–58; Konstantinopoulos, *Archaeology* 21 (1968): 115–23; Blackman, *ArchDelt* 27 (1972): B.686–87; *AEpigr* 1984, # 913; Konstantinopoulos, *Akten*, 207–13; Casson, *The Ancient Mariners* (1991), 142.

Rome

No specific information is preserved regarding any Herodian building in Rome, other than the questionable evidence of Moses Khorenats'i, who stated (2.25) that Herod built from Rome to Damaskos, a formulaic encompassing of the western world from an Armenian perspective. Yet Herod certainly provided monetary support for the projects of Augustan Rome: at the time of his third and last trip to the city (12 B.C.), he gave Augustus 300 talents for public spectacles (*AJ* 16.128). He may also have endowed a synagogue, but it is possible that the synagogue simply honored Herod without any personal involvement (supra, p. 75). There were places in Rome where client kings and eastern royalty were commemorated, and it is plausible that Herod was honored somewhere in the city (see Appendix 2).

Samos

Herod made *doreai* to the people of Samos (*BJ* 1.425), which he visited after he returned from the Bosporan expedition with Marcus Agrippa in the summer and autumn of 14 B.C. He spent several weeks on the island, receiving complaints about lack of religious freedom from Jewish communities (supra, pp. 50–51).

Josephus's text does not mention any architectural endeavors on Samos, but the passage concerning Herod's gifts is in the midst of a catalogue of Herodian building achievements, immediately after reference to his rebuilding of the Temple of Apollo on Rhodes. Thus it is safe to assume that during the time Herod was on the island, he commissioned building of some sort.

Samos prospered in the Augustan period, as is shown by its role as Agrippa's headquarters, as well as the several Roman villas discovered on the island. It had been the headquarters of Antonius and Cleopatra before Actium (Plutarch, *Antonius* 56), and perhaps that was why the new regime showed interest. One can speculate about any Herodian role in the establishment of the Augustan presence on Samos, but the Roman monument northeast of the ancient Temple of Hera, which may have held a colossal statue of Augustus—a type of monument Herod commissioned elsewhere (*BJ* 1.414)—seems a possibility.

Reuther, *Der Heratempel von Samos* (1957), 65–68; Tölle, *Die Antike Stadt Samos* (1969); Catling, *AR* 25 (1979): 36.

Sidon

Sidon, the most Hellenized of the Phoenician coastal cities, was always a place of importance. The city had a Jewish community, which had recorded the services of Hyrkanos II to Julius Caesar on a bronze tablet in both Greek and Latin, one of the earliest documented uses of Latin in the Levant (*AJ* 14.190–212). A few years later, Antonius upheld Jewish rights at Sidon, especially those of property (*AJ* 14.320–23). Herod demonstrated his interest in the city by building a theater (*BJ* 1.422), probably that discovered in the 1960's on the northern flank of the hill dominated by the medieval castle.

Dunand, *BMusBeyr* 20 (1967): 27–44; Rey-Coquais, in *PECS*, 837.

Sparta

Along with the Athenians, Nikopolitans, and Pergamenes, the Lakedaimonians were among those who received Herod's anathemata (*BJ* 1.425). Since Nikopolis is known to have received architectural benefits, so may the other cities on the list. Few cities in mainland Greece would have been more worthy of Herod's interest, because of a long history of relationships between Spartans and Jews, which culminated in the presence, however strangely and even disastrously, of the Spartan Eurykles at Herod's court (supra, pp. 59–60). In addition, Sparta had a particular reason to be favored by Augustus and his supporters, since the city had protected Livia and the young Tiberius during the Perusine War (Dio 54.7).

The friendship between Jews and Spartans allegedly originated at the time of the Spartan king Areus, whose reign began in the late fourth century B.C., and who wrote to the Jewish high priest Onias (I?) that he had discovered a common ancestry between Spartans and Jews and wanted to initiate contact (1 Macc. 12.21–23; *AJ* 12.225–28). Although there are many difficulties both textually and historically with Areus's letter, nevertheless the tradition of a relationship between the two peoples was well established by the late Hellenistic period, especially by the time of the Hasmonean Jonathan, around the middle of the second century B.C. (1 Macc. 12.6; *AJ* 13.166–70). Areus's interest in Judaea was doubtless political. There was increasing awareness of the Jews on the part of Greeks in the fourth century B.C., and he was probably seeking an eastern ally. Regardless, by the time of Herod, the connection seems to have been taken for granted, and this was not the only instance in which a Greek state claimed an ancestral relationship with the Jews. This tradition may have allowed the friendship to develop between Herod and Eurykles. They seem to have known each other from the early 20's B.C. or shortly after the battle of Actium and their involvement in the development of Nikopolis until the collapse of Eurykles' eastern intrigues, around 7 B.C., and Herod's patronage at Sparta could have fallen at any time during that period. There is no evidence that Herod was ever in Sparta, unless Eurykles' time at Herod's court was in return for a visit.

Ongoing excavations at Sparta have discovered details of the Roman city but nothing that can specifically be related to Herod's *anathemata*. One can only note the extant evidence for the type of constructions that might have interested Herod. Of importance is the theater, which was excavated extensively in the early twentieth century and reexamined in the 1990's. Lying to the west of the akropolis, it is one of the largest in Greece, and underwent an extensive reconstruction in the 20's B.C. Numismatic evidence suggests that the cavea was rebuilt at this time, and eventually statues of Gaius and Lucius Caesar stood in the structure, perhaps providing a *terminus ante quem* of the very end of the century for the rebuilding. In addition to the cavea, stage buildings and a colonnade were also constructed. All this suggests that during the Augustan period there was a renovation, which the excavators credited to Eurykles, who also built a gymnasium in the city (Pausanias 3.14.6). Yet it is equally possible that the theater was one of Herod's *anathemata*, as theaters were a known Herodian interest in Judaea and elsewhere.

The rebuilding of the theater seems to have been part of a general urban renewal in the Augustan period, which may have included the repair of a stoa at the southeast corner of the akropolis. Although there was activity in the area as early as the second century B.C. and as late as the time of Hadrian, the Augustan period was one of intense activity in and around the stoa, which perhaps represents part of Herod's and Eurykles' implementation of Augustus's interest in the city.

Woodward, *BSA* 26 (1923–24): 119–58; Woodward, *BSA* 27 (1925–26): 175–209; Ginsburg, *CP* 29 (1934): 117–22; Bowersock *JRS* 51 (1961): 112–18; Cardauns, *Hermes* 95 (1967): 317–24; Catling, *AR* 35 (1989): 35–36; Waywell et al., *BSA* 88 (1993): 219–86; French, *AR* 40 (1994): 20; Waywell and Wilkes, *BSA* 89 (1994): 377–432; Tomlinson, *AR* 41 (1995): 15–16; Tomlinson, *AR* 42 (1996): 13–14.

Tripolis

At the Phoenician port city of Tripolis, Herod built a gymnasium, one of three that he constructed at cities in southwestern Syria and Phoenicia (*BJ* 1.422). There is no obvious reason why Herod chose to build in one of the lesser cities of coastal Phoenicia, since he seems to have had no other association with the place. It had been favored somewhat by the Romans, inasmuch as Pompey had deposed the local tyrant Dionysios (*AJ* 14.39). The ancient city is virtually unknown, and there are no traces of Herod's gymnasium.

Dussaud, *Topographie historique* (1927), 75–76; Rey-Coquais, in *PECS*, 935.

Tyre

Herod's association with the famous and ancient Phoenician city of Tyre dated to before he was king. Cassius had used Roman forces from Tyre to assist Herod in avenging his father's death (*AJ* 14.288), and it was at Tyre that the second embassy of Jews accused Herod before Antonius (*BJ* 1.245; *AJ* 14.327). The city had a substantial Jewish community, whose rights Antonius upheld (*AJ* 14.305–22).

Herod favored Tyre by rebuilding its urban center (*BJ* 1.422). As at nearby Berytos, he constructed temples, exedrae, stoas, and the agora, where Antonius's decree regarding Jewish rights was set up in both Latin and Greek. The city had recovered from its siege by Alexander the Great and an earthquake, and by Roman times it had again become one of the great seaports of the eastern Mediterranean, retaining its historic independence (Strabo 16.2.23), although it was not the international power it had been (Pliny, *Natural History* 5.76). Little is known of the early Roman city, since it was rebuilt by Septimius Severus. Yet the agora of the Roman period, including a temple of Herakles, has been located southeast of the Crusader cathedral, and various Roman streets, including the *cardo* and *decumanus*, have been identified. Precise dating criteria are lacking, and none of these can be directly attributed to Herod; they are probably the later versions of some of his constructions.

MacDonald, in *PECS*, 944; Chéhab, *Tyre* [n. d.], 50; Bikai, *Heritage of Tyre* (1992), 15–16.

CHAPTER NINE

The Buildings of Herod's Descendants

When Herod died in 4 B.C., his kingdom was split among three of his surviving sons: Archelaos, who became *ethnarchos* of Judaea, Samaria, and Idumaea; Antipas, who became tetrarch of Galilee; and Philippos, who became tetrarch of Peraia. All were builders in their own right (map 5), and all had had an education in Rome,[1] which may have helped to encourage their architectural efforts.

Despite his brief and undistinguished period as *ethnarchos*, from 4 B.C. to A.D. 6, Archelaos built a new city, Archelais, and added notably to his father's palace at Jericho. He also provided Jericho with additional water supply, diverting it from a village named Neara and irrigating an expansion of the existing palm orchards.[2] Neara is probably biblical Na'aran, at springs 8 km northwest of Jericho, whose excavated remains consist of a synagogue of the sixth century A.C.[3] Aqueduct traces to the west lead to Jericho. At Jericho proper, no construction that can definitely be attributed to Archelaos has as yet been identified,[4] and his work may largely have been repair of fire damage, since in the disturbances after Herod's death, one of his slaves, a certain Simon, claimed the throne and burned a number of Herod's palaces, including that at Jericho, before he was killed by the

---

1. *BJ* 1.602; *AJ* 17.20. On Herod's successors generally, see Richard D. Sullivan, "The Dynasty of Judaea in the First Century," *ANRW* 2.8 (1977): 296–354; Schürer (NEV), 1: 336–57, 442–54, 471–83.

2. *AJ* 17.340.

3. Michael Avi-Yonah, "Na'aran," in *NEAEHL*, 1075–76.

4. Ehud Netzer, "The Winter Palaces of the Judaean Kings at Jericho at the End of the Second Temple Period," *BASOR* 228 (1977): 12.

Romans.[5] Nevertheless, whatever Archelaos did, it was renowned as a lavish reconstruction performed in a manner worthy of his father.

His new city, Archelais (fig. 38), was itself near Jericho, and may have been part of the same general reconstruction project. It has been identified with the site of Khirbet el-Beiyudat, 12 km to the north, although the only excavated remains are a Byzantine church,[6] and exact attribution must remain unclear. Since Josephus called Archelais a *kome*, not a *polis*, it cannot have been large. Regardless, the palm groves, already famous in the days of Herod the Great, were enlarged by Archelaos and became a major source of revenue, producing some of the best dates in the world.[7] When Archelaos was deposed, they passed to his aunt Salome, who eventually willed them to her confidante Livia, and they thus became imperial property.[8]

Archelaos's brother Antipas, whose rule as tetrarch of Galilee was more successful and more lengthy than his brother's brief time as *ethnarchos*, was a more extensive builder. Before he ran afoul of the emperor Gaius and was banished in A.D. 39,[9] he had founded at least one city and built at others.

His major construction was the new city of Tiberias, a rare example of a toponym honoring the emperor Tiberius. It was founded on the west shore of the Sea of Galilee in an area of hot springs[10] shortly after Tiberius became emperor.[11] The city immediately became controversial because a cemetery was destroyed to create it,[12] and because it was forcibly populated from the hinterland.[13] It was organized in the fashion of a Greek *polis*, with an archon and boule,[14] and issued its own coins.[15] It was designed to be

---

5. *BJ* 2.57–59; *AJ* 17.273–77; Tacitus, *Histories* 5.9.

6. Hanania Hizmi, "Khirbet el-Beiyudat," in *NEAEHL*, 181–82.

7. Horace, *Epistles* 2.2.184; Pliny, *Natural History* 13.44. The palm trees still flourished in the sixth century A.C., as the Mabada mosaic map testifies, and their descendants are there today.

8. *AJ* 18.31.

9. *BJ* 2.183; *AJ* 18.252.

10. *BJ* 2.168; *Life* 85. On Tiberias in its early years, see Tessa Rajak, "Justus of Tiberias," *CQ*, n.s., 23 (1973): 346–51.

11. Its era began in A.D. 20 (Barclay V. Head, *Historia Numorum: A Manual of Greek Numismatics* [Oxford, 1911], 802). For a discussion of the date, see Harold W. Hoehner, *Herod Antipas* (Society for New Testament Studies Monograph 17 [Cambridge, 1972]), 93–95, who would prefer A.D. 23. The official founding may have been in A.D. 18, to coincide with Tiberius's sixtieth birthday: see Michael Avi-Yonah, "The Foundation of Tiberias," *IEJ* 1 (1950–51): 169.

12. This resulted in a purification which itself become controversial: see Lee I. Levine, "R. Simeon b. Yohai and the Purification of Tiberias: History and Tradition," *HUCA* 49 (1978): 143–85.

13. *BJ* 2.641; *Life* 134.

14. Hoehner (supra, n. 11), 97–100.

15. Head (supra, n. 11), 802.

Antipas's capital[16] and was noted for its lavish palace, perhaps mentioned by Jesus of Nazareth,[17] whose decoration included figured wall paintings, probably in the Pompeian Second or Third style, a golden roof, and elaborate furniture, including Corinthian lamps.[18] The artwork and the controversies over the establishment of the city—Antipas was far less cautious than his father—resulted in the demolition of the palace during the 60's A.C.: Josephus himself was commissioned by the assembly in Jerusalem to undertake the task, but found that he had been anticipated by the archon of the city, a certain Jesus.

Literary sources indicate that Tiberias also had a synagogue[19] and a stadium, used during the civil disturbances of the 60's A.C. as a place of detention and execution.[20] Whether these were constructed by Antipas is unknown. Later coins of the city seem to indicate that it had a Temple of Zeus and perhaps a Sarapieion,[21] but these may not have been built by Antipas. Tiberias has remained an important city into modern times, and although its general plan is known, and public buildings and streets dating to the early second century A.C. have been excavated, nothing that directly relates to Antipas's city has been discovered, and it is probable that it was virtually destroyed in A.D. 66.[22]

Antipas's second most important construction was Autokratoris, founded at the site of Sepphoris, 25 km west of Tiberias. Although Antipas intended that Tiberias would supplant it,[23] Autokratoris remained the most important city in Galilee until at least the 60's A.C.[24] Herod the Great may have built at Sepphoris, but it had burned at the time of his death,[25] which might have stimulated Antipas to rebuild it, perhaps immediately after his accession.[26] No specifics are provided regarding Antipas's work, except that the city was fortified in A.D. 6 or 7,[27] and that by the time of Agrippa II, it

16. *Life* 37.

17. Matt. 11.8: see Gerd Theissen, "Das 'schwankende Rohr' in Mt. 11, 7 und die Gründungsmünzen von Tiberias," *ZDPV* 101 (1985): 51–52.

18. *Life* 65–68.

19. *Life* 277, 280, 293.

20. *BJ* 3.539; *Life* 91, 331.

21. BMC Palestine, 8; Head (supra, n. 11), 802.

22. Yizhar Hirschfeld, *A Guide to Antiquity Sites in Tiberias* (Jerusalem, 1992); id., "Tiberias," in *NEAEHL*, 1464–70. Two 1839 views of Tiberias, showing the city before modern tourist construction, are to be found in David Roberts, *The Holy Land* (London, 1989), pls. 62, 64.

23. *Life* 37.

24. *BJ* 2.511; *AJ* 17.289; *Life* 38, 232; David Adan-Bayewitz and Isadore Perlman, "The Local Trade of Sepphoris in the Roman Period," *IEJ* 40 (1990): 170–72.

25. *BJ* 2.68.

26. Hoehner (supra, n. 11), 85.

27. *AJ* 18.27.

contained royal archives and a treasury.[28] With Tiberias and Autokratoris, Antipas was following his father's policy of using both the personal name and title of the Roman emperor to name cities, but the toponym Autokratoris, although unique, was short-lived and never came into general use.

Sepphoris has seen extensive excavation, but attributions of material continue to be obscure.[29] Most of the major remains are second century A.C. or later,[30] although there is scattered material from the period of Antipas.[31] The summit of the site seems to have been continuously occupied from Hellenistic into Roman times,[32] and a palatial structure with painted decoration may mark the location of Antipas's palace,[33] although the bulk of the structure is as late as the third century A.C.[34]

The theater of Sepphoris may also be the work of Antipas (fig. 39). It lies at the northeast edge of the summit, and was a structure 73 m across, largely cut out of bedrock.[35] A date during the reign of Antipas has been presumed rather than proven.[36] The theater was filled with over six meters of debris, which had washed into it from the summit, some of it containing Hellenistic material; this, as well as its construction out of bedrock, has made dating difficult. It has even been suggested that it was the work of Herod the Great,[37] but this is unlikely. A date as late as the third century A.C. has also been proposed,[38] which would make it a significantly less important structure in the history of architecture than if it were the work of Antipas. The lack of chronological controls makes attribution as yet impossible.

28. *Life* 38.

29. For possible work by Herod the Great at this site, see supra, pp. 212–13.

30. Ehud Netzer and Zeev Weiss, "Sepphoris (Sippori), 1991–1992," *IEJ* 43 (1993): 190–96.

31. Eric Meyers et al., "Sepphoris (Sippori), 1986 (I)—Joint Sepphoris Project," *IEJ* 37 (1987): 275–78; James F. Strange and Thomas R. W. Longstaff, "Sepphoris (Sippori) 1986 (II)," *IEJ* 37 (1987): 280; James F. Strange et al., "Sepphoris (Sippori), 1987," *IEJ* 38 (1988): 188–90; Eric Meyers et al., "Sepphoris (Sippori), 1987 and 1988," *IEJ* 40 (1990): 219–22; James F. Strange, "Six Campaigns at Sepphoris: The University of South Florida Excavations, 1983–1989," in *The Galilee in Late Antiquity*, ed. Lee I. Levine (New York, 1992), 347–48; Samuel R. Wolff, "Archaeology in Israel," *AJA* 98 (1994): 511–12.

32. Meyers et al., *IEJ* 40 (supra, n. 31), 220.

33. Leroy Waterman et al., *Preliminary Report of the University of Michigan Excavations at Sepphoris, Palestine, in 1931* (Ann Arbor, 1937) 28.

34. Zeev Weiss, "Sepphoris," in *NEAEHL*, 1324–28.

35. Ibid., 1325–26.

36. Waterman (supra, n. 33), 29; Eric Meyers et al., "Sepphoris (Sippori), 1985 (I)," *IEJ* 35 (1985): 297; Strange and Longstaff, *IEJ* 37 (supra, n. 31), 280; Meyers et al., *IEJ* 37 (supra, n. 31), 277–78; Weiss (supra, n. 34), 1325; Strange, "Six Campaigns" (supra, n. 31), 342–43. For a recent summary of the evidence, see Arthur Segal, *Theatres in Roman Palestine and Provincia Arabia* (*Mnemosyne*, suppl. 140 [Leiden, 1995]), 41–43.

37. Waterman (supra, n. 33), 29.

38. W. F. Albright, review of *Preliminary Report of the University of Michigan Excavations at Sepphoris*," by Leroy Waterman et al., *Classical Weekly* 31 (1937–38), 148.

The only other well-documented building effort of Antipas was at the ancient city of Betharamatha, east of Jericho, which his father had probably named Livias. Antipas renamed it Julias, most likely in A.D. 14 when the newly widowed Livia officially took the name Julia Augusta.[39] The site is probably modern Tell er-Ramah, 18 km east of Jericho, which is unexcavated.[40]

Some other possible constructions of Antipas are not specifically cited. Work continued on the Temple in Jerusalem. The Tiberieion at Caesarea, known solely through its famous dedicatory inscription, which is the only epigraphic mention of Pontius Pilate,[41] was probably constructed by Antipas, who was always anxious to honor Tiberius. A stadium at Caesarea, which existed at the same time, may also be Antipas's work.[42] At Tarichaiai, north of Tiberias on the Sea of Galilee, more famous as biblical Magdala but little known archaeologically, a hippodrome existed in the 60's A.C.,[43] which may have been built by Antipas or perhaps Agrippa II, into whose territory it eventually passed.[44]

Although never holding a kingship, and thus not having the prestige of his father, Antipas continued to relate to Rome in much the same way his father had. Educated in the city, he had spent his youth surrounded by the dynamic architectural endeavors of the later years of the Augustan building program. He was also able to see the completed products of his father's architectural efforts. His close relationships with members of the ruling elite at Rome, especially Tiberius, paralleled his father's interests. Yet it is clear that Antipas did not build on his father's scale, and efforts outside his tetrarchy were thus limited. No specifics are preserved, but two or three inscriptions honoring him may be vestiges of his royal building in the Greek world. The most definite is from Delos, dated to around A.D. 6, recording a statue erected in the precinct of Apollo[45] at approximately the time of Archelaos's deposition and Antipas's hopes that his rule would be expanded into a kingship, when he would have been particularly anxious to show his respect for ancient Greek and Roman institutions. Inscriptions from Kos[46] and Chios[47] also seem to honor Antipas, although the interpretation of the

---

39. Tacitus, *Annals* 1.8, but see Hoehner (supra, n. 11), 89–91.

40. See Livias, supra, pp. 183–84.

41. Antonio Frova et al., *Scavi di Caesarea Maritima* (Rome, 1966), 217–20.

42. *BJ* 2.171; *AJ* 18.57. This may be the structure currently under excavation in the southern area of the city: see Yosef Porath, "Herod's 'amphitheatre' at Caesarea: A Multi-Purpose Entertainment Building," in *The Roman and Byzantine Near East: Some Recent Archaeological Research* (*JRA*, suppl. 14 [1995]), 15–27.

43. *BJ* 2.599; *Life* 132, 138.

44. *BJ* 3.445.

45. *OGIS*, 417.

46. *OGIS*, 416.

47. *SEG* 35.930B20.

latter is uncertain. But in none of the cases is there any specific building that can be attributed to the tetrarch.

A final curious note to Antipas's building concerns the peace talks between the Romans and Parthians at the very end of Tiberius's reign. The governor of Syria, L. Vitellius, met with the Parthian king Artabanos III in a luxurious pavilion erected in the middle of the Euphrates by Antipas, who also lavishly catered the meetings. Although temporary, the pavilion was elaborate, and its construction and remote location show the wide-ranging architectural reach of the Herodian dynasty.[48] Antipas's last attempt to assist the eastern policy of his patron Tiberius was in vain, however, because within a few months Tiberius was dead, and two years later Gaius accused Antipas of pro-Parthian sentiments and deposed him, banishing him to either Gaul or Spain.

The half-brother of Archelaos and Antipas, Philippos, ruled as tetrarch of Peraia from Herod's death until the twentieth year of Tiberius, A.D. 33 or 34.[49] He was not as aggressive a builder as Antipas, and seems to have built only during the first three years of his reign. There is no record of further building during his remaining thirty-five years, unlike the continuing efforts of his brothers. Nevertheless, he founded two cities, the Caesarea that came to be called after him, and a Julias. His building at these is documented in literature merely in a pair of sparse references by Josephus.[50]

Caesarea was located near the Paneion, where Herod the Great had built a temple of Augustus. Coins of the city show Herod's temple and identify Philippos as founder.[51] The city seems to have been established early in Philippos's reign, perhaps around 3–1 B.C.[52] The urban center is today marked by the remains of a monumental building, 9 by 75 m, consisting of parallel vaults similar to those at Herod's maritime Caesarea, and serving a similar function as granaries or warehouses. Nearby fragments of architectural ornamentation and the remnants of another large ashlar building, perhaps a basilica, may also belong to Philippos's city, although recent excavation suggests a later date. The site is still under excavation, and further definition of its urban core is in progress.[53]

48. *AJ* 18.102; see also Suetonius, *Gaius* 14, *Vitellius* 2; Dio 59.27; Barbara Levick, *Tiberius the Politician* (London, 1976), 146–47; Hoehner (supra, n. 11), 252–59.

49. *AJ* 18.106.

50. *BJ* 2.168; *AJ* 18.28.

51. See Paneion, supra, pp. 190–92.

52. Zvi Uri Ma'oz, "Banias," in *NEAEHL*, 138.

53. Ma'oz (supra, n. 52), 141–42. Blocks from the city (or even Herod the Great's Temple of Augustus at the Paneion) may have ended up in the thirteenth-century fortress now known as Qalat Nimrod, 3 km to the east. Limestone ashlars with marked anathyrosis are prominent in and around the west gate of the fortress (fig. 40).

Philippos's other foundation was Julias, named after Augustus's daughter.[54] This would make its establishment unlikely after her banishment in 2 B.C. Located at biblical Bethsaida, at the north end of the sea of Galilee (modern et-Tell), it, too, was a *polis*. Recent excavations have revealed remnants of public buildings of the late Hellenistic or early Roman periods, which were destroyed in the second century A.C., but specifics are as yet lacking as to whether these were constructed by Philippos.[55]

The Herodian architectural tradition continued into the following generation, that of Herod's grandsons. Agrippa I, son of Aristoboulos, had spent much time in Rome living in the imperial household.[56] Unfortunately, he fell out with Tiberius—an accusation against Tiberius's favorite, his uncle Antipas, was no help—and spent the last months of Tiberius's reign in prison, until Gaius upon accession released him and gave him his uncle Philippos's vacant tetrarchy to rule as king.[57] Within four years he was ruling a territory similar in extent to that of his grandfather, but only until A.D. 44, when he died suddenly in his grandfather's theater at Caesarea.[58]

Despite his short reign, Agrippa I was an active builder.[59] Only two places are specified, however: Jerusalem and Berytos. At Jerusalem, work continued on the Temple, and Agrippa began a new wall across the northern edge of the city, but the governor of Syria reported this possibly treasonable act to the emperor Claudius, who suggested that the construction stop, advice Agrippa followed.[60] It was hastily completed at the time of the Jewish revolt in the 6o's A.C. Various fragments several hundred meters northwest of the Antonia have been identified with this wall. Foundation blocks in the style characteristic of Herod and his descendants, up to 5.5 m long and 1.75 m

---

54. *AJ* 18.28. For the possibility that Julias was in fact named after Livia, and founded in A.D. 30, see Heinz-Wolfgang Kuhn and Rami Arav, "The Bethsaida Excavations: Historical and Archaeological Approaches," in *The Future of Early Christianity: Essays in Honor of Helmut Koester*, ed. Birger A. Pearson (Minneapolis, 1991), 87–91, and Fred Strickert, "The Coins of Philip," in *Bethsaida: A City by the North Shore of the Sea of Galilee*, vol. 1, ed. Rami Arav and Richard A. Freund (Kirksville, Mo., 1995), 181–84.

55. Rami Arav, "Bethsaida Excavations: Preliminary Excavation Report, 1987–1993," in *Bethsaida* (supra, n. 54), 3–63. An inscription from Herod the Great's Caesarea seems to refer to a person whose mother was named Cleopatra: if this is Philippos's mother, it may indicate building by him at that site, perhaps an otherwise-unknown Kleopatreion, but the text is highly fragmentary and seems to call Caesarea "Flavia Augusta," unlikely until well after Philippos's death (Baruch Lifshitz, "Inscriptiones latines de Césarée [Caesarea Palaestinae]," *Latomus* 22 [1963]: 783–84). A more probable candidate is the Cleopatra who was the wife of Gessius Florus, procurator in the 6o's A.C. (*AJ* 20.252), but even she is rather early.

56. *AJ* 18.167–237; Jones, *Herods*, 184–216.

57. *BJ* 2.178–83.

58. *BJ* 2.219; *AJ* 19.343–52; Acts 12.19–23.

59. *AJ* 19.335.

60. *BJ* 5.147–55; *AJ* 19.326–327.

high, may be Agrippa's work, but the interpretation is disputed.[61] He may also have been active in the Temple area, since numerous stone weights from his fifth year found southwest of the Temple Mount testify to economic reforms in A.D. 41–42.[62]

Agrippa I also built at Berytos, constructing a theater, amphitheater, baths, and stoas, all particularly lavish.[63] This is the most extensive known building program of a descendant of Herod the Great's outside the area of his rule. Herod himself had also built considerably at Berytos, but the structures erected by his grandson are all distinct, and it is unlikely that Josephus confused the work of the two. Baths of uncertain date are known west of Herod the Great's civic center,[64] but no other remains attributable to Agrippa are known, and most fieldwork at Berytos is neither recent nor interpreted with unanimity. No reason is preserved as to why Agrippa should have singled out Berytos for such extensive largesse, but it is possible that it was because the city had benefited heavily from the architectural and other interests of his namesake, Marcus Agrippa.

The brother of Agrippa I, Herod, was named king of the territory of Chalkis by Claudius in A.D. 41. He only lived for seven more years,[65] and both he and his kingdom are so shadowy that no record of building is preserved in either literary or archaeological sources, although he seems to have been honored by the city of Athens.[66] Upon his death, Chalkis was given to his nephew, the son of Agrippa I, who eventually became (as King Agrippa II) ruler of much of the territories of his father and great-grandfather.[67] He was particularly Greek in his culture and outlook,[68] and was an extensive builder. He is known to have built at Jerusalem, at Philippos's Caesarea, and at Berytos.

In Jerusalem, he enlarged the existing palace, a project that caused him difficulty, because it allowed him to look from a dining loggia into the Temple, a prospect offensive to many, and a wall was soon erected to block his view. The emperor Nero eventually had to mediate this dispute over rival

61. Hillel Geva, "Jerusalem: The Second Temple Period," in *NEAEHL*, 744–45. See also Jodi Magness, "The North Wall of Aelia Capitolina," in *Essays in Honor of James A. Sauer*, ed. Lawrence E. Stager and Joseph A. Greene (Cambridge, Mass., forthcoming).

62. Benjamin Mazar, *The Excavations in the Old City of Jerusalem near the Temple Mount* (Jerusalem, 1971), 17–21.

63. *AJ* 19.335–37.

64. Jean Lauffray, "Forums et monuments de Béryte," *BMusBeyr* 7 (1944–45): 26–33; id., "Beyrouth archéologie et histoire, époques gréco-romaines. I. Period hellénistique et Haut-Empire romain," *ANRW* 2.8 (1977): 156.

65. *BJ* 2.217–23.

66. *OGIS*, 427.

67. *BJ* 2.247; Jones, *Herods*, 217–61.

68. *Life* 359; *Apion* 1.51.

constructions and sided with the Temple authorities.[69] At the time of the Jewish revolt in A.D. 66, Agrippa II was preparing to raise the level of the Temple foundations, and had brought impressive beams from Lebanon for the task, but the beams were appropriated by the revolutionary forces and used to gain access to the Temple precinct.[70] He also paved the streets of Jerusalem with marble, seemingly a make-work project for those who had become unemployed when the Temple was finally finished.[71]

At Philippos's Caesarea, Agrippa II embarked on a program of enlargement and enhancement, renaming it Neronias, a name that did not outlast the emperor, although it appears on coins.[72] No details are preserved, and since the project seems only to have begun after A.D. 60,[73] the work may have been limited.

At Berytos, Agrippa II continued his forebears' interest in the city by building a lavish theater and erecting many public statues, including copies of famous Greek works. There was an annual and expensive festival, and the city was the beneficiary of gifts of grain and olive oil. Like his great-grandfather, he was accused of robbing his own territory to benefit a foreign city,[74] but his policy seems to have been a direct imitation of the public spectacles and doles of the Roman emperors, and it is clear he spent a great deal of time in Berytos,[75] perhaps even planning it as an ultimate place of refuge should he be deposed. In addition, a number of inscriptions, particularly from Syria, mention Agrippa II (although some are so fragmentary that it is not clear which Agrippa is meant). Some of these may record building. At Seia in Syria (where there was a statue of Herod the Great), a certain freedman named Aphareus, perhaps originally a member of the royal household, honored Agrippa with an inscription on the epistyle of a building.[76] Others come from nearby Kanatha,[77] Helbon near Damaskos,[78] and Eitha.[79]

In addition, Agrippa II was probably responsible for one of the most obscure sites of the Herodian dynasty, that of Agrippina, a point north of

69. *AJ* 20.189–96.

70. *BJ* 5.36–38.

71. *AJ* 20.222.

72. *BJ* 3.514; *AJ* 20.211; BMC Palestine, 239.

73. It was after the arrival of Festus as procurator, if the events recorded by Josephus are in chronological sequence: cf. *AJ* 20.182.

74. *AJ* 20.211–12.

75. *Life* 181, 357.

76. *OGIS*, 419. On the statue of Herod, see infra, p. 272.

77. *OGIS*, 424; J.-P. Rey-Coquais, "Canatha," in *PECS*, 191–92; Schürer (NEV), 2: 140–42.

78. *OGIS*, 420.

79. *OGIS*, 421. Eitha was called "Caesarea Eitha" at some time during its history (*IGRR*, 3: 1142; *SEG* 30.1670): it is possible that this name was given by Agrippa II or one of his predecessors, perhaps Philippos (Henry Innes MacAdam, *Studies in the History of the Roman Province of Arabia: The Northern Sector* [*BAR-IS*, 295 (1986)]: 61–67).

Alexandreion, on a route of signal stations leading north from Jerusalem, mentioned only in the *Mishna*.[80] The only attempt to locate it has placed it at Kochav ha-Yarden, where the ruins of the prominent Crusader fortress of Belvoir now stand, an identification that is probable but totally hypothetical.[81] There are no archaeological remains to support the hypothesis. Agrippina was probably one of the places Josephus fortified in the 60's A.C. defense of Galilee, but he did not mention it by name.[82] Yet its commemoration of a member of the Julio-Claudian family connects it securely to the Herodian dynasty. There are only two possibilities for the eponym: Agrippina the daughter of Marcus Agrippa and Julia, and her daughter, the mother of the emperor Nero.[83]

The elder Agrippina was born around 14 B.C.[84] and thus would have been only ten years old when Herod the Great died, which rules out any possibility that the Agrippina fortress was his foundation. It was in the territory of Antipas thereafter, but Agrippina's hostility toward Tiberius (especially after she suspected the emperor of complicity in the death of her husband, Germanicus), and Antipas's greater friendliness toward the Claudian side of the family, makes it unlikely that Antipas would have honored her. She died in A.D. 33, and can thus effectively be eliminated as the eponym of the fortress.

One is left with her daughter, born in A.D. 15.[85] Of no great prominence during the reigns of Antipas and Agrippa I, she married the emperor Claudius in A.D. 49, around the time the emperor made Agrippa II king of Chalkis. Agrippina's son Nero, when he became emperor, gave Galilee to Agrippa II, including the territory where Agrippina has been located. There thus seems no doubt that the Agrippina fortress was built by Agrippa II during the 50's A.C., following a pattern of toponymic honoring of the wives and mothers of Roman emperors. Agrippa II would have been aware of the relationship between his name and Agrippina's—his namesake was her

80. *Rosh Hashana* 2.4.

81. G. Dalman, "Nach Galiläa von 30. September bis 13. Oktober 1921," *PalJb* 18–19 (1922–23): 43–44.

82. *BJ* 2.573–74; *Life* 187–88; Michael Avi-Yonah, "The Missing Fortress of Flavius Josephus," *IEJ* 3 (1953): 95.

83. The name has been corrupted in the *Mishna* to Grofina. It is impossible to determine its exact proper form. The only other use of the name of Agrippina as a toponym is Colonia Agrippinensis, modern Cologne, where the younger Agrippina was born, which she renamed after her son became emperor (Tacitus, *Annals* 12.27; Pliny, *Natural History* 4.106). But the place came to be called simply Agrippina (Ammianus Marcellinus 15.5.15; 15.8.19; 16.3.1; 17.2.1): thus the Galilean site might also have been so named. Other possible forms, conforming more to the toponymic onomastics of the Herodian dynasty, are Agrippinas or Agrippineion.

84. J. P. D. V. Balsdon, *Roman Women: Their History and Habits* (London, 1962), 88–96.

85. Ibid., 107–22.

Berenike inscription, Berytos (center portion). Based on René Mouterde and Jean Lauffray. *Beyrouth, ville romaine: Histoire et monuments* (Beirut, n.d.), 8–9. Drawn by Letitia K. Roller.

grandfather—and the personal name (in the masculine form Agrippinos) appeared briefly in the Herodian family, the name of a son of a sister of Agrippa II's, Mariamme, who had married a prominent citizen of Alexandria, one Demetrios.[86] Their son Agrippinos was probably born between A.D. 54 (Nero's accession) and 59 (Agrippina's murder), the same period as the building of the fortress.

Another sister of Agrippa II's, Berenike, was the most prominent woman of the Herodian family, and the only one to carry the title "queen."[87] After the death of her second husband, her uncle Herod of Chalkis, she came to live with her brother in Jerusalem, where questions of propriety were repeatedly raised.[88] Her famous affair with the future emperor Titus was the ultimate evolution of the close relationship between the Herodian and imperial families, which had existed for a century, and made her an object of interest in Roman circles.[89] She was honored by the Athenians with a statue,[90] and at Berytos a record of her building program is preserved in an inscription that commemorates a hexastyle building adorned in marble.[91] The extant portions are as follows:

R]EGINA BERENICE REGIS MAGNI A[

QU]OD REX HERODES PROAVOS EORUM FECERAT VE[

MARBORIBUSQUE ET COLUMNIS [S]EX

EX[ORNAVERUNT

The use of the plural pronoun indicates that there was another builder, also a great-grandchild of Herod, so it is easy to restore her brother Agrippa II as co-donor. The inscription was found in a structure in the Corinthian and Ionic orders, which was probably a basilica, originally part of Herod the Great's monumental civic center, enhanced or rebuilt by Berenike and her brother.

No other members of the Herodian dynasty are specifically documented as builders. But it is hard to imagine any descendant of Herod the Great's who held royal power not being a builder. His grandson Tigranes IV and great-grandson Tigranes V were kings of Armenia. The son of Tigranes V, Alexandros, married into the royal family of Kommagene and ruled Kilikia

86. *AJ* 20.147; infra, Stemma 4.

87. *Life* 119; Tacitus, *Histories* 2.81.

88. *AJ* 20.145.

89. Suetonius, *Titus* 7; Tacitus, *Histories* 2.2; Dio 65.15; 66.18; Juvenal 6.156–60; Grace H. Macurdy, "Julia Berenice," *AJP* 56 (1935) 246–53; John A. Crook, "Titus and Berenice," *AJP* 72 (1951): 162–75; Ronald Syme, "*Titus et Berenice:* A Tacitean Fragment," in Ronald Syme, *Roman Papers,* vol. 7, ed. Anthony R. Birley (Oxford, 1991), 647–62.

90. *OGIS,* 428.

91. *AEpigr* 1928: 23.

in the time of Vespasian. Aristoboulos, son of Herod of Chalkis, ruled Lesser Armenia and Chalkidike at about the same time.[92] In any case, during his lifetime, Herod the Great directly and indirectly influenced his in-laws, who were themselves client kings.

The best example is Archelaos of Kappadokia, the father-in-law of Herod's son Alexandros.[93] He and Herod were in frequent contact (although not always on the best of terms), visited each other, and traveled together.[94] The career of Archelaos is a parallel to that of Herod. He was made king of Kappadokia by Antonius, either in 41 or 36 B.C., allegedly because of the triumvir's interest in his mother, Glaphyra.[95] Archelaos's position was confirmed by Octavian after Actium,[96] and like Herod, he embarked on a career of closeness to the Augustan elite and royal building. He was also a scholar, writing a work on natural history, which was used by Pliny.[97] Also like Herod, he was not universally beloved by his subjects, who brought accusations against him before the Roman government, probably in 26 B.C., but he was successfully defended by the future emperor Tiberius, then starting his public career.[98] He too was attentive to his dynastic relationships with the other royal families of the East. His daughter Glaphyra married Herod's son Alexandros around 16 B.C. After Alexandros's execution, Glaphyra married Juba II of Mauretania, himself a notable royal builder,[99] but eventually—perhaps after a divorce—returned to Judaea to marry Herod's son Archelaos.[100] Archelaos of Kappadokia himself eventu-

92. Descendants of Herod even became related to, or were themselves, officials in the Roman government. The earliest connection is when Herod's great-granddaughter Drusilla married Antonius Felix, procurator of Judaea during the reigns of Claudius and Nero, and the opponent of Paul of Tarsos (*AJ* 20.141–44; Acts 24.24). The best example is Herod's great-great-grandson Alexandros, who after a long career as king of Kilikia, came to Rome and was consul early in the second century A.C. (Richard D. Sullivan, "The Dynasty of Commagene," *ANRW* 2.8 [1977]: 794–95), perhaps in A.D. 106 or 108 (Syme [supra, n. 89], 655). The complexities of the eastern dynasties are still being revealed, especially through new epigraphic evidence, and it is possible that there were other connections. Forthcoming work by Nikos Kokkinos will illuminate further details about the family relationships of Herod the Great.

93. On Archelaos generally, see Mario Pani, *Rome e i re d'Oriente da Augusto a Tiberio* (Pubblicazioni della Facoltà di lettere e filosofia dell'Università di Bari, 11 [Bari (1972)]), 93–145; Richard D. Sullivan, "The Dynasty of Cappadocia," *ANRW* 2.7 (1980): 1149–61; Sullivan, *NER*, 182–85. Coin portraits of Archelaos show a strong profile, with features remindful of Alexander the Great and Octavian (fig. 41).

94. *BJ* 1.456, 499, 513; *AJ* 16.131.

95. Strabo 12.2.11; Tacitus, *Annals* 2.42; Appian, *Civil War* 5.7; Dio 49.32; Martial 11.20; Magie, *RR*, 435.

96. Dio 51.2.

97. *FrGrHist*, # 123. Archelaos is also probably one of the scholars of that name mentioned by Diogenes Laertios (2.17).

98. Suetonius, *Tiberius* 8; Dio 57.17; Bowersock, *Augustus*, 158–60.

99. The career of Juba II is an interesting parallel to that of Herod and would benefit from further study. Brought to Rome as a child by Julius Caesar, he was raised in the city and

ally married Pythodoris I of Pontos, a granddaughter of Marcus Antonius's and an important queen in her own right.[101]

Archelaos thus became the most powerful client king in Asia Minor. He built at least three cities, whose names follow the proper formulas: Sebaste, Caesarea, and Archelais. The coastal Kilikian city of Elaioussa became Sebaste, probably shortly after he obtained the territory around 20 B.C. Here Archelaos built a palace, and it seems to have become his favored residence.[102] The city was architecturally innovative, using *opus reticulatum* and concrete.[103] Extensive and evocative remains are visible in and around the sand dunes that today cover the site (fig. 42).[104]

---

eventually sent by Augustus to be king of Mauretania, probably about 25 B.C.: he thus spent the years 45–25 B.C. in Rome and saw the end of Caesar's architectural program and the first half of that of Augustus. In Mauretania he established his capital at Iol, which he renamed Caesarea about the time Herod began his Caesarea, and introduced the latest in Roman architecture there and elsewhere in his kingdom, particularly at the western city of Volubilis. A prolific scholar, he left copious writings, particularly on history and antiquarianism (*FGrHist*, # 275, frs. 1–6), which survived long enough to be used by Pliny and Plutarch but are no long extant. His work on the history of the theater (frs. 15–17) may have included an architectural study: his theater at Caesarea was one of the earliest outside Italy. He also wrote on painting (frs. 20–21). His first wife was Cleopatra Selene, daughter of Antonius and Cleopatra. He died around A.D. 23 and was succeeded by his son Ptolemaios, a descendant not only of his famous namesakes but of the aristocracy of Republican Rome and the native dynasts of North Africa, a fine example of the intermingling of prominent families in the early Imperial period. There is no evidence that Juba and Herod ever came into contact, despite being virtually in-laws, although as a boy Juba would probably have been in the household of Octavian when Herod was first in Rome, and presumably he and Herod had many of the same intimates. Like Herod, he showed the best of the client-king concept and its architectural dimensions. There is no good recent study of Juba; the best available is Felix Jacoby, "Iuba II" (# 2), in *RE*, 9 (1916): 2384–95, supplemented by the material in *FGrHist* and Stéphane Gsell, *Histoire ancienne de l'Afrique du nord* (Paris, 1914–28), 8: 205–76. On Juba's Caesarea, modern Cherchel, see Gilbert Picard, "La date du théâtre de Cherchel et les débuts de l'architecture théâtrale dans les provinces romaines d'occident," *CRAI* 1975: 386–97; Jean-Claude Golvin and Philippe Leaveau, "L'amphithéâtre et le théâtre-amphithétre de Cherchel: Monuments à spectacle et histoire urbaine à Caesarea de Maurétanie," *MEFRA* 91 (1979): 817–43; Philippe Leveau, *Caesarea de Maurétanie: Une ville romaine et ses campagnes* (*CEFR*, 70 [1984]).

100. *BJ* 2.114–16.

101. Strabo 12.3.29. On Pythodoris, see Richard D. Sullivan, "Dynasts in Pontus," *ANRW* 2.7 (1986): 920–22. The date of the marriage is unknown: see Sullivan, "Dynasty of Cappadocia" (supra, n. 93), 1158–59.

102. Strabo 12.2.7; 14.5.6.

103. Ward-Perkins, *RIA*, 305; Josef Keil and Adolf Wilhelm, *Denkmäler aus dem Rauhen Kilikien* (*MAMA* 3 [1931]), 222–23, pl. 177; Hazel Dodge, "Brick Construction in Rome, Greece, and Asia Minor," in *Roman Architecture in the Greek World*, ed. Sarah Macready and F. H. Thompson (Society of Antiquaries of London Occasional Papers, n.s., 10 [London, 1987]), 107.

Caesarea, his official capital, was founded in the shadow of Mount Argaios at the ancient city of Mazaka, which had been destroyed by Tigranes the Great of Armenia, its inhabitants becoming the population of Tigranes' own foundation, Tigranokerta.[105] Caesarea was dedicated ca. 13–9 B.C., very close to the time of Herod's own Caesarea, and eventually became the capital of the Roman province of Galatia.[106] It has remained an important city, and as Kayseri, it is the only modern city to retain the name Caesarea. Few ancient remains are, however, known.

The city of Archelais was founded late in Archelaos's reign at Garsaoura, in a fertile location on the main east-west route through Kappadokia. It became important enough to receive the status of a *colonia* under Claudius. The site, at modern Aksaray, is little known archaeologically.[107]

As with that of Herod, the building program of Archelaos was more extensive than suggested by the literature. At Komana, a religious center that had existed since at least Hittite times, located southeast of Archelaos's Caesarea, he was honored as founder.[108] Like Herod, he strengthened his rule by architecturally honoring himself, the Roman imperial family, and the ancient cults of his territory.

After fifty years on the throne, Archelaos was called to Rome by Tiberius shortly after the latter's accession. The reasons are uncertain, given the hostility of the literary tradition toward Tiberius: either the emperor was offended at some previous slight or, more probably, he felt that Archelaos had become too powerful and had overstepped the limits of client kingship, perhaps interfering with the royal succession in Armenia.[109] Archelaos's friendship with the late Gaius Caesar, Augustus's grandson, indicates that the traditional rivalries between the Julian and Claudian families may also have been a problem for him. A letter from Livia summoned him to Rome, and he was brought to trial before the Senate. But it was too much for the elderly dynast—he would have been nearly eighty, at least—and he died while at Rome, perhaps even by suicide. His kingdom became a province, although his widow Pythodoris continued to rule her own territories and to support the scholarly endeavors of Strabo.[110]

104. T. S. MacKay, "Elaeussa, Later Sebaste," in *PECS*, 294–95; Magie, *RR*, 475, 494.

105. Strabo 11.14.15; 12.2.7–10.

106. R. P. Harper, "Caesarea Cappadociae," in *PECS*, 182; Magie, *RR*, 1353.

107. Pliny, *Natural History* 6.8; Magie, *RR*, 1353–54.

108. *OGIS*, 358.

109. Levick (supra, n. 48), 140–41.

110. Strabo 12.3.31; Tacitus, *Annals* 2.42; Suetonius, *Tiberius* 37; Dio 57.17; on Pythodoris and Strabo, see supra, p. 65.

CHAPTER TEN

The Legacy of Herod

The Herodian building program established the pattern for Roman architecture in Syria and the Levant, and indeed much of the Roman East, a pattern that survived until the ultimate decline and collapse of Roman political control. Yet, ironically, Herod's architectural legacy was stronger outside his kingdom than within it. After the end of the Herodian dynasty, it was not until the early fourth century A.C. and the spate of Constantinian church building that the southern Levant was again significant architecturally.[1] Many Herodian sites quickly faded. The fortresses became less valuable as the Nabataean kingdom became more romanized and the frontier shifted to the east. Hyrkania does not seem to have been used much after Herod's time.[2] Alexandreion,[3] Judaean Herodeion,[4] Kypros,[5] Machairous,[6] and Masada[7] were of little importance after the insurrection of the 60's A.C. The palace at Jericho was burned at Herod's death, although it was rebuilt by Archelaos.[8] Antipatris,[9] Hebron,[10] and Jerusalem[11] all suffered extensive destruction in the 60's A.C. Sebaste was also destroyed at that time, although there was a Severan rebuilding.[12] Of all the Herodian sites within and near

1. Ward-Perkins, *RIA*, 313.
2. Joseph Patrich, "Hyrcania," in *NEAEHL*, 639.
3. Yoram Tsafrir and Itzhak Magen, "Sartaba-Alexandrium," in *NEAEHL*, 1320.
4. *BJ* 4.518–20, 555; 7.163.
5. Ehud Netzer, "Cypros," in *NEAEHL*, 317.
6. *BJ* 7.190–209.
7. *BJ* 7.252–407.
8. *BJ* 2.57; *AJ* 17.274, 340.
9. *BJ* 2.513–15.
10. *BJ* 4.554.
11. *BJ* 6.403–34.
12. Nahman Avigad, "Samaria (City)," in *NEAEHL*, 1302.

his kingdom, only two flourished into Byzantine times: Askalon and Caesarea, whose position as seaports allowed their survival and even enhancement.[13] As the preferred port for travel to Greece and Italy, Herod's Caesarea continued to be a major center. Ptolemais, Caesarea's predecessor, suffered a proportionate decline.

But the full impact was elsewhere. The effects of Herod's program appeared as soon as the Nabataean kings began to adopt Roman architecture, especially during the reign of Aretas IV—perhaps Herod's cousin—who came to the throne around 9 B.C., just as Herod's work was ending, and who may have wished to initiate his own building program as a replacement for or continuation of the virtually defunct Herodian one. Aretas's daughter had long been married to Herod's son Antipas,[14] which would have cemented relations between the dynasties. At Petra, the Temple of the Winged Lions and the large theater are both structures of Herodian inspiration;[15] the former is remindful of the Herodian temples to Augustus. To the north, in Syria, the great Temple of Juppiter at Baalbek (fig. 45) seems to have been started shortly after the town became part of the territory of the Roman *colonia* of Berytos around 15 B.C. The Temple of Juppiter had close affinities with Herod's temples at Sebaste and Jerusalem: the plan and architectural details reflect those of the former, whereas the sheer size of the complex is remindful of the latter, a fitting precedent for a shrine to another major eastern divinity.[16] At Palmyra, which came under Roman control only a few years after Herod's death, the Temple of Bel (fig. 44),

13. The Paneion also flourished, but not so much because of Herod's construction as because Philippos founded his Caesarea there.

14. *AJ* 18.109.

15. Philip C. Hammond, *The Excavation of the Main Theater at Petra, 1961–1962: Final Report* (London, 1965), 62–65; Arthur Segal, *Theatres in Roman Palestine and Provincia Arabia* (*Mnemosyne*, suppl. 140 [Leiden, 1995]), 91–92; Margaret Lyttleton and Thomas Blagg, "Sculpture in Nabataean Petra, and the Question of Roman Influence," in *Architecture and Architectural Sculpture in the Roman Empire*, ed. Martin Henig (Oxford University Committee for Archaeology, Monograph 29 [Oxford, 1990]), 106; Judith McKenzie, *The Architecture of Petra* (Oxford, 1990) 51, 92; Millar, *RNE*, 406–7. Theaters seem to have been particularly favored by the Nabataeans in the years immediately after the time of Herod the Great: see Segal (supra), 6–7.

16. Ward-Perkins, *RIA*, 314–17. The Temple of Juppiter in Damaskos is in the same tradition, although poorly known because of its incorporation, in part, into the Ummayed Mosque. Its huge enclosure, 305 by 385 m, although not as vast as Herod's Temple in Jerusalem, is a similar blend of indigenous and Roman styles. The construction technique of the *temenos* is remindful of the supposed Herodian enclosure at Hebron, although of poorer quality (David M. Jacobson, "The Plan of the Ancient Haram el-Khalil in Hebron," *PEQ* 113 [1981]: 79–80). The date is uncertain, but it was under way by A.D. 15–16, as building inscriptions testify (*SEG* 2.828–32; Ward Perkins, *RIA*, 328; Klaus Freyberger, "Untersuchungen zur Baugeschichte des Jupiter-Heiligtums in Damaskus," *Damaszener Mitteilungen* 4 [1989]: 61–86). These inscriptions are dated between 327 and 402 of an unspecified era, originally thought to be Pompeian (and thus between A.D. 264 and 340), but now generally believed to be Seleukid

started at about the same time as the Temple of Juppiter at Baalbek and dedicated in A.D. 32, was in a similar tradition.[17]

The Dekapolis was another region that felt the effects of Herod's program. Herod had avoided the area, perhaps because of its associations with Pompey, the opponent of Julius Caesar. The anomalous political situation of the Dekapolis—seemingly a Roman enclave surrounded by Herodian and Nabataean territory—caused its isolation in Herod's day. But early in the first century A.C., it began to prosper, architecturally and otherwise, especially Gerasa, where construction of the Temple of Zeus, modeled on the Herodian Temple of Augustus at Sebaste, initiated the urban renewal of the city.[18]

Other client kings and rulers of the east followed Herod's example. The career of his in-law Archelaos of Kappadokia has already been examined. The client kings of Kommagene, no strangers to monumental architecture, as the monument of Antiochos I at Nemrud Dag demonstrates, also began to be affected by the Herodian legacy. Buildings at their capital of Samosata, which Herod had visited in 36 B.C., and which was rebuilt in monumental fashion at some time during the Augustan period,[19] made use of *opus reticulatum*, even more unusual in eastern Anatolia than in Judaea.[20] The royal

---

(therefore A.D. 15–91). For the arguments, see Henri Seyrig, "Antiquités syriennes," *Syria* 27 (1950): 34–37.

17. Ward-Perkins, *RIA*, 354–57.

18. Ibid., 335; Millar, *RNE*, 38–39. Little is known about the initiation of work on the temple, but it was in progress in A.D. 22/23, when one Zabdias son of Aristomachos, priest of the imperial cult, contributed 1,000 drachmas toward its construction (C. Bradford Welles, "The Inscriptions," in *Gerasa: City of the Decapolis*, ed. Carl H. Kraeling [New Haven, 1938], 373–74, # 2). The temple may have been commissioned by the Nabataean king Aretas IV (Carl H. Kraeling, "The History of Gerasa," in ibid., 36–39).

19. Antiochos I died around 36 B.C., probably as a result of the Roman-Parthian engagements that swept over his kingdom, in which Herod played a part (*BJ* 1.321–22, *AJ* 14.439–47; Plutarch, *Antonius* 34; Dio 49.20–22). The next fifty years of Kommagene have a confusing history, with at least four kings known by name but with a contradictory chronology. Antiochos II and his brother Mithradates II seem to have been rival monarchs: the former was executed by Octavian after killing an ambassador sent to Rome by the latter (Dio 52.43). As survivor, Mithradates II seems to have lived until around 20 B.C., when he was succeeded by his nephew Mithradates III, but by A.D. 17 part of the territory, especially around Samosata, had become a Roman province, and his son Antiochos III ruled the remainder (see Stemma 13, and Sullivan, *NER*, 193–98). All four kings are shadowy, and which of them were royal builders cannot be determined. In 20 B.C. Augustus was in the vicinity, although Kommagene is not mentioned in the sources as a place he visited at this time (Helmut Halfmann, *Itinera principum* [Heidelberger Althistorische Beiträge und Epigraphische Studien, 2 (Stuttgart, 1986)], 158): if he did come to Samosata, it would have been a propitious time to inaugurate royal building, as happened elsewhere on this trip, such as at Caesarea Anazarbos (infra, n. 25). See also Strabo 16.2.3; Millar, *RNE*, 52–53.

20. Ahmet A. Tırpan, "Roman Masonry Techniques at the Capital of the Commagenian Kingdom," in *The Eastern Frontier of the Roman Empire*, ed. D. H. French and C. S. Lightfoot (*BAR-IS* 553 [1989]), 519–36; Ward-Perkins, *RIA*, 328–29.

house of Kommagene was eventually related to the Herodian one, as Herod's great-great-grandson Alexandros (who was also a great-great-grandson of Archelaos of Kappadokia) married Iotape VII, daughter of Antiochos IV of Kommagene and Iotape VI of Emesa, and became king of a district of Kilikia before going to Rome to become consul.[21]

As more is learned about the architecture of the periphery of Herod's kingdom, especially the remote areas of interior Syria, other examples of Herodian influence will emerge. Dynastic marriage with Herodians was commonplace throughout this region. An example is the small but influential client kingdom of Emesa. It had been under Roman influence since the time of Pompey, and Herod's grandson Aristoboulos married Iotape IV, the daughter of the local king, Sampsigeramos;[22] Aristoboulos's niece Drusilla married another king of Emesa, Azizos.[23] Drusilla's sister, Berenike, the rebuilder of Berytos, married two client kings: first her uncle Herod of Chalkis, and then Polemon II of Pontos, a descendant of Marcus Antonius's and son of the Thracian king Kotys VIII. Polemon became ruler of Kilikia, already a beneficiary of the patronage of Herod the Great.[24] Although such intermarriage did not make monumental architecture a certain result, those areas where Julio-Claudian material is known and where in-laws or descendants of Herod lived, such as Kappadokia, Kilikia, and Nabataea, demonstrate that the marrying of Herodian descendants to local royalty was a major way in which this ever-architecturally-conscious family spread its ideas about the architectural duties of client kingship.

21. *AJ* 18.140; *PIR*, 2d ed., A500. Josephus's text is corrupt, and the place Alexandros ruled has been emended to Ketis, a little-known city or district of Kilikia (see Jones, *Cities*, 195–96, 208; Richard D. Sullivan, "The Dynasty of Commagene," *ANRW* 2.8 [1977]: 794–95).

22. *AJ* 18.135; Richard D. Sullivan, "The Dynasty of Emesa," *ANRW* 2.8 (1977): 198–219. It was from the royal family of Emesa that Julia Domna, the wife of Septimius Severus, was descended, as well as her son and grand-nephew, the emperors Caracalla and Elagabalus, the final evolution of the intermingling of the eastern dynasties with Rome (Sullivan, *NER*, 202). Emesa, modern Homs, has few remains from any period (J.-P. Rey-Coquais, "Emesa," in *PECS*, 302).

23. *AJ* 20.139–41. Drusilla later married the procurator Antonius Felix.

24. *AJ* 19.354, 20.145–46. For the ancestry of Polemon II, see Stemma 13, and Richard D. Sullivan, "Papyri Reflecting the Eastern Dynastic Network," *ANRW* 2.8 (1977): 920. One wonders what Herodian influence there might have been on the founding of Kilikian Caesarea (Magie, *RR*, 275, 473), at Anazarbos in the northeastern part of the Kilikian plain. The evidence for the founding of Caesarea Anazarbos is obscure, but coins seem to connect it with Augustus's visit of 20 B.C. (BMC Lycaonia, Isauria, and Cilicia, cii–ciii) and the reestablishment of the local dynasty under Tarkondimotos (Dio 54.9; Sullivan, *NER*, 191): the era of the city began the following year (Michael Gough, "Anazarbus," *AnatSt* 2 [1952]: 93). Herod was known and active in this area—the territory of Archelaos of Kappadokia was nearby—and the later connections between his family and the dynasty of Kilikia are a further demonstration of the influence of the Herodian family in this region. The impressive remains of Caesarea Anazarbos are mostly from the third century A.C. (Gough, 99–127).

Even Rome itself saw the architectural legacy of Herod. His role in the developing harbor technology of the early Empire has been noted.[25] He was also important in the evolution of palatial construction. The Roman diffidence about the domestic trappings of royalty has meant that the antecedents of the great imperial residences are, to some extent, to be sought elsewhere than at Rome. Certainly, the aristocratic villas in Rome and Campania played a role, but the link between the Villa of the Mysteries and the Domus Aurea can be sought at Herodeion, which took the Roman rural villa and turned it into a royal palace. If the palaces of Archelaos of Kappadokia and Juba II of Mauretania were known, the evolution might be clearer. The only palace in Rome before the time of Nero, that credited to Tiberius, was largely the work of Gaius and others; its original Tiberian form would have been more conforming to the simple austerity of that emperor, who after his accession did practically no building in Rome.[26] A true palace was not built in Rome until Nero's Domus Transitoria and its successor, the Domus Aurea, effectively initiated palatial construction in the city.[27] The scanty remains of the former show the use of hydraulics in a manner that would have pleased Herod; the Domus Aurea, bringing the countryside into the city,[28] has as its most obvious precedent Herod's palace at Herodeion, with its curved forms and elaborate maze-like quality, and was the first structure in the Roman world to exceed it in size and lavishness. With the Domus Aurea, the villa-palace concept had come to Rome, and the way was clear for the great palaces of the later Empire.[29]

In terms of baths and amphitheaters, Judaea was better endowed than Rome before the time of Nero. The numerous baths Herod built, while rel-

25. Recent work by Robert L. Hohlfelder has suggested that some of the master builders of Herod's harbor at Caesarea may have moved on to Paphos on Cyprus, which was devastated by an earthquake in 15 B.C., almost exactly at the time the Caesarea harbor was finished. See his "Caesarea's Master Harbor Builders: Lessons Learned, Lessons Applied?" in *CMR*, 91–101.

26. Clemens Krause, "Domus Tiberiana," in *LTUR*, 2: 189–90; Richardson, *NTD*, 136–37. Even Tiberius's most famous and elaborate monument, the Villa Jovis on Capri, is simpler and more austere than its reputation suggests (Ward-Perkins, *RIA*, 198–201), and is smaller than the Herodian palace at Jericho. Both structures are similar in their use of apsidal forms and peristyles. On Gaius's elaboration of Tiberius's palace in Rome, see Henry Hurst, "Domus Gai," in *LTUR*, 2: 106–8.

27. Richardson, *NTD*, 138–39, 119–21.

28. Suetonius, *Nero* 31.

29. Hadrian's villa at Tivoli may be another legacy of Herodian architecture (fig. 46). Hadrian, whose personal and innovative interest in architecture is well known, probably saw the remains of Herod's buildings. Herodeion in particular, with its curved forms, seems to have been an inspiration at Tivoli, noted for incorporating the architecture of famous places (Aelius Spartianus, *Hadrian* [*HA*] 26: "provinciarum et locorum celeberrima"). See William L. MacDonald and John A. Pinto, *Hadrian's Villa and Its Legacy* (New Haven, 1995), 85–88. In Rome, Hadrian's Temple of Venus and Roma is in a similar eastern tradition, and looks backs to the complexes at Palmyra, Baalbek, and Damaskos, as well as Herod's Temple in Jerusalem.

atively modest and generally private rather than public, were forerunners of those at Rome: at the time of Herod's death, the city seems to have had only one public bath, that of Marcus Agrippa, completed between 19 and 12 B.C.[30] Although modest baths were built by Cn. Domitius Ahenobarbus, perhaps around the time of his consulship in A.D. 32,[31] another public bathing establishment was not constructed in Rome until the time of his son, Nero.[32] Similarly, Rome was lacking in amphitheaters long after they were common in Judaea. That of Statilius Taurus remained the only one in the city until it was destroyed in the fire of A.D. 64.[33] In the same area, Gaius started but never finished one,[34] and Nero built a temporary one, perhaps on the ruins of Taurus's structure, initiating the complex around his baths.[35]

Thus it was not until the middle of the first century A.C. that Rome began to have structures that Judaea had known for over half a century. And it is no accident that it was Nero who fulfilled at Rome the legacy of Herodian architecture. He had a close relationship with Agrippa II, the last Herodian king of Judaea, strengthening his territorial and political position.[36] He also made Herod's great-grandsons Tigranes and Aristoboulos kings of Greater and Lesser Armenia respectively.[37] In return for his favor to the Herodian family, Agrippa II gave Philippos's Caesarea a new foundation as Neronias,[38] and built a fortress named after Nero's mother.[39] Nero's architectural extravagance and innovation are well known, and it is perfectly reasonable that Herod, another great architectural creative mind and fellow philhellene, would have been a source of inspiration.

Herod's motivation for his building program has been endlessly debated. In one sense, the matter is not an important one, because it is the products of the motivation that are the legacy of Herod. But in another sense, the answer is obvious to the point of banality: Herod did what he did because it was reasonable and necessary within his cultural environment, part of his obligations as a late Hellenistic dynast and client king of Rome's. Yet there are three unusual qualities to the Herodian building program: its extent, throughout Greece, Asia Minor, Syria, and the southern Levant, a range

30. Richardson, *NTD*, 386–88.

31. Seneca, *Controversiae* 9.4.18.

32. Suetonius, *Nero* 12; Richardson, *NTD*, 393–95.

33. Dio 62.18.

34. Suetonius, *Gaius* 21; Domenico Palombi, "Amphitheatrum Caligulae," in *LTUR*, 1: 35.

35. Tacitus, *Annals* 13.31; Suetonius, *Nero* 12; Pliny, *Natural History* 16.200, 19.24; Richardson, *NTD*, 10–11; Domenico Palombi, "Amphitheatrum Neronis," in *LTUR*, 1: 30.

36. *BJ* 2.252; *Life* 38.

37. *BJ* 2.252; *AJ* 18.140.

38. *AJ* 20.211.

39. Supra, pp. 247–49.

equaled or surpassed only by the Roman emperors; Herod's quickness to adopt Roman forms when Hellenistic ones were more obvious; and the concentration of architecturally interesting buildings in a region that had had no history of monumental architecture, thus bringing Judaea, however briefly, into the Greco-Roman architectural mainstream.

But the building program had many other qualities: as Ronald Syme put it, Herod was "the earliest and most zealous to propagate the new faith"[40] represented by Augustan Rome and its deliberate replacement of the existing Hellenistic dynastic system with the personality of the emperor at Rome. This gives the program an almost religious quality: as the Temple in Jerusalem served the cultic needs of his people, Herod's secular constructions served the cultic needs of the new Augustan era. It is perhaps significant that Josephus's initial catalogue of the Herodian building program[41] described it as an act of *eusebeia* and listed the structures in order of to whom they were dedicated. First is the Temple in Jerusalem (dedicated to the God of Herod and his people), then those structures dedicated to Romans, then those dedicated to members of his family, and finally those dedicated to himself. Only when these buildings had been catalogued did Josephus consider those outside Herod's kingdom, dedicated to the Greek cities, ending with his benefits to Olympia, described as a gift to the entire world. Clearly this list, probably derived from Nikolaos, presented the Herodian program in a definite hierarchy, beginning with God, going on to Rome, Herod's family, and Greece, in that order, and ending with the entire world.[42] Although it shows the type of philosophical cataloguing in which Hellenistic historians delighted, the list gives Herod's work a motivational context.

The best evidence for Herod's motivation is Herod himself, and a speech of his is preserved in which he discussed his building program.[43] Although often dismissed as a historiographical fabrication, its source is more likely Herod's own memoirs or the testimony of Nikolaos, and it thus has a close, if not exact, relationship to what Herod said and what he believed. The occasion was the beginning of construction on the Temple in Jerusalem, probably autumn 18 B.C., when Sebaste was completed, Caesarea was under way, and Herod was about to make his second trip to Rome.

In the speech Herod specified that his building program was to benefit the population as a whole, not merely himself, and he linked it to the current state of prosperity in Judaea. He spoke of the physical beauty of his

40. Syme, *RR*, 474.

41. *BJ* 1.401–28.

42. Peter Richardson, *Herod: King of the Jews, Friend of the Romans* (Columbia, S.C., 1996), 191–96.

43. *AJ* 15.382–88.

buildings, and echoing Perikles,[44] described how they adorned the country. He admitted that he had neglected local religious concerns, but had had a good reason to do so, since his policy to date had brought about peace and prosperity, as well as a strong and profitable relationship with Rome. But now he was to rectify his neglect by beginning construction on the most pious—again the concept of *eusebeia*—and beautiful building of his career, and thereby honoring God, who had made his rule of Judaea possible.

There is no doubt that Herod was a persuasive speaker—one need only remember his masterful speech to Octavian after Actium—and his words at the Temple dedication offer a significant insight into his thinking as he began the last decade of his building career. As would any good orator, he attempted to anticipate criticism and skillfully to straddle the twin needs of duty to his patrons and to his subjects. Regardless of how close Josephus's words are to what Herod said that day in Jerusalem, they are his only extant comments on his own building program.

Clearly, Herod was driven by a certain megalomania: he wanted to leave behind physical monuments of his reign. There was nothing unusual about this, and he was the inheritor of a long tradition of royal building, which had originated in the most ancient cultures of the eastern Mediterranean. When pressed by the nationalistic elements within his kingdom, he would imply that he was forced to build by the Romans, but such a statement depended on the ignorance of those hearing it to have any credence. He also maintained that he was attempting to ingratiate himself with the Roman ruling elite,[45] but this too is implausible: if flattery were a primary motive, Herod not only completely misjudged Augustus and his colleagues but devoted a great deal of effort and expense to such a misbegotten goal.

No one reason can be isolated. His role as client king demanded that he create a secure frontier for Rome in the dangerous area between Syria and Egypt, and this may have been a major reason for starting his building.[46] He had a deep personal interest in architecture: this was inevitable in the world of Pompey, Gabinius, and Caesar, which was that of his youth. Whether or not he was an actual architect remains unproven and depends on how literally one interprets statements by Josephus, although he nowhere explicitly credited Herod with practical architectural ability, despite noting his talents as a scholar and athlete.[47] Nevertheless, Herod retained a close rela-

---

44. Plutarch, *Perikles* 12.

45. *AJ* 15.328–30.

46. M. Gihon, "Idumea and the Herodian Limes," *IEJ* 17 (1967): 27–42.

47. *BJ* 15.420 has been cited as proof that he was a practical architect. Here Herod is said to have undertaken (ἐπραγματεύετο) the stoas and peristyles around the Temple in Jerusalem, but the word does not seem ever to have had an actual constructional use (*LSJ*), and the silence of Josephus on Herod as an architect is persuasive. See Ehud Netzer, "Herod's Building Program: State Necessity or Personal Need," *JC* 1 (1981): 50–55; Lee I. Levine, "Towards an

tionship to his projects, and here the influence of his youth was paramount. His family was associated with the greatest builder of the previous generation, and it is no accident that much of the Herodian program sought to carry the interrupted vision of Julius Caesar to its conclusion. Like Augustus, Herod had an astute ability to mix the old and the new.

Herod was not alone: throughout the Roman world of the last part of the first century B.C., there was a significant amount of building, particularly by the client kings. Herod's in-laws Archelaos and Juba II were in the forefront. All played a part in the romanizing of the world. But the factors affecting Herod were unique, since he had to contend with the turbulent internal politics and religious sensitivities of Judaea, a dangerous frontier situation, and a society that was still economically primitive. In one sense he was a failure: his was the first of the great client kingdoms to come under direct Roman control, and his immediate architectural legacy did not outlive his dynasty. But in using architecture as a metaphor for proper exercise of political power and the establishment of a new world order, he was particularly successful. To him, it was "magnus ab integro saeclorum nascitur ordo," and he eagerly played his part.

Appraisal of Herod as a Builder," *JC* 1 (1981): 62–66; Ehud Netzer, "In Reply," *JC* 1 (1981): 73–80.

APPENDIX ONE

THE CURIOUS MATTER OF HERODIAN
BUILDING IN ARMENIA

One of the most peculiar references to Herodian building concerns activity in Armenia. The source is the *History of the Armenians* by Moses Khorenats'i,[1] a work whose date of authorship is greatly in dispute. According to his own text,[2] Moses was active around the time of the ecumenical council of Ephesos, in A.D. 431.[3] Other references mention the first half of the fifth century A.C. in contemporary terms, giving the impression that this was when Moses lived.[4] Yet he seems to have been unknown to Armenian historians before the tenth century A.C., and he used sources that appear to be later than his ostensible era of the fifth century A.C. In modern times there has been little agreement on the date of Moses, and although it seems clear that he could not have lived as early as his claimed date of the fifth century A.C., his actual date, and the date of the composition of his history, remain disputable.[5]

The scope of Moses' *History* is from the Creation to the fifth century A.C., allegedly his own period. There is a particular amount of detail on the Hellenistic and Roman periods: the middle of the three books of the *History*,

1. References to Moses Khorenats'i's *History of the Armenians* in this discussion refer to the translation and commentary by Robert W. Thomson (Cambridge, Mass., 1978), but Greek and Latin proper names have been reconciled with the forms used elsewhere in this work.

2. Moses, *History* 3.61.

3. For the date of this council, which is attested in the *Chronikon Paschale*, the anonymous chronology of the seventh century A.C., see *Chronicon Paschale, 284–628 A.D.*, trans. Michael Whitby and Mary Whitby (Translated Texts for Historians, 7 [Liverpool, 1989]), 71; George Ostrogorsky, *History of the Byzantine State*, 2d English ed., trans. Joan Hussey (Oxford, 1968), 58–59.

4. Moses, *History* 1.22, 3.61–68.

5. See the discussion in the Thomson edition of Moses' *History* (supra, n. 1), 1–8; Hans Gärtner, "Moses Chorenachi," in *KlPauly*, 3 (1979): 1438–39.

titled "The Intermediate Period," covers the time from Alexander the Great to Constantine. Herod is mentioned several times in this book, always from an Armenian point of view. He first appears when his father, Antipatros, was allied with a certain Mithradates, [6] whom Moses referred to as a nephew of King Tigranes the Great of Armenia, confusing several contemporaries who bore the same name: the famous Mithradates of Pontos,[7] Mithradates of Pergamon, who, according to Josephus,[8] was Antipatros's actual ally, and a Mithradates who was a member of the Georgian royal family, which was related to that of Armenia.[9] Moses' account of this episode involving Antipatros and Mithradates is based on the writings of Josephus, generally an important source for him, but in this case with spectacular confusion of the personalities involved. This minor reference to Herod serves as a paradigm for the difficulties in interpreting the text of Moses' *History*.

From the point of view of his building program, two citations of Herod in the *History* are of interest. After detailing Antonius's eastern campaigns of the early 30's B.C., Moses then described the reign of the Armenian king Arsham:

> After this there occurred a dissension between Herod, king of Judaea, and our King Arsham. Herod, after many valiant deeds, devoted himself to works of philanthropy, constructing many buildings in many cities from Rome to Damaskos. He asked Arsham for a multitude of unskilled workers to fill in the public squares of Antioch in Syria, which were impassable and impracticable because of the mud and mire. But Arsham refused and gathered his army to oppose Herod. Through messengers he sent word to the emperor at Rome not to place him under the authority of Herod. But the emperor not only did not free Arsham from Herod's authority but he also entrusted to the latter all the Mediterranean lands.[10]
>
> At that time, Herod, having taken into his service troops from Galatia and Pontos, established as king of the Mediterranean lands under his own authority the father-in-law of his son Alexandros, who on his father's side was descended from Timon and on his mother's side from the Median royal line from the seed of Daryavaush the Vishtaspan. When Arsham saw this he paid homage to Herod as sovereign lord and gave him the workers he had requested. With their help he filled in the public squares of Antioch over a

6. Moses, *History* 2.18.

7. Moses (*History* 2.15) inventively stated that Mithradates of Pontos was murdered by the father of Pontius Pilate.

8. *BJ* 1.187; *AJ* 14.128. On this Mithradates, see Sullivan, *NER*, 158–59.

9. Moses, *History* 2.11.

10. The word used by Moses here and in the following sentence is "Mijerkreayk", which Thomson (supra, n. 1, p. 82) called "a calque on 'Mediterranean'" and translated as "Anatolia."

length of 20 stadia, and he paved them with white marble paving stones so that the torrents might be more easily directed over the pavement to avoid damage to the city. [11]

This strange passage, typical of Moses, implies that Armenia would have gone to war with Herod over a request for workmen, and that Herod ruled the entire Mediterranean region. It is based ultimately on *BJ* 1.425, which mentions twenty stadia of marble paving at Antioch to lessen the effects of rainfall, and *BJ* 1.476, which discusses the ancestry of Alexandros's in-laws. What is lacking in the text of Josephus is any suggestion that Herod was involved in the establishment of the kingship of Alexandros's father-in-law, who was Archelaos, king of Kappadokia, and any mention of an Armenian king Arsham.

Arsham does not appear in the canonical lists of Armenian kings. The late first century B.C. in Armenia is a shadowy and unclear period,[12] especially after the death of Artavasd I, son of Tigranes the Great, who was captured by Marcus Antonius in 34 B.C. during his Armenian campaign—on which Herod accompanied him part of the way—and sent to Cleopatra, to be executed after Actium.[13] After describing Antonius's capture of Artavasd,[14] Moses stated that Arsham, said to have been the nephew of Tigranes the Great, was made king by the army. Moses was not clear about Arsham's name, however, calling him "Arjam, that is Arsham." Although Arsham is an Armenian royal name, having appeared in the Ervand-Orontid dynasty in the third century B.C.,[15] there is no evidence other than Moses' account of a King Arsham in the late first century B.C. His appearance in Moses' text has been plausibly explained: Eusebios's *Ecclesiastical History* described a letter sent to Jesus of Nazareth by one Abgaros Ouchama.[16] In the Armenian version of Eusebios's history, used by Moses, the name is "Abgar Arjamay," which became in part the "Arjam" of Moses, a nonexistent proper name, amended to a known Armenian royal name, Arsham.[17]

11. Moses, *History* 2.24–25, Thomson translation, with orthography of proper names standardized.

12. Charles Burney and David Marshall Lang, *The Peoples of the Hills* (London, 1971), 20; M. Chahin, *The Kingdom of Armenia* (London, 1987), 245.

13. For the sources, see Eleanor Goltz Huzar, *Mark Antony: A Biography* (London, 1978), 176–80; Sullivan, *NER*, 285–90; for Herod's involvement, see *AJ* 14.439–47.

14. Moses, *History* 2.23.

15. Chahin (supra, n. 12) 217–18: it was this Arsham (Arsames) who brought Greek-style coinage to Armenia (Burney and Lang [supra, n. 12], 89).

16. Eusebios, *Ecclesiastical History* 1.13.

17. The process is explained by Thomson (supra, n. 1) 160.

Since there was no Arsham as king of Armenia in the first century B.C., Armenian involvement in the urban renewal of Antioch is thrown into serious doubt. Rather, the tale seems to be an example of Moses' common technique of giving an Armenian element to incidents obtained from Hellenistic and Roman historians, especially Josephus.[18] Nevertheless, there was an Armenian presence in Antioch in the first century B.C., when Tigranes the Great spent the years 83–69 B.C. as nominal ruler of Syria; some of this time he was in Antioch.[19] Thus it is quite possible that half a century later, when Herod was rebuilding the city, Armenian workmen, perhaps a colony left from the years of Tigranes' rule, were available. But given the lack of evidence for such a colony, it is better to assume that the entire incident is one of Moses' inventive glosses on Armenian history.

The second mention of Herod by Moses in a context relevant to the Herodian building program concerns Abgar, the presumed son and successor of the mythical king Arsham. Unlike his father, however, Abgar was not a Mosaic creation but an actual dynast, although, expectedly, not as Moses described him. According to Moses,[20]

> there took place a quarrel between Abgar and Herod, for Herod commanded his own image to be set up near to the emperor's in the temples of Armenia. Since Abgar did not accept this, Herod sought a pretext against him. He sent an army of Thracians and Germans on a foray for plunder into Persia and commanded them to cross Abgar's land. But Abgar did not submit to this and opposed them, saying that it was the emperor's command that this army should cross into Persia through the desert. Herod became angered at this, but he was unable to do anything in person since he had to endure all sorts of pain; on account of his presumption against Christ, worms grew inside him, as Josephus narrates. He sent his nephew Joseph to whom he had given his sister, who had previously been the wife of his brother Pheroras. He took a great army, marched to Mesopotamia, and met Abgar in the province of Bugnan where he was encamped. In the battle he was killed and his army fled. Imme-

18. This seems to have been a device Moses particularly used when Josephus was his source: see Thomson (supra, n. 1), 25–31. Even one of the most famous events of the first century B.C., Crassus's defeat by the Parthians at Carrhae, taken by Moses from *BJ* 1.179–81, is emended: Moses (2.17) changed the victors from Parthians to Armenians led by Tigranes the Great.

19. Appian, *Syrian Wars* 48; Plutarch, *Lucullus* 21–36; *AJ* 13.419; see also Glanville Downey, *A History of Antioch in Syria from Selecus to the Arab Conquest* (Princeton, 1961), 136–39; Sullivan, *NER*, 101–5. Tigranes' presence in Antioch is assumed largely by coins he seems to have struck there from 83 B.C.: see George MacDonald, "The Coinage of Tigranes I," *NC*, 2d ser., 4 (1902): 193–201, and Paul Z. Bedoukian, "A Classification of the Coins of the Artaxiad Dynasty of Armenia," *ANSMN* 14 (1968): 53–55.

20. Moses, *History* 2.26 (Thomson), with standardization of proper names.

diately thereafter Herod also died, and Augustus made his son Archelaos *ethnarchos* of the Jews.

Moses' sources for most of this material are Josephus's two histories and Eusebios's *Ecclesiastical History*. The material on Herod's last illness is from *BJ* 1.656 and *AJ* 17.168, where it is seen as punishment for his impious deeds, with material added from *Ecclesiastical History* 1.8, which interpreted Josephus's nonspecific comment on Herod's punishment to refer to treatment of Jesus of Nazareth. At Herod's funeral, according to Josephus, a contingent of Thracians and Germans in full armor stood guard.[21] The death of Herod's relative Joseph is another of Moses' famous Armenizations of history: Josephus[22] described the death of Herod's *brother* Joseph (not his nephew Joseph, about whom little is known) at the hands of the Hasmonean Antigonos II near Jericho. Joseph's brother Pheroras, whose wives are unknown, ransomed the head of his brother. These events took place early in Herod's kingship, many years before his death.

Abgar was not mentioned by Josephus but played a prominent role in Eusebios's *Ecclesiastical History* as a major figure in the early history of Christianity.[23] According to Eusebios, he was the ruler of the Osrhoenes, with his capital at Edessa. He became seriously ill and appealed for help to Jesus of Nazareth, about whom he had heard. Jesus sent a letter, and Abgar was cured; eventually, a certain Thaddaeus was sent to Abgar to establish Christianity in the kingdom. Eusebios wrote that he had discovered the correspondence himself in the archives at Edessa, along with a Syriac addendum describing the mission of Thaddaeus, dated to the year 340 in the Seleukid era (ca. A.D. 28). These are events after Herod's death, but there is little doubt that Abgar was an actual king of Osrhoene in the early first century A.C. The name is an Osrhoenian royal name from the second century B.C. through the third century A.C., and there was an Abgar on the throne during the reign of the Roman emperor Claudius.[24]

As usual, Moses has taken his sources and given them an Armenian flavor. He claimed[25] that Eusebios stated that Armenian history was to be found in the archives in Edessa, especially material on Abgar, to Moses an Armenian king. Needless to say, such information does not appear in Eusebios' account. Nor is there anything in the works of Josephus—Moses' other

21. *BJ* 1.672.

22. *BJ* 1.323–25; *AJ* 14.448–50.

23. Eusebios, *Ecclesiastical History* 1; Hendrik Jan Willem Drijvers, "Hatra, Palmyra und Edessa," *ANRW* 2.8 (1977): 895–96.

24. Tacitus, *Annals* 12.12.

25. Moses, *History* 2.10.

source at this point—regarding Abgar: Abgar, Edessa, and Osrhoene were not mentioned anywhere by Josephus.

The one reference to Herodian art in these convoluted passages of Moses' *History* is Herod's command to Abgar regarding statues in the temples of Armenia. Although the incident is probably ultimately based on Josephus's description of the attempt by the emperor Gaius to set up his own statues in the Temple at Jerusalem, using military force if necessary,[26] it may contain some memory of Herodian building in the far east. Direct contact between Armenia and the Hellenistic-Roman world began at least at the time of the Roman invasion by Lucullus in the early first century B.C.[27] By the following century, when Garni was established as a royal Armenian residence, the Hellenistic architectural and artistic style was familiar, as the ruins of Garni testify. Remains at the site include a hexastyle Ionic temple, ashlar isodomic masonry, and Greek inscriptions, as well as other paraphernalia of the Greco-Roman world.[28] Garni is essentially post-Herodian, but in Herod's day Armenia was developing the elements of Hellenistic-Roman civilization that would make Garni possible a generation or two later. One might expect Herod's architectural reach to have extended to this area, which was just acquiring the arts of his world. Armenia was to become no stranger to Herodian dynasts: his grandson and great-grandson became rulers of the kingdom.[29]

Yet Moses' text is so convoluted that it is quite possible that the reference to Herod's statues is not to Armenia but to Edessa, where Abgar actually ruled. The city of Edessa lies only 250 km. northeast of Antioch, a much more plausible locale for Herodian artistic interest than remote Armenia. Edessa was founded, or at least named, by Seleukos Nikator at the end of the fourth century B.C.,[30] perhaps because its springs and waters reminded him of Makedonian Edessa,[31] itself noted even today for its attractive waterfalls. By the second century B.C., it was the capital of an independent kingdom of Osrhoene, which lasted at least until the third century A.C., sus-

26. *AJ* 18.261–67.

27. Plutarch, *Lucullus;* Freya Stark, *Rome on the Euphrates: The Story of a Frontier* (New York, 1966), 72–85.

28. B. Arakelyan, "Excavations at Garni, 1949–1950," in V. P. Alekseev, ed., *Contributions to the Archaeology of Armenia,* trans. Arlene Krimgold, ed. Henry Field (Russian Translation Series of the Peabody Museum of Archaeology and Ethnology, 3.3 [Cambridge, Mass., 1968]), 13–108; B. Arakelyan, "Excavations at Garni, 1951–1955," in ibid., 109–98.

29. The younger son of Alexandros of Judaea and Glaphyra of Kappadokia was Tigranes IV of Armenia (*BJ* 1.552; *AJ* 18.139–40; Augustus, *Res gestae* 27), on the throne perhaps by A.D. 10 (Magie, *RR,* 485, 1345–46); his nephew was Tigranes V, whom Nero made king (Magie, *RR,* 556–58). See infra, Stemma 13.

30. J. B. Segal, "Antioch-by-the-Callirhoe," in *PECS,* 61.

31. J. B. Segal, *Edessa, "The Blessed City"* (Oxford, 1970), 6–7.

pended between Rome and Parthia.[32] The Edessan king list runs from Aryu in 132 B.C. to Abgar X in A.D. 242; in Herod's day there were three kings named Abgar: Abgar III (29–26 B.C.), Abgar IV (26–23 B.C.), and Abgar V (4 B.C.–A.D. 7).[33] It is Abgar V whom Moses made Herod's opponent, but this king did not come to the throne until the year of Herod's death, a synchronism reflected somewhat in Moses' account. Yet the existence of two kings named Abgar on the throne during the period of Herodian building raises the possibility that one of them may have known Herod. He may have been related to the Osrhoenian royal family, which was partially of Nabataean stock.[34] Herod was in the region of Osrhoene early in his career, at Samosata in Kommagene, just north of Edessa.[35] Interestingly, Josephus's description of Herod at Samosata is immediately previous to his account of the death of Herod's brother Joseph, which in the text of Moses immediately follows the discussion of the disagreement between Herod and Abgar. Thus the account of Herod at Samosata is paralleled by Herod quarreling with the king of nearby Edessa, both accounts placing Herod—or his political reach—in almost the same area.

Unfortunately, little is known archaeologically of Edessa during the late first century B.C. The late Hellenistic period at the site is notorious in its obscurity.[36] Excavations, mostly in the 1950's, revealed material largely of the third century A.C. and later,[37] when the city was rebuilt after being destroyed by a flood in A.D. 201. Before the flood, however, it was known for its "charming and beautiful buildings,"[38] and perhaps a Herodian contribution was one of these structures.

---

32. Sullivan, *NER*, 106–7.

33. Segal, *Edessa* (supra, n. 31), 15.

34. Ibid., 16–17.

35. See supra, pp. 256–57.

36. Jules Leroy, "Nouvelles découvertes archéologiques relatives à Édesse," *Syria* 38 (1961), 159–69.

37. Segal, in *PECS* (supra, n. 30) 61; J. B. Segal, "New Mosaics from Edessa," *Archaeology* 12 (1959): 151–57.

38. *Chronicle of Edessa*, a Syriac account of the city, written shortly after the flood (quoted by Segal, *Edessa* [supra, n. 31], 24).

APPENDIX TWO

HERODIAN ICONOGRAPHY

The question of portraits or other representations of Herod is a vexing one. The Jewish prohibition of graven images—prescribed in the Second Commandment—meant that sculptural portraits would not be possible under strict observance of Jewish law.[1] On the other hand, dynastic portrait sculpture was a necessity in the Hellenistic-Roman world in which Herod functioned, and it is difficult to imagine that he completely ignored this important mode of artistic expression.[2]

As always, Herod, the master at compromise and assimilation, adopted a program that, in theory at least, blended his ambitions both as Jewish monarch and Hellenistic-Roman client king. Within his kingdom, in deference to the Jewish population, figured sculpture of any sort was virtually nonexistent. Even with this limitation, the possibility for misunderstanding was high, as demonstrated by confusion over trophies at the theater in Jerusalem, which certain Jewish leaders believed were graven images.[3] Although Herod defused this potentially sacrilegious incident, such problems were ever-present. Late in Herod's life, two rabbis named Judas and Matthias exhorted their followers to pull down the golden eagle Herod had placed at the entrance to the Temple in Jerusalem; they did so, only to be caught and executed (along with their teachers).[4] This incident had overtones of rebellion as well as theology, capitalizing on the weakening of

1. For the theology involved, see Boaz Cohen, "Art in Jewish Law," *Judaism* 3 (1954): 165–76; Schürer (NEV), 2: 81–82; and, as it specifically related to Herod, Peter Richardson, "Law and Piety in Herod's Architecture," *Studies in Religion* 15 (1986): 347–60.

2. There is a rich Christian iconography of Herod, but it lies outside the scope of this study. For further details, see Helmut Merkel and Dieter Korol, "Herodes der Grosse," in *Reallexikon für Antike und Christenthum*, 14 (Stuttgart, 1988), 833–40.

3. *AJ* 15.272–79.

4. *BJ* 1.649–55.

Herod's rule during his last illness; nevertheless, it demonstrates how seriously certain of Herod's subjects reacted to any perceived violation of the Second Commandment. Herod did erect statues at Caesarea, and after his death these were considered evidence that Caesarea was a Greek, not Jewish, city.[5]

Coinage was another typical mode of expression for a Hellenistic-Roman dynast. There was an ancient tradition of ruler portraits on coins, as well as one of using coinage to commemorate events of a reign. One might expect that Herod, with Greek, Roman, and Near Eastern traditions all providing a precedent, would have used coinage in a similar way. But such was not the case. Herodian coins have no indication of his artistic and architectural achievements, except in the most indirect way.[6] Opinions on the quality of Herodian coinage vary,[7] but certainly the art on Herodian coins is undistinguished, being mostly limited to anchors, shields, cornucopiae, and other symbols.[8] Ritual implements or details from the Temple in Jerusalem, including the altar and the ill-fated eagle, are the closest representations to architecture.[9] Dynastic portraits are totally absent,[10] and Herod thus shrewdly avoided the use of portraiture on an artistic medium that his subjects would handle every day.

Herodian portraiture must be sought in other media. Although figured sculpture was expressly prohibited in Jewish law, this does not seem to have applied (at least as strictly) to painting on flat surfaces,[11] and there were paintings of members of Herod's family. Most notable were the paintings Q. Dellius commissioned and sent to Marcus Antonius,[12] which caused a great deal of difficulty for Herod's wife Mariamme, leading, in fact, to her

5. *BJ* 1.414; 2.266–67.

6. Ya'akov Meshorer, *Ancient Jewish Coinage*, vol. 2: *Herod the Great through Bar Cochba* (Dix Hills, N.Y., 1982), 5.

7. Meshorer (ibid., 5) thought Herodian coins poor, whereas Uriel Rappaport ("Ascalon and the Coinage of Judea," *PP* 36 [1981], 363–64) felt that they represent some of "the finest workmanship in Jewish coinage."

8. BMC Palestine, 220–27.

9. Josef Meyshan, "The Symbols on the Coinage of Herod the Great and Their Meanings," *PEQ* 91 (1959): 109–20.

10. A coin of Sebaste with a female head, generally thought to date to the reign of Agrippa II, has recently been reinterpreted as a Herodian coin with a portrait of the Kore of Sebaste. Its provenience is clear from the inscription, but its date and iconography are far from certain. Those who date it to the reign of Agrippa II usually indentify the female bust as a contemporary member of the royal family, or even Augustus's wife Livia. If it is from the reign of Herod the Great, it would be unique, issued during the earliest years of Sebaste, but still probably does not show a dynastic portrait. For the reinterpretation, as well as previous interpretations, see Nikos Kokkinos, "A Coin of Herod the Great Commemorating the City of Sebaste," *Liber Annuus* 35 (1985): 303–6, and Sebaste, supra, p. 210.

11. Cohen (supra, n. 1), 166.

12. *AJ* 15.25–27.

death.[13] Although they indicate that portrait painting was a more acceptable means of dynastic iconography, there is no evidence of a painting of Herod himself.

Josephus felt that Herod resented the Jewish prohibition of sculpture and would have liked statues in his honor,[14] but even outside his kingdom, Herod seems to have made little use of sculptured portraiture. The best evidence comes from Seia in Syria (fig. 26), where a statue of Herod was erected, perhaps after 22 B.C. A major religious center of southern Syria, lying southeast of Damaskos in the district called Trachon or Trachonitis, Seia came under Nabataean influence in the early first century B.C., during the collapse of the Seleukids; a sanctuary and temple of Ba'al Shamin were built around 33 B.C.[15] The temple lay at the western end of a ridge in a prominent location overlooking the plain. Its façade was at the rear of an enclosed courtyard and contained two columns, creating a recessed porch in the center. Four statues stood in pairs along the line of the colonnade, two to the right and two to the left of the columns, with the doorway to the temple proper between the columns. The statues were badly destroyed when first examined, by Count de Vogüé in 1861, but the statue immediately to the right of the doorway still had a foot attached to the base, and fragments of the torso lay in the vicinity. It had apparently been willfully destroyed, and there was no trace of the head. The dedicatory inscription was recorded by de Vogüé but had disappeared by the time Howard Crosby Butler visited the site in 1904.[16] The inscription revealed, however, that the statue was of Herod, erected by a certain Obaisatos, or Obaisath, son of Saodes, at his own expense.[17]

---

13. *BJ* 1.439; supra, p. 28.

14. *AJ* 16.158.

15. The site was first examined by de Vogüé in 1861: see his *La Syrie Centrale: Architecture civile et religieuse du Ier au VIIe siècle*, vol. 1 (Paris, 1865–67), 31–38. Further bibliography on the site includes Charles Clermont-Ganneau, *Archaeological Researches in Palestine during the Years 1873–1874*, vol. 1 (London, 1899), 263 (probably merely based on de Vogüé and not autopsy); Howard Crosby Butler, *Architecture and Other Arts. Part II of the Publications of an American Archaelogical Expedition to Syria in 1899–1900* (New York, 1903), 334–40 (again based solely on de Vogüé); Howard Crosby Butler, *Publications of the Princeton University Archaeological Expeditions to Syria in 1904–1905 and 1909. Division II: Ancient Architecture in Syria. Section A: Southern Syria. Part 6: Sî' (Seeia)* (Leiden, 1916), the most detailed discussion, based on survey and excavations in 1904; J.- P. Rey-Coquais, "Seia," in *PECS*, 820. Excavations at Seia in the 1970's and 1980's did not further illuminate the matter of Herod's statue: see Jean-Marie Dentzer and Jacqueline Dentzer, "Le fouilles de Sî' et la phase hellénistique en Syrie du sud," *CRAI* 1981: 78–102; Jean-Marie Dentzer et al., "Six campagnes de fouilles à Sî': Développement et culture indigène en Syria méridionale," *Damaszener Mitteilungen* 2 (1985): 65–83.

16. See also Merkel and Korol (supra, n. 2), 836–51.

17. *OGIS*, 415.

Seia was added to Herod's territory by Augustus, probably at or shortly after 22 B.C.,[18] which may indicate a *terminus post quem* for Obaisatos's dedication. The dedicator was a Nabataean, and if erection of the statue was anything other than pure political pragmatism by this local philanthropist, it may have been that he was a relative of Herod's, who was half Nabataean.[19]

In the Boston Museum of Fine Arts there is a marble head, with some details in stucco, 0.64 m high, or three times life size (which would mean a full statue 4–5 m high), originally from Memphis in Egypt (fig. 48).[20] The face has a beard running along the point of the jaw and chin; the upper lip is clean-shaven. The marble is from the Greek mainland, perhaps Pentelic. The piece has been reworked, with the beard and other details added in stucco, and thus is difficult to date. When acquired by the museum, it was advertised as a portrait of the emperor Severus Alexander; it is now believed to have originally been Ptolemaios IV, Ptolemaios VI, Ptolemaios IX, or Marcus Antonius,[21] but is currently exhibited as "Hellenistic Ruler (A Ptolemy?)." Harald Ingholt has made a compelling argument, although not widely accepted, that in its reworked form it is a portrait of Herod.[22]

18. *AJ* 15.342–343.

19. Inscriptions from Athens (supra, p. 219) indicate that one or more statues of the king stood in that city. For the dubious tradition regarding statues of Herod in Armenia, see Appendix 1.

20. The piece is Boston Museum # 59.51. The head is turned slightly up and to the left, and has a beard from the sideburns around the point of the chin. The hair is in curls on the front. The beard and hair have been applied in stucco, and there is also stucco on the nose. There are flecks of gold in the hair and reddish color on the eyes and lips. Neither ear is apparent; on the right there are two small drill holes connected by a trough. On the left there may be a faint outline of the lobe and back part, but no holes. The forehead bulges out at the eyebrows, with the right eyebrow more prominent than the left. The eyes are sunk 33–35 mm. The ball of the right eye is a little flatter than the left, and the left eye is slightly larger than the right (65 by 31 mm vs. 60 by 28 mm). The nose is prominently formed, and has been altered by stucco. It stands out far (55 mm) from the face, and is hooked in two peaks with a slight dip near the lower part. The end curves around so that it ends in a knob. The nostrils are large; the right one (slightly better preserved) is 17 mm across. The upper lip recedes in comparison to the lower; there are many chisel marks on the upper lip, perhaps indicating that a mustache was removed. The lower lip is protruding (17 mm) and almost curved out. The chin is convex, yet flat below the point of the convexity. The beard runs under the chin to the neck. The neck is preserved for 0.208 m below the chin. There are intrusive areas of chiseling on the sides of the neck, especially the left, and there is stucco on the right side of the neck and down onto the right throat. The bibliography for the statue appears in Cornelius C. Vermeule III and Mary B. Comstock, *Sculpture in Stone and Bronze* (Boston, 1988), 110.

21. Mary B. Comstock and Cornelius C. Vermeule, *Sculpture in Stone* (Boston, 1976), 84–85.

22. Harald Ingholt, "A Colossal Head from Memphis, Severan or Augustan?" *JARCE* 2 (1963), 125–42; but see Louis H. Feldman, *Josephus and Modern Scholarship, 1937–1980* (Berlin, 1984), 288.

Ingholt suggested that the portrait was reworked in the period immediately after Actium when Herod assisted and supplied Octavian on his way to Egypt.[23] Herod eventually joined Octavian in Egypt and escorted him back to Antioch.[24] While in Egypt, Herod may have visited Memphis, where there was an extensive Idumaean population, and perhaps indulged in some architectural patronage.[25] There was also a famous Jewish temple nearby. It had been built in the second century B.C. on a tract of land 180 stadia from Memphis at Leontopolis, which King Ptolemaios VI Philometor had given to the priest Onias. The temple was impressive and had rich ornamentation; Onias evidently wanted to create a competitor to the Jerusalem temple. It was stripped of its furnishings and closed on Vespasian's orders because of disturbances in Egypt in the aftermath of the Jewish revolt.[26]

Particularly suggestive for Ingolt is the shaven upper lip and the roughness of the marble on the left of the neck. The treatment of the facial hair is neither Greek nor Roman, but remindful of Semitic representations. The roughness of the neck may be a remnant of the royal diadem Herod wore, which Octavian had placed on his head when the two met on Rhodes just after Actium.[27] In this context the suggestion by Mary Comstock and Cornelius Vermeule[28] that the portrait was originally one of Marcus Antonius has a peculiar appropriateness. One expects that there might have been quite an industry in reworking portraits of Antonius, especially in Egypt, immediately after 30 B.C., and Herod's glib transition from supporter of Antonius to supporter of Octavian is therefore mirrored in the transformation of a portrait of Antonius into one of Herod. The evidence is strongly circumstantial but points to the Boston head as a portrait originally of Antonius that was resculptured shortly after 30 B.C. into a portrait of Herod, perhaps by members of the Idumaean colony at Memphis wishing to honor their compatriot, because of some specific service, or merely as a recognition of Herod's enhanced status under the new Roman regime.

If the head is of Herod, it is the only extant visual contemporary record of the king.[29] The Boston head is the portrait of a serious, intense man, a pow-

23. *AJ* 15.187–201; *BJ* 1.386–97.

24. *AJ* 15.215–18.

25. Ingholt (supra, n. 22), 133–34. Such patronage is not documented by Josephus and is hypothetical, yet curiously he (*BJ* 4.532) describes the tombs of the descendants of Abraham at Memphis as built of especially fine marble and well constructed, terminology (especially the use of marble) he reserved for Herodian work.

26. *BJ* 7.420–25; *AJ* 13.70.

27. *AJ* 15.195; *BJ* 1.393; Ingholt (supra, n, 22), 139–41.

28. Comstock and Vermeule (supra, n. 21), 85.

29. Except for a statement that in old age Herod dyed his hair (*BJ* 1.490), no physical description has survived, although he was of great physical prowess and a skilled athlete (*BJ* 1.429–30).

erful personality. The largeness of the eyes and the set of the jaw, with the slight protrusion of the lower lip, all combine to transmit a strong feeling of authority and dignity, depicting someone about to make a major decision.[30]

It is clear, then, that the theological realities of Herod's world meant that unlike the typical Hellenistic-Roman dynast, he was not extensively commemorated in portrait sculpture. The few known examples of such memorials are consistent in that they were probably not instituted by Herod himself and were outside (or, in the case of Seia, at the fringe of) Herod's territory. Yet given Herod's primary role as a client king of Rome's, Rome's establishment of Herod as king, and Herod's own intimacy with the ruling elite at Rome, it seems plausible that Herod or his dynasty might have been commemorated in the city of Rome itself. Foreign rulers were depicted in sculpture at Rome: the most famous example is the golden statue of Cleopatra that adorned the Forum Julium.[31] Statues of famous persons were also set up in the Forum Augustum, including a full range of Roman military heroes.[32] The Theater of Pompey also had an extensive display of historical and allegorical statuary relating to Pompey's own career.[33] Augustus erected a structure that included a sculpture gallery of statues of all the nations of the world, whatever this meant, including one of the Punic god Melkart; it seems to have been called the Porticus ad Nationes.[34] Thus Rome of Herod's day had a regular program of commemorating in sculpture the far-flung corners of the world—Agrippa's world map in the Porticus Vipsania was a similar concept—and it is difficult to imagine that the Herodian dynasty was not somehow represented.

30. A head discovered in Jerusalem in 1873 has also been suggested to be a portrait of Herod, but the attribution is exceedingly weak. Since 1899 the head has been in the Hermitage in St. Petersburg (inventory A571), and it has consistently been identified as the emperior Hadrian. It is a severe, bearded portrait of a mature man wearing a crown, similar to other portraits of Hadrian from the East. The attribution to Herod seems to be due to a newspaper report of 1894 and is based solely on the provenience and the crown. It if were Herod, it would have been sculpted over a century after his death, which is unlikely given the local attitudes toward Herod even by the time of Josephus. When the Hermitage published the head, it ignored any suggestion that it might be Herod, but the possibility that it is a head of Herod was raised in 1988 by Dieter Korol, although probably merely in an attempt to create a complete potential iconography of the king rather than to make any new critical statement. See Emil Schürer, *Geschichte des jüdischen Volkes in Zeitalter Jesu Christu*, 3d–4th ed. (Leipzig, 1901), 1: 376–77; Musée de l'Ermitage, *Le Portrait romain* (Leningrad, 1974), 159–60, no. 32; Merkel and Korol (supra, n. 2), 831.

31. Appian, *Civil War* 2.102; Dio 51.22.

32. For the sources, see Richardson, *NTD*, 161; Paul Zanker, *The Power of Images in the Age of Augustus*, trans. Alan Shapiro (Ann Arbor, 1988), 210–13.

33. Pliny, *Natural History* 36.41; Richardson, *NTD*, 384.

34. Pliny, *Natural History* 36.39; Servius, *Aeneid* 8.271; the structure is unknown except for these two references. See also Richardson, *NTD*, 316–17.

The major commemorative sculptural document of the Augustan period is the Ara Pacis, and questions continue regarding the depiction of foreigners on its screen.[35] If individual personalities (and not idealized figures in the style of the Parthenon frieze) are depicted,[36] and if non-Romans were included, it would be a particularly appropriate place to show the role Herod played in Roman eastern policy.

Barbarian royalty has repeatedly been identified among those shown, most recently in the suggestion that figure # 30 on the south frieze is Queen Dynamis of Bosporos and that the child in front of her (# 31) is one of her children, Aspourgos.[37] If this attribution is correct, the Ara Pacis commemorates, in part, Marcus Agrippa's lengthy campaign in Asia Minor; Agrippa himself (# 28) stands just to the viewer's left of Dynamis and Aspourgos, with the latter holding his toga. Such an interpretation brings the events memorialized extremely close to Herod, who accompanied Agrippa on the Bosporan campaign and who smoothed over a potential diplomatic incident between the Roman entourage and Troy, a city itself of major relevance to the Ara Pacis.[38]

A close examination of the south frieze of the screen reveals that Agrippa and the three figures behind him (to the viewer's right) form a distinct unit (fig. 47). Between Agrippa and Dynamis is the left profile of a young man (# 29), in low relief, barely appearing out of the background of the frieze and only visible above shoulder height and often ignored by commentators.

35. The bibliography on the Ara Pacis is immense. Of particular relevance are the following: Richardson, *NTD*, 287–89; Charles Brian Rose, "'Princes' and Barbarians on the Ara Pacis," *AJA* 94 (1990): 453–67; Salvatore Settis, "Die Ara Pacis," in *Kaiser Augustus und die verlorene Republik* (Berlin, 1988), 400–426; John Pollini, "Ahenobarbi, Appuleii and Some Others on the Ara Pacis," *AJA* 90 [1986]: 453–60; Gerhard M. Koeppel, "Die historischen Reliefs der römischen Kaizerzeit, V: Ara Pacis Augustae, Teil 1," *BJb* 187 (1987): 101–57 (whose numbering of the figures is herein used); Mario Torelli, *Typology and Structure of Roman Historical Reliefs* (Ann Arbor, 1982), 27–61; Diana E. E. Kleiner, "The Great Friezes of the Ara Pacis Augustae: Greek Sources, Roman Derivations, and Augustan Social Policy," *MEFRA* 90 (1978): 753–85; Erika Simon, *Ara Pacis Augustae* (Greenwich, Conn. [1967]). A complete bibliography for the altar may be obtained through the bibliographies of these works; see also, most recently, Diana E. E. Kleiner, *Roman Sculpture* (New Haven, 1992), 119, who, however, identified figure # 31 as Roman, without totally rejecting the possibility that he might be a foreigner (p. 93), and Richard Billows, "The Religious Procession of the Ara Pacis Augustae: Augustus' *Supplicatio* in 13 B.C.," *JRA* 6 (1993): 80–93, who discussed the frieze in detail without dealing with figures ## 29–31.

36. Richardson, *NTD*, 288.

37. Rose (supra, n. 35); this child has also been identified as Gallic (Pollini [supra, n. 35], 453); see also Simon (supra, n. 35), 18, who first suggested that # 30 and # 31 were foreigners. For the bibliography on the various identifications of these figures, see Kleiner, *MEFRA* (supra, n. 35) nn. 15, 16.

38. Supra, pp. 49–50.

Although Roman in form (he is clean shaven and wears a wreath on his Roman-style hair), by all rights he should be a foreigner, since he is a component of the unit memorializing Agrippa's eastern campaign. There is one outstanding candidate for this Romanized eastener: Antipatros the eldest son of Herod, who, at about thirty years of age, came to Rome with Agrippa upon the latter's return from the Bosporos, and was so favored that he was soon living in Augustus's household. By the time of the dedication of the Ara Pacis in 9 B.C.[39] Agrippa himself was dead; hence the monument became in part a memorial to his legacy. Herod was elderly and losing favor with Augustus, but Antipatros would have represented the new generation of eastern dynasts. Already the Herodian dynasty was spreading itself through the eastern kingdoms, and Augustus would have hoped that whatever the problems with Herod in his old age, his offspring would continue to uphold Roman policy in the East. Sadly this was not to be the case with Antipatros, as he was executed by his father few years later, but when the altar was dedicated on 30 January 9 B.C.. he was Herod's and Augustus's hope for the future. Hence Antipatros was deserving of a place—however shadowy—on the Ara Pacis, a symbolic reminder of the achievements of both Agrippa himself, and the role the Herodian dynasty had played in the eastern policy of Rome.

39. Ovid, *Fasti* 1.709–22.

APPENDIX THREE
STEMMATA

The stemmata that follow show the family of Herod the Great, the client kings of Asia Minor (including Kappadokia, Kilikia, Kommagene, Emesa, Armenia, and Pontos, with Seleukid and Ptolemaic connections) and their genealogy, the Hasmoneans, and the Julio-Claudians. Only with the stemmata of the family of Herod (more properly the Antipatrids of Judaea) has any attempt been made at completeness; the others only illustrate their relationship with Herod. Repetition has been minimized. The family of Herod the Great is complete only on its own stemmata: when members of the family are shown on the Hasmonean and Asian stemmata, only immediate connections are shown. For the sake of clarity, each of Herod's wives (with offspring) has been shown in a separate stemma (nos. 3–12) with an additional stemma (no. 2) showing Herod's ancestry, siblings, and their offspring. Except in Stemma 13, that of the Asian Rulers, which follows accepted dynastic numbers, sequential numbers have been given to like-named persons, but this is merely to limit confusion (and to provide for cross references between stemmata), not any official or recognized dynastic numbering.

The stemmata of the family of Herod the Great are based largely on those by Otto, *RE*, after p. 14, and Schalit, end pocket of *KH*, supplemented somewhat by Sullivan, *NER*. The Hasmonean stemma is from Sullivan and from Carsten Colpe, "Hasmonäer," *KlPauly* 2 (1979): 950. The Julio-Claudian stemma is from H. H. Scullard, *From the Gracchi to Nero* (4th ed., New York, 1976) 331. Material has been blended to provide the most up-to-date information possible. The works of Josephus are almost the sole ancient source for the Herodian genealogies. Detailed information on the sources is provided in the works cited above.

It would be possible to show everyone in a single complex, but virtually unintelligible, stemma. Herod and his son Antipatros married into the Hasmonean family, there are numerous relationships between Herod's family and those of the Asian client kings, and Marcus Antonius twice provides a connection between the client kings and the Julio-Claudians. In the interests of clarity, however, separate stemmata have been shown, but the numerous relations are a fine example of what Sullivan called the "Eastern Dynastic Network."

STEMMA 1 The Hasmoneans

*This stemma has been simplified somewhat to emphasize the connections
of Herod the Great.*

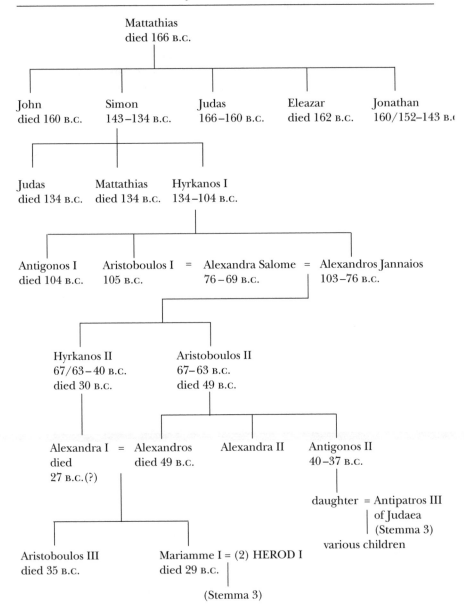

All of the descendants of Antipatros II were entitled to carry the nomen Julius or Julia because of the Roman citizenship bestowed by Julius Caesar; this has generally been omitted.

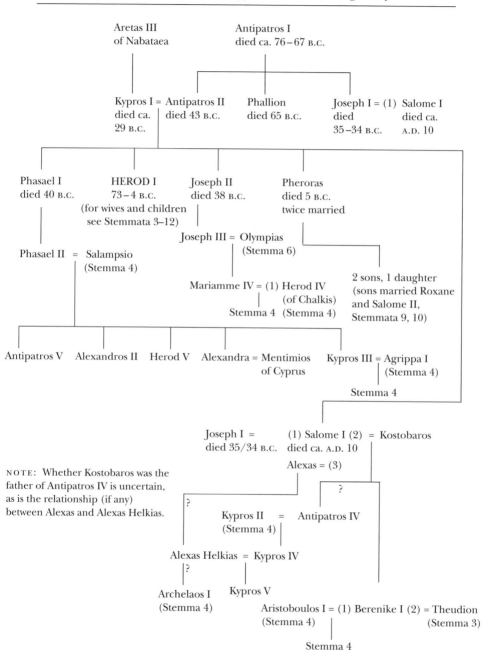

NOTE: Whether Kostobaros was the father of Antipatros IV is uncertain, as is the relationship (if any) between Alexas and Alexas Helkias.

*Doris's ancestry is not clear (see BJ I.241, 432; AJ 14.300): she was perhaps
an Idumaean or from Jerusalem.*

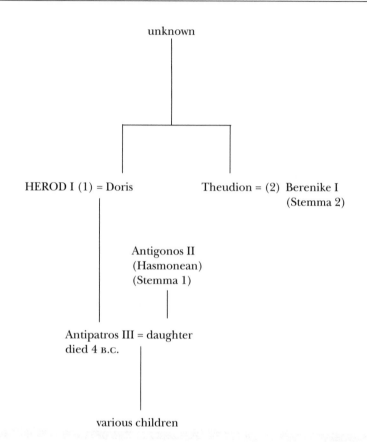

unknown

HEROD I (1) = Doris   Theudion = (2) Berenike I
                                                        (Stemma 2)

                    Antigonos II
                    (Hasmonean)
                    (Stemma 1)

Antipatros III = daughter
died 4 B.C.

            various children

STEMMA 4   Herod's Marriage to Mariamme the Hasmonean

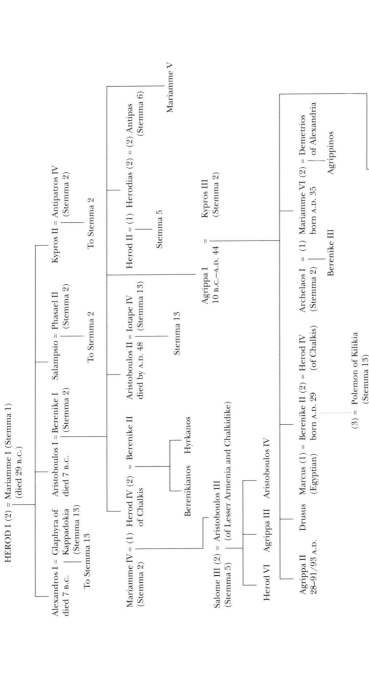

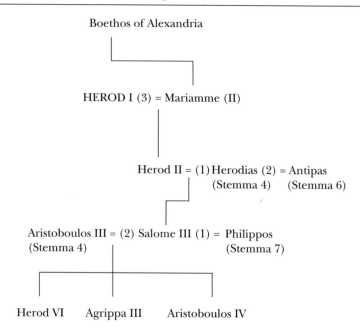

Boethos of Alexandria

HEROD I (3) = Mariamme (II)

Herod II = (1) Herodias (2) = Antipas
(Stemma 4)   (Stemma 6)

Aristoboulos III = (2) Salome III (1) = Philippos
(Stemma 4)   (Stemma 7)

Herod VI   Agrippa III   Aristoboulos IV

NOTE: According to the biblical tradition, Herodias was married first to Philippos
(Stemma 7) rather than to Herod II (Matt. 14.3; Mark 6.17).

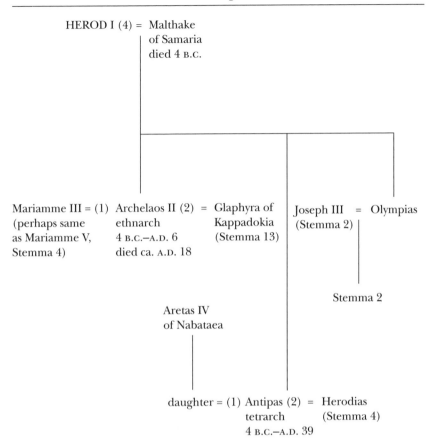

HEROD I (4) = Malthake
of Samaria
died 4 B.C.

Mariamme III = (1) Archelaos II (2) = Glaphyra of   Joseph III   = Olympias
(perhaps same   ethnarch   Kappadokia   (Stemma 2)
as Mariamme V,   4 B.C.–A.D. 6   (Stemma 13)
Stemma 4)   died ca. A.D. 18

                                                        Stemma 2
                    Aretas IV
                    of Nabataea

            daughter = (1) Antipas (2) = Herodias
                           tetrarch   (Stemma 4)
                           4 B.C.–A.D. 39

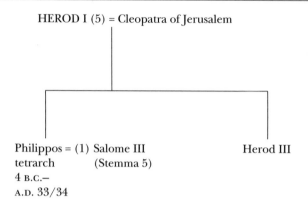

HEROD I (5) = Cleopatra of Jerusalem

Philippos = (1) Salome III   Herod III
tetrarch   (Stemma 5)
4 B.C.–
A.D. 33/34

NOTE: See note on Stemma 5.

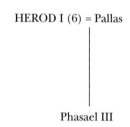

HEROD I (6) = Pallas

Phasael III

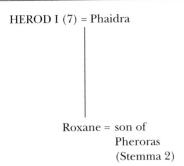

HEROD I (7) = Phaidra

Roxane = son of
Pheroras
(Stemma 2)

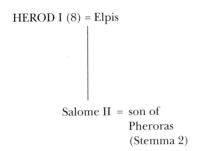

HEROD I (8) = Elpis

Salome II = son of
Pheroras
(Stemma 2)

HEROD I (9) = unknown cousin

NOTE: See note on Stemma 12.

HEROD I (10) = unknown niece (daughter of Pheroras, Stemma 2?)

NOTE: At *BJ* 1.563 (repeated with less detail at *AJ* 17.21) Josephus wrote that Herod had nine wives. He then listed eight by name (and their children) and wrote that two more, unnamed, were childless, for a total of ten. One of the unnamed wives was a cousin, another a niece. Only two nieces of Herod are known: Berenike I, and a daughter of Pheroras. Berenike I was twice married, particularly to Herod's son Aristoboulos I, so Herod's marriage might have been to the daughter of Pheroras, whose name is unknown and for whom there is no record of marriage. No female cousins are known. Since neither of the marriages produced children and both were within the family, it is best to assume they were early and brief.

STEMMA 13   Selected Asian Dynasts, Showing Their Relationships with
the Family of Herod the Great

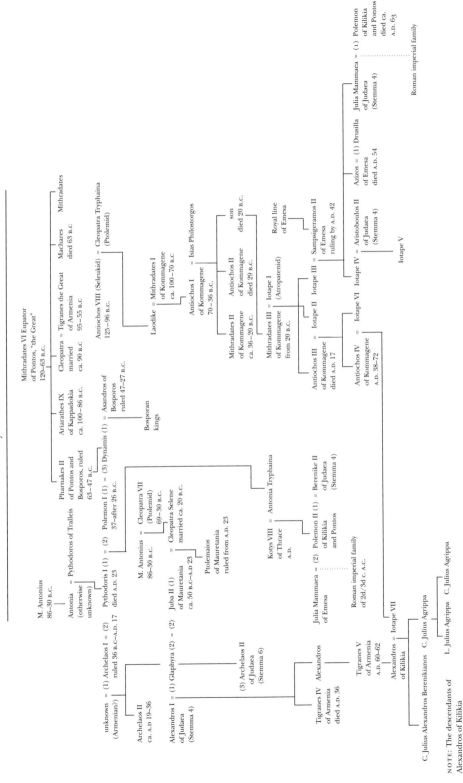

NOTE: The descendants of
Alexandros of Kilikia
are uncertain.

STEMMA 14   Selected Julio-Claudians

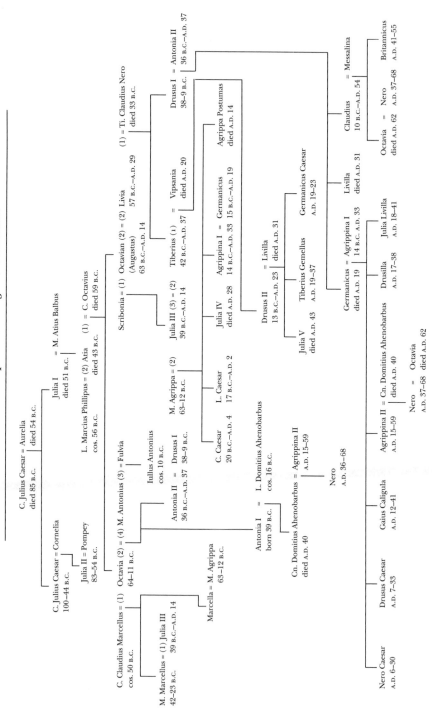

BIBLIOGRAPHY

Abel, F.-M. "De l'Ouady Far'a à Fasa'il—l'Alexandreion." *RBibl* 10 (1913): 227–34.
———. "Inscription grecque de l'aqueduc de Jerusalem avec la figure du pied byzantin." *RBibl* 35 (1926): 284–88.
———. *Géographie de la Palestine.* Paris, 1938.
———. "Les confins de la Palestine et de l'Égypte sous les Ptolèmées." *RBibl* 49 (1940): 55–75.
Adam, Jean-Pierre. *Roman Building: Materials and Techniques.* Translated by Anthony Mathews. Bloomington, Ind., 1994.
Adan-Bayewitz, David, and Isadore Perlman. "The Local Trade of Sepphoris in the Roman Period." *IEJ* 40 (1990): 153–72.
Africa, Thomas. "Worms and the Death of Kings: A Cautionary Note on Disease and History." *ClAnt* 1 (1982): 1–17.
Aharoni, Yohanan, and Sara Ben-Arieh. "Survey between Raphia and the Brook of Egypt." *'Atiqot* 7 (1974): 88–94.
Akten des XIII Internationalen Kongresses für klassiche Archäologie, Berlin 1988. Mainz, 1990.
Akurgal, Ekrem. *Ancient Civilizations and Ruins of Turkey.* 7th ed. Istanbul, 1990.
Albricci, Anna. "L'orchestra dipinta del teatro erodiano di 'Caesarea Maritima'." *BdA* 47 (1962): 289–304.
Albright, W. F. "Contributions to the Historical Geography of Palestine." *AASOR* 2–3 (1921–22): 1–46.
———. "The Site of Aphek in Sharon." *JPOS* 3 (1923): 50–53.
———. Review of *Preliminary Report of the University of Michigan Excavations at Sepphoris,*" by Leroy Waterman, N. E. Manasseh, S. Yeivin, and Catherine S. Bunnell. *Classical Weekly* 31 (1937–38): 148.
Alcock, Susan E. *Graeca Capta: The Landscapes of Roman Greece.* Cambridge, 1993.
Alekseev, V. P., ed. *Contributions to the Archaeology of Armenia.* Translated by Arlene Krimgold. Edited by Henry Field. Russian Translation Series of the Peabody Museum of Archaeology and Ethnology, 3.3. Cambridge, Mass. 1968.

Alexander, William Hardy. "The Enigma of Horace's Mother." *CP* 37 (1942): 385–97.

Aline de Sion, Marie. *La forteresse Antonia à Jérusalem et la question du Prétoire*. Paris, 1955.

Alt, A. "Die Reiterstadt Gaba." *ZDPV* 62 (1939): 3–21.

Aly, W. "Strabon von Amaseia" (# 3). *RE*, 2d ser., 7 (1931): 76–155.

———. *Strabon von Amaseia*. Bonn, 1957.

Amiran, D. H. K., E. Arieh, and T. Turcotte. "Earthquakes in Israel and Adjacent Areas: Macroseismic Observations since 100 B.C.E." *IEJ* 44 (1994): 260–305.

Amiran, Ruth, and A. Eitan, "Herod's Palace." *IEJ* 22 (1972): 50–51.

Amit, David. "Water Supply to the Alexandrium Fortress (Sartaba)." *AAP*, 215–21.

———. "The Water System of Dok Fortress (Dagon)." *AAP*, 223–28.

———. "What Was the Source of Herodion's Water." *Liber Annuus* 44 (1994): 561–78.

Anderson, J. G. C. "Some Questions Bearing on the Date and Place of Composition of Strabo's *Geography*." In *Anatolian Studies Presented to Sir William Mitchell Ramsay*, ed. W. H. Buckler and W. M. Calder, 1–13. Manchester, 1923.

André, J. *La vie et l'oeuvre d'Asinius Pollion*. Paris, 1949.

Andreou, Ioanna. "Το ἔργο της ΙΒ' Εφορείας Ἀρχαιοτήτων στη Νικόπολη." In *Nikopolis*, vol. 1, ed. Chrysos, 145–52.

Antioch-on-the Orontes. Vol. 3, *The Excavations, 1937–1939*. Edited by Richard Stillwell. Princeton, 1941.

Applebaum, Shimon. "Hellenistic Cities of Judaea and Its Vicinity—Some New Aspects." In *The Ancient Historian and His Materials: Essays in Honour of C. E. Stevens*, ed. Barbara Levick, 59–73. Farnborough, 1975.

———. "Judaea as a Roman Province: The Countryside as a Political and Economic Factor." *ANRW* 2.8 (1977): 355–96.

———. "Josephus and the Economic Causes of the Jewish War." In *Josephus, the Bible, and History*, ed. Louis H. Feldman and Gohei Hata, 237–64. Detroit, 1989.

Arakelyan, B. "Excavations at Garni, 1949–1950." In Alekseev, ed., *Contributions*, 13–108.

———. "Excavations at Garni, 1951–1955." In Alekseev, ed., *Contributions*, 109–98.

Arav, Rami. *Hellenistic Palestine: Settlement Patterns and City Planning, 337–31 B.C.E.* BAR-IS, 485. London, 1989.

———. "Some Notes on the Foundation of Straton's Tower. *PEQ* 121 (1989): 144–48.

———. "Bethsaida Excavations: Preliminary Excavation Report, 1987–1993." In *Bethsaida: A City by the North Shore of the Sea of Galilee*, vol. 1, ed. Rami Arav and Richard A. Freund, 3–63. Kirksville, Mo., 1995.

Atkinson, Kathleen M. T. "The Governors of the Province Asia in the Reign of Augustus." *Historia* 7 (1958): 300–330.

Avigad, Nahman. *Discovering Jerusalem*. Nashville, 1983.

———. *The Herodian Quarter in Jerusalem*. Jerusalem, 1991.

———. "Description of the Tombs." In *NEAEHL*, 750–53.

———. "Samaria (City)." In *NEAEHL*, 1300–1310.

Avi-Yonah, Michael. *Map of Roman Palestine*. 2d rev. ed. Jerusalem, 1940.

————. "Oriental Elements in the Art of Palestine in the Roman and Byzantine Periods." *QDAP* 10 (1944): 105–51.

————. "The Foundation of Tiberias." *IEJ* 1 (1950–51): 160–69.

————. "The Missing Fortress of Flavius Josephus." *IEJ* 3 (1953): 94–98.

————. *The Madaba Mosaic Map.* Jerusalem, 1954.

————. "The Third and Second Walls of Jerusalem." *IEJ* 18 (1968): 98–125.

————. *Gazetteer of Roman Palestine.* Qedem 5. Jerusalem, 1976.

————. *The Holy Land from the Persian to the Arab Conquests (536 B.C. to A.D. 640): A Historical Geography.* Rev. ed. Grand Rapids, Mich. 1977.

————. "Mareshah (Marisa)." In *EAEHL*, 782–90.

————. "Mareshah (Marisa)." In *NEAEHL*, 948–51.

————. "Na'aran." In *NEAEHL*, 1075–76.

————, ed. *The World History of the Jewish People.* Vol. 1, pt. 7, *The Herodian Period.* New Brunswick, N.J., 1975.

Avi-Yonah, Michael, and A. Negev. "Caesarea." *IEJ* 13 (1963): 146–48.

Babylonian Talmud, The. Translated and edited by I. Epstein. London, 1935–52.

Badian, Ernst. "The Early Career of A. Gabinius (cos. 58 B.C.)." *Philologus* 103 (1959): 87–99.

Bagatti, B. "La posizione del tempio erodiano di Gerusalemme." *Biblica* 46 (1965): 428–44.

Bahat, Dan. "The Western Wall Tunnels." In *Ancient Jerusalem Revealed,* ed. Hillel Geva, 177–90. Jerusalem, 1994.

Balsdon, J. P. V. D. *Roman Women: Their History and Habits.* London, 1962.

————. *Romans and Aliens.* London, 1979.

Barag, Dan. "Herod's Royal Castle at Samaria-Sebaste." *ErIsr* 23 (1992): 293–301.

————. "King Herod's Royal Castle at Samaria-Sebaste." *PEQ* 125 (1993): 3–17.

Bartlett, John R. *Jews in the Hellenistic World: Josephus, Aristeas, the Sibylline Orations, Eupolemus.* Cambridge Commentaries on the Writings of the Jewish and Christian World, 1.1. Cambridge, 1985.

Bauer, Heinrich. "Basilica Fulvia." In *LTUR*, 1: 173–75.

————. "Basilica Paul(l)i." In *LTUR*, 1: 183–87.

Baumann, Uwe. *Rom und die Juden.* Studia Philosophica et Historica, 4. Frankfurt a/M, 1983.

Bean, George. *Turkey's Southern Shore: An Archaeological Guide.* New York, 1968.

Bedoukian, Paul Z. "A Classification of the Coins of the Artaxiad Dynasty of Armenia." *ANSMN* 14 (1968): 41–66.

Beebe, H. Keith. "Caesarea Maritima: Its Strategic and Political Significance to Rome." *JNES* 42 (1983): 195–207.

Ben David, Chaim. "The Ancient Water Supply System of Hippus-Susita." *AAP*, 133–40.

Ben Zeev, Miriam Pucci. "Marcus Antonius, Publius Dolabella, and the Jews." *Athenaeum* 82 (1994): 31–40.

————. "Caesar's Decrees in the Antiquities: Josephus' Forgeries or Authentic Roman *Senatus Consulta?*" *Athenaeum* 84 (1996): 71–91.

Bengtson, Hermann. *Marcus Antonius: Triumvir und Herrscher des Orients.* Munich, 1977.

Benoit, P. "L'Antonia d'Hérode le Grand et le forum oriental d'Aelia Capitolina." *HThR* 64 (1971): 135–67.

Benzinger, I. "Balanaia." In *RE*, 2 (1896): 2816–17.

Berthold, Richard M. *Rhodes in the Hellenistic Age*. Ithaca, N.Y., 1984.

Bickerman, Elias J. *Chronology of the Ancient World*. 2d ed. Ithaca, N.Y., 1980.

———. *The Jews in the Greek Age*. Cambridge, Mass., 1988.

Biers, Jane C. *Corinth: Results of Excavations Conducted by the American School of Classical Studies at Athens*. Vol. 17, *The Great Bath on the Lechaion Road*. Princeton, 1985.

Bietenhard, Hans. "Die Dekapolis von Pompeius bis Traian." *ZDPV* 79 (1963): 24–58.

———. "Die syrische Dekapolis von Pompeius bis Traian." *ANRW* 2.8 (1977): 220–61.

Bikai, Patricia Maynor. "Classical Tyre." In *The Heritage of Tyre*, ed. Jowkowsky, 61–68.

Bikai, Pierre M. "The Land of Tyre." In *The Heritage of Tyre*, ed. Jowkowsky, 13–23.

Billows, Richard. "The Religious Procession of the Ara Pacis Augustae: Augustus' *Supplicatio* in 13 B.C." *JRA* 6 (1993): 80–93.

Binder, Wolfgang. *Der Roma-Augustus Monopteros auf der Akropolis in Athen und sein typologischer Ort*. Stuttgart, 1969.

Blackman, D. J. "Rhodes: Survey of Ancient Shipsheds." *ArchDelt* 27 (1972): B.686–87.

———. "Ancient Harbors in the Mediterranean, Part 1." *IJNA* 11 (1982): 79–104.

———. "Ancient Harbors in the Mediterranean, Part 2." *IJNA* 11 (1982): 185–211.

Blake, Marion Elizabeth. *Ancient Roman Construction in Italy from the Prehistoric Period to Augustus*. Washington, D.C., 1947.

Blakely, Jeffrey A. "A Stratigraphically Determined Date for the Inner Fortification Wall at Caesarea Maritima." In *The Answers Lie Below: Essays in Honor of Lawrence Edmund Toombs*, ed. Henry O. Thompson, 3–38. Lanham, Md., 1984.

———. *Caesarea Maritima: The Pottery and Dating of Vault 1: Horreum, Mithraeum, and Later Uses*. Vol. 4 of *CaesMarit*. Lewistown, N.Y. 1987.

Bloedhorn, Hanswulf. "Herodianische Architektur in Jerusalem." In *Akten*, 437.

Blomme, Yves. "Faut-il revenir sur la datation de l'arc de l''Ecce Homo'?" *RBibl* 86 (1979): 244–71.

Boardman, John. "The Ancient City of Chios." In J. K. Anderson, John Boardman, and M. S. F. Hood, "Excavation on the Kofinà Ridge, Chios." *BSA* 49 (1954): 123–28.

Boëthius, Axel. *Etruscan and Early Roman Architecture*. 2d ed. Harmondsworth, 1978.

Bokotopoulou, Ioulia. Ανασκαφικές και αναστηλωτικές εργασίες στη Νικόπολη κατά την δεκαετία 1967–1977." In Nikopolis, vol. 1, ed. Chrysos, 135–44.

Bol, Peter Cornelius, Adolf Hoffmann, and Thomas Weber. "Gadara in der Dekapolis." *AA* 1990: 193–266.

Bomgardner, David L. "A New Era for Amphitheatre Studies." *JRA* 6 (1993): 375–90.

Boraas, Roger S., and L. T. Geraty. *Heshbon, 1974: The Fourth Campaign at Tell Hes-bân*. Andrews University Monographs, Studies in Religion, 9. Berrien Springs, Mich., 1976.

Boraas, Roger S., and Siegfried H. Horn. *Heshbon, 1973: The Third Campaign at Tell Hesbân*. Andrews University Monographs, Studies in Religion, 8. Berrien Springs, Mich., 1975.

Bosworth, A. P. "Asinius Pollio and Augustus." *Historia* 21 (1972): 441–73.

Bowersock, G. W. "Eurycles of Sparta." *JRS* 51 (1961): 112–18.

————. *Augustus and the Greek World*. Oxford, 1965.

————. Review of *The Coins of the Decapolis and Provincia Arabia*, by A. Spijkerman. *JRS* 72 (1982): 197–98.

————. *Roman Arabia*. Cambridge, Mass., 1983.

Bowsher, Julian M. C. "Architecture and Religion in the Decapolis: A Numismatic Survey." *PEQ* 119 (1987): 62–69.

Braund, David. "Four Notes on the Herods." *CQ* 33 (1983): 239–42.

————. *Rome and the Friendly King: The Character of Client Kingship*. London, 1984.

Broshi, Magan. "Does 'State Necessity' Contradict 'Personal Need'?" *JC* 1 (1981): 67.

Broughton, T. Robert S. *The Magistrates of the Roman Republic*. 3 vols. Philological Monographs of the American Philological Association, 15. New York, 1951–52, 1986.

Brown, Frank E. Review of *Etruscan and Roman Architecture*, by Axel Boëthius and J. B. Ward Perkins. *ArtB* 54 (1972): 342–44.

Bruneau, Philippe. *Recherches sur les cultes de Délos à l'époque hellénistique et à l'époque impériale*. BEFAR, 217. Paris, 1970.

Bruun, Christer. *The Water Supply of Ancient Rome: A Study of Roman Imperial Administration*. Commentationes Humanarum Litterarum, 93. Helsinki, 1991.

Brzoska, J. "Apollonios" (# 85). In *RE*, 3 (1895): 141–14.

Bull, Robert J. "Caesarea and King Herod's Magnificent City Plan." *AJA* 100 (1996): 370.

Bull, Robert J., Edgar M. Krentz, Olin J. Storvick, and Marie Spiro. "The Joint Expedition to Caesarea Maritima: Eleventh Season, 1984." *AASOR* 51 (1994): 63–86.

Burney, Charles, and David Marshall Lang. *The Peoples of the Hills*. London, 1971.

Burrell, Barbara. "Palace to Praetorium: The Romanization of Caesarea." In *CMR*, 228–47.

Burrell, Barbara, and Kathryn Gleason, "The Promontory Palace at Caesarea, Israel: The 1993 and 1994 Seasons." *AJA* 99 (1995): 306–7.

Burrell, Barbara, Kathryn Gleason, and Ehud Netzer. "Uncovering Herod's Seaside Palace." *BAR* 19 (1993): 50–57, 76.

Busink, Th. A. *Der Tempel von Jerusalem*. Vol. 2. Leiden, 1980.

Butler, Howard Crosby. *Architecture and Other Arts. Part II of the Publications of an American Archaeological Expedition to Syria in 1899–1900*. New York, 1903.

————. *Publications of the Princeton University Archaeological Expeditions to Syria in 1904–1905 and 1909. Division II: Ancient Architecture in Syria. Section A: Southern Syria. Part 6: Sî' (Seeia)*. Leiden, 1916.

Cagnat, René. "Communication de M. René Cagnat." *CRAI* 1927: 243–44.

Campbell, W. A. "The Circus." In *Antioch-on-the-Orontes*, vol. 1: *The Excavations of 1932*, ed. George W. Elderkin, 34–41. Princeton, 1934.

————. "The Sixth Season of Excavation at Antioch-on-the Orontes, 1937." *AJA* 44 (1946): 417–27.

Cardauns, Burkhart. "Juden und Spartaner zur hellenistisch-jüdischen Literatur." *Hermes* 95 (1967): 317–24.

Cartledge, Paul, and Antony Spawforth. *Hellenistic and Roman Sparta: A Tale of Two Cities.* London, 1989.

Cassas, Louis-François. *Voyage pittoresque de la Syrie, de la Palestine, et de la Basse-Egypt.* Paris, 1799.

Casson, Lionel. *Ships and Seamanship in the Ancient World.* Princeton, 1971.

————. *The Ancient Mariners.* 2d ed. Princeton, 1991.

Catling, H. W. "Archaeology in Greece, 1978–1979." *AR* 25 (1979): 3–42.

————. "Archaeology in Greece, 1988–1989." *AR* 35 (1989): 3–116.

Cattalini, Dorianna. "Aqua Iulia." In *LTUR*, 1: 66–67.

Chahin, M. *The Kingdom of Armenia.* London, 1987.

Chéhab, Maurice H. "Fouilles de Tyr: La nécropole, I. L'arc de triomphe." *BMus-Beyr* 33 (1983): 1–131.

————. *Tyre.* Translated by Leila Badre. Beirut, n.d..

Chen, Doron. "The Design of the Ancient Synagogues in Judea: Masada and Herodium." *BASOR* 239 (1980): 37–40.

Chronicon Paschale, 284–628 A.D. Translated by Michael Whitby and Mary Whitby. Translated Texts for Historians, 7. Liverpool, 1989.

Chrysos, Evangelos, ed. *Nikopolis.* Vol. 1. Preveza, 1987.

Cichorius, Conrad. *Römische Studien.* Leipzig, 1922.

Clermont-Ganneau, Charles. *Archaeological Researches in Palestine during the Years 1873–1874.* Vol.1. London, 1899.

Coarelli, Filippo. *Guide archeologiche Laterza: Roma.* Bari, 1980.

————. "Atrium Libertatis." In *LTUR*, 1: 133–35.

————. "Bibliotheca Asinii Pollionis." In *LTUR*, 1: 196.

————. "Campus Agrippae." In *LTUR*, 1: 217.

————. "Curia Hostilia." In *LTUR*, 1: 331–32.

Cohen, Boaz. "Art in Jewish Law." *Judaism* 3 (1954): 165–76.

Cohen, Getzel M. "The Hellenistic Military Colony: A Herodian Example," *TAPA* 103 (1972): 83–95.

Cohen, Shaye J. D. *Josephus in Galilee and Rome: His Vita and Development as a Historian.* Columbia Studies in the Classical Tradition, 8. Leiden, 1979.

Cohn, Erich W. "The Appendix of Antonia Rock in Jerusalem." *PEQ* 111 (1979): 41–52.

Cohn, L. "Ammonios" (# 17). In *RE*, 1 (1894): 1866–67.

————. "Eirenaios" (# 6). In *RE*, 10 (1905): 2120–24.

Coleiro, E. "Quis Tiphys?" *Latinitas* 22 (1974): 109–16.

Colpe, Carsten. "Hasmonäer." In *KlPauly*, 2 (1979): 950.

————. "Herodes" (# 1). In *KlPauly*, 2 (1979): 1090–92.

Colvin, Howard. *Architecture and the After-Life.* New Haven, 1991.

Comstock, Mary B., and Cornelius C. Vermeule. *Sculpture in Stone.* Boston, 1976.

Corbishley, Thomas. "A Note on the Date of the Syrian Governorship of M. Titius." *JRS* 24 (1934): 43–49.

———. "The Chronology of the Reign of Herod the Great." *JThS* 36 (1935): 22–32.

———. "Quirinius and the Census: A Re-Study of the Evidence." *Klio* 29 (1936): 81–93.

Corbo, Virgilio C. "Macheronte: La Reggia-Fortezza Erodiana." *Liber Annuus* 29 (1979): 316–26.

———. *Herodion I.* Studium Biblicum Franciscanum Collectio Maior, 20. Jerusalem, 1989.

Corbo, Virgilio C., and Stanislao Loffreda. "Nuove scoperte alla fortezza di Macheronte." *Liber Annuus* 31 (1981): 257–86.

Cotton, Hannah M., and Joseph Geiger. *Masada.* Vol. 2, *The Latin and Greek Documents.* Jerusalem, 1989.

Cotton, Hannah M., Omri Lernau, and Yuval Goren. "Fish Sauces from Herodian Masada," *JRA* 9 (1996): 223–38.

Crawford, M. H. "Greek Intellectuals and the Roman Aristocracy in the First Century B.C." In *Imperialism in the Ancient World,* ed. P. D. A. Garnsey and C. R. Whittaker, 193–207. Cambridge, 1978.

Croke, Brian. "Malalas, the Man and His Work." In *Studies in John Malalas,* ed. Elizabeth Jeffreys, Brian Croke, and Roger Scott, 1–25. Byzantina Australiensia, 6. Sydney, 1990.

Crook, John A. "Titus and Berenice." *AJP* 72 (1951): 162–75.

Crowfoot, J. W., G. M. Crowfoot, and Kathleen M. Kenyon. *Samaria-Sebaste.* Vol. 3: *The Objects from Samaria.* London, 1957.

Crowfoot, J. W., Kathleen M. Kenyon, and E. L. Sukenik. *Samaria-Sebaste.* Vol. 1, *The Buildings at Samaria.* London, 1942.

Dalman, G. "Nach Galiläa von 30. September bis 13. Oktober 1921." *PalJb* 18–19 (1922–23): 10–80.

Daly, Lloyd W. "Roman Study Abroad." *AJP* 71 (1950): 40–58.

Dar, Shimon. *Landscape and Pattern: An Archaeological Survey of Samaria, 800 B.C.E.—636 C.E.* BAR-IS, 308. London, 1986.

D'Arms, John H. *Romans on the Bay of Naples: A Social and Cultural Study of the Villas and Their Owners from 150 B.C. to A.D. 400.* Cambridge, Mass., 1970.

Delorme, Jean. *Gymnasion: Étude sur les monuments consacrés a l'éducation en Grèce.* BEFAR, 186. Paris, 1960.

Dentzer, Jean-Marie. "Six campagnes de fouilles à Sî': Développement et culture indigne en Syria méridionale." *Damaszener Mitteilungen* 2 (1985) 65–83.

Dentzer, Jean-Marie, and Jacqueline Dentzer. "Les fouilles de Sî' et la phase hellénistique en Syrie du sud." *CRAI* 1981: 78–102.

Derenbourg, J. *Essai sur l'historie et la géographie de la Palestine d'après les Thalmuds et les autres sources rabbiniques.* Vol. 1. Paris, 1867.

De Vries, Bert. "Archaeology in Jordan." *AJA* 96 (1992) 503–42.

De Vries, Bert, and Pierre Bikai. "Archaeology in Jordan." *AJA* 97 (1993): 457–520.

Dihle, Albrecht. "Ptolemaios" (# 75). *RE,* 46 (1959), 1861.

Dilke, O. A. W. *Greek and Roman Maps.* Ithaca, N.Y., 1985.

Diplock, P. Russell. "The Date of Askalon's Sculptured Panels and an Identification of the Caesarea Statues." *PEQ* 103 (1971): 13–16.

Dittenberger, Wilhelm, and Karl Purgold. *Olympia.* Vol. 5, *Die Inschriften von Olympia.* Amsterdam, 1966.

Dodge, Hazel. "Brick Construction in Rome, Greece, and Asia Minor." In *Roman Architecture in the Greek World,* ed. Sarah Macready and F. H. Thompson, 106–16. Society of Antiquaries of London Occasional Papers, n.s., 10. London, 1987.

———. "The Architectural Impact of Rome in the East." In *Architecture and Architectural Sculpture in the Roman Empire,* ed. Martin Henig, 108–20. Oxford University Committee for Archaeology Monograph 29. Oxford, 1990.

Donner, Herbert. "Kallirrhoë." *ZDPV* 79 (1963): 59–89.

Dothan, Moshe. "Acre." *RBibl* 82 (1975): 566–68.

———. "Akko: Interim Excavation Report, First Season, 1973/4." *BASOR* 224 (1976): 1–48.

———. "Ashdod." In *NEAEHL,* 93–102.

Dothan, Trude, and Immanuel Dunayevsky. "Tell Qasile." In *EAEHL,* 963–68.

Doukellis, P. N. "Actia Nicopolis: Idéologie impériale, structures urbaines et devéloppement régional." *JRA* 3 (1990): 399–406.

Downey, Glanville. "The Architectural Significance of the Use of the Words *Stoa* and *Basilike* in Classical Literature." *AJA* 41 (1937): 194–211.

———. "Q. Marcius Rex at Antioch." *CP* 32 (1937): 144–51.

———. "Imperial Building Records in Malalas." *BZ* 38 (1938): 1–15, 299–311.

———. *A History of Antioch in Syria from Seleucus to the Arab Conquest.* Princeton, 1961.

———. *Ancient Antioch.* Princeton, 1963.

Dreizehnter, Alois. "Pompeius als Städtegründer." *Chiron* 5 (1975): 213–45.

Drijvers, Hendrik Jan Willem. "Hatra, Palmyra und Edessa. Die Städte der syrisch-mesopotamischen Wüste in politischer, kulturgeschichtlicher und religionsgeschichtlicher Bedeuchtung." *ANRW* 2.8 (1977): 799–906.

Dudley, Donald R. *Urbs Roma.* N.p., 1967.

Dunand, Maurice. "Kanata et Κάναθα." *Syria* 11 (1930): 272–79.

———. *Byblos: Son histoire, ses ruines, ses légendes.* Beirut, 1963.

———. "Rapport préliminaire sur les fouilles de Sidon en 1964–1965." *BMusBeyr* 20 (1967): 27–44.

Dupont-Sommer, A. "Les fouilles du Ramat-el-Khalil, près d'Hébron." *Syria* 11 (1930): 16–32.

Durrbach, Félix. *Choix d'inscriptions de Délos.* Paris, 1921–22.

Dussaud, René. *Topographie historique de la Syrie antique et médiévale.* Paris, 1927.

Edwards, Ormond. "Herodian Chronology." *PEQ* 114 (1982): 29–42.

Epstein, Claire. "Hippos (Sussita)." In *NEAEHL,* 634–36.

Étienne, Robert. "La naissance de l'amphithéâtre: Le mot et la chose." *REL* 43 (1966): 213–20.

Evans, Harry B. "Agrippa's Water Plan." *AJA* 86 (1982): 401–11.

———. *Water Distribution in Ancient Rome: The Evidence of Frontinus.* Ann Arbor, 1994.

Everman, Diane. "Survey of the Coastal Area North of Caesarea and of the Aqueducts: Preliminary Report." In *Caesarea Papers*, 181–93. *JRA*, suppl. 5. 1992.

Feldman, Louis H. "Jewish 'Sympathizers' in Classical Literature and Inscriptions." *TAPA* 81 (1950): 200–208.

———. "Asinius Pollio and His Jewish Interests." *TAPA* 84 (1953): 73–80.

———. *Josephus and Modern Scholarship (1937–1980)*. Berlin, 1984.

———. "Asinius Pollio and Herod's Sons." *CQ* 35 (1985): 240–43.

———. *Jew and Gentile in the Ancient World*. Princeton, 1993.

Fenn, Richard. *The Death of Herod*. Cambridge, 1992.

Ferroni, Angela Maria. "Concordia, Aedes." In *LTUR*, 1: 316–20.

Fiehn, K. "Menedemos" (# 12). In *RE*, 29 (1931): 795.

Fiema, Zbigniew T., and Richard N. Jones. "The Nabataean King-List Revised: Further Observations on the Second Nabataean Inscription from Tell esh-Shuqafiya, Egypt." *ADAJ* 34 (1990): 239–48.

Filmer, W. E. "The Chronology of the Reign of Herod the Great." *JThS*, n.s., 17 (1966): 283–98.

Finley, M. A., and H. W. Pleket. *The Olympic Games: The First Thousand Years*. New York, 1976.

Fischer, Moshe. "Die Strassenstation von Ḥȯrvat Məṣād (Ḥirbet el-Qaṣr): Ein Betrag zur Geschichte des Weges von Jerusalem nach Emmaus." *ZDPV* 103 (1987): 117–36.

———. "Marble Imports and Local Stone in the Architectural Decoration of Roman Palestine: Marble Trade, Techniques, and Artistical Taste." In *Classical Marble: Geochemistry, Technology, Trade*, ed. Norman Herz and Marc Waelkens, 161–70. NATO ASI Series, 153. Dordrecht, 1988.

———. *Das korinthische Kapitell im Alten Israel in der hellenistischen und römischen Periode*. Mainz, 1990.

———. "Some Remarks on Architectural Decoration in Palestine during the Hellenistic Period (3rd–1st Centuries B.C.E.)." In *Akten*, 434–36.

———. "The Basilica of Ascalon: Marble, Imperial Art and Architecture in Roman Palestine." In *The Roman and Byzantine Near East: Some Recent Archaeological Research*, 121–50. *JRA*, suppl. 14 (1995).

Fittschen, Klaus. "Zur Herkunft und Entstehung des 2. Stils—Probleme und Argumente." In *Hellenismus in Mittelitalien*, ed. Paul Zanker, 539–63. *AbhGött* 97 (1976).

Fitzmyer, Joseph A. "The Languages of Palestine in the First Century A.D." *Catholic Biblical Quarterly* 32 (1970): 501–31.

Flinder, Alexander. "A Piscina at Caesarea—A Preliminary Survey." *IEJ* 26 (1976): 77–80.

———. "The Piscinas at Caesarea and Lapithos." In *Harbour Archaeology*, ed. Avner Raban, 173–78. BAR-IS, 257. London, 1985.

Fluss, M. "C. Sosius" (# 2). In *RE*, 2, 15th ser. (1927): 1176–80.

Foerster, Gideon. "Hellenistic Baths in Israel." In *Akten*, 439.

———. "Beth-Shean at the Foot of the Mound." In *NEAEHL*, 223–35.

———. "Herodium." In *NEAEHL*, 618–21.

———. *Masada*. Vol. 5, *Art and Architecture*. Jerusalem, 1995.

Fossey, John M. *Topography and Population of Ancient Boiotia.* Chicago, 1988.

Fraenkel, Eduard. "Livius" (# 10a). In *RE*, suppl. 5 (1931): 598–607.

———. *Horace.* Oxford, 1957.

Fraser, P. M. *Ptolemaic Alexandria.* 3 vols. Oxford, 1972.

———. "A Syriac *Notitia Urbis Alexandrinae.*" *JEA* 37 (1951): 103–8.

French, E. B. "Archaeology in Greece, 1993–1994." *AR* 40 (1994): 3–84.

Frey, Jean-Baptiste. *Corpus of Jewish Inscriptions.* Vol. 1. New York, 1975.

Freyberger, Klaus. "Untersuchungen zur Baugeschichte des Jupiter-Heiligtums in Damaskus." *Damaszener Mitteilungen* 4 (1989): 61–86.

Frézouls, Edmond. "Recherches sur les théatres de l'orient syrien." *Syria* 36 (1959): 202–27.

Fritz, K. von. "Philostratos" (# 7). In *RE*, 19 (1941): 123–24.

Frova, Antonio, et al. *Scavi di Caesarea Maritima.* Rome, 1966.

Frumkin, Amos. "The Water Supply System of Sebastiya." In *AAP*, 157–67.

Fulco, W. J., and F. Zayadine. "Coins from Samaria-Sebaste." *ADAJ* 25 (1981): 197–225.

Gabba, Emilio. "The Historians and Augustus." In *Caesar Augustus: Seven Aspects*, ed. Fergus Millar and Erich Segal, 61–88. Oxford, 1984.

———. "The Finances of King Herod." In *Greece and Rome in Eretz Israel: Collected Essays*, ed. A. Kasher, U. Rappaport, and G. Fuks, 160–68. Jerusalem, 1990.

Gagé, J. *Recherches sur les jeux séculaires.* Collection d'études latines, 11. Paris, 1934.

Garbrecht, Günther, and Jehuda Peleg. "Die Wasserversorgung geschichtlicher Wüstenfestungen am Jordantal." *AntW* 20.2 (1989): 2–20.

———. "The Water Supply of the Desert Fortresses in the Jordan Valley." *BiblArch* 57 (1994): 161–70.

Gardiner, E. Norman. *Athletics of the Ancient World.* Oxford, 1930.

———. *Olympia: Its History and Remains.* Washington, D.C., 1973.

Gardner, E. A. "Inscriptions from Cos, etc." *JHS* 6 (1885): 248–60.

Garstang, John. "Askalon." *PEFQ* 1924: 24–35.

Gärtner, Hans. "Moses Chorenachi." In *KlPauly*, 3 (1979): 1438–39.

Gatt, G. "Bemerkungen über Gaza und seine Umgebung." *ZDPV* 7 (1884): 1–14.

Geffcken, J. "Krinagoras." In *RE*, 22 (1922): 1859–64.

Gelzer, Matthias. *Caesar: Der Politiker und Staatsmann.* Wiesbaden, 1960.

Gersht, Riva. "The Tyche of Caesarea Maritima." *PEQ* 116 (1984): 110–14.

Geva, Hillel. "The 'Tower of David'—Phasael or Hippicus?" *IEJ* 31 (1981): 57–65.

———. "Excavations in the Citadel of Jerusalem, 1979–1980: Preliminary Report." *IEJ* 33 (1983): 55–71.

———. "Jerusalem: The Second Temple Period." In *NEAEHL*, 735–56.

Ghini, Giuseppina. "Gymnasium Neronis." In *LTUR*, 2: 374.

Gianfrotta, Piero A. "Harbor Structures of the Augustan Age in Italy." In *CMR*, 65–76.

Gibson, Shimon. "The 1961–67 Excavations in the Armenian Garden, Jerusalem." *PEQ* 119 (1987): 81–96.

Gihon, M. "Idumea and the Herodian Limes." *IEJ* 17 (1967): 27–42.

Ginouvès, René, and Roland Martin. *Dictionnaire méthodique de l'architecture grecque et romaine.* CEFR, 84 (1985–92).

Ginsburg, Mich[a]el S. *Rome et la Judée.* Paris, 1928.

———. "Sparta and Judaea." *CP* 29 (1934): 117–22.

Gisinger, F. "Timagenes" (# 2). In *RE*, 2d ser., 11 (1936): 1063–73.

Giuliani, Cairoli F. and Patrizia Verducchi. "Basilica Iulia." In *LTUR*, 1: 177–79.

Gjerstad, Einer. "Die Unsprungsgeschichte der römischen Kaiserfora." *OpArch* 3 (1944): 40–72.

Gleason, Kathryn L. "Garden Excavations at the Herodian Winter Palace in Jericho, 1985–7." *Bulletin of the Anglo-Israel Archaeological Society* 7 (1987–88): 21–39.

———. "The Garden Portico of Pompey the Great." *Expedition* 32.2 (1990): 4–13.

———. "Ruler and Spectacle: The Promontory Palace." In *CMR*, 208–27.

Glucker, Carol A. M. *The City of Gaza in the Roman and Byzantine Periods.* BAR-IS, 325. London, 1987.

Glueck, Nelson. "Some Ancient Towns in the Plains of Moab." *BASOR* 91 (October 1943): 7–26.

———. *Explorations in Eastern Palestine IV. AASOR* 25–28 (1945–49 [1951]).

———. *Deities and Dolphins.* New York, 1965.

Goldschmidt-Lehmann, Ruth P. "The Second (Herodian) Temple, Selected Bibliography." *JC* 1 (1981): 336–59.

Golvin, Jean-Claude. *L'amphithéâtre romain: Essai sur la théorisation de sa forme et des ses fonctions.* Paris, 1988.

Golvin, Jean-Claude, and Philippe Leveau. "L'amphithéâtre et le théâtre-amphithéâtre de Cherchel: Monuments à spectacle et histoire urbaine à Caesarea de Maurétanie." *MEFRA* 91 (1979): 817–43.

Gomme, A. W. *The Population of Athens in the Fifth and Fourth Centuries B.C.* Oxford, 1933.

Goodfellow, Charlotte E. *Roman Citizenship.* Lancaster, Pa., 1935.

Goodman, Martin. *The Ruling Class of Judaea.* Cambridge, 1987.

———. "Judaea." In *CAH*, 2d ed. (1996) 10: 737–81.

Gough, Michael. "Anazarbus." *AnatSt* 2 (1952): 85–150.

Gracey, M. H. "The Armies of the Judaean Client Kings." In *The Defence of the Roman and Byzantine East*, ed. Philip Freeman and David Kennedy, 311–23. BAR-IS, 297. London, 1986.

Graf, David F. "The Nabataeans and the Decapolis." In *The Defence of the Roman and Byzantine East*, ed. Philip Freeman and David Kennedy, 785–96. BAR-IS, 297. London, 1986.

———. "Hellenisation and the Decapolis." *ARAM* 4 (1992): 1–48.

Grafman, R. "Herod's Foot and Robinson's Arch." *IEJ* 20 (1970): 60–66.

Grant, Michael. *Herod the Great.* London, 1971.

———. *The Jews in the Roman World.* New York, 1973.

The Greek Anthology: The Garland of Philip. Edited by A. S. F. Gow and D. L. Page. Cambridge, 1968.

Greenhalgh, Peter. *Pompey: The Roman Alexander.* London, 1980.

Grether, Gertrude. "Livia and the Roman Imperial Cult." *AJP* 67 (1946): 222–52.

Groag, E. "C. Julius Agrippa" (# 50). In *RE*, 19 (1917): 143.

Groebe, P. "C. Asinius Pollio Cn. f." (# 25). In *RE*, 2 (1896): 1589–1602.

Gros, Pierre. "Apollo Palatinus." In *LTUR*, 1: 54–57.

Gruen, Erich S. *The Last Generation of the Roman Republic*. 1975. Reprint, Berkeley, 1995.

Gsell, Stéphane. *Histoire ancienne de l'Afrique du nord*. 8 vols. Paris, 1914–28.

Gurval, Robert Alan. *Actium and Augustus: The Politics and Emotions of Civil War*. Ann Arbor, 1995.

Halfmann, Helmut. *Itinera principum*. Heidelberger Althistorische Beiträge und Epigraphische Studien, 2. Stuttgart, 1986.

Hall, Clayton M. *Nicolaus of Damascus' Life of Augustus*. Menasha, Wis., 1923.

Hamburger, H. "The Coin Issues of the Roman Administration from the Mint of Caesarea Maritima." *IEJ* 20 (1970): 81–91.

Hammer, Jacob. *Prolegomena to an Edition of the Panegyricus Messalae: The Military and Political Career of M. Valerius Messala Corvinus*. New York, 1925.

Hammond, Philip C. *The Excavation of the Main Theater at Petra, 1961–1962: Final Report*. London, 1965.

Hanfmann, George M. A. *Sardis from Prehistoric to Roman Times: Results of the Archaeological Exploration of Sardis, 1958–1975*. Cambridge, Mass., 1983.

Hanslik, Rudolf. "M. Titius" (# 18). In *RE*, 2d ser., 6 (1937): 1559–1652.

———. "M. Valerius Messalla Corvinus" (# 261). In *RE*, 2d ser., 15 (1955): 131–57.

Hanson, John Arthur. *Roman Theater-Temples*. Princeton, 1959.

Harder, Günther. "Herodes-Burgen und Herodes-Städte im Jordangraben." *ZDPV* 78 (1962): 49–63.

Harper, R. P. "Caesarea Cappadociae." In *PECS*, 182.

Harris, H. A. *Greek Athletics and the Jews*. Cardiff, 1976.

Head, Barclay V. *Historia Numorum: A Manual of Greek Numismatics*. Oxford, 1911.

———. *Catalogue of the Greek Coins of Lydia*. = BMC Lydia. 1901. Reprint, Bologna, 1964.

Hellmann, Marie-Christine. "A propos d'un lexique des termes d'architecture grecque." In *Comptes et inventaires dans la cité grecque: Actes du colloque international d'épigraphie tenu à Neuchâtel du 23 au 26 septembre 1986 en l'honneur de Jacques Tréheux*, ed. Denis Knoepfler, 239–61. Neuchâtel, 1988.

Herbert, Sharon. "Tel Anafa." In *NEAEHL*, 58–61.

Hesberg, Henner von, and Silvio Panciera. *Das Mausoleum des Augustus: Der Bau und Seine Inschriften*. Bayerische Akademie der Wissenschaften, Philosophisch-Historische Klasse, Abhandlungen, n.s., 108. Munich 1994.

Hill, George Francis. *Catalogue of the Greek Coins of Palestine (Galilee, Samaria, and Judaea)*. =BMC Palestine. London, 1914.

———. *Catalogue of the Greek Coins of Lycaonia, Isauria, and Cilicia*. =BMC Lycaonia, Isauria, and Cilicia. 1900. Reprint, Bologna, 1964.

Hirschfeld, Yizhar. *A Guide to Antiquity Sites in Tiberias*. Jerusalem, 1992.

———. "Tiberias." In *NEAEHL*, 1464–70.

———. "The Early Roman Bath and Fortress at Ramat Hanadiv near Caesarea." In *The Roman and Byzantine Near East: Some Recent Archaeological Research. JRA*, suppl. 14 (1995): 28–55.

Hirschfeld, Yizhar, and R. Birger-Calderon. "Early Roman and Byzantine Estates near Caesarea." *IEJ* 41 (1991): 81–111.

Hizmi, Hanania. "Khirbet el-Beiyudat." In *NEAEHL*, 181–82.

Hodge, A. Trevor. *Roman Aqueducts and Water Supply*. London, 1992.

Hoehner, Harold W. *Herod Antipas*. Society for New Testament Studies Monograph 17. Cambridge, 1972.

Hoepfner, Wolfram. "Nikopolis: Zur Stadtgründung des Augustus." In *Nikopolis*, vol. 1, ed. Chrysos, 129–33.

————. "Von Alexandreia über Pergamon nach Nikopolis: Städtebau und Stadtbilder Hellenistischer Zeit." In *Akten*, 275–85.

Hohlfelder, Robert L. "The Building of the Roman Harbour at Kenchreai: Old Technology in a New Era." In *Harbour Archaeology*, 81–86. BAR-IS, 257. London, 1985.

————. "Caesarea's Master Harbor Builders: Lessons Learned, Lessons Applied?" In *CMR*, 77–101.

Holloway, R. Ross. "The Tomb of Augustus and the Princes of Troy." *AJA* 70 (1966): 171–73.

Hölscher, G. "Πανίας." In *RE*, 36 (1949): 594–600.

Holum, Kenneth G., and Avner Raban. "Caesarea." In *NEAEHL*, 270–72.

————. "Caesarea: The Joint Expedition's Excavations, Excavations in the 1980s and 1990s, and Summary." In *NEAEHL*, 282–86.

Holum, Kenneth G., Robert L. Hohlfelder, Robert J. Bull, and Avner Raban. *King Herod's Dream: Caesarea on the Sea*. New York, 1988.

Honigmann, E. "Mariame" (# 3). In *RE*, 14 (1930): 1745–46.

Horn, S. H. "Heshbon." In *EAEHL*, 510–14.

Horowitz, Gabriel. "Town Planning of Hellenistic Marisa: A Reappraisal of the Excavations after Eighty Years." *PEQ* 112 (1980): 93–111.

Hultsch, F. "Dositheos" (# 9). In *RE*, 10 (1905): 1607–8.

Humphrey, John H. *Roman Circuses: Arenas for Chariot Racing*. London, 1986.

————. "'Amphitheatrical' Hippo-Stadia." In *CMR*, 121–29.

Hunt, D. W. S. "An Archaeological Survey of the Classical Antiquities of the Island of Chios Carried Out between the Months of March and July 1938." *BSA* 41 (1940–45): 29–52.

Hurst, Henry. "Domus Gai." In *LTUR*, 2: 106–8.

Huzar, Eleanor Goltz. *Mark Antony: A Biography*. London, 1978.

Iliffe, J. H. "A Copy of the Crouching Aphrodite." *QDAP* 2 (1933): 110–12.

Ingholt, Harald. "A Colossal Head from Memphis, Severan or Augustan?" *JARCE* 2 (1963): 125–42.

Isaac, Benjamin. "A Donation for Herod's Temple in Jerusalem." *IEJ* 33 (1983): 86–92.

Ita of Sion, Marie. "The Antonia Fortress." *PEQ* 100 (1968): 139–43.

Jacobson, David M. "Ideas concerning the Plan of Herod's Temple." *PEQ* 112 (1980): 33–40.

————. "The Plan of the Ancient Haram el-Khalil in Hebron." *PEQ* 113 (1981): 73–80.

————. "The Design of the Fortress of Herodium." *ZDPV* 100 (1984): 127–36.

————. "King Herod's 'Heroic' Public Image." *RBibl* 95 (1988): 386–403.

————. "The Plan of Herod's Temple." *Bulletin of the Anglo-Israel Archaeological Society* 10 (1990): 36–66.

Jacobson, David M., and Shimon Gibson, "A Monumental Stairway on the Temple Mount." *IEJ* 45 (1995): 162–70.

Jacobson, David M. , and M. P. Weitzman. "What Was Corinthian Bronze?" *AJA* 96 (1992): 237–47.

Jacoby, Felix. "Hekataios aus Abdera" (# 4). In *RE*, 14 (1912): 2750–69.

———. "Iuba II" (# 2). In *RE*, 9 (1916): 2384–95.

———. *Die Fragmente der griechischen Historiker.* =FGrHist. Berlin and Leiden, 1923–.

Jameson, Shelagh. "Chronology of the Campaigns of Aelius Gallus and C. Petronius." *JRS* 58 (1968): 71–84.

Jerusalem Revealed: Archaeology in the Holy City, 1968–1974. Jerusalem, 1975.

Jex-Blake, K., and E. Sellers. *The Elder Pliny's Chapters on the History of Art.* Edited by Raymond V. Schoder. 2d American ed. Chicago, 1976.

Jidejian, Nina. *Byblos through the Ages.* Beirut, 1968.

Jolivet, Vincent. "Domus Pompeiorum." In *LTUR*, 2: 159–60.

Jones, A. H. M. "The Urbanization of Palestine." *JRS* 21 (1931): 78–85.

———. *The Herods of Judaea.* Oxford, 1938.

———. "I Appeal unto Caesar." In *Studies Presented to David Moore Robinson, vol.* 2, ed. George E. Mylonas and Doris Raymond, 918–30. St. Louis, 1953.

———. *The Cities of the Eastern Roman Provinces.* 2d ed. Oxford, 1971.

Josephus, Flavius. *Josephus with an English Translation.* Loeb ed. 10 vols.: 1–4 by H. St. J. Thackeray, 5 by H. St. J. Thackeray and Ralph Marcus, 6–7 by Ralph Marcus, 8 by Ralph Marcus and Allen Wikgren, and 9–10 by L. H. Feldman. Cambridge, Mass., 1926–65.

Jowkowsky, Martha Sharp, ed. *The Heritage of Tyre: Essays on the History, Archaeology, and Preservation of Tyre.* Dubuque, 1992.

Kadman, Leo. *The Coins of Caesarea Maritima.* Corpus Nummorum Palaestinensium, 2. Jerusalem, 1957.

Kahn, Lisa. "King Herod's Temple of Roma and Augustus at Caesarea Maritima." In *CMR*, 130–45.

Kaimio, Jorma. *The Romans and the Greek Language.* Commentationes Humanarum Litterarum, 64. Helsinki, 1979.

Kanael, B. "The Partition of Judea by Gabinius." *IEJ* 7 (1957): 98–106.

Kashtan, Nadav. "Akko-Ptolemais: A Maritime Metropolis in Hellenistic and Early Roman Times, 332 BCE–70 CE, As Seen through the Literary Sources." *Mediterranean Historical Review* 3 (1988): 37–53.

Keil, J. "P. Vedius Pollio" (# 8). In *RE*, 2d ser., 15 (1955): 568–70.

Keil, Josef, and Adolf Wilhelm. *Denkmäler aus dem Rauhen Kilikien.* MAMA, 3. 1931.

Kelso, James L., and Dimitri C. Baramki. *Excavation at New Testament Jericho and Khirbet en-Nitla.* AASOR 29–30 (1949–51 [1955]).

Kennedy, David. "Syria." In *CAH*, 2d ed. (1996), 10: 703–36.

Kennedy, George. *The Art of Persuasion in Greece.* Princeton, 1963.

Kenyon, Kathleen. *Jerusalem: Excavating 3000 Years of History.* New York, 1967.

———. "Some Aspects of the Impact of Rome on Palestine." *JRAS* 1970: 181–91.

———. *Digging Up Jerusalem.* London, 1974.

Kindler, Arie. "Akko, a City of Many Names." *BASOR* 231 (1978): 51–55.

Klein, S. "Batira-Petor." *BJPES* 4 (1936): 33–34.

Kleiner, Diana E. E. "The Great Friezes of the Ara Pacis Augustae: Greek Sources, Roman Derivatives, and Augustan Social Policy." *MEFRA* 90 (1978): 753–85.

———. *Roman Sculpture.* New Haven, 1992.

Kochavi, Moshe. "The History and Archeology of Aphek-Antipatris." *BiblArch* 44 (1981): 75–86.

Kockel, Valentin. "Forum Augustum." In *LTUR*, 2: 289–95.

Koeppel, Gerhard. "Die historischen Reliefs der römischen Kaiserzeit, V: Ara Pacis Augustae, Teil 1." *BJb* 187 (1987): 101–57.

Kokkinos, Nikos. "A Coin of Herod the Great Commemorating the City of Sebaste." *Liber Annuus* 35 (1985): 303–6.

———. "The Herodian Dynasty: Origins, Role in Society, and Eclipse." Ph.D. diss., Oxford, 1993.

Kondis, Ioannis D. "Zum Antiken Stadtbauplan von Rhodos." *AM* 73 (1958): 146–58.

Konstantinopoulos, Gregory. "Rhodes: New Finds and Old Problems." Translated by J. Walter Graham. *Archaeology* 21 (1968): 115–23.

———. "Städtebau im Hellenistischen Rhodos." In *Akten*, 207–13.

Korfmann, Manfred. "Troia—Reinigungs- und Dokumentationsarbeiten 1987, Ausgrabungen 1988 und 1989." *Studia Troica* 1 (1991): 1–34.

Kraeling, Carl H. "The History of Gerasa." In *Gerasa: City of the Decapolis*, ed. id., 27–69. New Haven, 1938.

———. *Excavations at Dura-Europos.* Vol. 8, pt. 1, *The Synagogue.* New Haven, 1956.

Kraft, Konrad. "Der Sinn des Mausoleums des Augustus." *Historia* 16 (1957): 189–206.

Krause, Clemens. "Domus Tiberiana." In *LTUR*, 2: 189–97.

Krawczuk, Aleksander. "Herod Wielki i Rzym." *Sprawozdanie PAN* (Kraków) 1963: 144–45.

———. *Herod Król Judei.* Warsaw, 1965.

———. "Herodowy Mecenat." *Meander* (Warsaw) 33 (1978): 3–5.

Kuhn, Heinz-Wolfgang, and Rami Arav. "The Bethsaida Excavations: Historical and Archaeological Approaches." In *The Future of Early Christianity: Essays in Honor of Helmut Koester*, ed. Birger A. Pearson, 77–106. Minneapolis, 1991.

Kushnir-Stein, Alla. "The Predecessor of Caesarea: On the Identification of Demetrias in South Phoenicia." In *The Roman and Byzantine Near East: Some Recent Archaeological Research. JRA*, suppl. 14 (1995): 9–14.

Kuttner, Ann L. *Dynasty and Empire in the Age of Augustus: The Case of the Boscoreale Cups.* Berkeley, 1995.

La Rocca, Eugenio. *Ara Pacis Augustae.* Rome, 1983.

Lämmer, Manfred. "Eine Propaganda-Aktion des König Herodes in Olympia." In *Perspektiven der Sportwissenschaft: Jahrbuch der Deutschen Sporthochschule, Köln, 1972*, 160–73. Schorndorf, 1973.

———. "The Introduction of Greek Contests into Jerusalem through Herod the Great and Its Political Significance." In *Physical Education and Sports in the Jewish History and Culture*, ed. Uriel Simri, 18–38. N.p., 1973.

———. "Griechische Wettkämpfe in Jerusalem und ihre politischen Hintergründe." *Kölner Beiträge zur Sportwissenschaft* 2 (1974): 182–227.

————. "Die Aktischen Spiele von Nikopolis." *Stadion* 12–13 (1986–87): 27–38.

Lang, David Marshall. *Armenia: Cradle of Civilization.* London, 1970.

Laqueur, Richard. "Teukros" (# 4). In *RE,* 2d ser., 9 (1934): 1131–32.

————. "Nikolaos" (# 20). In *RE,* 33 (1936): 362–424.

————. *Der jüdische Historiker Flavius Josephus.* 1920. New ed. Darmstadt, 1970.

Lasserre, François. "Strabon devant l'Empire romain." *ANRW* 2.30 (1982–83): 867–96.

Lassus, Jean. "La ville d'Antioche à l'époque romaine d'après l'archéologie." *ANRW* 2.8 (1977): 54–101.

Lauffray, Jean. "Forums et monuments de Bèryte." *BMusBeyr* 7 (1944–45): 13–80.

————. "Beyrouth archéologie et histoire, époques gréco-romaines. I. Periode hellénistique et Haut-Empire romain." *ANRW* 2.8 (1977): 135–63.

Lawrence, A. W. *Greek Architecture.* 4th ed. Revised by R. E. Tomlinson. Harmondsworth, 1983.

Le Pera, Susanna. "Aqua Virgo." In *LTUR,* 1: 72–73.

Leaf, Walter. "Strabo and Demetrios of Skepsis." *BSA* 22 (1916–18): 23–47.

Leon, Harry J. "The Synagogue of the Herodians." *JAOS* 49 (1929): 318–21.

————. *The Jews of Ancient Rome.* Philadelphia, 1960.

Leroy, Jules. "Nouvelles découvretes archéologiques relatives à Édesse." *Syria* 38 (1961): 159–69.

Leveau, Philippe. *Caesarea de Maurétanie: Une ville romaine et ses campagnes.* CEFR, 70 (1984).

Levi Della Vida, G. "Una bilingue greco-nabatea a Coo." *ClRh* 9 (1938): 139–48.

Levick, Barbara. *Roman Colonies in Southern Asia Minor.* Oxford, 1967.

————. *Tiberius the Politician.* London, 1976.

Levine, Lee I. *Caesarea under Roman Rule.* Studies in Judaism in Late Antiquity, 7. Leiden, 1975.

————. *Roman Caesarea: An Archaeological-Topographical Study. Qedem* 2. Jerusalem, 1975.

————. "R. Simeon b. Yoḥai and the Purification of Tiberias: History and Tradition." *HUCA* 49 (1978): 143–85.

————. "Towards an Appraisal of Herod as a Builder." *JC* 1 (1981): 62–66.

————. "Josephus' Description of the Jerusalem Temple: *War, Antiquities,* and Other Sources." In *Josephus and the History of the Greco-Roman Period: Essays in Memory of Morton Smith,* ed. Fausto Parente and Joseph Sievers, 233–46. Studia Post-Biblica, 41. Leiden, 1994.

Levine, Lee I., and Ehud Netzer. *Excavations at Caesarea Maritima, 1975, 1976, 1979: Final Report. Qedem* 21. Jerusalem, 1986.

————. "Caesarea: Excavations in the 1970s." In *NEAEHL,* 280–82.

Lieberman, Saul. *Greek in Jewish Palestine.* 2d ed. New York, 1965.

Lifshitz, Baruch. "Inscriptions latines de Césarée (Caesarea Palaestinae)." *Latomus* 22 (1963): 783–84.

————. "Césarée de Palestine, son histoire et ses institutions." *ANRW* 2.8 (1972): 490–518.

————. "Jérusalem sous la domination romaine. Histoire de la ville depuis la conquête de Pompée jusqu' à Constantin (63 a.c—325 p.c)." *ANRW* 2.8 (1977): 444–89.

Lindsay, Hugh. "Augustus and Eurycles." *RhM* 135 (1992): 290–97.

Ling, Roger. *Roman Painting.* Cambridge, 1991.

Lipschitz, Nili, and Simcha Lev-Yadun. "The Botanical Remains from Masada: Identification of the Plant Species and Possible Origin of the Remnants." *BASOR* 274 (1989): 27–32.

Loffreda, Stanislao. "Alcuni vasi ben datati della fortezza di Macheronte." *Liber Annuus* 30 (1980): 377–402.

Lyttleton, Margaret, and Thomas Blagg. "Sculpture in Nabataean Petra, and the Question of Roman Influence." In *Architecture and Architectural Sculpture in the Roman Empire,* ed. Martin Henig, 91–107. Oxford University Committee for Archaeology Monograph 29. Oxford, 1990.

MacAdam, Henry Innes. *Studies in the History of the Roman Province of Arabia: The Northern Sector.* BAR-IS, 295. London, 1986.

Macalister, R. A. S. "The Nicophorieh Tomb." *PEFQ* 1901: 397–402.

MacDonald, George. "The Coinage of Tigranes I." *NC,* 2d ser., 4 (1902): 193–201.

MacDonald, M. C. A. "Herodian Echoes in the Syrian Desert." In *Trade, Contact, and the Movement of Peoples in the Eastern Mediterranean: Studies in Honour of J. Basil Hennessy,* ed. Stephen Bourke and Jean-Paul Descoeudres, 285–90. MeditArch, suppl. 3. Sydney, 1995.

MacDonald, William L. "Tyrus." *PECS,* 944.

———. *The Architecture of the Roman Empire II: An Urban Appraisal.* Yale Publications in the History of Art, 35. New Haven, 1986.

MacDonald, William L., and John A. Pinto. *Hadrian's Villa and Its Legacy.* New Haven, 1995.

MacKay, T. S. "Elaeussa, Later Sebaste." In *PECS,* 294–95.

MacMullen, Ramsay. "Provincial Languages in the Roman Empire." *AJP* 87 (1966): 1–17.

Macurdy, Grace H. "Julia Berenice." *AJP* 56 (1935): 246–53.

McDermott, William C. "C. Asinius Pollio, Catullus, and C. Julius Caesar." *AncW* 2 (1979): 55–60.

McKay, Alexander G. *Houses, Villas and Palaces in the Roman World.* Ithaca, N.Y., 1975.

McKenzie, Judith. *The Architecture of Petra.* Oxford, 1990.

Madden, Frederic W. *History of Jewish Coinage and of Money in the Old and New Testament.* 1864. Reprint, New York, 1967.

Mader, Evaristus. "Les fouilles allemandes au Ramat el Khalil." *RBibl* 39 (1930): 84–117.

———. *Mambre.* Freiburg, 1957.

Magie, David, Jr. "The Mission of Agrippa to the Orient in 23 B.C." *CP* 3 (1908): 145–52.

———. *Roman Rule in Asia Minor to the End of the Third Century after Christ.* Princeton, 1950.

Magness, Jodi. "The North Wall of Aelia Capitolina." In *Essays in Honor of James A.*

Sauer, ed. Lawrence E. Stager and Joseph A. Greene. Cambridge, Mass., forthcoming.

Maisler, B. "The Excavations at Tell Qasile: Preliminary Report. *IEJ* 1 (1950–51): 61–76, 125–40, 194–218.

———. "The Excavation of Tell Qasile." *BiblArch* 14.2 (1951): 43–49.

———. "Beth She'arim, Gaba, and Harosheth of the Peoples." *HUCA* 24 (1952–53): 75–84.

Malalas, John. *The Chronicle of John Malalas.* Translated by Elizabeth Jeffreys, Michael Jeffries, and Roger Scott. Byzantina Australiensia, 4. Melbourne, 1986.

Mallon, Alexis. "Deux forteresses au pied des monts de Moab." *Biblica* 14 (1933): 400–407.

Mantzoulinou-Richards, Ersie. "From Syros: A Dedicatory Inscription of Herodes the Great from an Unknown Building." *AncW* 18 (1988): 87–99.

Ma'oz, Zvi Uri. "On the Hasmonean and Herodian Town Plan of Jerusalem." *ErIsr* 18 (1985): 46–57.

———. "Banias." In *NEAEHL,* 136–43.

Marble in Antiquity: Collected Papers of John Bryan Ward-Perkins. Edited by Hazel Dodge and Bryan Ward-Perkins. Archaeological Monographs of the British School at Rome, 6. London, 1992.

Marrou, H. I. *A History of Education in Antiquity.* Translated by George Lamb. New York, 1964.

Maurer, Christian. "Der Struthionteich und die Burg Antonia." *ZDPV* 80 (1964): 137–49.

Mazar, Amihai. "Jerusalem." In *Die Wasserversorgung Antiker Städte,* 185–88. Geschichte der Wasserversorgung, 2. Mainz, 1987.

———. "A Survey of the Aqueducts Leading to Jerusalem." In *AAP,* 169–95.

———. "Beth-Shean: Tel Beth-Shean and the Northern Cemetery." In *NEAEHL,* 214–23.

Mazar, Benjamin. "The Excavation South and West of the Temple Mount in Jerusalem: The Herodian Period." *BiblArch* 33 (1970): 47–60.

———. *The Excavations in the Old City of Jerusalem near the Temple Mount.* Jerusalem. 1971.

———. "Les fouilles près du mont du temple à Jerusalem." *Dossiers de l'archéologie* 10 (May–June 1975): 34–39.

———. "Herodian Jerusalem in the Light of the Excavations South and South-West of the Temple Mount." *IEJ* 28 (1978): 230–37.

Meritt, Benjamin D. "Greek Inscriptions." *Hesperia* 21 (1952): 340–80.

Merkel, Helmut, and Dieter Korol. "Herodes der Grosse." In *Reallexikon für Antike und Christenthum,* 14: 815–49. Stuttgart, 1988.

Meshel, Ze'ev, and David Amit. "Water Supply to Cyprus Fortress." *AAP,* 229–42.

Meshorer, Ya'akov. *Ancient Jewish Coinage.* Vol. 2, *Herod the Great through Bar Cochba.* Dix Hills, N.Y., 1982.

Meyers, Eric M. "Roman Sepphoris in Light of New Archeological Evidence and Recent Research." In *The Galilee in Late Antiquity,* ed. Lee I. Levine, 321–38. New York, 1992.

Meyers, Eric M., Ehud Netzer, and Carol Meyers. "Sepphoris (Sippori), 1985 (I)." *IEJ* 35 (1985): 295–97.

———. "Sepphoris (Sippori), 1986 (I)—Joint Sepphoris Project." *IEJ* 37 (1987): 275–78.

———. "Sepphoris (Sippori), 1987 and 1988." *IEJ* 40 (1990): 219–23.

Meyshan, Josef. "The Symbols on the Coinage of Herod the Great and Their Meanings." *PEQ* 91 (1959): 109–20.

Millar, Fergus. "The Roman *Coloniae* of the Near East: A Study of Cultural Relations." In *Roman Eastern Policy and Other Studies in Roman History*, ed. Heikki Solin and Mika Kajava, 7–58. Commentationes Humanarum Litterarum, 91. Helsinki, 1990.

———. *The Roman Near East, 31 B.C.—A.D. 337.* Cambridge, Mass., 1993.

Miller, Stephen G. *Arete: Greek Sports from Ancient Sources.* 2d expanded ed. Berkeley, 1991.

Mishnah: A New Translation by Jacob Neusner. New Haven, 1988.

Mitchell, Stephen. "Imperial Building in the Eastern Roman Provinces." *HSCP* 91 (1987): 333–65.

———. *Anatolia: Land, Men, and Gods in Asia Minor.* 2 vols. Oxford, 1993.

Mitford, Terence Bruce. "Roman Rough Cilicia." *ANRW* 2.7 (1980): 1230–61.

Modona, Aldo Neppi. *L'isola di Coo nell'antichità classica.* Memorie dell'Istituto storico-archeologico di Rodi, 1. Rhodes, 1933.

Momigliano, Arnoldo. "Herod of Judaea." In *CAH*, 1st ed., corrected (1966), 10: 316–39.

Monceaux, Paul, and Léonce Brossé. "Chalcis ad Belum: Notes sur l'histoire et les ruines de la ville." *Syria* 6 (1925): 339–50.

Moretti, Giuseppe. *Ara Pacis Augustae.* Rome [1948].

Moretti, Luigi. *Iscrizioni agonistiche greche.* Studi pubblicati dall'Istituto italiano per la storia antica, 12. Rome, 1953.

Morselli, Chiara. "Forum Iulium." In *LTUR*, 2: 299–306.

Moses Khorenats'i. *History of the Armenians.* Translated with commentary by Robert W. Thomson. Cambridge, Mass., 1978.

Moulton, Warren J. "A Visit to Qarn Sartabeh." *BASOR* 62 (April 1936): 14–18.

Mouterde, René, and Jean Lauffray. *Beyrouth ville romaine: Histoire et monuments.* Beirut, n.d.

Mowry, Lucetta. "Settlements in the Jericho Valley during the Roman Period (63 B.C.–A.D. 134)." *BiblArch* 15.2 (1952): 26–42.

Mühll, P. von der. "A. Gabinius" (# 11). In *RE*, 13 (1910): 424–30.

Münzer, F. "L. Cornelius Lentulus" (# 194). In *RE*, 7 (1900): 1369–71.

———. "Cn. Cornelius Lentulus Clodianus" (# 216). In *RE*, 7 (1900): 1380–81.

———. "P. Cornelius Lentulus Sura" (# 240). In *RE*, 7 (1900): 1399–1402.

———. "L. Sempronius Atratinus" (# 26). In *RE*, 2d ser., 2 (1923): 1366–68.

Musée de l'Ermitage. *Le Portrait romain.* Leningrad, 1974.

Nash, Ernest. *Pictorial Dictionary of Ancient Rome.* 2 vols. 2d ed. New York, 1968.

Nedergaard, Elizabeth. "Arcus Augusti (a. 29 a. C.). " In *LTUR*, 1: 80–81.

———. "Arcus Augusti (a. 19 a. C.)." In *LTUR*, 1: 81–85.

Negev, A. "The High Level Aqueduct at Caesarea." *IEJ* 14 (1964): 237–49.
———. *Caesarea.* Translated by H. Arvay. Tel Aviv, 1967.
———. "Hyrcania." In *PECS*, 401.
Negev, A., Antonio Frova, and Michael Avi-Yonah. "Caesarea: Excavations in the 1950s and 1960s." In *NEAEHL*, 272–80.
Netzer, Ehud. "Cypros." *Qadmoniyot* 8 (1975): 54–61.
———. "The Hasmonean and Herodian Winter Palaces at Jericho." *IEJ* 25 (1975): 89–100.
———. "The Winter Palaces of the Judaean Kings of Jericho at the End of the Second Temple Period." *BASOR* 228 (1977): 1–13.
———. *Greater Herodium. Qedem* 13 (1981).
———. "The Herodian Triclinia—A Prototype for the 'Galilean-Type' Synagogue." In *Ancient Synagogues Revealed*, ed. Lee I. Levine, 49–51. Jerusalem, 1981.
———. "Herod's Building Program: State Necessity or Personal Need." *JC* 1 (1981): 48–61.
———. "In Reply." *JC* 1 (1981): 73–80.
———. "Ancient Ritual Baths (*Miqvaot*) in Jericho." *JC* 2 (1982): 106–19.
———. "Herodium—Herod the Great's Prestige Building Project." In Επιστη-μονικη επετήρις της Φιλοσοφικης σχολής του Πανεπιστημίου Αθηνών 28 (1979–85): 524–47.
———. "The Augusteum at Samaria-Sebaste: A New Outlook." *ErIsr* 19 (1987): 97–105.
———. "Herod the Great's Contribution to Nikopolis in the Light of His Building Activity in Judea." In *Nikopolis*, vol. 1, ed. Chrysos, 121–28.
———. *Herodium: An Archaeological Guide.* Jerusalem, 1987.
———. "Masada." In *Die Wasserversorgung Antiker Städte*, 189–92. Geschichte der Wasserversorgung, 2. Mainz, 1987.
———. "The Water Supply Network of Masada." *AAP*, 261–71.
———. "Architecture in Palaestina prior to and during the Days of Herod the Great." In *Akten*, 37–50.
———. *Masada*, vol. 3: *The Buildings, Stratigraphy, and Architecture.* Jerusalem, 1991.
———. "Cypros." In *NEAEHL*, 315–17.
———. "Lower Herodium." In *NEAEHL*, 621–26.
———. "The Promontory Palace." In *CMR*, 193–207.
Netzer, Ehud, and Sara Ben-Arieh. "Remains of an Opus Reticulatum Building in Jerusalem." *IEJ* 33 (1983): 163–75.
Netzer, Ehud, and Eric M. Meyers. "Preliminary Report on the Joint Jericho Excavation Project." *BASOR* 228 (1977): 15–27.
Netzer, Ehud, and Zeev Weiss. "Sepphoris (Sippori), 1991–1992." *IEJ* 43 (1993): 190–96.
Nicolet, Hélène. "Une monnaie de bronze frappée à Pella (Décapole) sous Commode." In *Coins, Culture, and History in the Ancient World: Numismatic and Other Studies in Honor of Bluma L. Trell*, ed. Lionel Casson and Martin Price, 51–55. Detroit, 1981.
Nielsen, Inge. *Thermae et Balnea: The Architecture and Cultural History of Roman Public Baths.* Aarhus, 1990.

————. *Hellenistic Palaces: Tradition and Renewal.* Studies in Hellenistic Civilization, 5. Aarhus, 1994.

Niese, B. "Alexas von Laodikeia" (# 1a). In *RE*, suppl. 1 (1903): 56.

————. "Eurykles" (# 5). In *RE*, 11 (1907): 1330–31.

Nikolaos of Damaskos. *Life of Augustus.* Edited by Jane Bellemore. Bristol, 1984.

Olami, Yaacov, and Yehudah Peleg. "The Water Supply System of Caesarea Maritima." *IEJ* 27 (1977): 127–37.

Oleson, John Peter. "Herod and Vitruvius: Preliminary Thoughts on Harbour Engineering at Sebastos, the Harbour of Caesarea Maritima." In *Harbour Archaeology*, 165–72. BAR-IS, 257. London, 1985.

————. "Artifactual Evidence for the History of the Harbors of Caesarea." In *CMR*, 359–77.

Oleson, John Peter, and Graham Branton. "The Technology of King Herod's Harbor." In *Caesarea Papers*, ed. Robert Lindley Vann, 49–67. *JRA*, suppl. 5 (1992).

Ostrogorsky, George. *History of the Byzantine State.* 2d English ed. Translated by Joan Hussey. Oxford, 1968.

Otto, Walter. "Herodes I" (# 14). In *RE*, suppl. 2 (1913): 1–158.

Ovadiah, Asher. *Geometric and Floral Patterns in Ancient Mosaics.* Rome, 1980.

————. "Was the Cult of the God Dushara-Dusares Practiced in Hippos-Susita?" *PEQ* 113 (1981): 101–4.

————. "Mosaic Pavements of the Herodian Period in Israel." *Mediterranean Historical Review* 5 (1990): 207–21.

Ovadiah, Ruth, and Asher Ovadiah. *Hellenistic, Roman and Early Byzantine Mosaic Pavements in Israel.* Bibliotheca Archaeologica, 6. Rome, 1987.

Palombi, Domenico. "Amphitheatrum Caligulae." In *LTUR*, 1: 35.

————. "Amphitheatrum Neronis." In *LTUR*, 1: 36.

Pani, Mario. *Roma e i re d'Oriente da Augusto a Tiberio.* Pubblicazioni della Facoltà di lettere e filosofia dell'Università di Bari, 11. Bari [1972].

Papi, Emanuele. "Domus: M. Antonius." In *LTUR*, 2: 34.

Parnham, Edith Diane. "Motivations for the Building Program of Herod the Great." M.A. thesis, Wilfrid Laurier University, 1976.

Paton, W. R., and E. L. Hicks. *The Inscriptions of Cos.* Oxford, 1891.

Patrich, Joseph. "Reconstructing the Magnificent Temple Herod Built." *Bible Review* 4.5 (October 1988): 16–29.

————. "The Aqueducts of Hyrcania." *AAP*, 243–60.

————. "The Buildings of Masada." *JRA* 6 (1993): 473–75.

————. "Hyrcania." In *NEAEHL*, 639–41.

————. "The Structure of the Second Temple—A New Reconstruction." In *Ancient Jerusalem Revealed*, ed. Hillel Geva, 260–71. Jerusalem, 1994.

Patterson, John R. "The City of Rome: From Republic to Empire." *JRS* 82 (1992): 186–215.

Peleg, Jehuda. "Caesarea Maritima." In *Die Wasserversorgung Antiker Städte*, 176–78. Geschichte der Wasserversorgung, 2. Mainz, 1987.

————. "The Water System of Caesarea." In *AAP*, 115–22.

Pelling, C. B. R. "Plutarch's Method of Work in the Roman Lives." *JHS* 99 (1979): 74–96.

Perowne, Stewart. *The Life and Times of Herod the Great.* London, 1956.

Peter, Hermann. *Historicorum Romanorum Reliquiae.* 1906. Reprint, Stuttgart, 1967.

Petrie, Flinders. *Anthedon. BSAE* 58 (1937).

Phillimore, J. S. "Crinagoras of Mytilene." *Dublin Review* 139 (1906): 74–86.

Philon of Alexandria. *Philonis Alexandrini Legatio ad Gaium.* Translated and edited by E. Mary Smallwood. Leiden, 1970.

Phythian-Adams, W. J. "Reports on Soundings at Gaza, Etc." *PEFQ* 1923: 11–17.

Picard, Gilbert. "La date du théâtre de Cherchel et les débuts de l'architecture théâtrale dans les provinces romaines d'occident." *CRAI* 1975: 386–97.

Piccirillo, Michele. "Le monete della fortezza di Macheronte (El-Mishnaqa)." *Liber Annuus* 30 (1980): 403–14.

———. *I mosaici di Giordania.* Rome, 1986.

———. "Ricerca storico-archeologica in Giordania, VII (1987)." *Liber Annuus* 37 (1987): 373–436.

———. "Ricerca storico-archeologica in Giordania, VIII (1988)." *Liber Annuus* 38 (1988) 449–70.

———. *The Mosaics of Jordan.* Edited by Patricia M. Bikai and Thomas A. Dailey. Amman, 1993.

Picozzi, M. G. "Syros." In *PECS,* 874.

Pixner, Bargil. "The History of the 'Essene Gate' Area." *ZDPV* 105 (1989): 96–104.

Pixner, Bargil, Doron Chen, and Shlomo Margarlit. "Mount Zion: The 'Gate of the Essenes' Reconsidered." *ZDPV* 105 (1989): 85–95.

Platner, Samuel B. *A Topographical Dictionary of Ancient Rome.* Completed and revised by Thomas Ashby. London, 1929.

Pleket, H. W. "Olympic Benefactors." *ZPE* 20 (1976): 1–17.

Plöger, Otto. "Die makkabäischen Burgen." *ZDPV* 71 (1955): 141–72.

Plutarch. *Life of Antony.* Edited by C. B. R. Pelling. Cambridge, 1988.

Pollini, John. "Ahenobarbi, Appuleii and Some Others on the Ara Pacis." *AJA* 90 (1986): 453–60.

Porath, Yosef. "Herod's 'amphitheatre' at Caesarea: A Multi-Purpose Entertainment Building." In *The Roman and Byzantine Near East: Some Recent Archaeological Research,* 15–27. *JRA,* suppl. 14 (1995).

———. "The Evolution of the Urban Plan of Caesarea's Southwest Zone: New Evidence from the Current Excavations." In *CMR,* 105–20.

Porte, Ilana d'Ancona. "The Art and Architecture of Palestine under Herod the Great: A Survey of Major Sites." Ph.D diss., Harvard University, 1966.

———. "Summary of 'The Art and Architecture of Palestine under Herod the Great: A Survey of Major Sites." *HSCP* 26 (1966): 341–44.

Pritchard, James B. *The Excavations at Herodian Jericho, 1951. AASOR* 32–33 (1952–54 [1958]).

Purcell, Nicholas. "*Atrium Libertatis.*" *BSR* 61 (1993): 125–55.

———. "Forum Romanum (the Imperial Period)." In *LTUR,* 2: 335–42.

———. "Forum Romanum (the Republican Period)." In *LTUR,* 2: 325–36.

Raban, Avner. *The Harbours of Caesarea Maritima, 1: The Site and the Excavations.* BAR-IS, 491. London, 1989.

———. "Maritime Caesarea." In *NEAEHL,* 286–91.

————. "Caesarea Maritima—Area I1: The Eastern Quay to the End of the Byzantine Era." *CMS News* (Haifa) 22 (August 1995).

Raban, Avner, Kenneth L. Holum, and Jeffrey A. Blakely. *The Combined Caesarea Expeditions: Field Report of the 1992 Season.* Haifa, 1993.

Radt, Wolfgang. *Pergamon.* Cologne,1988.

Rajak, Tessa. "Justus of Tiberias." *CQ,* n. s., 23 (1973): 345–68.

————. *Josephus: The Historian and His Society.* London, 1983.

————. "The Jews under Hasmonean Rule." In *CAH,* 2d ed. (1994), 9: 274–309.

Rakob, Friedrich. "Hellenismus in Mittelitalien: Bautypen und Bautechnik." In *Hellenismus in Mittelitalien,* ed. Paul Zanker, 366–85. *AbhGött* 97 [1976].

Rappaport, Uriel. "Ascalon and the Coinage of Judea." *PP* 36 (1981): 353–66.

Raven, Susan. *Rome in Africa.* 3d ed. London, 1993.

Rawson, Elizabeth. *Intellectual Life in the Late Roman Republic.* London, 1985.

Reeder, Jane Clark. "Typology and Ideology in the Mausoleum of Augustus: Tumulus and Tholos." *ClAnt* 11 (1992): 265–307.

Reifenberg, A. "Caesarea: A Study in the Decline of a Town." *IEJ* 1 (1950–51): 20–32.

————. *Ancient Jewish Coins.* 4th ed. Jerusalem, 1965.

Reinhold, Meyer. *Marcus Agrippa: A Biography.* Geneva, N.Y., 1933.

Rengstorf, Karl Heinrich, ed. *A Complete Concordance to Flavius Josephus.* Leiden 1973–83.

Renov, I. "A View of Herod's Temple from Nicanor's Gate in a Mural Panel of the Dura-Europos Synagogue." *IEJ* 20 (1970): 67–74.

Reuther, Oscar. *Der Heratempel von Samos: Der Bau Seit der Zeit des Polykrates.* Berlin, 1957.

Rey-Coquais, J.-P. "Byblos." In *PECS,* 176.

————. "Canatha." In *PECS,* 191–92.

————. "Emesa." In *PECS,* 302.

————. "Laodicea ad Mare." In *PECS,* 482.

————. "Paneas." In *PECS,* 670.

————. "Seia." In *PECS,* 820.

————. "Sidon." In *PECS,* 837.

————. "Tripolis." In *PECS* 935.

————. "Syrie romaine, de Pompée à Dioclétien." *JRS* 68 (1978): 44–73.

Reynolds, Joyce. *Aphrodisias and Rome. JRS* Monographs, 1. London, 1982.

Richardson, L., Jr. "A Note on the Architecture of the *Theatrum Pompei.*" *AJA* 91 (1987): 123–26.

————. *A New Topographical Dictionary of Ancient Rome.* Baltimore, 1992.

Richardson, Peter. "Law and Piety in Herod's Architecture." *Studies in Religion* 15 (1986): 347–60.

————. *Herod: King of the Jews, Friend of the Romans.* Columbia, S.C., 1996.

Richter, Gisela M. A. *The Sculpture and Sculptors of the Greeks.* 4th ed., rev. New Haven, 1970.

Ridgway, Brunilde Sismondo. *Roman Copies of Greek Sculpture: The Problem of the Originals.* Ann Arbor, 1984.

Riesner, Rainer. "Josephus' 'Gate of the Essenes' in Modern Discussion." *ZDPV* 105 (1989): 105–9.

Ringel, Joseph. *Césarée de Palestine: Étude historique et archéologique.* Paris [1975].

Ritmeyer, Kathleen, and Leen Ritmeyer. *Reconstructing Herod's Temple Mount in Jerusalem.* Washington, D.C., 1990.

Robert, Louis. *Études épigraphiques et philologiques.* Bibliothèque de l'École des hautes études, Sciences historiques et philologiques, 272. Paris, 1938.

Roberts, David. *The Holy Land.* London, 1989.

Roddaz, Jean-Michel. *Marcus Agrippa.* BEFAR, 253. Rome, 1984.

Roll, Israel, and Etan Ayalon. "Apollonia-Arsuf." In *NEAEHL*, 72–75.

Roller, Duane W. "The Northern Plain of Sharon in the Hellenistic Period." *BASOR* 247 (1982): 43–52.

———. "The Wilfrid Laurier University Survey of Northeastern Caesarea Maritima." *Levant* 14 (1982): 90–103.

———. "Straton's Tower: Some Additional Thoughts." In *Caesarea Papers*, ed. Robert Lindley Vann, 23–25. *JRA*, suppl. 5 (1992).

Rose, Charles Brian. "'Princes' and Barbarians on the Ara Pacis." *AJA* 94 (1990): 453–67.

———. "The Theater of Ilion." *Studia Troica* 1 (1991): 69–77.

———. "The 1991 Post-Bronze Age Excavations at Troia." *Studia Troica* 2 (1992): 43–60.

———. "The 1992 Post-Bronze Age Excavations at Troia." *Studia Troica* 3 (1993): 97–116.

Rosenfeld, Ben-Zion. "The 'Boundary of Gezer' Inscriptions and the History of Gezer at the End of the Second Temple Period." *IEJ* 38 (1988): 233–45.

Rossbach, O. "Antiphilos" (# 6). In *RE*, 2 (1894): 2525.

Rostovtzeff, M. "Queen Dynamis of Bosporus." *JHS* 39 (1919): 88–109.

———. *The Social and Economic History of the Hellenistic World.* Oxford, 1941.

———. *The Social and Economic History of the Roman Empire.* 2d ed. Oxford, 1957.

Ruge, W. "Soloi" (# 1). In *RE*, 2d ser., 5 (1927): 935–38.

Rutgers, Leonard Victor. "Roman Policy toward the Jews: Expulsions from the City of Rome during the First Century C.E." *ClAnt* 13 (1994): 56–74.

Sacks, Kenneth S. *Diodorus Siculus and the First Century.* Princeton, 1990.

Sandmel, Samuel. *Herod: Profile of a Tyrant.* Philadelphia, 1967.

Sanford, Eva Matthews. "The Career of Aulus Gabinius." *TAPA* 70 (1939): 64–92.

Sauer, James A. "Area B." In *Hesbon, 1971: The Second Campaign at Tell Hesbân*, ed. Roger S. Boraas and Siegfried H. Horn, 35–71. Andrews University Monographs, 6. Berrien Springs, Mich., 1973.

Sauvaget, J. "Le plan de Laodicée-sur-mer." *BEO* 4 (1934): 81–114.

———. "Le plan antique de Damas." *Syria* 25–26 (1946–49): 314–58.

Scardigli, Barbara. "Asinius Pollio und Nikolaos von Damaskos." *Historia* 32 (1983): 121–23.

Schalit, Abraham. *Namenwörterbuch zu Flavius Josephus.* Leiden, 1968.

———. *König Herodes: Der Mann und Sein Werk.* Studia Judaica, 4. Berlin, 1969.

———. "The Fall of the Hasmonean Dynasty and the Roman Conquest." *HP*, 26–43.

———. "The End of the Hasmonean Dynasty and the Rise of Herod." *HP*, 44–70.

Schick, Barauth C. "Recent Discoveries at the 'Nicophorieh'." *PEFQ* 1892: 115–20.

Schläger, Helmut, and Jörg Schäfer. "Phaselis: Zur Topographie der Stadt und des Hafengebietes." *AA* 86 (1971): 542–61.

Schmitt, Götz. "Gaba, Getta und Gintikirmil." *ZDPV* 103 (1987): 22–48.

Schottroff, W. "Horonaim, Nimrim, Luhith und der Westrand des 'Landes Ataroth'." *ZDPV* 82 (1966): 163–208.

Schult, Hermann. "Zwei Häfen aus römischer Zeit am Toten Meer." *ZDPV* 82 (1966): 139–48.

Schürer, Emil. *Geschichte des jüdischen Volkes im Zeitalter Jesu Christu.* 3d–4th eds. Leipzig, 1901.

————. *The History of the Jewish People in the Age of Jesus Christ (175 B.C.—A.D. 135).* A New English version, edited by Geza Vermes, Fergus Millar, Pamela Vermes, and Matthew Black. Edinburgh, 1973–87.

Schwartz, G. "Alexandros von Milet" (# 88). In *RE*, 1 (1894): 1449–52.

————. "Chronicon Paschale." In *RE*, 6 (1899): 2460–77.

Schwartz, Seth. *Josephus and Judaean Politics.* Columbia Studies in the Classical Tradition, 18. Leiden, 1990.

Scullard, H. H. *From the Gracchi to Nero.* 4th ed. London, 1976.

Segal, Arthur. "Herodium." *IEJ* 23 (1973): 27–29.

————. "Herodium and the Mausoleum of Augustus." *Qadmoniyot* 7 (1974): 46–49.

————. "The Stages of Construction of Herodium." *ErIsr* 12 (1975): 109–15.

————. "Theatres in Ancient Palestine during the Roman-Byzantine Period (An Historical-Archaeological Survey)." *Scripta classica Israelica* 8–9 (1985–88): 145–65.

————. "Theatres in Eretz-Israel in the Roman- Byzantine Period." *ErIsr* 19 (1987): 106–24.

————. *Theatres in Roman Palestine and Provincia Arabia.* Mnemosyne, suppl. 140. Leiden, 1995.

Segal, Arthur, and Yehuda Naor. "Four Seasons of Excavations at an Hellenistic Site in the Area of Kibbutz Sha'ar ha-Amakim." In *The Eastern Frontier of the Roman Empire*, ed. D. H. French and C. S. Lightfoot, 421–35. BAR-IS, 553. London, 1989.

————. "Sha'ar ha-'Amaqim." In *NEAEHL*, 1339–40.

Segal, J. B. "New Mosaics from Edessa." *Archaeology* 12 (1959): 151–57.

————. *Edessa, "The Blessed City."* Oxford, 1970.

————. "Antioch-by-the-Callirhoe." In *PECS*, 61.

Seigne, Jacques. "Découvertes récentes sur le sanctuaire de Zeus à Jerash." *ADAJ* 27 (1993): 341–51.

Settis, Salvatore. "Die Ara Pacis." In *Kaiser Augustus und die Verlorene Republik*, 400–426. Berlin, 1988.

Seyrig, Henri. "Antiquités syriennes." *Syria* 27 (1950): 5–56.

Sherwin-White, A. N. *The Roman Citizenship.* 2d ed. London, 1973.

————. *Roman Foreign Policy in the East, 168 B.C. to A.D. 1.* London, 1984.

————. "Lucullus, Pompey, and the East." In *CAH*, 2d. ed. (1994), 9: 229–75.

Sherwin-White, Susan M. *Ancient Cos.* Hypomnemata, 51. Göttingen, 1978.

Shipley, Frederick W. "Chronology of the Building Operations in Rome from the Death of Caesar to the Death of Augustus." *MAAR* 9 (1931): 7–60.

————. *Agrippa's Building Activities in Rome.* St. Louis, 1933.

Siegelmann, Azriel. "The Identification of Gaba Hippeon." *PEQ* 116 (1984): 89–93.

Simon, Erika. *Ara Pacis Augustae*. Greenwich, Conn. [1967].

Simpson, Christopher J., and Nadine Brundrett, "Innovation and the Baths of Agrippa: An Exaggerated Claim?" *AJA* 100 (1996): 391–92.

Sivan, Renée, and Giora Solar. "Excavations in the Jerusalem Citadel, 1980–1988." In *Ancient Jerusalem Revealed*, ed. Hillel Geva, 168–76. Jerusalem, 1994.

Sjöqvist, Erik. "Kaisareion: A Study in Architectural Iconography." *OpRom* 1 (1954): 86–108.

Small, David B. "Studies in Roman Theater Design." *AJA* 87 (1983): 55–68.

———. "Late Hellenistic Baths in Palestine." *BASOR* 266 (1987): 59–74.

———. "Phasing Masada's Architecture." *Levant* 22 (1990): 139–47.

Smallwood, E. Mary. *The Jews under Roman Rule*. Studies in Judaism in Late Antiquity, 20. Leiden, 1976.

Smith, Robert Houston. "Pella." In *NEAEHL*, 1174–80.

Sordi, Marta. "Timagene di Alessandria: Uno storico ellenocentrico e filobarbaro." *ANRW* 2.30 (1982–83): 775–97.

Spijkerman, Augustus. *The Coins of the Decapolis and Provincia Arabia*. Edited by Michele Piccirillo. Studi Biblici Francisciani Collectio Maior, 25. Jerusalem, 1978.

Spoerri, Walter. "Hekataios von Abdera." In *Reallexikon für Antike und Christenthum*, 14: 275–310. Stuttgart, 1988.

Stager, Lawrence E. "Ashkelon." In *NEAEHL*, 103–12.

Stähelin, F. "Antipatros" (# 20b). In *RE*, suppl. 3 (1918): 124–25.

Stark, Freya. *Rome on the Euphrates: The Story of a Frontier*. New York, 1966.

Steinby, Eva Margareta. "Basilica Aemilia." In *LTUR*, 1: 167–68.

———, ed. *Lexicon Topographicum Urbis Romae*. Rome 1993–.

Stern, Mehanem. *Greek and Latin Authors on Jews and Judaism*. 3 vols. Jerusalem, 1974–80.

———. "The Reign of Herod." *HP*, 71–123.

———. "The Herodian Dynasty and the Province of Judea at the End of the Period of the Second Temple." *HP*, 124–78.

Strange, James F. "The Capernaum and Herodium Publications." *BASOR* 226 (1977): 65–73.

———. "Six Campaigns at Sepphoris: The University of South Florida Excavations, 1983–1989." In *The Galilee in Late Antiquity*, ed. Lee I. Levine, 339–55. New York, 1992.

Strange, James F., and Thomas R. W. Longstaff. "Sepphoris (Sippori), 1986 (II)." *IEJ* 37 (1987): 278–80.

Strange, James F., Dennis F. Groh, and Thomas R. W. Longstaff. "Sepphoris (Sippori), 1987." *IEJ* 38 (1988): 188–90.

Strickert, Fred. "The Coins of Philip." In *Bethsaida: A City by the North Shore of the Sea of Galilee*, vol. 1, ed. Rami Arav and Richard A. Freund, 165–89. Kirksville, Mo., 1995.

Strobel, August. "Zur Ortslage von Kallirrhoë." *ZDPV* 82 (1966): 149–62.

———. "Observations about the Roman Installations at Mukawer." *ADAJ* 17 (1972): 101–27.

————. "Auf der Suche nach Machärus und Kallirrhoe." *ZDPV* 93 (1977): 247–67.

Strong, Donald. *Roman Art.* 2d ed., annotated. Harmondsworth, 1988.

Sullivan, Richard D. "The Dynasty of Commagene." *ANRW* 2.8 (1977): 732–98.

————. "The Dynasty of Emesa." *ANRW* 2.8 (1977): 198–219.

————. "The Dynasty of Judaea in the First Century." *ANRW* 2.8 (1977): 296–354.

————. "Papyri Reflecting the Eastern Dynastic Network." *ANRW* 2.8 (1977): 908–39.

————. "Dynasts in Pontus." *ANRW* 2.7 (1980): 913–30.

————. "The Dynasty of Cappadocia." *ANRW* 2.7 (1980): 1125–68.

————. *Near Eastern Royalty and Rome, 100–30 B.C.* Phoenix, suppl. 24. Toronto, 1990.

Swoboda, Karl. *Römische und Römanische Palaste.* 3d, enlarged ed. Vienna, 1969.

Syme, Ronald. "Pollio, Saloninus and Salonae." *CQ* 31 (1937): 39–48.

————. *The Roman Revolution.* Oxford, 1939.

————. "Who Was Vedius Pollio?" *JRS* 51 (1961): 23–30.

————. "Problems about Janus." *AJP* 100 (1979):188–212.

————. *The Augustan Aristocracy.* Oxford, 1986.

————. "*Titus et Berenice*: A Tacitean Fragment." In Ronald Syme, *Roman Papers*, vol. 7, ed. Anthony R. Birley, 647–62. Oxford, 1991.

————. *Anatolica: Studies in Strabo.* Edited by Anthony R. Birley. Oxford, 1995.

Talbert, Richard J. A. *The Senate of Imperial Rome.* Princeton, 1984.

Taylor, Lily Ross, and Russell T. Scott. "Seating Space in the Roman Senate and the *Senatores Pedarii*." *TAPA* 100 (1969): 529–82.

Thackeray, H. St. John. *Josephus: The Man and the Historian.* 1929. New ed. New York, 1967.

Theissen, Gerd. "Das 'schwankende Rohr' in Mt. 11, 7 und die Gründungsmünzen von Tiberias." *ZDPV* 101 (1985): 43–55.

Thouvenot, R. *Essai sur la province romaine de Bétique.* BEFAR, 189. Paris, 1940.

Tırpan, Ahmet A. "Roman Masonry Techniques at the Capital of the Commagenian Kingdom." In *The Eastern Frontier of the Roman Empire*, ed. D. H. French and C. S. Lightfoot, 519–36. BAR-IS, 553. London, 1989.

Toher, Mark, "The Date of Nicolaus' Βίος Καίσαρος," *GRBS* 26 (1985): 199–206.

Tölle, Renate. *Die Antike Stadt Samos.* Mainz, 1969.

Tomlinson, R. A. "Archaeology in Greece, 1994–1995." *AR* 41 (1995): 1–74.

————. "Archaeology in Greece, 1995–1996." *AR* 42 (1996): 1–47.

Torelli, Mario. *Typology and Structure of Roman Historical Reliefs.* Ann Arbor, 1982.

Treggiari, Susan. *Roman Freedmen in the Late Republic.* Oxford, 1969.

Tsafrir, Yoram. "Symmetry at Herodium, 'Megalomania' in Herodian Architecture, and the Place of Roman Technology." *JC* 1 (1981): 68–72.

————. "The Desert Fortresses of Judaea in the Second Temple Period." *JC* 2 (1982): 120–45.

Tsafrir, Yoram, and Itzhak Magen, "Sartaba-Alexandrium." In *NEAEHL*, 1318–20.

Tsafrir, Yoram, Leah di Segni, and Judith Green. *Tabula Imperii Romani: Iudaea Palaestina.* Jerusalem, 1994.

Tsaravopoulos, A. "A Mosaic Floor in Chios." In *Chios: A Conference at the Homerieon in Chios, 1984*, ed. John Boardman and C. E. Vaphopoulou-Richardson, 305–15. Oxford, 1986.

Tuchelt, Klaus. *Frühe Denkmäler Roms in Kleinasien, 1: Roma und Promagistrate. Ist-Mitt*, suppl. 23. 1979.

Tushingham, A. D. *Excavations in Jerusalem, 1961–1967*. Vol. 1. Toronto, 1985.

———. "The Western Hill of Jerusalem: A Critique of the 'Maximalist' Position." *Levant* 19 (1987): 137–43.

Ulrich, Roger B. "Julius Caesar and the Creation of the Forum Julium." *AJA* 97 (1993): 49–80.

Valvo, Alfredo. "M. Valerio Messalla Corvino negli studi più recenti." *ANRW* 2.30 (1982–83): 1663–80.

Van der Vliet, E. Ch. L. *Strabo over landen, volken en steden.* Assen, 1977.

Van Ooteghen, J. *Lucius Marcius Philippus et sa famille.* Académie royale de Belgique, *Memoires*, 55.3. Brussels, 1961.

Vann, Robert L. "The Drusion: A Candidate for Herod's Lighthouse at Caesarea Maritima." *IJNA* 20 (1991): 123–39.

Vardaman, E. Jerry. "The History of Herodium." In *The Teacher's Yoke: Studies in Memory of Henry Trantham*, ed. id. and James Leo Garrett, Jr., 58–81. Waco, 1964.

———. "Herodium: A Brief Assessment of Recent Suggestions," *IEJ* 25 (1975): 45–46.

Vermeule, Cornelius C., III. *Roman Imperial Art in Greece and Asia Minor.* Cambridge, Mass., 1968.

———. *Jewish Relationships with the Art of Ancient Greece and Rome.* Art of Antiquity, 4.2. Boston, 1981.

Vermeule, Cornelius C., III, and Mary B. Comstock. *Sculpture in Stone and Bronze.* Boston, 1988.

Ville, Georges. *La gladiature en occident des origines à la mort de Domitien.* BEFAR, 245. 1981.

Vincent, L. H., E. J. H. MacKay, and F. M. Abel. *Hébron: Le Haram el-Khalil: Sépulture des Patriarches.* Paris, 1923.

Viscogliosi, Alessandro. "Amphitheatrum Statilii Tauri" In *LTUR*, 1: 36–37.

———. "Apollo, Aedes in Circo." In *LTUR*, 1: 49–54.

Vogel, Eleanor K. *Bibliography of Holy Land Sites, vol.* 1. [Cincinnati] 1982.

Vogel, Eleanor K., and Brooks Holtzclaw. *Bibliography of Holy Land Sites.* Vol. 2. [Cincinnati] 1982.

Vogüé, Charles-Melchior, Comte de. *Syrie Centrale: Architecture civile et religieuse du Ier au VIIe siècle.* Vol. 1. Paris, 1865–77.

Volkmann, Hans. "Ptolemaios" (## 54–55). In *RE*, 46 (1959): 1765–66.

Vos, Mariette de. "Domus Transitoria." In *LTUR*, 2: 199–202.

Wacholder, Ben Zion. *Nicolaus of Damascus.* Berkeley, 1962.

———. "Josephus and Nicolaus of Damascus." In *Josephus, the Bible, and History*, ed. Louis H. Feldman and Gohei Hata, 147–72. Detroit, 1989.

Waelkens, Marc. "The Adoption of Roman Building Techniques in the Architecture of Asia Minor." In *Roman Architecture in the Greek World*, ed. Sarah Macready and F. H. Thompson, 94–105. Society of Antiquaries of London Occasional Papers, n.s., 10. London, 1987.

————. "Hellenistic and Roman Influence in the Imperial Architecture of Asia Minor." In *The Greek Renaissance in the Roman Empire*, ed. Susan Walker and Averil Cameron, 77–88. *BICS* 55 (1989).

Wagner-Lux, Ute, Ernst W. Kreuger, Karel S. H. Vriezen, and Tootje Vriezen–van der Flier. "Bericht über die Oberfälchenforschung in Gadara (Umm Qēs) in Jordanien im Jahre 1974." *ZDPV* 94 (1978): 135–44.

Wagner-Lux, Ute, Karel S. H. Vriezen, Ferdinand van den Bosch, Nicole F. Mulder, and Robert Guineé. "Vorläufiger Bericht über die Ausgrabungs- und Vermessungsarbeiten in Gadara (Umm Qēs) in Jordanian in Jahre 1992." *ZDPV* 109 (1993): 64–72.

Walbank, F. W. "Monarchies and Monarchic Ideas." In *CAH*, 2d ed. (1984), 7.1: 62–100

Ward-Perkins, J. B. "Tripolitana and the Marble Trade." *JRS* 41 (1951): 89–104.

————. *Roman Imperial Architecture*. 2d ed. Harmondsworth, 1981.

Waterman, Leroy, N. E. Manasseh, S. Yeivin, and Catherine S. Bunnell. *Preliminary Report of the University of Michigan Excavations at Sepphoris, Palestine, in 1931*. Ann Arbor, 1937.

Waywell, G. B., and J. J. Wilkes, "Excavations at Sparta: The Roman Stoa, 1988–91, Part 2." *BSA* 89 (1994): 377–432.

Waywell, G. B., J. J. Wilkes, Donald M. Bailey, and G. D. R. Sanders. "Excavations at Sparta: The Roman Stoa, 1988–91. Preliminary Report, Part 1." *BSA* 88 (1993): 219–86.

Weber, Wilhelm. "Studien zur Chronik des Malalas." In *Festgabe für Adolf Deissmann*, 20–66. Tübingen, 1927.

Weiss, Zeev. "Sepphoris." In *NEAEHL*, 1324–28.

Welch, Katherine. "The Roman Arena in Late-Republican Italy: A New Interpretation." *JRA* 7 (1994): 61–80.

Welles, C. Bradford. "The Inscriptions." In *Gerasa: City of the Decapolis*, ed. Carl H. Kraeling, 355–494. New Haven, 1938.

Wenning, Robert. "Die Stadtgöttin von Caesarea Maritima." *Boreas* 9 (1986): 113–29.

————. "Hellenismen Augusteischer Zeit in Herodianischen und in Nabatäischen Reich: Ein Vergleich." In *Akten*, 438.

————. "Die Dekapolis und die Nabatäer." *ZDPV* 110 (1994): 1–35.

Wiesenberg, E. "The Nicanor Gate." *Journal of Jewish Studies* 3 (1952): 14–29.

Wightman, Gregory J. "Temple Fortresses in Jerusalem, Part II: The Hasmonean *Baris* and Herodian Antonia." *Bulletin of the Anglo-Israel Archaeological Society* 10 (1990): 7–35.

————. *The Walls of Jerusalem from the Canaanites to the Mamluks. MeditArch*, suppl. 4. Sydney, 1993.

————. "Ben Sira 50:2 and the Hellenistic Temple Enclosure in Jerusalem." In *Trade, Contact, and the Movement of Peoples in the Eastern Mediterranean: Studies in Honour of J. Basil Hennessy*, ed. Stephen Bourke and Jean-Paul Descoeudres, 275–83. *MeditArch*, suppl. 3. Sydney, 1995.

Wilkinson, John. "Ancient Jerusalem: Its Water Supply and Population." *PEQ* 106 (1974): 33–51.

————. "The Streets of Jerusalem." *Levant* 7 (1975): 118–36.

————. *Jerusalem as Jesus Knew It: Archaeology as Evidence.* Jerusalem, 1978.

Will, Ernest. "La Tour de Straton: Mythes et réalités." *Syria* 64 (1987): 245–81.

Williams, Caroline. "Hellenistic and Roman Buildings in the Medieval Walls of Mytilene." *Phoenix* 38 (1984): 31–76.

Williams, Caroline, and Hector Williams. "Excavations at Mytilene, 1988." *EchCl* 33, n.s., 8 (1989): 167–81.

————. "Excavations at Mytilene, 1990." *EchCl* 35, n. s., 10 (1991): 175–91.

Williams, Hector. "Notes on Roman Mytilene." In *The Greek Renaissance in the Roman Empire*, ed. Susan Walker and Averil Cameron, 163–68. *BICS*, suppl. 55 (1989).

Williams, Richard S. "The Role of *Amicitia* in the Career of A. Gabinius (cos. 58)." *Phoenix* 32 (1978): 195–210.

————. "*Rei publicae causae*: Gabinius' Defense of His Restoration of Ptolemy Auletes." *CJ* 81 (1985–86): 25–38.

Willrich, Hugo. "Dositheos" (## 3–5). In *RE*, 10 (1905): 1605–6.

————. "Euaratos." In *RE*, 11 (1907): 847–48.

————. *Das Haus des Herodes zwischen Jerusalem und Rom.* Heidelberg, 1929.

Wiseman, T. Peter. *New Men in the Roman Senate, 139 B.C.—A.D. 14.* Oxford, 1971.

————. "Campus Martius." In *LTUR*, 1: 220–24.

Wissowa, Georg. "Q. Dellius." In *RE*, 4 (1901): 2447–48.

Wolff, Samuel R. "Archaeology in Israel." *AJA* 97 (1993): 135–63.

————. "Archaeology in Israel." *AJA* 98 (1994): 481–519.

————. "Archaeology in Israel," *AJA* 100 (1996): 725–68.

Woodward, A. M. "Excavations at Sparta, 1924–1925: The Theatre." *BSA* 26 (1923–24): 119–58.

————. "Excavations at Sparta, 1926: The Theatre." *BSA* 27 (1925–26): 175–209.

Wright, G. R. H. "The Archaeological Remains at El Mird in the Wilderness of Judaea." *Biblica* 42 (1961): 1–21.

Wroth, Warwick. *Catalogue of the Greek Coins of Galatia, Cappadocia, and Syria.* =BMC Galatia, Cappadocia, and Syria. 1899. Reprint, Bologna, 1964.

Yadin, Yigael. *Masada: Herod's Fortress and the Zealots' Last Stand.* New York, 1966.

Yalouris, E. "Notes on the Topography of Chios." In *Chios: A Conference at the Homereion in Chios, 1984*, ed. John Boardman and C. E. Vaphopoulou-Richardson, 141–68. Oxford, 1986.

Yavetz, Zvi. "The *Res Gestae* and Augustus' Public Image." In *Caesar Augustus: Seven Aspects*, ed. Fergus Millar and Erich Segal, 1–36. Oxford, 1984.

Yegül, Fikret. *Baths and Bathing in Classical Antiquity.* New York, 1992.

Yellin, Joseph, and Jan Gunneweg. "The Flowerpots from Herod's Winter Garden at Jericho." *IEJ* 39 (1989): 84–90.

Zanker, Paul. *The Power of Images in the Age of Augustus.* Translated by Alan Shapiro. Ann Arbor, 1988.

Zecchini, Giuseppe. "Asinio Pollione: Dall'attività politica alla riflessione storiographica." *ANRW* 2.30 (1982–83): 1265–96.

LIST OF PASSAGES CITED

Italicized numbers are citations in ancient texts; romanized numbers are page numbers in this volume.

INDEX

Roman proper names are generally alphabetized under the portion of the name (whether nomen or cognomen) which is most familiar; this has resulted in some inconsistencies but, perhaps, fewer than in any other system. Roman numerals in parentheses after dynastic names are for convenience of distinction, not any recognized dynastic numbering. Toponyms are normally alphabetized by the name itself, not any geographical or demographic feature (e.g. Wadi Qelt under Qelt, Khirbet Drousia under Drousia). Constructions and districts within cities are entered under the name of the city.

Compositor: Braun-Brumfield, Inc.
Text: 10/12 Baskerville
Display: Baskerville
Printer and binder: Braun-Brumfield, Inc.